RELIGIOUS FREEDOM

JEFFERSONIAN AMERICA

Jan Ellen Lewis, Peter S. Onuf, and
Andrew O'Shaughnessy, *Editors*

RELIGIOUS FREEDOM

JEFFERSON'S LEGACY

AMERICA'S CREED

John Ragosta

UNIVERSITY OF VIRGINIA PRESS
Charlottesville and London

University of Virginia Press
© 2013 by the Rector and Visitors of the University of Virginia
All rights reserved

First published 2013

1 3 5 7 9 8 6 4 2

LIBRARY OF CONGRESS CATALOGING-IN-PUBLICATION DATA
Ragosta, John A.
Religious freedom : Jefferson's legacy, America's creed / John Ragosta.
p.   cm. — (Jeffersonian America)
Includes bibliographical references and index.
ISBN 978-0-8139-3370-2 (cloth : alk. paper) — ISBN 978-0-8139-3371-9 (e-book)
1. Jefferson, Thomas, 1743–1826—Religion. 2. Jefferson, Thomas, 1743–1826—Political
and social views. 3. Freedom of religion—United States—History—18th century.
4. Freedom of religion—Virginia—History—18th century. 5. Church and state—
United States—History—18th century. 6. Church and state—Virginia—History—
18th century. 7. Virginia. Act for establishing religious freedom. I. Title.
E332.2.R35 2013
973.4'6092—dc23

2012033620

Preparation of this volume has been supported by the Thomas Jefferson Foundation.

MONTICELLO

To Liz—for everything.

[The Virginia Statute for Establishing Religious Freedom] is a true standard of Religious liberty: its principle the great barrier agst usurpations on the rights of conscience. As long as it is respected & no longer, these will be safe.

JAMES MADISON

The "Act for Establishing Religious Freedom" is not a mere application of, or a supplement to the principles as expressed by the Declaration of Independence, but the essential counterpart of it.

WILLIBALD M. PLÖCHL

Who but JEFFERSON, could have so clearly defined the inalienable rights of mankind, and the legitimate objects of Government. . . . What other statesman could have broken down, at once, the connexion between Church and State?

Vermont Patriot & State Gazette, June 22, 1835

Contents

Preface

In writing a history book, the author often seeks to place him or herself into the historic time and place about which he or she writes. I had the privilege of writing most of this book while on Thomas Jefferson's "little mountain," a welcome opportunity to try to immerse myself in Jefferson's perspective. I am deeply grateful to the Gilder Lehrman Institute of American History and the Thomas Jefferson Foundation for the opportunity to serve as the Gilder Lehrman Junior Research Fellow at the Robert H. Smith International Center for Jefferson Studies (ICJS) at Monticello. I wonder how different a book this might have been had it not been written on Mr. Jefferson's mountain. Far more important than the place, however, was the kind assistance and support from Andrew O'Shaughnessy, the ICJS director, and all of the staff at the Jefferson Library, the Jefferson Papers, and the various fellows who visited Monticello during 2010–11. Without their thoughtful guidance, encouragement, and friendship this book could not have been completed.

In some respects, this effort was a direct outgrowth of my first book, *Wellspring of Liberty: How Virginia's Religious Dissenters Helped Win the American Revolution and Secured Religious Liberty.* One reviewer praised that work but noted ruefully that I had failed to give Jefferson his due on the question of religious liberty. This volume should correct any shortcoming in that regard.

This book, then, is about Jefferson's role and the principle of religious liberty. It is not a survey of all religious freedom issues or even all church/state issues. As a result, there is much that this book does not do, does not attempt to do. It does not grapple fully with conflicting views on establishment in the eighteenth and nineteenth centuries or with continued, sometimes successful, political intervention by religionists. It does not seek systematically to answer modern questions concerning church/state interaction, nor to resolve the complicated question of how should religion be used, or avoided, in political discourse. Nor does the book focus extensively on the important impact of religion on early American culture. Those are all worthwhile topics, and each is touched upon in this volume, but they are topics for other works. (A detailed review of Madison's views on religion would also be particularly useful.) The issue that this book seeks to address is the role that Jefferson and the Jeffersonian vision played in the development of American religious freedom in a constitutional and principled sense.

Readers of *Wellspring* will find much of chapters 2 and 3 familiar, although that material has been updated and the focus here is somewhat different. A very early version of some of the arguments in chapters 4 and 5 was presented at the conference "John Adams & Thomas Jefferson: Libraries, Leadership and Legacies" in June 2009, jointly sponsored by the Boston Public Library, the Massachusetts Historical Society, and the Robert H. Smith International Center for Jefferson Studies.

One note on sources: Where possible, I cite Jefferson to the excellent *Papers of Thomas Jefferson*. If that source is not available, I generally cite to Ford, Bergh, or the Library of Congress files, in that order. Since the Library of Congress files are digital images, they are the most definitive, but they are also not as easily accessible to a broad audience. Bergh, on the other hand, has the annoying habit of changing Jefferson's capitalization and punctuation (earlier editions of the *Papers of Thomas Jefferson* also did so on occasion, but with less impact on meaning). While this is normally not a significant issue, Bergh does, for example, capitalize "Him" or "Himself" when Jefferson is referring to Jesus, something that Jefferson normally did not do. What Bergh italicizes is also often simply a larger print style that Jefferson sometimes used. Nonetheless, given the ease of access, I generally referenced Bergh in preference to the Library of Congress unless there was some specific reason to do otherwise, and I use the formatting of the source referenced.

Of course, many people contributed to this effort. Peter Onuf's consistent support and invaluable insight seem to undergird my work. Other fellows at ICJS offered ideas and timely encouragement, particularly Csaba Levai, Alan Gibson, Simon Newman, Dan Clinkman, Iain McLean, and David Konig. My colleague and friend William Brent Jones provided helpful insights on Baptist theology. ICJS was also kind enough to sponsor a book workshop at which an early version of the manuscript was discussed, dissected, and reformed. Each participant at the workshop has my heartfelt thanks: Peter Onuf, Dick Holway, Gaye Wilson, Taylor Reveley IV, Simon Newman, Max Edelson, Chuck McCurdy, Andrew O'Shaughnessy, and Johann Neem. Chuck McCurdy's contribution, as well as his subsequent support and encouragement, are especially noteworthy; chapters 5–7 would have been very different but for his thoughtful commentary. Of course, I could not end such a list without noting the assistance of the editors and staff at the University of Virginia Press and the kind and insightful comments of the reviewers.

I dedicate this book to my wife, Liz. Only someone who has been married for thirty years can fully appreciate how much she has contributed to my ability to finish this project—her thoughtful reading of chapters (when she had other things to do) being the very least of it. Sadly, I can probably not list all that she has done to help me—I won't even try.

RELIGIOUS FREEDOM

INTRODUCTION

THE FOUNDER OF AMERICAN RELIGIOUS FREEDOM WAS THOMAS Jefferson, or so said the conventional wisdom, and the Supreme Court, for most of the twentieth century.

At one level, perhaps that is not surprising. Jefferson often seems the most tangibly present of America's Founders. He is quoted more often, reportedly, and referenced more commonly in the blogosphere than any other early American. Political campaigns, from right and left, seek to embrace Jefferson's wisdom and capture his image on everything from debt reduction, to race relations, to the structure of government. Celebration of our "nation's birthday" is intimately linked with Jefferson's most famous production. To those who have spent time at the University of Virginia or at Monticello, his presence seems particularly palpable. Why not seek his vision on a topic that has tended to define the American experience at home and abroad?

Certainly, Jefferson had much to say on the topic. Issuing a vehement, almost angry, demand for religious liberty, he famously declared, "I have sworn upon the altar of God eternal hostility against every form of tyranny over the mind of man," a phrase engraved on his monument on the Tidal Basin in Washington, D.C. Even more well-known is his Letter to the Danbury Baptists explaining his view that the First Amendment to the U.S. Constitution builds a "wall of separation between Church & State."[1]

Until relatively recently, the notion that Thomas Jefferson—and his wall of separation—stood at the center of American religious freedom was largely noncontroversial. Since 1879, the Supreme Court has defined the principle of American religious freedom by reference to the learning of Jefferson and his devoted lieutenant, James Madison, particularly Jefferson's Statute for Establishing Religious Freedom and 1802 Letter to the Danbury Baptists and Madison's Memorial & Remonstrance Against Religious Assessments, which played an important role in the adoption of Jefferson's Statute. While application of the principle by courts and legislatures sometimes suffered, the principle itself was exceedingly important, and rooted in Jefferson. Chief Justice Earl Warren explained in 1961 that the Court "considered the happenings surrounding the Virginia General Assembly's enactment of 'An act for establishing religious freedom,' . . . written by Thomas Jefferson and sponsored by James Madison, as best reflecting the long and intensive struggle for religious freedom in America, and as particularly relevant in the search for First Amendment meaning." A similar near consensus triumphed in the academy.[2]

The Jeffersonian vision was equally active beyond the courts. In fact, that vision permeated the consciousness of America so thoroughly that arguments before the courts are in many respects only around the periphery. William Lee Miller explains that "the American tradition thus built [by Jefferson and his allies] was to have a much larger meaning than could be found, two centuries later, simply by looking at issues generating heat under the headings 'church and state,' 'religious freedom,' 'religion-in-politics.'" Today, two-thirds of Americans agree that separation of church and state is part of our constitutional heritage.[3]

Yet, in recent years, as one approaches the divisive issue of religion and its proper place in the modern polity, the image of Jefferson that had been dominant on the question of religious freedom has become somewhat less clear or, perhaps, tarnished. Voices on both the right and the left alternately use or disavow Jefferson's authority. Two developments feed the present unease with the sage of Monticello.

First, while Jefferson became the favorite spokesman for twentieth-century Supreme Court justices determined to construct a high and solid wall between church and state, in the past thirty-five years serious questions have been raised about the centrality of Jefferson to the historic development of American religious freedom. Critics of too strict a separation point out that Jefferson was hardly the only Founder and that, in fact, many others had a far more robust notion of church/state cooperation, making Jefferson an outlier. They argue that fixation on Jefferson to understand the First Amendment is ahistorical. Others, seeking a similar result, take a different tact: Jefferson's own religious actions in the public square—from his attendance at church services in the House of Representatives in Washington, D.C., to his invocation of divine providence in his inaugural addresses—lead to questions concerning the scope of Jefferson's vision for separation of church and state. Conservative sponsors of the National Prayer Breakfast invoke Jefferson's support for the "pure principles which Jesus taught." Both views question the legitimacy of our historic memory.[4]

In a seminal 1985 case, Justice William Rehnquist insisted in dissent that relying on Jefferson and Madison and their experience in adoption of the Virginia Statute to define religious freedom and, particularly, to understand the First Amendment is "demonstrably incorrect as a matter of history." A group of historians have joined a rising drumbeat of opposition to a Jeffersonian view of American religious freedom.[5]

Critics rightly observe that when the Constitution was drafted, twelve of thirteen states had some form of religious establishment or, at least, a test oath for office, and many of those requirements continued well into the early republic. Why, they ask, should Jefferson's views be privileged rather than those of other Founders who had a more fulsome concept of government's role in promoting religion? Jefferson, after all, appears to be outside of the mainstream on this issue. The First Amendment, binding only on the federal government, left states free to accommodate or regulate religion or even to form religious establishments, and Justice Clarence Thomas questions why that is not paramount in our understanding of religious liberty during the Founding.[6]

Certainly Jefferson saw his contribution to religious freedom as central to his legacy, asking that the Virginia Statute for Establishing Religious Freedom be remembered on any monument as one of only three accomplishments he wished to be listed from a remarkably full political and private life. The question, though, is whether Jefferson's vision of religious liberty and separation of church and state was as powerful in the new nation as it was in his own imagined legacy (and that of the Supreme Court) and whether our understanding of that vision has been misguided.

A second, related development also requires reconsideration of our understanding of Jefferson and his role in establishing religious liberty: Much of the modern dialogue presents a dichotomy between a "Christian nation" and a "secular" one, a dichotomy in which Jefferson's image is often used as the tool of choice to promote a secular result. Alternatively, supporters of a "Christian nation" model often fixate on actions that Jefferson took that seem to evidence that his "wall of separation" was, perhaps, not so high and impregnable.

This dichotomy is fed by a growing perception that a strong wall of separation is inconsistent with a vibrant public religion. Court cases contribute to this view by pitting the Establishment Clause of the First Amendment—"Congress shall make no law respecting an establishment of religion"—against the Free Exercise Clause—"or prohibiting the free exercise thereof." As one former judge and commentator put it, "At times, the Religion Clauses of the First Amendment are seen as a tug-of-war between a 'pro-religion' Free Exercise Clause and an 'anti-religion' Establishment Clause." Some academics play a part, equating "*separation* between church and state" with a system in which "religious influences [are] separated from public life and policy."[7]

The result is a continuing battle fought not usually over dry, abstract principles but over deeply felt actions: crosses and flags in cemeteries, prayers at pubic ceremonies, tax credits and expenditures for religiously affiliated schools. In these battles, history is too often used as a blunt weapon rather than a vehicle for understanding. Justice Goldberg, in 1963, spoke in Jeffersonian terms when he urged that the First Amendment was not intended to create such a tension, that both the Establishment and Free Exercise Clauses have a single goal: "to promote and assure the fullest possible scope of religious liberty and tolerance for all and to nurture the conditions which secure the best hope of attainment of that end." A unitary vision of religious freedom, though, seems sorely lacking in the modern debate.[8]

In spite of the volume and extent of the debate, unanswered questions abound. Was Jeffersonian thought the foundation upon which American religious freedom was built? How would Jefferson have perceived the suggested dichotomy between a "Christian nation" and secular state? If Jefferson's views on religious liberty and separation of church and state are central to understanding the First Amendment, must religion be relegated to a secondary status?

Unfortunately, the rhetoric on these topics seems rarely to match the research, and history has much to tell us, first on Jefferson: What were his beliefs and how did they influence his position on religious freedom? Second, careful consideration should be given to the role of Jefferson's vision in the development of the First Amendment and, more generally, the principle of American religious liberty. Finally, without engaging in an extended, anachronistic, and somewhat quixotic discussion of how Jefferson might have addressed modern church/state issues, Jefferson's actions regarding religion should be considered to determine if they, too, speak to our understanding of religious freedom.

With Jefferson having been put on a pedestal at the center of American religious freedom, this book was precipitated by legitimate questions about that placement of the sage, questions that have not been adequately answered from a historic perspective.

This study begins with Jefferson and the development of his personal religious views and how they influenced his views on religious freedom. Then the historic milieu in which he operated is considered, including Virginia's efforts to adopt religious freedom and, eventually, the Virginia Statute for Establishing Religious Freedom. This "Virginia Experience" is viewed as central to the development of the First Amendment by the Supreme Court justices who put Jefferson at its center. A careful review of the adoption of the First Amendment and of the role that a Jeffersonian vision played in the understanding of religious liberty in America through 1879, when the Supreme Court declared Jefferson's thinking seminal, follows. The historic objections to reliance on Jefferson are then more particularly considered, as are various actions of both Jefferson and Madison that require a more nuanced view of a strict separation and a vibrant pubic religion. Finally, the significance of this discussion to our modern understanding is briefly considered.

Of course, the development of principled constitutional understanding does not always match practices on the ground. Several recent books have diligently traced the application of the principle of religious freedom in mundane legal and social circumstances in the nineteenth and twentieth centuries, and those issues deserve careful consideration. Still, principles matter, as do the constitutions (federal and state) that seek to encapsulate those principles. Whatever its implementation in local laws, the foundation for the principled understanding should be clear, and that requires a better appreciation of Jefferson's role.[9]

Referring to the Declaration of Independence, Andrew O'Shaughnessy, the director of the International Center for Jefferson Studies at Monticello, is fond of reminding us that Jefferson wrote the "mission statement" for the United States. True enough, but Jefferson's Statute for Establishing Religious Freedom has also defined our nation and its pursuit of freedom and was an essential element of the reforms that Jefferson sought through the Declaration. Not only does the Statute provide a ringing endorsement of religious liberty, but Jefferson understood that freeing the human mind from the tyranny of religious oppression—in which church/state cooperation played such a central role—would be essential to the growth of the republic and the principles enunciated in the Declaration. A leading religious historian concludes that, "from the perspective of more than two centuries later, it is possible to add that the Jeffersonian law [the Statute for Establishing Religious Freedom] set Western Civilization and democratic republics everywhere upon a dramatically different path," becoming a cornerstone of the development of liberal democracy for the past two hundred years. If Jefferson was at the center of American developments of religious freedom—he wrote not only our "mission statement" but America's creed—that is a fitting legacy and an important heritage for us all. His role deserves careful consideration.[10]

1

THOMAS JEFFERSON'S RELIGION AND RELIGIOUS LIBERTY

TODAY, ALMOST TWO HUNDRED YEARS AFTER HIS DEATH, THOMAS JEF-ferson's views on religion and religious freedom continue to occupy the courts and the public. Not only do violent arguments contend with the centrality of Jefferson and his Statute for Establishing Religious Freedom to our under-standing of religious liberty, but an almost equally contentious dispute exists on what Jefferson intended by religious freedom. Part of the confusion is gen-erated by a veil that lies over Jefferson's own religious beliefs, a veil that is not entirely happenstance or the product of historic forgetfulness.

Jefferson was adamant about not discussing his religious views publicly, insisting that "religion is a matter which lies solely between Man & his God, that he owes account to none other for his faith or his worship." His warning to one correspondent—"Say nothing of my religion. It is known to God and myself alone"—bespeaks a difficult subject for historic inquiry. Late in life he told another that "I never told my own religion, nor scrutinized that of another." For Jefferson, a number of factors recommended this course: not only was his religion the subject of vicious political attacks—attacks that could not have easily been answered by a more detailed public statement of his own unortho-dox beliefs—but he also was deeply suspicious of public, dogmatic statements of faith, especially by those seeking to use religion to promote their political agenda. "[I]t is in our lives," he explained, "and not from our words, that our religion must be read. By the same test, the world must judge me."[1]

The matter of his personal religious beliefs is further complicated by Jeffer-son's manipulation of terms. For example, he emphatically declared himself a "Christian," and some authors have been willing to accept that assertion at face value or, more cynically, to use it to their own ends. What Jefferson said in this regard is considerably more nuanced; he explained that "*I am a real Christian, that is to say, a disciple of the doctrines of Jesus.*" By that he meant that he embraced Jesus's moral teachings, but he rejected Jesus's divinity, the resurrection, original sin, the atonement, and the Trinity. Certainly, most modern or eighteenth-century Christians would not accept such a claim to the moniker "Christian." Jefferson might as correctly have declared "we are all Trinitarians, we are all Unitarians . . ." and expected anyone to agree.[2]

Equally misleading are statements from Jefferson's political supporters who responded to attacks on his religion by insisting on his orthodoxy, with questionable arguments and authority. For example, during the heated presidential campaign of 1800 that pitted Jefferson against his once and future friend John Adams, one supporter responded to claims of Jefferson's infidelity by rushing into print *Serious Facts* including the rather remarkable assertion that Jefferson's religious beliefs were "wholly unexceptionable" and that he was "at least as good a christian as Mr. Adams, and in all probability a much better one." Shortly after the election, another paper referred to "that great Statesman, Patriot and Christian Philosopher Jefferson." This pattern was to continue long after his death.[3]

Serious interpretive problems also arise from a tendency to treat the beliefs of the Founding Fathers as if they were set in stone and immutable in their own time, allowing individual quotes or actions to be taken out of context and declared emblematic. Holding historical figures to a higher than human standard may simplify our understanding and analysis, but it is not consistent with the human experience. Beliefs change over time, particularly as people mature. Given the nature of religious inquiry, even with such a powerful mind as Jefferson's, doubt might well cloud specifics, or what seemed to be clear one day might seem less certain the next. The truth is that Jefferson, like so many others, might lean toward deism on one day, and later be convinced of an active divine providence. This is not to say that he was fickle, only that he was human.

Further, in evaluating statements from a very public figure, one should consider whether what was expressed might be a political or legal statement. Founders, like any politicians, learned to speak in an effective public idiom. For example, when in 1774 Jefferson urged the designation of a day of fasting and prayer in Virginia to demonstrate solidarity with Massachusetts's resistance to Britain's Intolerable Acts, he later explained that he had "rummaged" precedent and "cooked up" the resolution "under the conviction of the necessity of arousing our people." In such circumstances, one might well question the depth of Jefferson's religious motivation in urging prayer.[4] Similarly, when Jefferson in his official capacity signed a legal form that dated a transaction "in the year of our Lord Christ"—language mandated by the terms of a treaty with the Netherlands—one can hardly take that to be a personal religious affirmation, although some have tried to make it so.[5] Finally, one should not discount social conventions and kindness; agreeing to pray for a sick friend or offering the condolences of an afterlife to one who is bereaved should be viewed with some caution in evaluating personal beliefs about the efficacy of prayer and immortality. All of these factors are at work in evaluating Jefferson's religion.

Yet, if Jefferson's vision of religious freedom is so central to our vision of America, his own religious views, and the religious milieu in which he was raised and developed those views, should be first considered. While it is commonly and rightfully remembered that Jefferson was deeply committed to very broad religious liberty, including separation between church and state, the extent to which that belief is grounded in his own religious beliefs is often forgotten. A better understanding of his religious views will provide a better understanding of his views on religious freedom.[6]

Thomas Jefferson was born on April 13, 1743 (n.s.), in Shadwell, Virginia, at the base of the small mountain that he would name Monticello, and, as was appropriate for a member of the gentry in the king's dominion, he was baptized and raised in the Church of England, the established church of colonial Virginia. (While no baptismal records survive, Jefferson's Anglican christening was inevitable and is widely credited.) Jefferson's father was a vestryman of the Church of England—both a political and religious position in colonial Virginia, and as a young man Jefferson, too, was elected to an Anglican vestry. His parents were buried in the established church, and he was married in it. His children were baptized and married in what was called after 1784 the Episcopal Church of Virginia, and an Episcopal minister officiated at his funeral. Weddings and births were carefully recorded by Thomas in the Jefferson family copy of the Anglican Book of Common Prayer, which came into Jefferson's possession from his father, Peter. He owned another well-worn copy that he reportedly carried to services in his pocket. While such evidence is enough for some to conclude simply that Jefferson "was a lifelong member of the Episcopal Church," family tradition and historic affiliation, even attendance at worship and ceremonial events, is not doctrinal acceptance and leaves the question of Jefferson's religious beliefs unanswered.[7]

As was common in colonial Virginia, his first formal schooling, away from home, was under the tutelage of the local minister of the Church of England, the Reverend William Douglas, an education that Jefferson saw as mediocre at best. After his father's untimely death when Jefferson was fourteen, and before he matriculated at the College of William and Mary at the age of sixteen, he sought to improve his classical education under the Reverend James Maury, an Anglican minister from Scotland with relatively traditional beliefs. While Maury was deeply opposed to the growing influence of evangelical dissenters in Virginia, Jefferson remembered him warmly for his assistance in the classics, but not for his religious influence.[8]

Little else is known about the details of Jefferson's early religious upbringing, although he certainly learned the liturgy and hymns of the church. Later in life, he remembered fondly his sister Jane singing hymns, and a granddaughter reported that she would "not unfrequently" hear him humming hymns to himself. He also had a sound grounding in the Bible and knew how to quote it to his advantage when appropriate, for example, reminding opponents of disestablishing the Church of England in 1776 that government support of religion was unnecessary as the "Gates of Hell shall not prevail" against the church. Similarly, when appointed to a committee by the Continental Congress to develop a national seal, he suggested that the seal might show the children of Israel led by pillars of fire and smoke through the desert, an image that would have sent a powerful message to most eighteenth-century Americans. (One should hesitate to draw much from this suggestion in terms of Jefferson's personal views, as he also suggested that the reverse side show Hengist and Horsa, legendary Anglo-Saxon Britons who, if legend is credited, kept Christianity out of Britain for several centuries. For Jefferson, as with other Founders, "all of these references were understood to be allegorical, not theological.")[9]

As a young man, Jefferson's theological views were apparently relatively traditional, influenced by his upbringing and social convention. In 1763, in one of his earliest preserved letters, he encourages his dear friend John Page to "assume a perfect resignation to the Divine will, to consider whatever does happen, must happen; . . . till we arrive at our journey's end, when we may deliver up our trust into the hands of him who gave it, and receive such reward as to him shall seem proportioned to our merit," but any orthodoxy was not to last.[10]

As Jefferson matured, Enlightenment ideals were permeating America, and Jefferson embraced an "Enlightenment humanism [which] regarded man as rational, reasonable, and free." During his time at the College of William and Mary, Jefferson studied primarily under William Small, a student of the Scottish Enlightenment and the only nonclerical member of the college's faculty. Consistent with a system of rational inquiry, he began to question some of the traditional tenets of the Anglican faith and, more generally, Christianity. During those years, the rather unorthodox Viscount Henry St. John Bolingbroke seems to take precedence in Jefferson's literary commonplace book. While Bolingbroke's impact on Jefferson's religious thought is complex, he certainly influenced Jefferson to challenge orthodox assumptions, "to trust . . . reason with discussions of right and wrong," as Jefferson would later explain. Two Bolingbroke entries in the commonplace book are emblematic:

> We must not assume for truth, what can be proved neither à priori, nor à posteriori. . . . [A]nd inspiration is become a mystery, since all we know of it is, that it is an inexplicable action of the divine on the human mind[.] [I]t would be silly, therefore, to assume it to be true.

> It is absurd to affirm that a god sovereignly good, and at the same time almighty and alwise, suffers an inferior dependent being to deface his work in any sort, and to make his other creatures both criminal and miserable.[11]

By the end of his college days, it would appear that Jefferson had rejected many of the traditional teachings of the Christian faith and pursued a natural religion or philosophy consistent with the rational inquiry of the Enlightenment. For example, he recounted later how "from a very early part of . . . life" he had rejected the notion of the Trinity, explaining he had "difficulty of reconciling the ideas of Unity and Trinity." Generally, though, as his 1763 letter to John Page indicates, these views matured with time; unorthodox views did not spring full-blown to the young scholar.[12]

Nor should the latitudinarianism of eighteenth-century Anglicans confuse this issue. It is certainly true that, "whereas earlier generations of Anglicans had defined religious identity in dogmatically narrow theological terms—which had resulted in civil war and regicide—post-Restoration churchmen embraced a broader, latitudinarian theology that made virtuous behavior and not strict adherence to doctrine the linchpin of Christianity and the harbinger of human happiness." Yet, while Anglicans of the eighteenth century were often far more focused on moral behavior than doctrinal conformity, as was Jefferson, and one might readily conclude that Jefferson's mature religious thought owed a debt to the widely read Bishop Tillotson's insistence that "Moral Duties" were "the great business of Religion," simply concluding that Jefferson was a latitudinarian Anglican is troubling. While Tillotson and other Anglican hierarchs may have focused primarily on conduct rather than dogma, they certainly could not have accepted Jefferson's views on Jesus, the resurrection, atonement, and miracles. As Tillotson would have put it, moral behavior and natural religion should be pursued through the "mediation of our Savior." Certainly Jefferson was aware that he had fallen away from even the latitudinarian attitudes common in the Anglican Church in late eighteenth-century Virginia: Seeking support for a candidate for the Anglican priesthood, he wrote Peyton Randolph in 1770 that "I have no interest at our episcopal palace, and indeed any application if known to come from me would rather be of disservice."[13]

Over time, Jefferson's religious beliefs became increasingly nonconventional, but also increasingly a matter of deeply thought and deeply felt convictions consistent with his commitment to reason. In 1771, when asked to suggest books for a gentry library, the religious authors to whom he turned were hardly traditionalists, including Locke, Xenophon, Epictetus, Antoninus, Seneca, Cicero, Bolingbroke, Hume, Kames, and Sterne. By 1781, Jefferson was advising others to follow his own path of inquiry and empiricism. In *Notes on the State of Virginia*, he urged the use of "[r]eason and free enquiry" against error: "Give a loose to them, they will support true religion, by bringing every false one to their tribunal, to the test of their investigation." Several years later, Peter Carr, a young nephew, was famously advised to "[f]ix reason firmly in her seat, and call to her tribunal every fact, every opinion. Question with boldness even the existence of a god; because, if there be one, he must more approve the homage of reason, than that of blindfolded fear." Evidencing the seriousness with which he took his own advice, in 1788, Jefferson regretfully declined the request of a friend, Philip Mazzei's stepson-in-law, to act as godparent for a child at its christening, explaining: "The person who becomes a sponsor for a child, according to the ritual of the church in which I was educated, makes a solemn profession, before god and the world, of faith in articles [of the Episcopal Church], which I had never sense enough to comprehend, and it has always appeared to me that comprehension must precede assent." While most people in the eighteenth century or today, even if questioning some of the tenets of the church, would have quietly subscribed the requisite terms to accommodate a friend and participate in this happy event, the sensitive and contemplative Jefferson would not; he was too religious, in his own way.[14]

Certainly, over time, Jefferson rejected many standard Christian dogmas. He concluded that the ostensible followers of Jesus had created a whole host of "misconstructions," including "the immaculate conception . . . , his [Jesus's] deification, the creation of the world by him, his miraculous powers, his resurrection and visible ascension, his corporeal presence in the Eucharist, the Trinity; original sin, atonement, regeneration, election . . ." For Jefferson, "[o]f this band of dupes and impostors, [the Apostle] Paul was the great Coryphaeus, and first corruptor of the doctrines of Jesus." Calvinism—at the heart of eighteenth-century Congregationalism and Presbyterianism—was also a target. Jefferson rejected the idea of original sin—believing it irrational and unjust for a loving god to punish one person for the fault of another—and vehemently opposed the notion of predestination. He insisted that God, as imagined by John Calvin, was a "daemon of malignant spirit." He fumed to another correspondent that Calvinism "has introduced into the Christian religion more new absurdities than it's leader had purged it of old ones," concluding that "our saviour did not come into the world to save metaphysicians only."[15]

Notice here the use of the term "our saviour." Yet, while deeply devoted to Jesus's moral teaching by the time of this letter, Jefferson continued to reject Jesus's divinity, resurrection, and the atonement. As with his description of himself as Christian, Jefferson was willing to use terms in the most flexible manner, particular when it allowed him to make a point by agreeing with someone on a broader issue.[16]

Of course, Jefferson's belief in rational inquiry and his wandering from an orthodox path are relatively easily established. Discerning the details of what he did believe is more difficult, in part because Jefferson believed that religion is between each individual and his or her god(s), stating that "my religion . . . is known to my god and myself alone." After his religious views were viciously attacked during the 1800 presidential campaign, in particular by Federalist clergy in New England, he insisted that public assaults on his beliefs were based upon speculations and crass political interests.

> The priests indeed have heretofore thought proper to ascribe to me religious, or antireligious sentiments, of their own fabric. . . . They wished him to be thought Atheist, Deist, or Devil, who could advocate freedom from their religious dictations. But I have ever thought religion a concern purely between our god and our consciences, for which we were accountable to him, and not to priests.

The political attacks, if possible, made him even more publicly protective of his own beliefs. Jefferson was not being obtuse; rather, he recognized that the public inquiries often masked partisan interests and intolerance, and public faith statements could mask hypocrisy. "I never will, by any word or act," he vowed, "bow to the shrine of intolerance, or admit a right of inquiry into the religious opinions of others."[17]

In spite of his public silence, Jefferson deeply felt the sting of the accusations against his religious beliefs. Even many years later, asked by a supporter to set forth his religious beliefs to silence public attacks, he refused indignantly:

> No, my dear Sir, not for all the world. Into what a nest of hornets would it thrust my head! . . . Don Quixote undertook to redress the bodily wrongs of the world, but the redressment of the mental vagaries would be an enterprise more than Quixotic. I should as soon undertake to bring the crazy skulls of Bedlam to sound understanding, as inculcate reason into that of an Athanasian. I am old, and tranquility is now my *summum bonum*. Keep me, therefore, from the fire and faggots of Calvin and his victim Servetus.

(The Athanasian creed focuses on Jesus's divinity and the Trinity.) Asked by another correspondent to write a book on his religion, he similarly replied, "I should as soon think of writing for the reformation of Bedlam." Late in life, he turned aside another request to publish his religious views by making a taunt of biblical miracles: "But have they not the Gospel? If they hear not that, and the charities it teacheth, neither will they be persuaded though one rose from the dead." Always cryptic in this regard, he insisted simply that he was "of a sect by myself."[18]

Goaded by the attacks, Jefferson's own developing views required him both to think about religion systematically and to keep his religion a matter between God and himself. On the latter point, publicly responding to "mental vagaries" of others would be more than Quixotic, would be a discourse with Bedlam, because the mind itself, "created . . . free" by God, was "altogether insusceptible of restraint" and "follow[ed] involuntarily the evidence proposed" to it (as he said in his version of the Virginia Statute). On the other hand, the gift of a mental faculty demanded that one think for oneself, and Jefferson spent considerable time and energy trying to understand his own relationship with God, even if modern readers can only see the result dimly.

Attempting to piece together those beliefs, one might begin by noting that Jefferson's mature religion was conceptually nondogmatic, less concerned with authoritative statements of perceived "truths" than with morality; in this sense, it was consistent with the thrust of latitudinarian Anglicanism. Shortly after the campaign of 1800, he told one clerical correspondent that he relished his nondogmatic faith: "When I was young I was fond of the speculations which seemed to promise some insight into that hidden country [spirits], but observing at length that they left me in the same ignorance in which they found me, I have for very many years ceased to read or to think concerning them, and have reposed my head on that pillow of ignorance which a benevolent creator has made so soft for us, knowing how much we should be forced to use it." When he did occasionally note what might be viewed as a dogma—for example, his rejection of spiritualism in favor of materialism—he was often quick to suggest that he might be wrong and that the issue was not essential. In retirement, he wrote his good friend John Adams:

> Mr. Locke, you know, and other materialists, have charged with blasphemy the spiritualists who have denied the Creator the power of endowing certain forms of matter with the faculty of thought. These, however, are speculations and subtleties in which, for my own part, I have little indulged myself. When I meet with a proposition beyond finite comprehension, I abandon it as I do a weight which human strength cannot lift. . . . Were it necessary, however, to form an opinion, I confess I should, with Mr. Locke, prefer swallowing one incomprehensibility rather than two.[19]

He was particularly suspicious of the claims of each of the competing sects to have discovered true dogmas, reminding one correspondent that, with principles of religion, it is not "given to us in this life to know whether your's or mine, our friend's or our foe's are exactly the right." By comparison, for Jefferson, avoiding dogmatic disputes could provide a positive good, especially in a growing republic with a diverse people seeking to form a new nation with a commonality of interests. Jesus, "the benevolent and sublime Reformer . . . has told us only that God is good and perfect, but has not defined Him. I am, therefore of His theology, believing that we have neither words nor ideas adequate to that definition. And if we could all, after this example, leave the subject as undefinable, we should all be of one sect, doers of good, and eschewers of evil." He chided the various denominations that "every religion consists of moral precepts & of dogmas. [I]n the first they all agree. . . . [A]nd these are the articles necessary for the preservation of order, justice, & happiness in society. [I]n their particular dogmas all differ; . . . & [these are] unimportant to the legitimate objects of society." Trying to explain his opposition to sectarianism in a more lighthearted manner, he wrote: "[W]ere I to be the founder of a new sect, I would call them Apiarians, and, after the example of the bee, advise them to extract the honey of every sect. [M]y fundamental principle would be the reverse of Calvin's, that we are to be saved by our good works which are within our power, and not by our faith which is not within our power."[20]

The contribution of religion (defined broadly to include ethics and morals) to the "legitimate objects of society" should not be missed. This was a view of long standing with Jefferson and a belief broadly shared in early America. In his *Notes on the State of Virginia*, Jefferson explained that the relatively liberal provisions on religious freedom in colonial New York and Pennsylvania had not undermined the essentials of religion: "Religion is well supported [in those states]; of various kinds, indeed, but all good enough; all sufficient to preserve peace and order or if a sect arises, whose tenets would subvert morals, good sense has fair play, and reasons and laughs it out of doors, without suffering the state to be troubled with it." Thus, while religion played an important role in society and, particularly, a republic, the state had only to maintain order and protect free inquiry. That, for Jefferson, should have been enough.[21]

Not only did Jefferson see moral principles and actions as central to society and dogmas as unessential and divisive, but his deep suspicion of religious dogmas was fed by an ugly history of religious wars and persecution. "On the dogmas of religion as distinguished from moral principles, all mankind, from the beginning of the world to this day, have been quarrelling, fighting, burning and torturing one another, for abstractions unintelligible to themselves and to all others, and absolutely beyond the comprehension of the human mind." He thought the search for uniformity among theological dogmatists was a fool's errand: "[I]s uniformity of opinion desirable? . . . The several sects [differing in opinion] perform the office of a Censor morum over each other. Is uniformity attainable? Millions of innocent men, women, and children, since the introduction of Christianity, have been burnt, tortured, fined, imprisoned; yet we have not advanced one inch towards uniformity." His good friend and collaborator James Madison, also abjuring the notion of a uniform dogma, made the same point: "[T]orrents of blood have been spilt in the world in vain attempts of the secular arm to extinguish religious discord, by proscribing all differences in religious opinion." (Madison, of course, would later famously argue in *Federalist* No. 10 that it was the equipoise among competing interests and differing sects that protected the liberty of all, especially minorities.) Jefferson agreed with the French philosopher Comte de Volney that dogmatic differences among the sects contributed to conflict and warfare but harmony would be promoted by agreement on the essential moral principles of rational religion. Building on this theme, early commentators made a point that Jefferson's views on religious freedom were most clear to those familiar with the wars of dogma evident in ecclesiastic history.[22]

A principled opposition to a dogmatic system of beliefs allowed Jefferson to avoid what he saw as unnecessary and unsolvable metaphysical disputes while at the same time allowing him to read his own beliefs into those of people who agreed with him on fundamental moral issues while disagreeing on dogma. Thus, for example, he claimed an affinity with the beliefs of Joseph Priestley even though Priestley was emphatic that Jesus was on a divine mission, performed miracles, and that much of this could be known through revelation—each of which propositions Jefferson rejected. As Paul Conkin observes, in seeking to understand Jefferson's religion it might be best to remember that "he was a creature of mood and sentiment much more than a rigorous thinker." Furthermore, having spent a life in public service, Jefferson was all too familiar with a human tendency to say one thing, to claim to support a particular dogma, and to do another, a particularly troubling practice in both religion and politics. This, too, contributed to a flexible, nondogmatic approach to religion and to his insistence that his religion "be read" in his action rather than words.[23]

In addition to his aversion to dogmatic religious disputes, Jefferson developed by adulthood a serious distrust of and antipathy toward the power of any religious clergy and their all-too-common intolerance, what he repeatedly referred to as "priestcraft." Several factors combined to generate his hostility to the clergy as an institution. First, clergy often seemed to base their power and influence on a "revealed" faith in opposition to reason; thus, credulous congregants might be convinced to support the church, and clergy, through fabrications and fantasies. Revelation had an aristocratic tone to it for the quintessential republican and offended Jefferson's rational epistemology. Good republicans needed to think and learn for themselves, and failing to do so is the "last degradation of a free and moral agent"—something that would both threaten the republic and insult the creator of the mental faculty. It was on this basis that Jefferson included in the preamble to the Virginia Statute for Establishing Religious Freedom the admonition that true religion would "extend ... by its influence on reason alone," and he was deeply annoyed when legislators, many devoted to a revealed religion, deleted this phrase.[24]

More broadly, throughout history, clergy had repeatedly aligned themselves with governmental authority as a means to maintain their position of power (and wealth) at the expense of the mass of people and to the detriment of free thought and a more rational religion. Nothing evidenced Jefferson's disdain for an organized, politicized clergy more than his references to the trilogy of "kings, nobles, and priests." Jefferson referred to the "loathsome combination of church and state" that tends to reduce men to "dupes & drudges of these Montebanks." After he became a great devotee of Jesus's teaching, he made this argument pointedly, noting that Jesus's crucifixion was the fruit of church/state cooperation by a religious order meddling in politics and seeking to maintain its own position of power. This understanding made it essential that a separation of church and state not only keep government out of the realm of religion, but also that the church be kept out of the business of government. He warned that the clergy, seeking to defend their positions of power against a broad disestablishment, "wish it to be believed that he can have no religion who advocates it's freedom." Casting himself as a martyr, and with a bit of a Christ-complex, he told his attorney general, Levi Lincoln: "They [the clergy] crucified their Saviour who preached that their kingdom was not of this world, and all who practice on that precept must expect the extreme of their wrath."[25]

Third, his enmity was certainly increased by the brutal attacks on his character and religion by New England's federalist clergy, particularly in the election of 1800 (although his aversion to "priestcraft" did not originate in that election as is sometimes suggested). Timothy Dwight, a Congregationalist minister and president of Yale College, warned that under Jefferson the people would "see the Bible cast into a bonfire, the vessels of the sacramental supper borne by an ass in public procession, and our children, either wheedled or terrified, uniting in the mob, in chanting mockeries against God." The *Hartford Courant* published a screed that concluded that Jefferson's election would mean that "[m]urder, robbery, rape, adultery, and incest will be openly taught and practiced, the air will be rent with the cries of distress, the soil will be soaked with blood, the nation black with crimes." The result, according to the New England clergy: "children writhing on the pike and the halberd."[26] Parents were warned, only a bit less ominously for eighteenth-century ministers, that Jefferson's election would result in "wresting the bible from the hands of your children." One trope used by New England federalist clergy was to preach that to vote for Jefferson was "no less than rebellion against God." In his popular pamphlet, the Reverend William Linn referred to Jefferson as the "arch-infidel." Such calumny filled pages. "The very fact that he was sympathetic with the French Revolution . . . and led the forces of religious freedom to victory in Virginia was sufficient to convince the Federalist clergy of New England that he was an atheist." The campaign continued well into the nineteenth century. One of America's first religious historians wrote: "Now, none of Mr. Jefferson's admirers will consider it slanderous to assert that he was a very bitter enemy to Christianity, and we may even assume that he wished to see not only the Episcopal church separated from the state in Virginia, but the utter overthrow of everything in the shape of a church throughout the country." (Ironically, this type of hyperbole from nineteenth-century religionists contributed to the erroneous view that Jefferson was entirely secular and opposed to any public religious action.)[27]

Jefferson maintained his public silence on religion but was deeply wounded and angered by these libels. He wrote a friend: "What an effort, my dear Sir, of bigotry in Politics & Religion have we gone through! The barbarians really flattered themselves they should be able to bring back the times of Vandalism, when ignorance put everything into the hands of power & priestcraft."[28]

Fourth, as the adult Jefferson became increasingly enamored with Jesus's philosophy, he blamed clergy for its perversion: "I abuse the priests indeed, who have so much abused the pure and holy doctrines of their master, . . . the genuine system of Jesus, and the artificial structures they have erected, to make them the instruments of wealth, power, and preeminence to themselves, are as distinct things in my view as light and darkness." Thus, the "priests" had not only abused the public by imposing upon their reason, their wallets, and their liberties, but they also imposed on what Jefferson saw and revered as pure Christian doctrines.[29]

As a result, Jefferson's republican campaign for political freedom and rational inquiry melded tightly with his opposition to priestcraft and any exercise of power by the church on the state. As Peter Onuf writes:

> Jefferson defined the old regime as an unholy alliance of "kings, nobles, and priests" that divided the people in order to rule them. Jefferson's Bill for Religious Freedom, he told John Adams in 1813, "put down the *aristocracy* of the clergy, and restored to the citizen the freedom of the mind," thus making possible the progressive development of that "entire union of opinion" that alone could guarantee the survival of republican government.[30]

As a rule, Jefferson's concerns focused on the "church," that is, institutionalized religion; he was close friends with a number of ministers. At times, though, his dislike and fear of the church ran so deep that he crossed the line to what might itself be called persecution of clergy, for example, initially insisting that ministers should be ineligible for public office, reasoning that history demonstrates that clergy's political influence resulted in "too many atrocities not to merit a proscription from meddling with government." When James Madison cautioned that exclusion of ministers would be a violation of their rights (and that the Constitution forbids only an institutional role for religion or any special privileges or position, not the participation of individual clergy in politics), Jefferson desisted, but only so far as to concede that there was no legal impediment to their participation. He still objected to the discussion of "public affairs *in the pulpit*," conceding ministers' right to discuss them "in *general conversation,* and *in writing*"; he concluded that a minister's involvement in politics was a "breach of contract" as a congregation hired a minister to preach religion, not politics, and ministers meddling in politics should be fired. The central point remains: Jefferson would not tolerate any official or special role for religion or religionists in politics.[31]

Jefferson, then, was nondogmatic and highly suspicious of sectarianism and the organized clergy. All of this, though, is still to define Jefferson's religion by what it is not. Yet, he was a deeply religious person. Moving beyond his disagreements with Christian dogma and ministers, Jefferson was an empiricist deeply devoted to reason, insisting in old age that "[w]hen once we quit the basis of sensation, all is in the wind." Still, he was devoutly theistic, believing that rational inquiry, without priestly revelation, would lead anyone to such a belief. He wrote to John Adams:

I hold (without appeal to revelation) that when we take a view of the universe, in its parts, general or particular, it is impossible for the human mind not to perceive and feel a conviction of design, consummate skill, and indefinite power in every atom of its composition. . . . [T]here is, in all this, design, cause and effect, up to an ultimate cause, a Fabricator of all things from matter and motion, their Preserver and Regulator while permitted to exist in their present forms, and their regeneration into new and other forms.

His voluminous correspondence is replete with references to a benevolent and rational creator. (He believed the same "free exercise of reason" would "vindicat[e] . . . the character of Jesus" as an inspired, but nondivine being.)[32]

Central to his understanding of that creator was that God had embodied man with the mind, the central element of human nature, essential for progress, rational religion, and republicanism. He explained to Adams that the beginning of the Gospel of John had been mistranslated; where translations read, "In the beginning, God existed, and the Word was with God," it should have read that "reason" or "mind" was with God. He concluded that in seeking to answer religious questions, "our reason at last must ultimately decide, as it is the only oracle which god has given us to determine between what really comes from him, & the phantasms of a disordered or deluded imagination." (In this his views paralleled those of Thomas Paine's *Age of Reason*.) The historian Johann Neem explains that Jefferson "believed firmly that God had created each person with the ability to reason, and thus to regulate belief was to insult God's creation." In addition to the dangers of church/state relations evident in history, then, "the freedom of conscience must be 'on the broadest bottom' to respect each person's private correspondence with God."[33]

Beyond his belief in a creator God, as a young man, Jefferson seemed to share a relatively conventional view of heaven, as his 1763 letter to John Page suggests. Over time, though, his views on the question of an afterlife became somewhat less clear. Jefferson certainly understood that a belief in a life after death and some rewards and punishment offered "an important incentive" to moral behavior. In this context, he praised Jesus for responding to Moses, who "had either not believed in a future state of existence, or had not thought it essential to be explicitly taught to his people." Such pragmatism hardly proves personal acceptance. In fact, materialism was important to Jefferson's understanding of the world, and Charles Sanford argues that "this materialism . . .

made grave difficulties for Jefferson in believing in the human soul and life after death." On the other hand, Jefferson was particularly fond of Psalm 15, which speaks of living on God's "holy mountain" as a result of good works. Declining one request to publish his religious beliefs, he told the correspondent: "[F]ollowing the guidance of a good conscience, let us be happy in the hope that . . . we shall all meet in the end. and that you and I may there meet and embrace is my earnest prayer." Later in life, he spoke passionately of meeting loved ones after death. For example, Jefferson's kind letter to John Adams after Abigail Adams's death concluded that "it is of some comfort to us both, that the term is not very distant, at which we are to deposit in the same cerement, our sorrows and suffering bodies, and to ascend in essence to an ecstatic meeting with the friends we have loved and lost, and whom we shall still love and never lose again." While such social gestures must be viewed with care, particularly given his own deep grief for the loss of children and a beloved wife, it is not insignificant that this letter is addressed to Adams, by this time one of Jefferson's most intimate correspondents. Sanford concludes that Jefferson's materialism must have waned over time in a debate about the afterlife that his heart won over his head. Perhaps, although Jefferson had always understood that matter could be enervated by God (one "incomprehensibility" rather than the two of an independent spirit and enervated matter). In the end, while the issue is not devoid of doubt, it seems that Jefferson's belief in a rational creator and the idea that one would be judged based on good deeds suggests some belief in an afterlife, even if this was an issue on which he vacillated while hoping for a reunion with loved ones. Beyond that, he was willing to rest his head on the "pillow of ignorance."[34]

Since Jefferson's rational god created man and obviously endowed him with an independent intellect, he also endowed him with fundamental rights. In his first important Revolutionary and literary work, *Summary View of the Rights of British America*, he declared that "[t]he god who gave us life, gave us liberty at the same time: the hand of force may destroy, but cannot disjoin them." Two years later he was famously to write that men are "endowed by their creator with certain unalienable rights." Michael Novak goes so far as to claim that "Jefferson's sole way of reaching the natural rights to religious liberty was by way of his Jewish-Christian convictions about the nature of the Creator and the Creator's relation to men and women, whom He created to be free." While intellectual lineage is notoriously hard to trace, it is certainly true that the linkage between his view that God created man and that essentials rights were inalienable was important for Jefferson's thought and had important implications for his views on religious freedom. Both Jefferson and Madison were clear that these God-given rights of free thought and free choice predate the social compact and could not be given up to government in that compact. Neem concludes that, for Jefferson, "because God had created 'the mind free,' each person had to make his or her own determinations about faith. . . . Since God had granted us the ability to think, to deny us that right was sinful as well as tyrannical." In an oft-quoted passage from the *Notes on the State of Virginia*, Jefferson asked, "Can the liberties of a nation be thought secure when we have removed their only firm basis, a conviction in the minds of the people that these liberties are of the gift of God?" (Ominously, this comment was made in the context of slavery.) Whether the intellectual antecedents of this view can be found in Christian doctrines of the equality of the individual (the soul) before God, as Novak claims, or in Enlightenment rationalism (or both) is not entirely clear. It is clear, though, that Jefferson believed that since God created the mind free, "and manifested his supreme will that free it shall remain," it was inappropriate—heretical, really—for human institutions to restrict that intellectual freedom. The primary nature of man's relationship to God, precedent to his relationship with government, contributed importantly to Jefferson's view on separation of church and state.[35]

Belief in an afterlife and god-created rights are consistent with deism, but Jefferson was not a deist, at least not a strict deist. Deistic Enlightenment thinkers often referred to God as the great "clock-maker" or Aristotle's "First Cause," who, having created the universe and established the laws of nature, allows creation to run without interference. While Jefferson certainly evidenced deistic tendencies—for example, in his rejection of biblical miracles—and recognized God as the author of the laws of nature, he believed in some level of divine intervention in the world, some providence. For example, he reasoned that God acted to sustain species from extinction and to keep planets and comets on their course: "We see, too, evident proofs of the necessity of a superintending power, to maintain the universe in its course and order. . . . [W]ere there no restoring power, all existences might extinguish successively, one by one." While one might conclude that a more thorough understanding of astrophysics and evolutionary science would have relieved Jefferson of his belief in providence, that is speculative. At other times, Jefferson speaks more generally about God's active role, telling the Reverend David Barrow, who sent Jefferson abolitionist tracts: "We are not in a world ungoverned by the laws and power of a superior agent. Our efforts are in his hand, and directed by it; and he will give effect in his own time."[36]

Here, too, Jefferson's use of terms can confuse; he uses the term "deism" to refer generally to a monotheistic belief. For example, he wrote approvingly to Joseph Priestly that Jesus taught "principles of pure deism." Elsewhere he concluded that the Jewish "system was Deism; that is, the belief of one only God." It is not surprising, then, that many sources refer to Jefferson simply as a deist, but that characterization is not wholly accurate.[37]

Some notion of a belief in providence also appears in Jefferson's use of prayer, although, as with many mere mortals, Jefferson could demonstrate some confusion and shifting beliefs in this regard as well. In his Second Inaugural Address, for example, he explained that "I shall need, too, the favor of that Being in whose hands we are, who led our forefathers, . . . who has covered our infancy with his providence, and our riper years with his wisdom and power; and to whose goodness I ask you to join with me in supplications." He wrote to one group of political correspondents: "I supplicate a protecting providence to watch over your own and our countrys freedom & welfare." Occasionally, those who seek to find more traditional beliefs in Jefferson point to his willingness to pray. Yet, care must be taken here as well. Jefferson's statements about prayer often occurred in social exchanges, for example, asking Priestley, in farewell, to "[a]ccept my sincere prayers for your health and life." At other times, he explained that "I am never tempted to pray but when a warm feeling for my friends comes athwart my heart." Jefferson's public invocations were of the most general sort, and the significance of social and political convention should not be dismissed. None of this suggests an active prayer life or a belief in the miraculous efficacy of prayer. In fact, his denial of biblical miracles would suggest otherwise. Rather, he seems to be willing to pray as a social (and political) matter and, while perhaps not believing devoutly in the value of prayer to elicit divine intervention, he believed that God actively sustained his creation and was not willing to preclude the possibility of more active intervention. Prayer was also justified for Jefferson as part of the human duty to praise the beneficence of God; "we are bound, with peculiar gratitude," he wrote once, "to be thankful to him [the 'beneficent Being'] that our own peace has been preserved."[38]

Jefferson often attended church and contributed to a number of churches, although the pattern of his attendance varied greatly over the course of his life. Given his beliefs, particularly his opposition to dogmatism, and his attendance at a broad variety of different services, one must conclude that his attendance was as much to foster the social benefits of church society and to provide an opportunity to meditate and pray, as any type of endorsement of a particular sect or dogma. (In this, Jefferson was much like Benjamin Franklin, who famously supported a broad variety of churches although no one would mistake him for a devout adherent.) Manasseh Cutler, a federalist minister, suggested that Jefferson's attendance at church, especially while in office, was more political than religious. This is not entirely fair. While Jefferson certainly was deeply cognizant of the image he projected as president—for example, playing the part of "everyman" in greeting White House guests wearing slippers—and this may have contributed to his attendance at various services in Washington, his church attendance spanned the years long after he had retired from public life.[39]

Certainly, Jefferson was deeply moralistic. As noted earlier, he believed that good deeds, rather than faith, were the measure of a life. Not only did he renounce Calvinism and expressly endorse a philosophy of works, but his parental advice was of a similar nature. He wrote to his young daughter Martha: "Be sure to obey it [your conscience]. Our maker has given us all, this faithful internal Monitor, and if you always obey it, you will always be prepared for the end of the world: or for a much more certain event which is death." (Here, too, Jefferson suggests a belief in a postmortem judgment.) He believed in an instinctive human moral sense, attributing a broad congruence among various religions and denominations on basic moral obligations to this faculty. Interestingly, "because Jefferson believed in an innate moral sense," and the primacy of action over belief, "he feared the corrupting influence of the clergy but not atheism."[40]

It was in this context of moralism that Jefferson became a great believer in the doctrines of Jesus, particularly teachings concerning obligations to strangers and to society. These views developed in middle age, when Jefferson began to rethink his religious beliefs. This process was encouraged by repeated reading of the Unitarian Joseph Priestley's *An History of the Corruptions of Christianity*, which convinced Jefferson that his rejection of Christianity was based upon the perversion of the teachings of Jesus by priestcraft. This did not change Jefferson's view on Jesus's divinity or the nature of his human experience, but it did change dramatically his analysis of Christianity and the way in which he expressed his own religious beliefs. Here, too, Jefferson might be criticized theologically for "finding, or creating, a Jesus that matched [his] doctrines," as Conkin suggests, but the implications for his own belief system are clear nonetheless.[41]

With his interest renewed by his reading of Priestley and by the vicious religious criticism heaped upon him during the election of 1800, Jefferson remarkably found time during his first term as president to turn to the fundamental questions of religion and the teachings of Jesus in a more systematic manner. As his thinking at this time developed considerably, it is his views after 1800 that must be understood as his considered, mature judgments. (Jefferson's views also seem to be influenced in this period by Thomas Paine's publication of *The Age of Reason*, although evidence of this is more indirect.)[42] Significantly, his views on religion developed in parallel with his views on how the young republic that he had helped to birth should develop.

Based in part upon a short comparison that Priestley had prepared of the virtue of Socrates and Jesus, *Socrates and Jesus Compared* (1803), Jefferson concluded that Jesus's "morality was the most benevolent and sublime probably that has been ever taught." Jefferson then encouraged Priestley to create a more systematic comparison of the ethics and morals of various great thinkers from classical history. While Priestley's final work, *The Doctrines of Heathen Philosophy, Compared with Those of Revelation*, disappointed Jefferson, he concluded based on his own study that while the Greek and Roman thinkers offered an admirable system of controlling personal passions, they and the Jewish tradition were all deficient in "peace, charity & love to our fellow men," whereas Jesus preached "universal philanthropy, not only to kindred and friends, to neighbors and countrymen, but to all mankind, gathering all into one family, under bonds of love, charity, peace, common wants and common aids." Jefferson concluded that "the morality of Jesus, . . . freed from the corruptions of latter times, is far superior" to that of other philosophers; had Jesus's doctrines "been preached always as pure as they came from his lips, the whole civilized world would now have been Christian." While Jefferson's view of the Stoics and Jews may have been cramped, as Conkin also observes, Jefferson increasingly identified himself as a follower of the teachings of Jesus based in large part on Jesus's teachings concerning moral obligations to all humans. Jefferson titled his own short comparative analysis prepared at this time "Syllabus of an Estimate of the merit of the doctrines of Jesus, compared with those of others" and made a few copies available to dear friends and family members, with a strict admonition not to publish it.[43]

Having rethought his views of Jesus, Jefferson then recast the Bible by excerpting from the New Testament only those fragments that he believed were the true ethical teachings of Jesus. While lesser mortals might shy from rewriting scripture, Jefferson insisted that the real words of Jesus could be distinguished easily from the corruptions of centuries of priests and prophets, "as easily distinguishable as diamonds in a dunghill." Jefferson created a rough edition of Jesus's "authentic" statements from the gospels by 1804; this compilation he referred to as "The Philosophy of Jesus." Later, in retirement, he was to continue this effort, creating from the gospels what he understood to be a more accurate report of Jesus's life and teachings uncorrupted by the interests of priestcraft; by 1820, he had completed (in English, French, Latin, and Greek) this more thorough and detailed version of a redacted gospel, entitling the work "The Life and Morals of Jesus." The extended time and effort that Jefferson took painstakingly cutting out each relevant verse with a razor from versions of the gospels in four different languages (two copies each), and reconstructing them, speaks to how seriously Jefferson took this exercise.[44]

As a preliminary matter, it is noteworthy that Jefferson worked only with the New Testament and only the Gospels, omitting, for example, Paul's letters. Given Jefferson's views, this compilation also omits any reference to Jesus's divinity or miracles and ends with Jesus being laid in the tomb. These segments, often referred to as the "Jefferson Bible," cast Jesus as a great moral philosopher and reformer. In that role, Jefferson had enormous respect, even a devout respect, for Jesus. Jefferson referred to his admiration of "the innocence of His [Jesus's] character, the purity and sublimity of his moral precepts, the eloquence o [sic] His inculcations, the beauty of the apologues in which He conveys them." He concluded that "the world will see, after the fogs shall be dispelled, in which for fourteen centuries He [Jesus] has been enveloped by jugglers to make money of Him, when the genuine character shall be exhibited, which they have dressed up in the rags of an impostor, the world, I say, will at length see the immortal merit of this first of human sages." Investigation of Jesus's real views, as he understood them, "must end in a return to primitive christianity." Of course, this would be a Christianity devoid of any notion of Jesus's divinity and, for example, "the disbandment of the unintelligible Athanasian jargon of 3. being 1. and 1. being 3."[45]

Given his views of the private nature of religion, "The Life and Morals of

Jesus" was not intended for publication and was not published broadly until after the Smithsonian Institute bought a copy from Jefferson's great-granddaughter Carolina Randolph in 1895. Jefferson's effort in this regard, though, was known much earlier, with one mid-nineteenth-century publication defending Jefferson against claims of infidelity by noting that a visitor to Monticello "might have had pointed out to him the spot where, ever at the hand, stood his beautifully bound copy of the 'morals of Jesus,' textually extracted by himself, exhibiting to the glance of the eye each verse in four languages." Edwin Gaustad provides a fair context for our understanding of the "Jefferson Bible," both what Jefferson intended and did not intend: He did not delete scriptural passages to "shock or offend," even priests; rather, "he composed it for himself, for his devotion, for his assurance, for a more restful sleep at nights and a more confident greeting of the mornings."[46]

This affinity for Jesus's teachings was the basis of Jefferson's oft-quoted statement that "I am a Christian, in the only sense in which he [Jesus] wished anyone to be; sincerely attached to his doctrines, in preference to all others; ascribing to himself every *human* excellence; and believing he never claimed any other." Later he used the term "Christianism," teachings that he saw as a "rational creed . . . universal and eternal," to describe his views. He sometimes made a point to note that he had differences even with his rewritten Jesus— "I am a Materialist; he takes the side of Spiritualism; he preaches the efficacy of repentance towards forgiveness of sin; I require a counterpoise of good works"—but he generally cherished Jesus's moral and ethical teachings. It was not insignificant that as Jefferson's affinity for Jesus's teaching increased, he saw Jesus's crucifixion as the result of "the jealousy & combination of the altar and the throne," that is, the fruit of a combination of church and state.[47]

Given his views on the private nature of religion and its abuse by public figures, not to mention his belief that rational inquiry would bring people to embrace fundamental moral doctrines, he was affirmatively opposed to proselytizing his newfound faith. He even questioned the appropriateness of foreign religious missions, explaining, "I do not know that it is a duty to disturb by missionaries the religion and peace of other countries, who may think themselves bound to extinguish by fire and fagot the heresies to which we give the name of conversions, and quote our own example for it."[48]

He was equally concerned about proselytizing to children, an effort that threatened the "tyranny over the mind" that he had vowed to oppose. While

Jefferson was willing to parse the Bible carefully to support his own views, and so remodeled found it a deeply useful moral guide, he objected to "putting the Bible and Testament into the hands of the children at an age when their judgments are not sufficiently matured for religious enquiries." Jefferson's concern for the maturity of children's judgment must be understood in light of his belief that so much of the Bible was later fabrication or embellishment by Jesus's disciples and his own commitment to personal, reasoned inquiry. It was absolutely essential for the future of the republic that these future citizens learn to think and reason on their own. In a letter that was not finally sent, a more unguarded Jefferson wrote:

> [B]ut a short time elapsed after the death of the great reformer of the Jewish religion [Jesus] before his principles were departed from by those who professed to be his special servants, & perverted into an engine for enslaving mankind, and aggrandizing their oppressors in church & state: that the purest system of morals ever before preached to man has been adulterated & sophisticated, by artificial constructions, into a mere contrivance to filch wealth & power to themselves, that rational men not being able to swallow their impious heresies, in order to force them down their throats, they raise the hue & cry of infidelity, while themselves are the greatest obstacles to the advancement of the real doctrines of Jesus, and do in fact constitute the real anti-Christ.

Yet, while Jefferson thought that the Bible was deeply corrupted by some of Jesus's disciples and thought it a wholly inappropriate text for the education of children, he certainly recognized that it also contained much of value. Thus, when a retired Jefferson was approached by a minister raising funds to provide Bibles to families in Virginia who were lacking, he contributed fifty dollars for those "wishing without having the means to procure one."[49]

Critically, Jefferson's religious views and support for a moralistic, rational "Christianity" merged with his vision for a growing republic. He explained that "the Christian religion when divested of the rags in which they [the clergy] have inveloped it, and brought to the original purity & simplicity of its benevolent institutor, is a religion of all others most friendly to liberty, science, & the freest expression of the human mind." It struck Jefferson with great force that people could be united by the moral teachings of Jesus but that they were bitterly divided by dogmas that had been engrafted onto Christianity over the centuries and that were propagated by sects and "priestcraft." In his First Inaugural Address, he made a point of explaining that the American people were "enlightened by a benign religion, professed indeed and practiced in various forms, yet all of them inculcating honesty, truth, temperance, gratitude and the love of man, acknowledging and adoring an overruling providence." He was certainly not here embracing the all too ubiquitous sectarian dogmas or what he viewed as the perversions of religion. If Christianity might be returned to its historic purity, he reasoned—that is, if the moral teaching of Jesus could be separated from miracles, divinity, atonement, original sin, predestination, trinitarianism, and, most especially, priestcraft—the American people would support a civic religion that buttressed the growth of the new republic. Given the political upheaval of the 1790s and the ugly use of religion in the campaign of 1800, his interest was fed by a growing belief that a sound, rational religion, adopted broadly by the American people, would support republicanism by encouraging free inquiry and ending divisive, potentially dangerous, and certainly unproductive dogmatic disputes.[50]

Jefferson's views belie any suggestion of a strict secularization of society; he would have emphatically distinguished a secular society from the necessity of removing church—and "priestcraft"—from entanglement with government. He urged rational inquiry but linked that to his own religious convictions, admonishing that "[f]or the use of . . . reason . . . every one is responsible to the God who has placed it in his breast, as a light for his guidance, and that, by which alone he will be judged." Beyond the broad value of such inquiry for republicanism, Jefferson thought that this rational inquiry would foster Unitarianism consistent with his own beliefs and, one might add, a "low" Unitarianism at that. As a largely demystified Unitarianism displaced many of the traditional Congregational meeting houses in New England in the early nineteenth century, Jefferson boasted that "I confidently expect that the present generation will see Unitarianism become the general religion of the United States," and that "there is not a *young man* now living in the United States who will not die an Unitarian." For Jefferson, this rational religion could play a crucial role in growth of the "Empire of Liberty." Yet, religion it was; while Jefferson demanded a firm wall of separation between church and state, he neither feared nor opposed a flourishing religious society beyond that wall.[51]

That Jefferson was to prove wrong about the direction for American religion does not change the nature of his beliefs nor his expectation that a vibrant religion would flourish under a wholly secular government. Nor does it change

his expectation that rational religious inquiry would, itself, promote republican institutions. In fact, the very freedom of thought and practice that he
insisted upon was, to his chagrin, to propel the revivals of the Second Great
Awakening and the popular success of the evangelical Methodists, Baptists,
and a number of new sects that paid even less obeisance to reason over revelation. The noted New England evangelical minister Lyman Beecher, initially a
determined opponent of Jefferson's disestablishment of religion and separation
of church and state, eventually admitted that forcing voluntarism on Congregational clergy was *"the best thing that ever happened to the State of Connecticut.*
It cut the churches loose from dependence on state support. It threw them
wholly on their own resources and on God." Beecher also conceded the danger
that a church/state alliance posed Christianity, noting that with the explosion
of religion under the voluntary principle, Christianity "has survived the deadly
embrace of establishments nominally Christian." Thus, Jeffersonian disestablishment played a key role in propelling the profusion of Christianity and new
Christian sects in a free religious market, feeding "a period of religious ferment,
chaos, and originality unmatched in American history." As one devout republican newspaper editor explained the working of the Jeffersonian "voluntary
principle," "God is taking care of his own cause, for never since the settlement
of this country has there been such glorious revivals of religion as since President Jefferson presided."[52]

While Jefferson might well be seen as the progenitor of the movement, the
result was not what Jefferson anticipated, or, in its particular form, a result
that he would have supported. Witnessing the evangelical explosion, he wrote
worriedly to one correspondent that "[t]he atmosphere of our country is unquestionably charged with a threatening cloud of fanaticism." Here, too, one
can overstate Jefferson's views. While he continued to express deep suspicion
of many evangelicals, it is worth noting that the Second Great Awakening was
not wholly negative from a Jeffersonian perspective: It resulted in a vibrant discourse, encouraged some to focus on nondogmatic religion (the origins of the
Disciples of Christ, for example), was based on a very democratic ecclesiology,
and many of the evangelicals continued to embrace, emphatically, separation
of church and state. In the end, he took to his death his belief that "truth" had
"nothing to fear from the conflict unless by human interposition disarmed of
her natural weapons" and his belief in the use of a rational, demystified religion
to move the young republic forward.[53]

This leads to a key point: Jefferson, while not a Christian in any traditional sense, was certainly not hostile to religion as a general matter. Arguably the attacks by his political opponents were far too successful in suggesting otherwise. He was a devoted theist; he seemed to believe in an afterlife, and he believed that an enlightened, reformed religion could play an important role in breaking the hold that the clergy historically held over the mind of man, a tyranny that threatened republican government itself. His religion, his view of the American religion, was to be a religion devoid of priestcraft and any spark of a dangerous liaison between church and state. It was to be a religion that was soundly based upon observance of nature and reason. The universal appeal of such a religion would help to glue the sinews of the new nation, which, in the 1790s especially, had faced deep political division that threatened the social harmony that Jefferson believed to be essential for the working of a republic. "In order to accomplish this task, Jefferson sought to 'sweep away' the 'gossamer fabrics of factitious religion,' to refashion Christianity in accordance with the 'light of science' and the needs of civil society, and to incorporate a nonsectarian God who promotes the cause of freedom into American public life." But a theistic religion, not secularism, it would be.[54]

Central to this religion, though, and to his vision of the republic, had to be broad religious freedom, including a separation of church and state. "If the freedom of religion, guaranteed to us by law *in theory*, can ever rise *in practice* under the overbearing inquisition of public opinion, truth will prevail over fanaticism, and the genuine doctrines of Jesus, so long perverted by His pseudo-priests, will again be restored to their original purity. This reformation will advance with the other improvements of the human mind." Thus, while his commitment to religious freedom was certainly a political position, it was also consistent with, if not compelled by, his personal religious beliefs. Believing that God endowed men with their fundamental rights, Jefferson explained that "[t]he rights of conscience we never submitted [to government]. We could not submit. We are answerable for them to our God. The legitimate powers of government extend to such acts only as are injurious to others. But it does me no injury for my neighbour to say there are twenty gods, or no god." In essence, Jefferson would agree with the evangelical tradition that each person is responsible for his or her own salvation and, as a result, must be free of government restraint on conscience or encouragement to a particular belief. (From a Baptist perspective, for example, even government encouragement of religion would interfere with a "free will offering" to God.)[55]

James Madison—whose views of religious liberty and separation of church and state intimately paralleled Jefferson's and who played a leading role in the implementation of the Jeffersonian vision in the American body politic—made just this point in the first paragraph of his famous Memorial & Remonstrance Against Religious Assessments. In explaining religious liberty, he notes:

> This right is in its nature an unalienable right. It is unalienable, because the opinions of men, depending only on the evidence contemplated by their own minds cannot follow the dictates of other men: It is unalienable also, because what is here a right towards men, is a duty towards the Creator. It is the duty of every man to render to the Creator such homage and such only as he believes to be acceptable to him. This duty is precedent, both in order of time and in degree of obligation, to the claims of Civil Society. . . . We maintain therefore that in matters of Religion, no man's right is abridged by the institution of Civil Society and that Religion is wholly exempt from its cognizance.

Jack Rakove concludes that "for Madison as for Jefferson, then, the easy acceptance of freedom of conscience was not some mere antecedent condition from which one might or might not proceed to attack the more difficult matter of establishment. The attack on establishment flowed logically, perhaps even necessarily, from the commitment to freedom of conscience." As Jefferson explained in the Virginia Statute, governments could regulate "overt acts," but they lacked authority to "intrude . . . into the field of opinion." In summarizing his views in this regard, one can do little better than quoting part of the preamble to the Statute (as he wrote it):

> Almighty God hath created the mind free, and manifested his supreme will that free it shall remain by making it altogether insusceptible of restraint; that all attempts to influence by temporal punishments, or burthens, or by civil incapacitations, tend only to beget habits of hypocrisy and meanness, . . . that the impious presumption of legislators and rulers, civil as well as ecclesiastical, who, being themselves but fallible and uninspired men, have assumed dominion over the faith of others, . . . hath established and maintained false religions over the greatest part of the world through all time.

The Statute spoke to Jefferson's understanding of human nature, of religion, and of republican government, and he was more than a little pleased with himself when he explained to John Adams that the Statute had "put down the aristocracy of the clergy, and restored to the citizen the freedom of the mind."[56]

Certainly, Jefferson referred to the suggestion that he intended a "government without religion" as a "slander." Jefferson did not expect or desire a secularization of society or that government officials, acting in their private capacity, would be areligious. Jefferson's own actions demonstrated that he expected all officials to act as moral beings and that he, like most people in the eighteenth century, believed that religion would promote virtue. While he was extremely reticent to speak about his religious views publicly, he did not attempt to hide his personal religiosity while a public official; for example, he attended church and invoked God in his inaugural addresses. Isaac Kramnick and R. Laurence Moore could have been speaking for Jefferson when they noted that the Founders' opposition to any alliance between church and state was

> not the product[. . .] of personal godlessness. Far from it. Almost everyone who participated in the debates about the Constitution shared a concern about the health of religion. The success of democracy depended upon a moral citizenry; and for most American thinkers of the eighteenth century, morality rested on some sort of religious convictions. So did a theory of human rights. . . . They respected the moral teachings of Christ and hoped that they would prosper among Americans and in the churches that Americans attended.

What Jefferson and others rejected was that government had any role to play, or should have any role to play, in promoting religion and that religionists would have any particular sway in government.[57]

Jefferson attributed the slander of a "government without religion" to conservative political opponents, citing Reverend Linn's attack during the campaign of 1800. His supporters made the same point: Politics have "converted the elegant reasoning of Jefferson against *religious establishments*, into a blasphemous argument against *religion* itself." Again in 1804, a friendly editor asked sarcastically why Jefferson's opponents insist that "religion is in danger," answering that they complain "because Mr. Jefferson in his political capacity *lets it alone*, lets it have its own free course, is not inclined to interpose with his power in favor of any sect, but is a friend to free, complete and perfect toleration.— The inference they draw from this, is, that he must be an infidel, possessing no regard for religion and of course, (reasoning Calvinistically) must hate it, and will embrace the first opportunity to destroy it!"[58]

Yet, while he might eschew a government, or government officials, without religion, he did emphatically and repeatedly advocate that government "let[ ] it alone," that there be a government without interference of ministers (in any official capacity), with no alliance between religion and government, no aid to religion, and no official recognition. During the difficult campaign of 1800, William Duane's *Aurora* expressed Jefferson's platform as "good government without the aid of priestcraft or religious politics, and justice administered without religious interference," criticizing Federalists for having mixed religion and politics, "equally polluting the holy altars of religion and the seats of justice." At the conclusion of the election, Jefferson's political-religious philosophy was summed up by one Republican minister as "Our Statesmen to the Constitution and our Clergy to the Bible."[59]

Combining his concerns for an ethical religion and growth of an "empire of liberty," he was convinced that any alliance between church and state would prostitute both and undermine the noble republican experiment, and it is clear that his concern went both to governmental interference with religion and religion's interference with government: "[I]n every country and in every age, the priest has been hostile to liberty. [H]e is always in alliance with the Despot." He told another correspondent that "history furnishes no example of a priest-ridden people maintaining a free civil government." Madison, concerned about the same potential of government when allied with the church to restrict free thought and action, warned that any church/state alliance would result in "pride and indolence in the Clergy; ignorance and servility in the laity; in both, superstition, bigotry and persecution."[60]

Thus, while many have noted Jefferson's contribution to a theistic American civil religion, Jefferson believed that such a civic religion must develop devoid of government influence and would be a rationalistic religion of liberty. The Statute was central to this understanding. The historian Johann Neem places Jefferson's famous 1802 Letter to the Danbury Baptists declaring a "wall of separation" between church and state in the same context:

> The real point of the letter ... lies in the next sentence, which concerns what would happen on the other side of the wall, in civil society: "I shall see with sincere satisfaction the progress of those sentiments which tend to restore to man his natural rights, convinced he has no natural right in opposition to his social duties." Jefferson believed that by erecting a wall between church and state, he could protect free inquiry and, by so doing, aid the process by which a purified Christianity housed in reason rather than faith would become Amer-

ica's civil religion. The wall of separation was not intended to banish religion from the public sphere of civil society. Instead, it was intended to prohibit an alliance between ministers and politicians that would limit free inquiry.

In constitutional terms, disestablishment and free exercise are inseparable. The Statute, and separation of church and state, protected free inquiry, which Jefferson, as with Madison, believed crucial to protect minorities and a vibrant public discourse. For religious freedom, the "maxim of civil government being reversed," he concluded "divided we stand, united we fall."[61]

One should not forget that it was in the context of opposition to any religious establishment that Jefferson wrote his good friend Benjamin Rush, "I have sworn upon the altar of god eternal hostility against every form of tyranny over the mind of man." For Jefferson, "the oldest and bloodiest and most deeply entrenched form of such tyranny had been in the name of religion." As early as 1776, he had called for "totally and eternally restraining the civil magistrate from all pretensions of interposing his authority or exercise in matters of religion." Jefferson saw in that policy a dual necessity, both protecting the republic from such an alliance but also protecting religion from the corruptions of "priestcraft." He confidently predicted that "a recollection of our former vassalage in religion & civil government, will unite the zeal of every heart, & the energy of every hand, to preserve that independence in both which, under the favor of heaven, a disinterested devotion to the public cause first achieved, and a disinterested sacrifice of private interests will now maintain." Jefferson saw separation as eliminating the "vassalage" of both religion and government. Tunis Wortman, a New York Republican lawyer working to rehabilitate Jefferson's religion in the context of the 1800 election, made the same point: "Religion and government are equally necessary, but their interests should be kept separate and distinct. No legitimate connection can ever subsist between them. Upon no plan, no system, can they become united, without endangering the purity and usefulness of both—the church will corrupt the state, and the state pollute the church."[62]

Given its antecedents in rationalism, republicanism, and religion, this core belief in religious liberty was largely unbounded for Jefferson. He made very clear that the Statute for Establishing Religious Freedom was to be understood to cover by the "mantle of it's protection, the Jew and the Gentile, the Christian and Mahometan, the Hindoo, and infidel of every denomination." He specifically rejected Locke's view that Catholics, for example, need not be tolerated because of an allegiance to a "foreign prince." By contrast, Jefferson suggested that "[p]erhaps the single thing which may be required others before toleration to them would be an oath that they would allow toleration to others." Even this minor limitation, with interesting modern implications, was not ultimately included in the Statute. He argued that in a free republic any restrictions on religious (and mental) freedom were unnecessary and counterproductive. "Reason and free enquiry are . . . the natural enemies of error, and of error only. Had not the Roman government permitted free enquiry, Christianity could never have been introduced. Had not free enquiry been indulged, at the era of the reformation, the corruptions of Christianity could not have been purged away. If it be restrained now, the present corruptions will be protected, and new ones encouraged." Over time, he believed that experience demonstrated the correctness of his views. In 1808, he told Baptist supporters that "we have solved, by fair experiment, the great & interesting question Whether freedom of religion is compatible with order in government." By 1823, Madison spoke for Jefferson when he wrote confidently to another correspondent:

> The settled opinion here is that religion is essentially distinct from Civil Gov^t. and exempt from its cognizance; that a connexion between them is injurious to both; that there are causes in the human breast, which ensure the perpetuity of religion without the aid of the law; that rival sects, with equal rights, exercise mutual censorships in favor of good morals; that if new sects arise with absurd opinions or overheated maginations [sic], the proper remedies lie in time, forbearance and example.[63]

Given this foundation, any effort to minimize the strength of Jefferson's belief in religious liberty and the separation of church and state is revisionist and ill-founded, inconsistent with both his religious and political understanding. Thus, when a rising chorus of late twentieth-century voices sought to curtail the separation of church and state in defining American religious freedom and civil religion, one device was to suggest that it was not central to Jefferson's views. For example, James Hutson, former chief of the Manuscript Division at the Library of Congress, argued that Jefferson's Letter to the Danbury Baptists insisting upon a "wall of separation between church and state" was a political diversion, merely a "short note of courtesy," not reflecting his considered views and of no constitutional significance. Hutson went on to urge that because Jefferson struck the term "eternal" before "wall of separation" and attended church services in the House of Representatives, "he seems to have . . . believed that, provided that the state kept within its well-appointed limits, it could provide 'friendly aids' to churches." A bevy of historians properly protested. Hutson's argument flies in the face not only of Jefferson's religious and political beliefs and consistent statements and actions, but his own characterization of the letter in a contemporaneous note that he wrote to his attorney general, Levi Lincoln, in which he saw the letter as an opportunity of "sowing useful truths & principles among the people" and making a "condemnation of the alliance between church and state." Postmaster General Gideon Granger advised Jefferson that the letter "is but a declaration of Truths which are in fact felt by a great Majority of New England, & publicly acknowledged by near half the People of Connecticut," but it will help "germinate among the People' and in time fix 'their political Tenets'" to church-state reform. The problem with the revisionist view goes beyond our understanding of the Danbury Letter's "wall of separation" and speaks to our fundamental understanding of Jefferson. Leonard Levy explains that those who find the Danbury Letter was "a little address of courtesy" with an unconsidered "figure of speech" or "motivated by an impish desire to heave a brick at the Congregationalist-Federalist hierarchy of Connecticut," do a grave injustice to Jefferson. "Jefferson had powerful convictions on the subject of religious liberty which he always approached most solemnly." The attacks that he had experienced, and his own conviction, determined his approach. He told Benjamin Rush that "it behooves every man who values liberty of conscience for himself, to resist invasions of it in the case of others."[64]

Jefferson was not alone in placing religious freedom, including separation of church and state, at the core of his political philosophy. As James Madison wrote in 1774, "[r]eligious bondage shackles and debilitates the mind and unfits it for every noble enterprize every expanded project." Members of the Supreme Court have noted that "[f]or Madison, as also for Jefferson, religious freedom was the crux of the struggle for freedom in general." Jefferson's legacy as the prophet of democratic freedom, then, must be seen in this light. As Gaustad concludes: "Just as Americans were to be politically free, so they were to be religiously free. It would be impossible to sustain one without the other." In fact, Jefferson might have mildly corrected Gaustad: If Americans were to be politically free, they must be religiously free.[65]

As with most people, Jefferson's views on religion were complex and shifting. Still, a broad understanding of his views can be formed from his mature writings and practices, and these views clearly influenced Jefferson's role in the development of American religious and political freedom.

In the end, Jefferson must be understood as deeply religious, theistic, but emphatically not a Christian, at least not in the conventional sense. He did, though, see Jesus as the world's greatest moral teacher. Jefferson believed in a doctrine of works, rejecting unequivocally Calvinism. Providence worked in Jefferson's world, but his statements and actions would suggest that it did so in the broadest, and somewhat impersonal, manner. He believed in rational inquiry and was deeply opposed to constraints on reason and personal investigation and understanding, and he was perhaps even more adamantly opposed to priestcraft and its tool: cooperation between church and state.

Critically, for Jefferson, both true religion and the republic depended upon liberty of the mind, including full religious liberty. Of necessity, such liberty included separation of church and state. These deeply felt beliefs were to drive his vision of religious liberty as embodied in the Statute for Establishing Religious Freedom.

2

VIRGINIA'S ESTABLISHMENT
AND THE REVOLUTIONARY BATTLE
FOR RELIGIOUS LIBERTY

JEFFERSON'S CAMPAIGN FOR RELIGIOUS LIBERTY AND THE SIGNIFI-
cance of his vision in the development of American religious freedom can be
best understood on the stage on which his views and commitment to religious
liberty developed. In particular, an understanding of the role of religious dissent in early Virginia is essential. Not only did discrimination against and
persecution of dissenters (primarily Presbyterians and Baptists) provide the
backdrop on which Jefferson acted, but their political support was to prove
essential in the fight for religious freedom, giving their views unusual significance in understanding that freedom.

Colonial Virginia had an established church. Equally important, it had a
well-entrenched political hierarchy drawn from that church and devoted to
its (the church's and the hierarchy's) continuance in power. As Jefferson began
to develop his own views on religion and religious freedom, the Church of
England in Virginia was strong and growing, increasing its already impressive
power. Beyond Jefferson's well-developed appreciation for the role of religious
persecution in history, it was this powerful, established church and the discrimination and later persecution imposed in its name that framed Jefferson's
deep concern and ultimately played a critical role in encouraging adoption of
the Virginia Statute for Establishing Religious Freedom.

Religious discrimination and persecution in colonial Virginia were far more
serious than many have suggested. Yet, despite the legal discrimination against
dissenters that accompanied the Church of England's status as the established
church, despite the growing violent persecution of dissent, and despite the efforts of Virginia's Anglican leaders to maintain political hegemony, the ranks

of Virginia's dissenters grew rapidly from the Great Awakening onward. Once war with Britain broke out, the Virginia Establishment quickly realized that it needed the support of Virginia's dissenters for effective mobilization. The situation was ripe with potential. Having suffered grievously at the hands of the Establishment, Virginia's dissenters might have resisted efforts to mobilize in support of a rebellion against the British Crown championed by the same leaders who had denied them toleration and, in many cases, participated in their persecution. In fact, historically, British officials had tended to protect American religious dissenters against some of the worst abuses of local colonial establishments; as a result, dissenters in other colonies had a noted, and dangerous, penchant for loyalism.

Not so in the Old Dominion. As a rule, Virginians tended to support the war as much or more than other colonists, but the relative lack of loyalism among Virginia's dissenters is striking. Understanding why is critical for understanding the development of religious freedom.

In Virginia, when the necessity of a broad mobilization became clear, dissenters abandoned forever pleas to the Establishment for improved toleration and instead insisted upon religious freedom in return for their full support for the war effort. The ensuing negotiations—incrementally, slowly, with difficulty—dramatically liberalized religious freedom in Virginia. Ecclesiastic taxes were suspended, then eliminated. Some vestry and marriage reforms were adopted. All the while, dissenters were encouraged to support the war effort, and the evidence is that they delivered that support. While Jefferson and Madison provided important intellectual leadership, the chorus of complaints from the evangelical dissenters, newly made important to Virginia's political leadership by the demands for mobilization, was essential for religious liberty in Virginia.

Still, by the time that Cornwallis surrendered at Yorktown, dissenters had not yet achieved full religious liberty: Marriage restrictions continued, and vestry reform had been very limited. Jefferson's draft Bill for Establishing Religious Freedom had been tabled, and a movement for renewed government financial support of religion seemed to be growing. With the need for mobilization removed, prospects for further reform were uncertain at best. Recognizing that the war and the resulting necessity of a united front against Britain's military power were essential for encouraging liberalization, Jefferson warned that "[f]rom the conclusion of this war we shall be going down hill. . . . The shackles . . . which shall not be knocked off at the conclusion of this war, will remain on us long, will be made heavier and heavier, till our rights shall revive or expire in convulsion." Within a few years, his concerns seemed prescient.[1]

Virginia's royal charter of 1606 presupposed that the new colony's mission was, in part, religious. King James I insisted that "the true word, and service of God and Christian faith be preached, planted and used" in Virginia "according to the doctrine, rights, and religion now professed and established within our realm of England." The 1609 charter proclaimed the necessity of "the Fear and true Worship of Almighty God" by demanding the Anglican Oath of Supremacy from everyone entering the colony. By 1619, the first colonial legislature formally established the Church of England for His Majesty's colony.[2]

When Puritan fever swept England, old and New, in the early years of the seventeenth century, a few Virginia settlers did seek to attract Puritan ministers. Yet, by 1643, in spite of the Civil War in England, only Anglican ministers were permitted in Virginia, and "nonconformists" were to be ordered out. While enforcement of such laws was often episodic, hundreds of dissenters who entered the colony over the course of almost four decades fled to Maryland or North Carolina. The laws were strengthened in 1659, during the Commonwealth period in England, in order to prevent the immigration of dissenters from the Church of England, especially Quakers.[3]

For Jefferson, the very nature of political control by a particular sect was rife with Puritanical intolerance; writing about this early period, he noted that when "[p]ossessed ... of the powers of making, administering, and executing the laws, they [early Virginia colonists] shewed equal intolerance ... with their Presbyterian brethren, who had emigrated to the northern government." (In another example of his self-definition of terms, Jefferson at times referred to all Calvinists, including New England Congregationalists, as Presbyterians.)[4]

Notwithstanding its official status, by the early eighteenth century, the established church of Virginia was an odd mixture of official power and internal weakness. In 1725, there were fifty-one parishes in Virginia, but only about two-thirds to three-quarters had ministers, and even this greatly overstates the effective presence of the Church of England as many of the parishes were so large as to impair practical, regular ministrations by a single rector. The problem was exacerbated by the Anglican requirement that priests be ordained by a bishop, with bishops resident only in England. Not only did colonials seeking ordination have to make an expensive and dangerous voyage to London (death rates among those seeking ordination were over 20 percent well into the eighteenth century), but the formal education expected of an Anglican priest was more readily available in England.[5]

While the College of William and Mary had been chartered in 1693 in part to provide a local priesthood, in the early eighteenth century, it was still not coming close to filling that need. As a result, almost all of the Anglican priests in Virginia in this period were from Great Britain, and it was not uncommon that the priests who found their way to Virginia were those unable to find positions in Britain (or those fleeing debt, unwelcome wives or children, or other serious problems). In 1751, the bishop of London had to concede that of the priests "sent from hence, a great part are of the Scotch and Irish, who can get no employment at home and enter into the service more out of necessity than choice. Some others are willing to go abroad to retrieve either lost fortunes or lost Characters." Although the problem is subject to exaggeration, James Madison later referred to "the indolence of most & the irregular lives of many of the established Clergy, consisting, in a very large proportion, of foreigners, and these in no inconsiderable proportion, of men willing to leave their homes in the parent Country where their demerit was an obstacle to a provision for them, and whose degeneracy here was promoted by their distance from the controuling eyes of their kindred & friends, by the want of Ecclesiastical superiors."[6]

Yet, despite the condition of the church and clerics in the earlier period, in the latter half of the century, while Jefferson was coming to maturity, the church's power and stature improved considerably, as did the performance of its clergy. By 1776, the number of parishes in Virginia had almost doubled from the inadequate levels of 1725, and the ninety-five parishes were almost completely occupied by resident ministers. Equally important, two-thirds to three-quarters of those ministers were American natives or had lived in America for a considerable period before seeking ordination, significantly reducing clerical problems. By the time of the Revolution, while as many as three-quarters of the clergy were from America, three-quarters of the complaints about clergy related to British priests who had come to America to find a benefice. With priests increasingly from local families, a number of Virginia clergy were appointed as civil magistrates as well. As the same Virginia gentry families dominated Anglican vestries and leadership in the House of Burgesses, politically active priests helped to form an apparently seamless bond between church and state. The local nature of the clergy also ensured that the vast majority of Virginia's ministers were patriots in the upcoming war (refuting, at least in Virginia, claims that Toryism among the clergy undermined the Church of England's power as the war approached).[7]

In fact, the Establishment was well-entrenched and strengthening as the Revolution approached. Unfortunately, the poor reputation from the earlier period haunted the priesthood into the second half of the eighteenth century (and into history books), tending to obfuscate rather than enlighten on the broader question of Establishment authority and development of religious freedom. Part of the reason for this was political, with the reputation of the Virginia clergy suffering from conflicts with powerful lay leaders, evident in both the Parsons' Cause and the Bishop's Controversy.

The Parsons' Cause arose primarily over the question of British control of local economic regulation. In colonial Virginia, a number of fees and taxes were paid in tobacco, not least of which was the regular parish assessment of 16,000 pounds of tobacco to pay the local Anglican minister. When tobacco crops were plentiful, tobacco prices dropped and ministers, receiving a fixed amount of tobacco, effectively received less money; when tobacco prices rose, ministers received what seemed like a windfall to small farmers and taxes weighed more heavily. In 1758, after several years of particularly bad crops and wartime disruption to the trade, tobacco prices had risen dramatically. In an effort to provide tax relief, the House of Burgesses—dominated by Anglican vestry members—passed a law valuing a pound of tobacco at two pence (about half of the market value) and permitting fees and taxes to be paid using currency rather than the (temporarily) more valuable tobacco. Anglican ministers, angered by the willingness of their congregants to see their pay shrink in years of abundant tobacco but unwilling to allow their pay to rise in years of scarcity, successfully petitioned the king, acting through the Privy Council, to disallow the law. Several ministers then sued for full payment of their annual allowance in tobacco or at the inflated tobacco prices. Appearing on behalf of a local vestry in what seemed to be a losing case, the young Patrick Henry made a name for himself by convincing a jury to award the Reverend James Maury (Jefferson's former teacher) only one pence in damages. For these purposes, the point is that the dispute was primarily about the power of the House of Burgesses to regulate local economic matters in opposition to the edicts of a distant king; secondarily, the case evidenced tension between vestry and clergy. It was not about the power of the Anglican establishment per se. While Henry—always the showman—effectively railed against priests as "rapacious harpies" who would take the "last hoe-cake, from the widow and her orphan children," the dispute did not end the increase in Anglican parishes and ministers or, certainly, compromise the role of the vestry.[8]

Similarly, the Bishop's Controversy—ignited when New England Congregationalists and Presbyterians came to fear that Parliament might send an Anglican bishop to America with ecclesiastic and political power to match that of bishops in England—was of a limited significance in Virginia. Virginia vestries tended to oppose a local bishop for fear that they would lose control over their own ministers, and many Anglican priests were equally concerned with the possibility of more immediate and effective supervision by a bishop. Few Virginians saw the possibility of a local bishop as a real threat to their personal freedom (one suspects that a mature Jefferson, with his antipathy to priestcraft and the power of church hierarchy, may have, although his contemporary correspondence does not speak of the matter). While the Bishop's Controversy resulted in a heated exchange in the *Virginia Gazette*, "in Virginia," these disputes "are best understood as dealing between parson and squire—between clergy and the vestrymen who were the lay governors of the parish churches." (Perhaps a more significant result of the Bishop's Controversy is that it contributed to the decision of James Madison Sr. to send his son to Princeton under the tutelage of the liberty-loving Jonathan Witherspoon in part because James Horrocks, a supporter of a colonial bishop, then controlled William and Mary.)[9]

Whatever the status of Anglican clergy as the Revolution approached, this should not be confused with the sociopolitical dominance of the Anglican hierarchy. In the fifty years from 1690 to 1740, 60 percent of the members of the House of Burgesses served on Anglican vestries, and that pattern did not change as the Revolution approached. Bishop Meade reported that only three members of the Virginia Convention that seized power from Lord Dunmore, the last British governor, had not been vestry members. Even this can understate the effective dominance of Anglicans in pre-Revolutionary Virginia politics. All of the members of the governor's council and, thus, of the highest court were Anglican. As Jack Greene adds, the religion of the leaders of the House of Burgesses was "remarkably homogenous. Of the 80 per cent ascertainable, all were Anglicans." The key leaders who controlled both the House of Burgesses and, after 1776, the House of Delegates were not only Anglican by birth, but tended to be strong supporters of the established church. Of the seven local men who dominated Virginia's late colonial politics—Richard Bland, Archibald Cary, Benjamin Harrison, Richard Henry Lee, Robert Carter Nicholas, Edmund Pendleton, and Peyton Randolph—the majority were dedicated churchmen. Cary and Pendleton, confirmed Anglicans who actively opposed religious dissenters, became the Speakers of the new Virginia Senate and House of Delegates respectively. Anglican dominance also permeated many local offices, including appointed county magistrates and justices of the peace, with a justice of the peace in Orange County losing his position in 1768 based upon a report that he was an "Anabaptist." The church that Jefferson knew as he struggled with his own religious beliefs, the church that he confronted as he worked for disestablishment, maintained broad power and prestige and was a formidable foe.[10]

The political power of Virginia's established church was reflected in a series of discriminatory laws. Anglican priests were paid and churches maintained through tax assessments of all landowners, including dissenters. Anglican vestries were given responsibility for a number of civic functions and enjoyed a commensurate taxing power. Vestries were responsible for poor relief and could create and fill workhouses. Combined, the vestry tax for the Anglican minister and for poor relief was generally the highest tax paid in eighteenth-century Virginia. Regular attendance at Anglican worship, or one of the few licensed dissenting meeting houses, was mandatory. Anglican vestries were required to report drunkenness, swearing, blasphemy, adultery, fornication, or whoredom to grand juries, not only significant authority in itself, but authority, like the mandatory attendance laws, that could be used selectively to discriminate against dissenters from the Church of England. Vestries were also responsible for periodically walking the bounds of each parish, marking property boundaries and initially resolving property disputes. Vestries had a role in policing Virginia's system of slavery, having authority to seize and sell a slave who was manumitted without the approval of the governor and council. Marriages had to be consecrated by an Anglican minister, making children of dissenters who failed to marry within the Church of England (or pay the local Anglican priest for his cooperation) subject to claims of bastardy, with potentially serious legal consequences, especially in probate. Vestries had responsibility for placing orphans and for the "binding out" of children when their parents could not care for them. In theory, schoolmasters had to be approved by the bishop of London. William and Mary, the only college in the colony, was controlled by Anglicans, with Anglican ministers accounting for almost its entire faculty throughout the period. Anglican priests enjoyed other special privileges, including exemption from militia musters and some taxes.[11]

Non-Anglicans were sometimes elected to a vestry, especially in the western counties, where dissenters, particularly Scotch-Irish Presbyterians, outnumbered Anglicans by the middle of the century. This, though, did not compromise the church's political dominance. In fact, continuance of Anglican vestries in these areas at all is testament to the power of the established church in colonial Virginia. Moreover, the law made it clear that dissenters could be removed from vestries, an authority that was exercised if Anglican hegemony was at risk. In the one case when a non-Anglicans majority on a colonial vestry was challenged, the governor ordered its dissolution and a new one elected "conformable to . . . the church of England." Nonconforming congregations in the Valley, both Lutheran and Presbyterian, were more likely to avoid conflict if they did not challenge Anglican social and political authority.[12]

Of course, laws on the book did not necessarily translate into significant discrimination in favor of Anglicans in practice. Edmund Randolph, a leader in the Virginia church and later governor of Virginia and George Washington's first attorney general, argued after the war that the Anglicans' "spirit of mildness was an antidote to the licensed severity of the law" in late colonial Virginia. Yet, claims made by members of the Establishment of lenient enforcement must be considered skeptically and, to the extent accurate, may be more evidence of selective enforcement rather than nonenforcement. While it is certainly true that discrimination and persecution were not always serious or monolithic, from the perception of religious dissenters, Randolph's statement is simply wrong. Certainly no one suggests that dissenters were not required to pay the tax for Anglican ministers, and failure to attend church—for all practical purposes, this meant failure to attend the Anglican Church—was apparently the most common crime prosecuted in eighteenth-century colonial Virginia. A study of grand jury presentments from 1750 to 1770 in eleven Virginia counties found that "missing church" was the most frequent offense in six of the counties and among the top three offenses in four others. Swearing—also cognizable by Anglican vestries—made the top three list in five counties. Fines were assessed in scores of cases, and anecdotal evidence suggests that dissenters were disproportionately the object of enforcement. As one leading Baptist minister explained, "[l]ittle notice was taken of the omission [in church attendance], if members of the established church; but so soon as the new-lights [evangelical Baptists and Presbyterians] were absent they were presented by the grand jury, and fined according to law." Similarly, while some dissenting ministers were able to start schools, when a dissenter sought a position that conflicted with an Anglican minister's school, the requirement that teachers be licensed by the bishop of London could be invoked. Tax laws, too, were subject to selective enforcement.[13]

In theory, the 1689 English Act of Toleration—endorsed by King William and Queen Mary shortly after they seized the British throne from Mary's too-Catholic father, James II—provided some relief to Protestant dissenters, but in Virginia there was an ongoing dispute as to whether the act applied at all. Even when the political establishment licensed dissenting ministers ostensibly under the authority of the Act of Toleration, the licensing process was more a matter of control than of license. To obtain a license, dissenting ministers were required to travel to Williamsburg for one of the semi-annual meetings of the General Court (often a difficult, lengthy, and costly trip) and present a petition from a local congregation that they proposed to serve and certification of orthodoxy from an Anglican minister (demonstrating support for the basic doctrines of the Anglican Church even if disagreement with the church's hierarchical structure). These limitations and requirements went well beyond the English statute.[14]

A minister who preached before seeking a license could be denied on that ground alone, and this, too, could be used in a strategic manner. When Establishment leaders wanted to limit early Presbyterian incursions, they used the fact that John Rodgers had preached before traveling to Williamsburg for a license as a reason to deny a license, declaring, "[W]e have Mr. Rodgers out, and we are determined to keep him out." Even when the requirements were met, sometimes licenses were still denied, or limited in terms of the number of meeting houses that could be served (to prevent anything that could be characterized as itinerancy and to discourage the socially destabilizing tendencies of evangelicals preaching to free and enslaved blacks). One Baptist minister reported: "I knew the general court to refuse a license for a Baptist meeting house, in the county of Richmond, because there was a Presbyterian meeting house already in the county."

> [T]hro' the whole process of this business, from the beginning to the end, obstructions and difficulties lay in the way—first to get signers to a petition, second to get a certificate from two acting magistrates in the county from which

the petition was sent, thirdly to find the court in such a temper and capable of exercising such generosity as to grant a license, and after all this, it was left uncertain and precarious, and depended on the will and temper of the clergy whether we should succeed or not.

Some dissenting ministers, particularly "New Light" Separate Baptists, refused to even apply for a license, insisting that their license came from "King Jesus," but this simply left them subject to legal persecution.[15]

Resenting these restrictions and harassment, the first dissenting minister licensed by the Virginia General Court, the renowned Presbyterian Samuel Davies, traveled to England and, in 1752, received an opinion from the English attorney general, Sir Dudley Rider, that the Act of Toleration did apply in the colonies. This, though, did not prevent Virginia's Anglican leadership from interpreting the act as narrowly as possible or, when convenient, ignoring it altogether. In 1772, a letter commonly attributed to John Randolph, the colony's attorney general and brother of the Speaker of the House of Burgesses, observed that most colonial lawyers believed that the Act of Toleration did not apply to Virginia and that opponents of the Establishment were engaged in "Heresy and Schism, and a Breach of the Laws." Other means to frustrate the growing tide of dissent were found as necessary. An indictment was issued against Joshua Morris for allowing a Presbyterian minister to preach at his house before receiving a license; Thomas Watkins was presented for speaking ill of the established church.[16]

Significantly, the legal dominance of the Virginia Anglican hierarchy and its efforts to restrain dissent were apparently supported by the Anglican laity which still accounted for a majority of the populace. Opposition to dissent among the laity meant that dissenters from the established church suffered not only legal infirmities but considerable social ostracism. Evangelical Baptists, in particular, "weare held in contempt by most of the people" according to one Piedmont planter. An evangelical preacher in the Southside of Virginia (south of the James River) decided not to seek ordination as a dissenter because "[t]he general prejudice of the people at the time against dissenters and in favor of the [Anglican] church, gave me a full persuasion that I could do more good in the church than anywhere else."[17]

In spite of this serious legal discrimination and social ostracism, in the mid-eighteenth century two independent movements—one physical, one religious—resulted in a dramatic increase in dissent in the British Crown's most populous colony. The first movement was the migration of Scotch-Irish (mostly Presbyterians) and Germans (Lutherans, Reformed, and Mennonites) down the valleys of Pennsylvania into the Shenandoah Valley of Virginia. Initially, their presence was not viewed as a threat; in fact, in 1738, when the Philadelphia Synod specifically requested the right to have Presbyterians settle in the Valley, Lieutenant Governor William Gooch gladly agreed in an effort to provide a buffer from Indian attacks for the Piedmont and Tidewater (although Gooch was later to join in opposition to Presbyterian incursions into the Piedmont). As midcentury approached, the majority of inhabitants west of the Blue Ridge were non-Anglican immigrants from the north, welcome interlopers to a government that had been plagued with Native American conflicts on the western frontier.[18]

The second movement feeding rapidly rising dissent was the Great Awakening, which stirred religious fervor across the mainland colonies and England. As evangelical ministers sowed enthusiasm and with it, often, schism, they found fertile ground for conversion in Virginia, where the Awakening was accompanied by a dramatic growth in Presbyterian and Baptist influence, especially in the Piedmont and Valley. This process started in the 1730s when some residents of Hanover and surrounding counties in the Piedmont began to absent themselves from the local Anglican Church—which they saw as unmoved by the Spirit—and to gather on Sundays to read homilies and prayers in local homes, particularly the home of Samuel Morris. As time went on, Presbyterian missionaries sent to the Valley brought their religious brethren in the Piedmont into the fold. As a result, Samuel Davies was sent by the Philadelphia Presbytery and received from Governor Gooch and the General Court a license to preach in four meeting houses in the Hanover area in 1747. In spite of the very real impediments, other licenses followed—although Anglican ministers still controlled marriage, Anglican vestries still controlled poor relief, and Anglican church taxes were still due from all residents.[19]

As Presbyterianism gained ground in the Valley and central Piedmont, Baptist preachers began to appear in the northern Piedmont and, shortly thereafter, Southside in the 1750s. The influx was led by "Separate" Baptists, deeply evangelical and opposed to social and religious hierarchy; the same enthusiasts led numerous schisms from New England's Congregational churches. The Baptist ministers often lacked formal education, and they generally opposed a professional clergy, favoring preaching by those "called by the Spirit" and itinerancy. Separate Baptist preachers were reluctant even to seek a formal license. When questioned, they might defiantly declare that their license came in Jesus's Great Commission (Matthew 28:18–20), and they recognized no authority to deny them the right to preach. Heightening the inevitable tension with the Establishment, Baptists, and to some extent Presbyterians, made a point of seeking to convert blacks and women and then permitted them to have a formal role in their churches—both assaults on the Old Dominion's social system. Opposition to horse racing, card playing, fiddling, drinking, and dancing further alienated "enthusiastic" New Light dissenters from Virginia's leaders.[20]

The precise number of dissenters in colonial Virginia is impossible to know for several reasons. First, many people who might have favored a dissenting minister practiced occasional conformity, that is, attended an Anglican Church for special ceremonies, for example, baptism, communion, or marriage. Further, when figures for dissenting congregations were kept, they were usually for the "membership" of the congregations, but membership in a colonial evangelical church generally required public recitation of a conversion experience to the congregation, and it was not uncommon for a congregation to have several times as many regular attendees as formal members. Patricia Bonomi concludes that a ratio of three or four noncommunicants to each member was probably too low, and Baptist David Benedict, writing in 1813, says "we may reckon seven adherents to one communicant." Finally, of course, membership was constantly shifting. Still, the overall success of dissenters was undoubted. When asked about the number of dissenters, one Anglican minister complained, "I might almost as well pretend to count the gnats that buzz around us in a summer's evening."[21]

This uncertainty as to the precise extent of dissent is evident in both the contemporary and later records. Jefferson on various occasions reported the dissenting population at the time of the Revolution as two-thirds of Virginia's white residents (a figure Madison deferentially debunked), one-half, and about one-fifth. Realistically, by 1775, Virginia's dissenters accounted for from one-fifth to as much as one-third or a bit more of the white population, and their membership was growing rapidly. Their presence, though, was not equally distributed throughout the state; in the Valley, dissenters were a majority, with their presence generally decreasing as one moved east through the Piedmont and into the Tidewater. This distribution was not insignificant since in Virginia, as in a number of the colonies, the western (newer) counties were underrepresented in the legislature; as a result, the Anglican Tidewater, with approximately one-third of Virginia's population, had approximately one-half of the representatives in the House of Burgesses. It was also easier for members from the Tidewater and eastern Piedmont to attend the assembly. With their continuing numerical superiority and dominance among the gentry, Anglican control of the government was easily maintained.[22]

As the 1760s progressed, and evangelical Presbyterians and, especially, Baptists began moving frequently into areas previously dominated by Anglicans, an explosion was almost inevitable. (Quakers, Lutherans, German Reformed, and Mennonites elicited far less opposition in large part because they were not enthusiastic evangelists. Methodists did not enter Virginia in significant numbers until the Revolution and, even then, were nominally part of the Anglican Church until 1784.) With dissent growing rapidly in spite of formal discrimination, threats were enlisted in an effort to quell the tide. For example, when Presbyterian James Waddell accepted the request of some congregants to preach at Lunenburg Parish Church one Sunday in the Anglican rector's absence, Minister Giberne issued a public rebuke, labeling Waddell a "pick pocket, dark-lantern, moon-light preacher, and an enthusiast," and initially called upon parishioners to seize him and take him to a public whipping post "to be dealt with according to law."[23]

More effective means of control were clearly necessary. As legal discrimination and threats had apparently failed, physical abuse of dissenting ministers became more common in the 1760s. Attacks on dissenting ministers and their supporters generally took on the manner of ruffian assaults. The Baptist preacher John Waller, known as "Swearing Jack" Waller before his conversion, wrote of one incident in August 1771: "[W]hilst Brother William Webber was addressing the congregation, . . . there came running towards him, in a most furious rage, Captain James Montague, a Magistrate of the county, followed by the Parson of the parish, and several others, who seemed greatly exasperated. . . . Brother Wafford was severely scourged, and Brother Henry Street received one lash from one of the persecutors, who was prevented from proceeding to further violence by his companions." Samuel Harriss was attacked with whips and clubs. Magistrates hunted one minister with dogs. Others were pelted with apples and stones or faced guns. Many other ministers suffered similar beatings until mob opposition became "the usual" practice.[24]

Baptist ministers were sometimes seized at prayer meetings and dunked in the closest body of water in parody of their baptism rituals. The ordeal could be intimidating. "A mob collected at one of their [Baptist] meetings and seized the preachers, Barrow and Mintz, and carried them to a water not far distant. There they dipped them several times, holding them under the water until they were nearly drowned, asking them if they believed. At length Mr. Barrow replied 'I believe you mean to drown me.'"[25]

Assaults were not limited to dissenting ministers. William Fristoe, a Baptist minister, told of one incident:

> At another time, ... while at devotion, a mob having collected, they immediately rushed upon them in the meeting house, and began to inflict blows on the worshippers, and produce bruises and bloodshed, so that the floor shone with the sprinkled blood the days following; upon which the few Baptists in the place concluded they would aim at a redress of their grievances, by bringing the lawless mob to justice. ... A warrant was applied for, and obtained, for the principal leaders of the mischief. ... [T]he result was, in [sic] was deemed a riot, and all were discharged.

In Stafford County, a hornets' nest was thrown into one prayer meeting, a snake into another. Baptisms in rivers and ponds were sometimes greeted with men on horseback riding through the participants gathered in the water, a frightening and dangerous game. Attendees at "illegal" preaching could also be charged for attending or fined for failing to disburse when ordered to do so or failing to testify against their ministers. Indictments in Caroline County in 1768 for assembling at unlawful preaching were ultimately discharged, but the harassing effect could still be significant. When dissenters were not readily available for abuse, their meeting houses could be attacked. This was hardly the mild toleration of an indulgent establishment that permeated much of the historiography.[26]

Many plantation owners were incensed at evangelical preaching to their slaves, insisting that slave conversion could undermine their authority; this created an additional cause of Establishment-dissenter tension. (Preaching to slaves by Anglican priests was also often found objectionable, but it did not threaten the additional disruptive tendency of the evangelicals' relatively egalitarian polity.) As a result, dissenting congregants were particularly likely to be attacked if black. James Ireland, a Baptist preacher who himself suffered persecution, recounted how at one meeting "the patrolers were let loose upon them [blacks]. . . . I was equally struck with astonishment and surprise, to see the poor negroes flying in every direction, the patrolers seizing and whipping them, whilst others were carrying them off prisoners, in order, perhaps, to subject them to a more severe punishment."[27]

With dissent continuing to increase in spite of legal discrimination and physical assault, Establishment leaders turned to incarceration. In June 1768, four Baptist ministers were arrested in Spotsylvania for preaching without a license. Refusing an offer of clemency if they agreed not to preach in the county for a year, they were marched off from the courthouse to the jail singing hymns along the way. Scores of other arrests followed, and dissenting ministers, particularly Baptists, found themselves facing extended stays in eighteenth-century jails for disturbing the peace, preaching without a license, and, in at least one case, alleged sedition. Brought before county magistrates, sometimes after weeks in jail, the dissenters were often offered freedom if they would give a bond not to preach in the county for a year; this offer was commonly rejected or later ignored as a bargain with the devil, a "perfidious wretch," according to one recently released preacher. Violation of such a bond, though, could lead to further jail time.[28]

Uncowed, many dissenters took the opportunity of their incarcerations to preach from their jail cells, recognizing the powerful witness that such preaching could provide. James Greenwood, jailed in King and Queen County, reported that "as the sound of salvation was heard from the grated windows of his cell, the multitudes without, wept, and many believed unto eternal life." One lawyer who had defended dissenting ministers warned that they "were like a Bed of chamomile, the more they were trod, the more they would spread." The Anglican hierarchy, at least initially, did not see the power of the tool that they were handing dissenters, and additional abuse was heaped upon the imprisoned preachers and their listeners. Pepper was burned at the windows or doors of some dissenters' jail cells; stones and sticks thrown at others. Crowds gathered to hear jailed preachers were dispersed by men on horseback. Blacks who gathered were brutally beaten. Bells were rung or obscene songs sung in an attempt to interfere with preaching. One minister, coming to his cell window to preach, was urinated on; another, his arms outstretched through his jail window in prayer, was cut by a knife. In Caroline County, a leading burgess and future Speaker of the Virginia Senate, Archibald Cary, had a wall erected around the jail and broken glass placed atop the wall in a vain effort to stop preaching by imprisoned ministers. (These precautions were for naught when dissenters gathered to hear a jailed preacher would wave a handkerchief on a stick above the new brick wall, a signal for preaching to commence.)[29]

Of course, not all Anglicans supported such persecution, far from it. Rhys Isaac notes that "those who took part in such actions were not typical of either the Anglican clergy or the country gentlemen." Perhaps so, but those who took part were, by and large, Anglican country gentlemen, Anglican clergy, and their supporters. Even when direct participation by Anglican leaders in an assault was not evident, dissenters rightfully saw the persecution as originating in the Establishment; the discrimination and persecution obviously did not originate with other dissenters. One dissenter declared that "[s]carcely a persecution took place . . . but had a Priest at the head of it, and received the hearty concurrence of their parish[i]oners."[30]

While the physical persecution certainly does not rival the abuses of previous ages, the extent of these attacks and their impact upon the dissenting population and their Enlightenment neighbors should not be underestimated. By the time the Revolutionary War arrived, more than half the Baptist ministers in Virginia had spent time in jail for preaching; scores of other Baptists and Presbyterians had been indicted or fined for attendance at unlicensed preaching, failure to attend Anglican services, or failure to testify against a preacher. Virtually every dissenter must have been familiar with the persecution. Of course, the full extent of the persecution cannot be known, and one might question the independence of sources in many cases. Yet, court and other records confirm much of the persecution, and it is more likely that what became known as a "usual" practice was underreported or records were lost than reports of assault (unchallenged contemporaneously) were fabricated.

James Madison's views in this regard are telling. Madison, an Anglican, was no friend of evangelical proselytizing, declaring later in life that the Baptists' "enthusiasm contributed to render them obnoxious to sober opinion," but he was absolutely infuriated by the religious persecution. Writing a college friend in early 1774, Madison bemoaned the presence in Virginia of "pride ignorance and Knavery among the Priesthood and Vice and Wickedness among the Laity," but said that much worse was the "diabolical Hell conceived principle of persecution . . . to their eternal Infamy the Clergy can furnish their Quota of Imps for such business. This vexes me the most of any thing whatever. There are at this [time] in the adjacent County not less than 5 or 6 well meaning men in close Goal for publishing their religious Sentiments which in the main are very orthodox." Madison had little doubt about where the problem arose: "Union of religious sentiments begets a surprizing confidence and Ecclesiastical Establishments tend to great ignorance and Corruption all of which facilitate the Execution of mischievous Projects." Madison "spared no exertion to save them [Baptists] from imprisonment & to promote their release from it," but incarcerations continued unabated through 1774. As incarcerations and persecution were less prevalent in Jefferson's Albemarle County than in Madison's Orange and surrounding counties, it is not surprising that Madison wrote more directly of his abhorrence, but Jefferson was undoubtedly equally vexed, as is evident in his 1776 speech in support of disestablishment and an end to legal discrimination.[31]

As persecution of dissenters increased, particularly after 1768, calls for greater toleration increased as well. In the early 1770s, dissenters began to petition the Virginia House of Burgesses seeking improved tolerance and an end to the arrests that plagued their preaching. Initially, their requests for legislative reform asked that they be allowed to preach outside of licensed meeting houses and that dissenting ministers, like Anglican ministers, be exempted from militia musters, but the Burgesses' Committee for Religion was not created to facilitate dissenters' interests. Rather, it "was yet another instrument by which Virginia's elite sought to maintain its internal cohesion and its dominant position during an era of multiple and interacting, internal and imperial crises. Its fundamental task was to bolster the hegemony of the provincial ruling class by reforming the established church and dealing with dissenter denominations." In 1770, dissenters' request that their ministers share the exemption from militia musters enjoyed by Anglican ministers was simply rejected. The Committee for Religion, initially tasked with seeking a system of improved toleration in light of dissenters' protests, was later "discharged" of that responsibility. No action was taken.[32]

As arrests continued, a number of Baptist petitions focused on improved toleration consistent with the "spirit" of the English Act of Toleration. Notably, at this time, many dissenters went out of their way to assure the Establishment that they were not seeking full religious freedom or equality with the Anglicans and were willing, for example, to continue to pay the Anglican religious tax. One group of Baptists insisted that they only sought the same treatment as Presbyterians, Quakers, and other dissenters. David Thomas, a Baptist preacher who had been incarcerated, conceded that dissenters were not seeking an end to the Establishment or its taxes, explaining that "[w]e freely pay all taxes, levies, &c." A 1774 Presbyterian petition from Peaks of Otter in Bedford County was clear that only tolerance was sought.[33]

Responding to calls for reform, a bill was introduced into the House of Burgesses in 1772, but the committee drafting the bill was controlled by Establishment leaders, in particular Robert Carter Nicholas, treasurer of the colony, chairman of the Burgesses' Committee for Religion, and devout churchman. As a result, it soon became clear that religious freedom for dissenters was not under serious consideration. The bill introduced by the committee would have arguably created more restrictions than it eliminated: continuing to require licensing, restricting meeting houses, making express penalties for attendance at unlawful preaching and for landowners who permitted it, and particularly targeting itinerancy and night preaching (often used to preach to slaves). For Nicholas, the purpose was not to improve the lot of dissenters, but to "guard against the Corruption of our Slaves . . . and to confine the [dissenting] Teachers to certain Places and Times of Worship." Others saw the legislation as an opportunity to bring "unordained preachers of that denomination [Baptists] under law and order."[34]

This pattern continued until the war. In early 1774, with Anglicans in firm control of the government and seeking even greater restrictions on dissent, Madison wrote a friend that he was "very doubtful" of the success of Baptist and Presbyterian petitions.

> [I]ncredible and extravagant stories were told in the House [of Burgesses] of the monstrous effects of the Enthusiasm prevalent among the Sectaries and so greedily swallowed by their Enemies that I believe they lost footing by it and the bad name they still have with those who pretend too much contempt to examine into their principles and Conduct and are too much devoted to the ecclesiastic establishment to hear of the Toleration of Dissentients, I am apprehensive, will be again made a pretext for rejecting their requests. . . . That liberal catholic and equitable way of thinking as to the rights of Conscience, which is one of the Characteristics of a free people . . . is but little known among the Zealous adherents to our Hierarchy.

Jefferson shared Madison's pessimism about reform in the prewar years, writing later that the established church in this period was "cruelly intolerant" and that the "unrighteous compulsion to maintain teachers of what they [dissenters] deemed religious errors was grievously felt during the regal government, and without a hope of relief."[35]

Persecution of dissenters by the Virginia Establishment effectively stopped with the war.

While the period from 1768 to 1774 saw a dramatic escalation in raw persecution of Virginia's Baptist and Presbyterian dissenters, facing a war with the most powerful empire in the world, Virginia's leaders recognized early that the support of the entire population was necessary. The need for the support of the rifle-wielding Presbyterians of the Shenandoah Valley and frontier was particularly noted, as was the potential of dissenting ministers to preach support for the new political regime among their congregants.

As armed conflict began, and as the necessity of broad support for mobilization became apparent to Establishment leaders, dissenters quickly became aware of emerging possibilities. As a result, the petitions from the dissenters, previously seeking only improved toleration, became far more insistent. Initially, they simply salted their petitions with analogies or references to the patriot cause or support for the Continental Congress, noting, for example, that opposition to British tyranny and an end to taxation without representation were conceptually consistent with their claims to improved religious toleration and an end to persecution. A petition from the Presbytery of Hanover, drafted in November 1774 (although not received by the legislature until May 1775—after word of Lexington and Concord had reached Williamsburg), assured Establishment leaders that Presbyterians were willing to register their places of worship and take an oath of loyalty.[36]

Dissenters' historically low social status and lack of experience in effective political participation initially resulted in some restraint. Thus, while among themselves dissenters were increasingly discussing the possibility of dramatic changes to the Establishment, including an end to church taxes, in 1775, those demands were not made directly to the legislature dominated by members of the Church of England. For example, the Anglican tax was apparently denounced in an August 1775 meeting of the Virginia Baptist General Association, but the association's 1775 petition to the Virginia Convention that had taken over effective governance of the colony after the colonists' break with Lord Dunmore did not mention the establishment tax at all, asking only that Baptist ministers be allowed to preach to soldiers of their own denomination. Even newspaper accounts of the meeting that noted complaints about the religious tax stressed that the association left members to decide whether to pay the tax "or to suffer the spoiling of goods, for conscience sake, without resistance." While the limited formal demands that were made by the dissenters in 1775 were quickly granted, with Patrick Henry bringing the issue of dissenters preaching to their troops to the floor of the Convention, even that was a "bitter pill" for many Establishment leaders—although only a taste of what was to come.[37]

By 1776, it was becoming clear to patriot leaders (and to dissenters) that they faced a long war and a daunting problem of recruiting and mobilization. In the spring, Jefferson wrote to leaders in Williamsburg from the Continental Congress in Philadelphia that "the ensuing [military] campaign is likely to require greater exertion than our unorganized powers may at present effect." Virginia political leaders who had only recently been protecting the Anglican hierarchy and persecuting dissenters found themselves working desperately to organize mobilization. Archibald Cary—scion of Anglican gentry, first Speaker of the Virginia Senate, and rabid prewar persecutor of dissenters—was charged with organizing mobilization in the central Piedmont. With dissenters accounting for as much as a third or more of the population and their numbers growing, it was clear that their support for the war effort was sorely needed.[38]

Certainly the Establishment could not risk a significant number of dissenters becoming loyalists as occurred elsewhere in the south. Virginia's patriot leaders must have watched with deep concern when many dissenters in the piedmont of North Carolina rose in defense of the king in early 1776, and sighed with considerable relief when news reached Williamsburg that the North Carolina loyalists who charged across Moore's Creek Bridge on February 27 shouting, "King George and Broadswords!" were met by devastating cannon fire and musketry from entrenched patriots. The *Virginia Gazette* welcomed the news that the Scottish Highlanders and former Regulators, "who had lately become very formidable and threatened much mischief to the southern colonies, as well as the glorious cause wherein all America is engaged," had been defeated. Yet, while the North Carolina loyalists were suppressed, for the time, Virginia leaders surely knew that their treatment of religious dissent had been far worse than that of their North Carolina compatriots. Moore's Creek was an ominous warning for Virginia.[39]

As the reality of the mobilization crisis became evident to both Establishment leaders and dissenters, the tone and content of dissenter petitions changed dramatically. Rejecting forever the role of a repressed minority seeking the favor of improved toleration from an entrenched Establishment, dissenters began to agitate for broad religious freedom, including an end to the establishment tax, the political power of Anglican vestries, and restrictions on marriage. Within weeks of news of the Battle of Moore's Creek Bridge reaching Williamsburg, an article in the *Virginia Gazette*, signed only "A Dissenter," demanded equal liberty for all Virginians, specifically calling for an end to the establishment tax and restrictions on marriage. There was no mistaking the author's intent when he noted that the struggle with Britain required that the colonists be united and that, as a result, dissenters should demand religious freedom, concluding portentously, "a word to the wise is enough."[40]

The Establishment was in no position to deny these demands entirely, and some of Virginia's leaders, notably Jefferson and Madison, welcomed the opportunity to promote religious freedom. The first indication that things had fundamentally changed and that dissenters might be successful in their efforts to improve their legal rights came in the Virginia Convention that was drafting a new constitution in the late spring of 1776. (Jefferson was in Philadelphia during this period, among other things, drafting the Declaration of Independence, but he was deeply interested in the convention's proceedings and always regretted his inability to have a more direct influence on the Virginia Constitution, although his draft of a constitution, sent belatedly from Philadelphia, did have some influence.)[41]

In a draft Declaration of Rights for the new state, George Mason proposed that Virginia provide "the fullest tolerance in the exercise of religion." This, though, was inadequate for the twenty-five-year-old James Madison, in Williamsburg in his first term as a representative. Madison had been deeply moved by the plight of dissenters and viewed their persecution with abhorrence. Committed to the natural rights doctrines that undergird much of the patriot movement and well aware of the necessity of unanimity in opposition to a powerful British empire, he insisted that toleration—the granting of a privilege by the Anglican hierarchy—was not enough; dissenters had a natural right to full religious freedom. Initially, Madison proposed that the convention recognize that "all men are equally entitled to the full and free exercise of it [Religion] accordg to the dictates of Conscience; and therefore that no man or class of men ought, on account of religion to be invested with peculiar emoluments or privileges." The convention rejected this proposal when Patrick Henry, who introduced it at the request of the shy young delegate, eschewed any intent to end the privileges of the established church. Madison, turning to Edmund Pendleton for assistance, had a second, narrower amendment introduced, which provided that "all men are equally entitled to the free exercise of religion, according to the dictates of conscience." This became part of Section 16 of the Virginia Declaration of Rights, adopted on June 12, 1776. At that time, it is unlikely that Madison had seen Jefferson's draft of a constitution, but their thinking on this matter was consistent. Jefferson proposed: "All persons shall have full and free liberty of religious opinion; nor shall any be compelled to frequent or maintain any religious institution."[42]

Inclusion of language calling for the "free exercise of religion" in a written constitution was a remarkable development in the history of religious liberty, and Madison later argued that in removing any notion of "toleration," the delegates "substituted a phraseology which—declared the freedom of conscience to be a *natural and absolute* right." Still, considerable ambiguity on the scope and impact of this language remained. While the Virginia Convention acceded to Madison's language in the name of promoting unity, it made it clear that it was not disestablishing the Anglican Church nor ending its own authority to regulate religion. For example, within weeks of having adopted the Declaration of Rights, the convention ordered ministers of the Church of England to eliminate prayers for the king from their services and replace them with prayers for local leaders, and the convention continued to regulate vestries and church property. As a result, the new state was launched with a somewhat hobbled mandate for religious freedom.[43]

With a new constitution in place, Virginia's leaders were quickly forced to focus on governance during a war crisis. While the convention had been debating the Declaration of Rights and a new state constitution, the war had been going poorly. In Canada, invading American armies were repelled with the loss of five thousand men, and a devastating defeat was waiting for General Washington's still novice army in New York. As the year wore on, the fortunes of war would continue to turn against the patriots, and problems with mobilization only increased. Washington, having suffered debilitating losses around New York in August and early September, was deeply frustrated with the short-term support of militias and volunteer companies and made clear that he needed long-term recruits in a disciplined national army.[44]

With money, supplies, and troops all in desperately short supply, the difficulties of effective mobilization were everywhere presenting themselves, and Virginia—the most populous of the new states (even excluding slaves)—was expected to lead in this essential effort. It was in this context of a mobilization crisis that the dissenters' previous pleas for improved toleration were forever abandoned to be replaced by increasingly forceful insistence that religious freedom was needed. Pointedly, dissenters made clear that their wholehearted support for the war effort depended upon the granting of religious liberty, including an end to establishment taxes and restrictions on worship and marriage. "*These things granted,*" they explained, "we will gladly unite with our Brethren of other denominations, and to the utmost of our ability, promote the common cause of Freedom." This was a threat and an opportunity that Virginia's leaders could ill afford to ignore.[45]

In the fall of 1776, dissenters flooded the new legislature with petitions demanding complete religious freedom. A petition sponsored by the Baptists garnered "10,000 names"—probably accounting for over 10 percent of the adult, white, male population (including many Anglicans)—and lamented the establishment tax, writing that "their property hath been wrested from [illegible] and given to those from whom they have received no equivalent." Another petition from the Hanover Presbytery noted that its members had

> hitherto submitted to several ecclesiastic burthens and restrictions that are inconsistent with equal liberty. But now when the many & grievous oppressions of our mother Country, have laid this continent under the necessity of casting off the yoke of tyranny, ... we flatter ourselves, that we shall be freed from all the incumbrances which a spirit of Domination, prejudice, or bigotry hath interwoven with most other political systems.

That petition went on to insist that spiritual regulation was not a legitimate object of government. Other petitions from dissenters peppered the assembly.[46]

These petitions continued implicitly, and sometimes not so implicitly, to demand religious freedom as the price for support for mobilization. The "10,000 Name" petition referred to the establishment levy as taxation without representation and called on the legislature to end it so that internal "animosities may cease"—a serious concern for leaders seeking to energize flagging mobilization. An October petition from the militia of heavily Presbyterian Augusta County reminded Establishment leaders that "unanimity" was needed in the war effort but warned that "their unanimity will be ever preserved by giving *equal liberty* to them all; nor do the[y] crave this as the pittance of courtesy but ... as their patrimony which cannot be withheld from them without the most flagitious fraud, pride and injustice, which if practiced may shake this continent and demolish provinces." Should the assembly fail to meet their expectations, they advised their representatives, "tell them, that your constituents are neither guided, nor will ever be influenced, by that slavish maxim in politicks, 'that whatever is enacted by that body of men in whom the supreme power of the state is vested must in all cases be implicitly obeyed,' and that they firmly believe attempts to repeal an unjust law can be vindicated beyond a simple remonstrance addressed to the legislators." (The Augusta Presbyterians, warming to the public and political nature of the battle, had their plea printed in the *Virginia Gazette*.) Less than a week later, in a dramatic change of tone from their prior missive, the Hanover Presbytery asked the assembly's assistance "in removing every species of religious, as well as civil bondage" so that "the religious Grievances under which we have hitherto laboured, ... no longer may be continued in our present form of Government." "[T]his being done," the Presbytery both warned and offered, it will serve the "great honour and interest of the State." Other dissenting petitioners assured the assembly of their support of the patriot movement, but denounced "the great Injustice" of the Establishment and advised that they were prepared "to bleed ... before they submit, to any form of Government, that may be subversive of these religious Privileges that are a Natural Right." If there was any chance that the threat and opportunity could be missed, a November letter to the *Virginia Gazette*, reportedly penned by Caleb Wallace, the moderator of the Hanover Presbytery, was even more clear: "[A]t a time when the salvation of our country confessedly depends on the aid and exertions of every party, does not policy loudly forbid any irritating refusal to the reasonable demands of thousands of valuable citizens?" Dissenting ministers, actively lobbying the new legislature, made clear the need for an end to the Establishment and linked reform to support for mobilization.[47]

The dissenters' task was not made easier by the composition of the new government. Edmund Pendleton—the Speaker of the new Virginia House of Delegates—had been an ardent supporter of the Establishment and had sat on a magistrates' bench that convicted dissenting preachers. Seeking to control any changes, Pendleton appointed a conservative Committee of Religion in the new House, including Carter Braxton, Richard Henry Lee, and Robert Carter Nicholas—all strong churchmen.[48]

Luckily for dissenters, Jefferson, recently returned from his service in the Second Continental Congress, was also placed on the committee. Beyond his own powerful inclinations to reform, Jefferson's constituents had pointedly warned him that the prospect of the new state adopting "laws in favour of the Episcopal Church," particularly the taxation of dissenters for support of the established church, "disturbs the minds of a great portion of our Community"; they urged Jefferson to make this "one of the first matters you will go upon, in order that they [religious dissenters] may be made sensible by some prudent and decent method, as soon as possible, that their suspicion is groundless."[49]

With more and more dissenting petitions being received by the House, it must have become evident that the conservative Committee of Religion would not be adequate to address mounting pressure in the face of the pressing necessity of support for mobilization. As a result, on November 6, the House made the highly unusual decision to open the committee to all members, allowing Madison to join Jefferson's efforts to encourage reform. By November 19, after the matter was removed from Braxton's committee altogether, the House voted a resolution, apparently drafted in part by Jefferson, calling for an end to all laws that "render criminal the maintaining any opinions in matters of religion, forbearing to repair to church, or the exercising any mode of worship whatsoever, or which prescribes punishments for the same," an end to taxing dissenters for establishment ministers, and an end to the church tax altogether. To Jefferson's dismay, the resolution also called for regulating "publick assemblies of societies for divine worship" and their clergy.[50]

At this point, Jefferson and Madison were appointed to a smaller committee to bring in a bill consistent with the November 19 resolution. Unfortunately, Jefferson left the House on personal business on November 29, and the next day, "a curious coincident" for one reporter, a watered-down resolution was introduced into the House effectively limited to exempting dissenters from the establishment tax, and a similarly limited bill was introduced on the floor the next business day. On the same day, a proposal that had previously been endorsed to dissolve the Anglican vestries, thereby ending their civil functions, was also abruptly tabled, perhaps only another curious coincident. Apparently recalled by friends of reform, Jefferson rushed back to the House, at which point floor amendments were introduced making clear that not only would the ecclesiastic tax be suspended, but penalties for religious violations were also to be terminated.[51]

While at least one early reporter credits Jefferson's return with the critical amendment, the editors of the *Papers of Thomas Jefferson* point out that the amendment was written in the hand of George Mason. Of course, this does not necessarily mean that Jefferson's presence was not instrumental in ensuring that the amendment was made and adopted. Given his prominence in the House as well as his obvious intimate involvement in the committee, not to mention his personally unwelcome decision to rush back to the House, one can certainly say that he played a key role in rescuing the reform from the lukewarm proposal that surfaced upon his departure. In any case, on December 9, after receiving the concurrence of the Virginia Senate, the establishment tax on dissenters was eliminated (and suspended on Anglicans), and other Parliamentary laws penalizing religious dissent were repealed. Later in life, Jefferson described these legislative battles as "the severest contests in which I have ever been engaged." Given Jefferson's experiences, this is a dramatic statement. The "severe" nature of these conflicts speaks both to the difficulty of overcoming the entrenched Establishment as well as Jefferson's own dedication to and involvement in the effort. It certainly indicates that the Establishment fought disestablishment and did not crumble in the face of an evangelical revolt.[52]

Further evidence of Jefferson's role in this critical development can be found in his notes. Facing considerable opposition to reform and deeply dedicated to the effort, Jefferson apparently made one of his rare legislative speeches to encourage an end to the Establishment and an end to all discrimination based on religion. Jefferson began his argument with an extended discussion of the legal discrimination visited upon dissenters in Virginia, specifically engaging the view among some members of the Establishment that Virginia's colonial toleration was adequate.

> Gent. w^{ll}. b. surpriz^d at det^l. y^{se} persecut^g. stat.
>
> mo^s. men imag^{ne}. persecn unkn^n t. our l^s.
>
> leg^l. sta. Relig^n. little undst^d.
>
> ye persecn go^s. n^t t. death b^t in 1. case—Fi. Impr.

Which is to say: "Gentlemen will be surprised at the details of these persecuting statutes. Most men imagine persecution is unknown to our laws. The legal status of religion is little understood. The persecution goes not to death but in 1 case—[but it extends to] fines [and] imprisonment." Dissenters had to pay for Establishment ministers and glebes as well as raising funds for their own churches: "y^{se} peop. p dble Contribns" ("these people pay double contributions"). He concluded, these laws "leave ev^y. one at [the] mercy of [a] **Bigot**," a point that he was to repeat in his *Notes on the State of Virginia*. It is clear that even by this time Jefferson's goal was a complete separation of church and state; in one early draft of the November 19 resolutions calling for an end to the establishment tax and penalties for religious violations, Jefferson called for "totally and eternally restraining the civil magistrate from all pretensions of interposing his authority or exercise in matters of religion." That, though, would take much more time to achieve.[53]

Jefferson's argument to the assembly presaged both his own Statute for Establishing Religious Freedom as well as arguments later made by Madison in his famous Memorial & Remonstrance Against Religious Assessments. For example, as he would in the Statute, Jefferson insisted that the "True line" of legislation had "noth^g. t. d. wth. Opn or tend^{cy}.—only **Overt** acts" ("nothing to do with opinion or tendency—only overt acts"). Anticipating Madison's argument in the Memorial, he noted that Islamic countries stifled free inquiry, suggesting that Christianity could only flourish (and convert Muslims) through an open system. Like Madison, Jefferson relied on Lockean theory concerning the nature of a civil contract, asking, "Has the State a right to adopt an opinion in matters of religion?," and answering that an individual is only answerable to God for his religious views, unable to surrender that natural right even in a Lockean contract:

> H^s. **State Right** to adopt an Opn in matt^r. Relig^n
> wh^n m^n. ent. Soc^{ty}. **Surrend^r.** litt. as posble
> Civ^l. r^{ts}. all y^t r. nec. to Civ^l govmt
> **Relig^s.** r^{ts} n^t nec. surr^d.
> Indivd. c^{nt} surr^{dr}.—answble to God.

Which is: "Has the State a right to adopt an opinion in matters of religion? When men enter society, they surrender as little as possible. Civil rights are all that are necessary to Civil Government. Religious rights are not necessary to surrender. An individual cannot surrender them—for them he is answerable to God." While the contribution of the Baptist and Presbyterian evangelicals to the fight for religious freedom in Virginia should not be minimized, these early views of Jefferson show that dissenters' later claims that the Statute for Establishing Religious Freedom and Memorial & Remonstrance owe a direct provenance to their own texts are excessive, or, as the editors of the *Papers of James Madison* point out, "assertions of intellectual dependence are often based on slender textual coincidences."[54]

Interestingly, Jefferson's work arguably suggested the argument later made famous by Madison in *Federalist* No. 10, that a multiplicity of sects in a large republic would protect religious freedom just as a multiplicity of political interests would prevent any single faction from gaining and abusing power. In his speech notes, Jefferson explained "ye pres^t ch^{ch}. too strong for any 1 sect, b^t too weak ag^t all." Similarly, in writing his *Notes on Virginia*, he observed that "[d]ifference of opinion is advantageous in religion. The several sects perform the office of a Censor morum over each other." (The argument was not original to Jefferson, either; both Voltaire and Adam Smith made similar points. As was often the case, Jefferson's contribution involved careful synthesis and extraordinary expression.)[55]

Importantly, at this time Jefferson was also sitting on the House of Delegate's War Committee, with a direct responsibility for mobilization. Jefferson would have been keenly aware of the difficulty of mobilization and the need to enlist dissenters, and he apparently used that position to support the dissenters' interests and the campaign for full religious liberty. His papers from 1776 include a "Memorandum concerning Military Service of Baptists" noting that "[t]here is but one Young man who is a Baptist and in a single State in the Neighbourhood that has not enlisted" (neighborhood of minister Elijah Craig) and that in the neighborhood of Baptist minister Jeremiah Walker, "[t]here is but one Young Man . . . who is a Baptist and in a single State, that has not enlisted, and he is so much an Invalid that he is not on the Militia List." Jefferson must have hoped to find good use for this information in his efforts to mobilize effective war support while pursuing broad religious freedom.[56]

While recognizing the important progress that had been made in 1776, Jefferson also recognized that much was left to be done. He later explained that "our opponents carried in the general resolutions of the comm[itt]ee of Nov. 19, a declaration that religious assemblies ought to be regulated, and that provision ought to be made for continuing the succession of the clergy, and superintending their conduct." All of this was an anathema to Jefferson's idea of full religious liberty. More immediately, the Church of England maintained its legal monopoly on marriage and the control of poor relief. The Anglican Church was still nominally an established church regulated by the assembly.

Ominously, proposals had been tabled for a general religious tax assessment that would benefit all Christian sects—exactly the type of government intervention in ecclesiastic matters that Jefferson had been arguing against—and the law ending the tax on dissenters deferred that matter, noting that "nothing in this act . . . shall be construed to affect or influence the said question of a general assessment."[57]

While Jefferson's and Madison's efforts at this time were absolutely essential, there should be little question that dissenting evangelicals were at least equally important. Absent wartime necessity and the dissenters' insistence on religious freedom, and their willingness to link religious freedom to mobilization, the experience of 1770–74 and both Jefferson's and Madison's ruminations suggest that little would likely have been accomplished. Jefferson and Madison were deftly able to use the mobilization crisis and the support and growing political presence of the dissenters to achieve reforms that they supported on principle. For their part, dissenters not only gained important rights to practice their religion but also a newfound ability to participate effectively in the polity. This pattern of cooperation between Enlightenment rationalists and previously disenfranchised evangelicals was to continue into the young republic.

Anglican petitions from 1777 and 1778 tend to confirm both the importance of the dissenters' role as well as the fact that dissenters were threatening to withhold support for mobilization if religious restrictions were not liberalized. An Anglican petition from Mecklenburg County, copied in other counties, sought a continuation of the establishment tax, but conceded that the petitioners "would by no means wish to see Churchmen adopt the principles of Dissenters, withhold their concurrence in the common cause until their particular requests are granted, for by such conduct all may be lost." Still, these Anglicans understood that the new government needed to "make men unanimous in the defence of liberty." Recognizing the pressure that the Assembly was under to encourage mobilization, and the inordinate leverage that this gave dissenters, the Anglican petitions urged that these matters "should be debated at a time when you have nothing of more importance to engage your attention." They conceded, though, that "if only withholding from a competent number of ministers of the gospel fixed salaries is the most likely means to make men unanimous in the defence of liberty, as has been urged, we should be very sorry indeed if there could be one found of that reverend order who would repine at the success of the measure." If anything, these Anglican petitions confirmed the wisdom of the legislature's decision to provide dissenters whatever liberalization was necessary to maintain their support for the war effort. Conservative Anglicans might protest, but with their leaders deeply engaged in the Revolution, they were simply not in a position to make demands (or threats) comparable to those coming from dissenters.[58]

As the war proceeded, efforts to improve religious freedom and relax old laws followed the wax and wane of mobilization needs. Requests for liberalization of the marriage and vestry regimes were particularly heated. Facing pressure from dissenters and the difficulty in recruiting for the patriot army, the Virginia General Assembly made sporadic reforms throughout the war. In 1775, after having failed to win an exemption in 1770, dissenting ministers were exempted from militia musters, like their Anglican counterparts, if they could show that they were duly "licensed" by the General Court or their sect—a difficult requirement for many Baptists in particular. In 1777, the exemption from militia service was clarified, making it easier for dissenting ministers to avoid service; all that was needed was to show that they complied with "the rules of their sect." This is a particularly interesting reform, and further evidence of dissenters' growing clout, as other exemptions from militia service were generally eliminated or narrowed in this critical period for mobilization. In 1777, in a further effort to encourage mobilization, dissenting sects were given authority to raise their own Continental companies. In 1778, Presbyterians complained of the requirement of oaths in legal proceedings, a requirement that was relaxed early the next year. In 1779, the establishment tax was finally ended, rather than simply being suspended from year to year. In June 1780, vestries were replaced by overseers of the poor in seven, primarily Presbyterian, western counties. In December 1780, after repeated complaints from dissenting interests, Virginia at last permitted dissenting ministers to perform the marriage ceremony legally. Unlike Anglican ministers, though, they still had to obtain a license that was restricted to one county, and the number of dissenting ministers who could perform marriages in any given county was limited.[59]

In June 1779, shortly after Jefferson left the House to take up his duties as Virginia's second governor, his Bill for Establishing Religious Freedom was first introduced in the General Assembly. In spite of the progress that had been made, members of the Establishment rallied against a bill that would have eliminated its vestiges of power and prohibited any tax to support religion. At the time, petitions and newspaper articles opposing Jefferson's bill outnumbered those in support, and the bill was simply left to languish. In the fall session of the House of Delegates, a new bill was introduced for a general assessment, a tax to support all Christian sects. One Presbyterian minister warned Jefferson of the danger, confirming that "the old detested establishment had warm advocates in the house [of Delegates]." Yet, while supported by many members of the Establishment, the dissenting sects had made clear their opposition to any tax to support religion. With the war still raging, indeed, having turned south—figuratively and literally—and with the need for support for mobilization again waxing hot, this, too, proved too controversial.[60]

Of course, as the prewar experience demonstrates, the Establishment was not agreeing to reform based on the principle of unbridled religious freedom. Quite the contrary, it expected something in return for the reforms that were made. In 1776, in what would have been anomalous before the war, dissenting ministers were officially asked to assist in gathering funds for those dispossessed in Norfolk. In February 1777, the state's first governor, Patrick Henry, publicly called for the assistance of the clergy in recruiting, and contemporaries saw the request as being particularly targeted at dissenters. If there was any doubt, early the next year Henry specifically sought and received the agreement of his governor's council to approach Jeremiah Walker, one of Virginia's most popular Baptist preachers, to assist with recruiting. Neither could have missed the significance of the fact that Walker had suffered incarceration and assault for preaching without a license before the war and was personally deeply engaged in the dissenters' petitioning campaign. By 1781, Samuel Davies son, Colonel William Davies, was put in charge of the state's war department, an honor that certainly would have been unexpected before the war. Nor did the dissenters miss the opportunity to use their improved political position to push their case for freedom. In 1778, Walker and Elijah Craig, who had also been repeatedly jailed for preaching, were appointed by the Baptist General Association to lay grievances before the assembly, especially opposition to a proposed general assessment. This pattern of an exchange of government requests for support and dissenters' petitions for reform continued throughout the war.[61]

Efforts to encourage support for mobilization from the dissenters appear to have met with considerable success. After their initial threats not to support the war effort, Virginia's dissenting ministers were apparently among the state's best recruiters. It is particularly striking that at least nine Baptist ministers who had personally suffered incarceration or physical abuse for preaching served in a military capacity (not simply as chaplains) during the war. And while records are incomplete, a comparison of the county-by-county returns that are available suggests that support for mobilization among dissenters was as strong as, if not stronger than, that among Anglicans, in spite of the dissenters' limited participation in the prewar polity and noted loyalism in other states.[62]

Not surprisingly, negotiations between Establishment leaders and dissenters for the latter's support for mobilization were not publicly embraced either during or after the war. Anglican petitions in 1777 and 1778 sought to make political capital of the fact that dissenters were seeking to use the necessity of mobilization to gain political advantage during the crisis. After the war, both Anglicans and former dissenters found it convenient to deny any contingency in the process. Anglicans wanted to efface previous religious intolerance and persecution. Edmund Randolph insisted that Anglicans "dreaded nothing so much as a schism among the people, and thought the American principle too pure to be adulterated by religious dissension. They therefore did in truth cast the Establishment at the feet of its enemies." Edmund Pendleton reportedly drafted a 1786 petition claiming "that at the period of the late glorious revolution in America they chearfully consented to an abolition of the old Church establishment."[63]

Similarly, former dissenters hoped to bury any suggestion that their support for the war effort was anything but unqualified, claiming the role of disinterested patriots who had wholeheartedly supported the war rather than a disenfranchised minority who demanded reforms as their price for mobilization. Thus, in 1784 the Hanover Presbytery wrote that "we have hitherto restrained our complaints . . . that we might not be thought to take any advantage from times of confusion, or critical situations of Government in an unsettled state of Convulsion and war, to obtain what is our clear and uncontestable right." Some Baptists made a similar claim that "we have patiently waited, while the great matters of the war, was the subject of deliberation." These claims seem to make some sense; after all, the new state was struggling with the war effort and its own birthing pains, and the legislature was almost overwhelmed with demands. Yet, at the time, noting the crisis besetting the new state, Anglicans had tried in vain to push the question of disestablishment off until after the war (and the necessity of mobilization) had passed. Rejecting any delay, Presbyterians and Baptists well understood what Jefferson would later relate in his *Notes*: The time for reform was while the war and the polity's desperate needs were most active. Post hoc assertions of restraint are simply inconsistent with the Presbytery's and Baptists' actions throughout the war, actions that provided the foundation and essential support for Jefferson's efforts at disestablishment.[64]

As the Revolution approached, the Anglican Establishment was in firm control of both church and state in Virginia. Dissenters, while a substantial and rapidly rising share of the population, were facing persistent and serious discrimination and growing persecution. By the time of the Revolution, more than half of the Baptist ministers in Virginia had suffered jail time; scores of others—Baptists and Presbyterians—had been jailed, beaten, dunked, fined, or otherwise harassed. The condition of the records and the apparent common nature of the harassments and beatings suggest that the recorded instances of physical persecution and arrest probably significantly underreport the actual experience of Virginia's dissenters.

Jefferson and Madison were deeply disturbed by these limitations on civil liberty and the active persecution that was increasingly visited upon dissenters from the Anglican hierarchy as the Revolution approached. Jefferson referred to the conditions in Virginia as "religious slavery." "I doubt whether the people of this country would suffer an execution for heresy, or a three years imprisonment for not comprehending the mysteries of the Trinity," he wrote during the war, but this was cold comfort to the apostle of freedom.

> [I]s the spirit of the people an infallible, a permanent reliance? Is it government? . . . Besides, the spirit of the times may alter, will alter. . . . A single zealot may commence persecutor, and better men be his victims. It can never be too often repeated, that the time for fixing every essential right on a legal basis is while our rulers are honest, and ourselves united. From the conclusion of this war we shall be going down hill. It will not then be necessary to resort every moment to the people for support. They will be forgotten, therefore, and their rights disregarded.

Looking back at the history of religious discrimination and persecution, he explained that "[i]f no capital execution took place here, as did in New-England, it was not owing to the moderation of the church, or spirit of the legislature, as may be inferred from the law itself; but to historical circumstances which have not been handed down to us."[65]

Yet, while persecution of dissenters escalated through 1774, once war with Britain became inevitable, their support was desperately needed as Virginia's political leaders, the same Anglican Establishment that had supported legal discrimination and persecution, sought to mobilize Virginia to fight the world's most powerful empire. With as much as one-third of the populace dissenting, Virginia could not mobilize effectively without their help. The stage was set for dramatic change, and Jefferson seized the opportunity.

By the end of the American Revolution, as a result of the complex negotiations between Virginia's Establishment leaders and dissenters that accompanied the campaign for mobilization, the religious Establishment in Virginia had been substantially liberalized, with Jefferson playing a central part in the reforms.

Still, restraints remained. Most immediately, marriage by dissenting ministers was still restricted and Anglican vestries continued to administer considerable political power, especially as related to poor taxes and orphans—authority that some believed was exercised under the influence of "Party Motives."[66] In addition, the proposal for a general assessment that had been tabled in 1779 was still being pursued by supporters of the old Establishment.

What the Establishment seemed not to realize, however, was that the process of negotiation for religious reform had not only liberalized religious regulation in Virginia, but had fundamentally politicized the dissenters, and they would not again long absent themselves from the political fray. Jefferson and Madison had found among the dissenters a powerful and faithful chorus to support their efforts to obtain complete religious freedom.

THE VIRGINIA STATUTE
FOR ESTABLISHING
RELIGIOUS FREEDOM

WITH THE AMERICAN VICTORY AT YORKTOWN IN 1781, THE NEED
for mobilization quickly evaporated. So, too, evaporated the solicitousness
of Virginia's Establishment leaders for religious dissenters. In the immediate
postwar years, petitions from Presbyterians and Baptists asking for an end to
the vestiges of religious discrimination continued to arrive in Richmond, but,
given the change in circumstances, they fell largely on deaf ears. In fact, with
the war won, Virginia's Anglican leaders, clergy and laity, saw an opportunity
to retrench and strengthen their troubled church (the "Episcopal Church of
Virginia" after 1784) with renewed government assistance. The primary means
for doing so was a proposed general tax assessment to support all Christian
sects; with Anglicans still nominally the largest denomination in the state, the
assessment would have disproportionately benefited them.

This reactionary proposal failed. With Jefferson in Paris acting as U.S. ambassador, James Madison led the effort against the general assessment. With
the aid of evangelical dissenters who had been deeply politicized by the negotiations during the course of the Revolution and who shared Jefferson's and
Madison's opposition to any alliance between church and state, the general assessment bill was defeated. Instead, riding the upwelling of political support
for religious liberty, Jefferson's Statute for Establishing Religious Freedom was
finally enacted. Jefferson, advising and watching from France, was ecstatic. Virginia, which had the strongest colonial Establishment leading up to the American Revolution and which persecuted dissenters more violently than any other
British North American colony in the eighteenth century, entered the constitutional period with the strongest, and certainly the most eloquent, guarantee

of religious freedom, including a disestablishment of the remaining vestiges of state religion and a guarantee of the free exercise of religion.

In spite of the robust negotiations between dissenters and Establishment leaders from 1775 through 1781, full religious freedom was not achieved in Virginia by the end of the Revolution. Restrictions on the ability of dissenting ministers to perform marriage ceremonies were still in place. Vestries from the Church of England continued to control some municipal functions, including poor relief and care of orphans (except in several western counties where use of an Anglican vestry had simply become impractical). The Church of England still had quasi-official status and was still nominally regulated in its form of worship and polity by the General Assembly. Jefferson's Bill for Establishing Religious Freedom had been tabled. Most troubling, after the war, a proposal for a general assessment—a tax to support all sects, or at least all Christian sects (largely the same thing in eighteenth-century Virginia)—which had been suggested in 1776 and tabled in 1779, was again under consideration.

At the same time, after Lord Cornwallis's surrender at Yorktown in October 1781, the need for dissenters' cooperation in the difficult task of mobilization quickly faded. While the war nominally continued for two years during the negotiation of the final Paris Peace Treaty, the pressure on the states to encourage recruiting and obtain military supplies quickly dissipated. As a result, in a sharp departure from the wartime pattern, continued pleas from dissenters for further liberalization of religious freedom were largely ignored. Petitioners complained that continued privileges for Anglican ministers were a violation of the Virginia Declaration of Rights, but to no avail. Proposals to expand vestries to include dissenters in their civil function were deferred and then rejected. Requests to end discrimination in marriages and to remove remaining civil authority from vestries were similarly deferred, then tabled. Dissenters reminded the legislature that they had "joined with our Brethren in the same Cause of Liberty," but Establishment leaders now seemed uninterested. Frustrated Baptists complained: "We cannot conceive that our conduct has been such in the late important Struggle [the Revolution] as to forfeit the Confidence of our Countrymen, or that the Church-of-England-Men have rendered such peculiarly meritorious Services to the State, as to make it necessary to continue the invidious Distinctions which still subsist." Full liberty, they insisted, "is what we have a just claim to as Freemen of the Commonwealth." Yet, with no more need for military recruits, the Establishment leaders who still controlled the Virginia Assembly were unmoved.[1]

By comparison, a few years after Yorktown, supporters of the Church of England (renamed the Episcopal Church of Virginia in a June 1784 convention) began to agitate for an improved official status for religion. The timing was not happenstance. The Reverend David Griffith, who would become the first Virginia nominee for ordination as an Episcopal bishop, sought to organize his Anglican colleagues to reinvigorate the struggling church. Griffith specifically recognized that during the war it would have been ill-advised to "interrupt that union which was so necessary for our mutual security and preservation" by angering dissenters with calls for government aid to religion. With victory, however, Griffin urged his brethren on, insisting that the need for restraint had passed: "that time, God be thanked, is happily over, and those reasons no longer exist." In September 1783, an editorialist urged the General Assembly that it was now time to act to support all Christian sects since "no proud or lordly prelate; no presbytery can awe your deliberations."[2]

The agitation for renewed state support of religion was made all the more urgent because the Anglicans were in desperate straits; while all religious denominations endured setbacks during the conflict, the Anglican Church was especially battered. Not only had it suffered from its affiliation with the British Crown, but, as the formerly established church had always been supported by tax dollars and its ministers had never been required to raise funds for regular operations, it found itself particularly exposed to the loss of tax revenues. Adding to the church's difficulties, a number of Anglican priests had died during the war or, after government tax support was suspended, had left the cloth to find employment, and their ranks could not be easily filled. Anglican priests had to be ordained by bishops; the only bishops were in Britain, and ordination had been curtailed by the war. After the war, British bishops were initially unwilling to consecrate ministers who would not take the prescribed oath of loyalty to the king. Facing what seemed a bleak future, Anglican petitions sought to frame a plan for church renewal in a manner that they hoped would garner broad support from those concerned about religion, including other denominations.

While a return to the former exclusive establishment was highly unlikely, state support for religion generally seemed an achievable goal to Anglican leaders. Their hope for improved relations between church and state was buttressed by the common perception that the war had impaired public morals and the broadly held eighteenth-century belief that a republic required virtuous citizens, and virtuous citizens required a vibrant religion. Thus, supporters of a general assessment saw their effort as aiding not only religion but also the state, and, by not discriminating among Christian sects, doing so in a manner that was quite liberal by eighteenth-century standards. Still, with a majority of the citizens nominally Anglican, a general religious tax distributed based upon church affiliation would provide enormous benefits to the Anglican Church.

In such circumstances, state support for religion seemed a natural expedient to many officials. The popular revolutionary and devoted Anglican Richard Henry Lee told a skeptical James Madison that "[r]efiners may weave as fine a web of reason as they please, but the experience of all times shows Religion to be the guardian of morals—and he must be a very inattentive observer in our Country, who does not see that avarice is accomplishing the destruction of religion, for want of a legal obligation to contribute something to its support."[3]

By the end of 1783, the Virginia General Assembly, still dominated by Anglicans, had received several petitions urging that something be done to improve morality and the condition of churches and their clergy. Warwick County petitioners advised the assembly that "it is essentially necessary for the good Government of all free states, that some legislative attention should be paid to religious Duties." A number of petitioners asked specifically that the assembly adopt a general assessment for religion and permit churches to incorporate (so that they could more easily hold and transfer property). Petitioners from Lunenburg County noted that during the war, ministers had been neglected and propagation of the gospel had suffered; they expressed a "wish to see the reformed Christian religion supported and maintained by a General and equal Contribution of the Whole State upon the most equitable footing that is possible to place it." From Amherst County, the assembly heard that while citizens welcomed the results of the Revolution, "One Thing is wanting to render Our Prospects of Future Happiness Compleat. And That so important, that without It we shall be so far from being a happy People, that we must be more miserable than the Beasts that Perish. Long have we Groand under & secretly Lamented the miserable Declension, Nay in some Places almost total Annihilation of our Divine Religion." They called on their representatives to be "Nursing Fathers to the Church" and "put a stop to these swiftly increasing Evils, to Check the Torrent of Iniquity before it Overspread Our Land like a Flood" by supporting religion through a general assessment. Episcopalians from Powhatan County offered to "chearfully pay any moderate or reasonable Contribution that may be levied on us for supporting in a liberal and plentiful Manner Ministers of the Gospel."[4]

Notably, while the assembly received eight petitions supporting an assessment from November 1783 through early November 1784 (when a resolution calling for an assessment was adopted by the House of Delegates), the assembly received no petitions opposing an assessment during that period. The same pattern of support for an assessment in light of the decline in religion was evident in the newspapers.[5]

Apparently recognizing that support for a general assessment might not, standing alone, be enough to ensure its adoption, especially if dissenters maintained a united opposition to any religious tax as they had during the war, additional concessions were suggested that might encourage support for the assessment from religious dissenters or at least placate any opposition. Reversing a long-standing position, Episcopalians in the House of Delegates decided to support reform of marriage and vestry laws. In addition, recognizing some of the legal challenges affecting local churches in terms of their ability to hold land or accept bequests, a proposal for nondiscriminatory incorporation of churches was devised which would have relieved any church that applied for incorporation of the risk of having property held by a small group of trustees. (As there was no general incorporation law at the time, the alternative was for each congregation to seek a separate law to incorporate or, as was usually done, to forego the benefits of incorporation.)

Initially, the plan seemed to be working. In the spring 1784 session of the General Assembly, the House Committee for Religion adopted a resolution in support of a general assessment at the urging of Patrick Henry. Several weeks later, the committee endorsed nondiscriminatory incorporation and marriage and vestry reform. The House promptly adopted marriage reform, but momentum was arrested when that reform died in the more conservative Senate with the end of the session. Still, the proposals for a general assessment, marriage and vestry reform, and incorporation were carried over to the next session, and the prospects for renewed state support for religion looked good to both supporters and opponents. A worried Madison reported the vote on a general assessment and Episcopal proposal for incorporation to Jefferson in Paris, noting that "[e]xtraordinary as such a project was, it was preserved from a dishonorable death by the talents of Mr. Henry. It lies over for another Session."[6]

In the October 1784 session, the plan to encourage marriage and vestry reform effectively linked with a general assessment was again introduced and seemed to be on solid ground. On November 11, on a 47 to 32 vote, the House of Delegates adopted a resolution to enact a law for citizens to "pay a moderate tax or contribution annually for the support of the Christian religion, or of some Christian church, denomination, or communion of Christians, or of some form of Christian worship." Led by Patrick Henry, the most popular politician in Virginia, and supported by important leaders, including Edmund Pendleton, Richard Henry Lee, Benjamin Harrison, Spencer Roane, Philip Barbour, John Page, and John Marshall, this effort seemed headed for success. Even George Washington appeared to provide lukewarm support for an assessment; declining George Mason's request that he join the opposition, Washington explained "[a]ltho' no mans Sentiments are more opposed to *any kind* of restraint upon religeous principles than mine are; yet I must confess, that I am not amongst the number of those who are so much alarmed at the thoughts of making People pay towards the support of that which they profess, ... if of the denominations of Christians; or declare themselves Jews, Mahomitans or otherwise, & thereby obtain proper relief." Madison wrote to the watching Jefferson that the resolution for a general assessment had passed "in spite of all the opposition that could be mustered."[7]

In fairness, while a number of authors report simply that Washington supported an assessment, his position was more nuanced. Washington understood that an assessment would create civil discord, which he sought to avoid. His note to Mason continued:

> I wish an assessment had never been agitated—& as it has gone so far, that the Bill could die an easy death; because I think it will be productive of more quiet to the State, than by enacting it into a Law; which, in my opinion, wou'd be impolitic, admitting there is a decided majority for it, to the disgust of a respectable minority.—In the First case, the matter will soon subside;—in the latter it will rankle, & perhaps convulse the State.

This is hardly a ringing endorsement. Washington also assumed that the bill exempted non-Christians; in fact, funds not designated for a Christian denomination would go to "seminaries of learning," generally run by Christian ministers. This was understood by careful observers at the time. Beverley Randolph, for example, wrote that "Turks, Jews & Infidels were to contribute, to the support of a Religion whose truth they did not acknowledge." In any case, Washington's failure to support Madison and Mason must have landed as another serious blow to the effort to block the assessment.[8]

Less than a week after adopting the general assessment resolution, the House adopted resolutions supporting marriage and vestry reform and non-discriminatory incorporation, providing further political support to the effort.[9]

The assessment effort received an unexpected but highly significant boost when the Presbytery of Hanover, which had helped to lead the wartime negotiations for religious freedom and had consistently opposed any assessment for religion, appeared to accept the need for a general assessment and endorsed the legislature's authority to act. In a lengthy petition dated November 12, 1784, and apparently written by John Blair Smith of Hampden-Sydney Academy, the Presbytery renewed its call for reform of marriage and vestry laws and nondiscriminatory incorporation. Most of the petition, however, provided a detailed opposition to any plan that might incorporate clergy separately from their laity or, in the act of incorporation, suggest any legislative authority over church polity or modes of worship, results that Smith thought possible based upon various incorporation proposals from the Episcopal clergy that had been floated over the spring and summer. For Smith, such proposals threatened an unholy alliance between ministerial authority and government.

> The Legislature in that case would be the head of a religious party. . . . We conceive that human Legislation ought to have human affairs alone for its concern. . . . [M]odes of worship, lie beyond their [legislators'] reach and are ever to be referred to a higher and more penetrating tribunal. . . . It is the duty of every man for himself to take care of his immortal interests in a future state, where we are to account for our conduct as individuals; and it is by no means the business of a Legislature to attend to this.

At the same time, Smith's petition for the presbytery urged that "it is wise policy in Legislation to seek its [religion's] alliance & solicit it's aid in a civil view because of it's happy influence upon the morality of the citizens." On this basis, the petition noted that the legislature had a "right" to adopt an assessment, a change in the presbytery's former insistence that such actions were beyond the purview of civil authorities. The presbytery cautioned only that any general assessment should follow "the most liberal plan," that is not impose any doctrinal uniformity or modes of worship on those accepting funds, as had been proposed in 1779.[10]

While Smith quibbled over the proper form of incorporation, the assessment proposal proceeded apace. With the House having voted a resolution in favor of a general assessment on November 11, the receipt of the presbytery's November 12 petition with its support of an assessment, even if conditional, made passage seem highly likely. It was also noteworthy that a November 11 petition from the newly formed Virginia Baptist General Committee did not expressly address the assessment, but asked only "that no order, or Denomination of Christians in this Commonwealth, have any Separate Privileges allowed them more than their Brethren of other Religious Societies. . . . And that in every Act, the bright beams of equal liberty, and impartial Justice may shine." While the Baptists indicated an interest in marriage and vestry reform, their plea for equal treatment could also be read to endorse a nondiscriminatory assessment. Certainly their petition expressed no opposition to an assessment at this crucial moment. Oddly, church records indicate that the General Committee had specifically discussed a general assessment at its meeting and, as the Baptists had done throughout the war, opposed it, but that opposition did not make its way into their petition at this critical moment. Madison noted wanly the Baptists' silence, writing Jefferson that "[t]he other Sects [other than Presbyterian] seemed to be passive."[11]

In fact, by November, no systematic opposition to the general assessment had appeared, and with Jefferson serving as American ambassador to France, any likely opposition was hobbled. John Holt Rice, a leading Presbyterian publisher and later founder of Union Theological Seminary, recounted some years later that "the general belief was that the measure [the assessment] would be carried in spite of all opposition." This, though, was to underestimate the political acumen of James Madison.[12]

Madison was outraged at the presbytery's apparent apostasy, and recognized the danger that it posed. Contrary to Irving Brant's suggestion that John Blair Smith "held to [his] principles" and opposed incorporation but was "equally vehement against the assessment," the presbytery appeared not simply to have abandoned the lists, but to have taken up an alliance with those supporting church-state integration, at least as to funding. Madison was in an uncharacteristic lather, explaining to James Monroe that

[t]he Episcopal people are generally for it [a general assessment], tho' I think the zeal of some of them has cooled. The laity of the other Sects are equally

unanimous on the other side. So are all the Clergy except the Presbyterian who seem as ready to set up an establishment which is to take them in as they were to pull down that which shut them out. I do not know a more shameful contrast than might be formed between their Memorials on the latter & former occasion.

As a result, Madison's first efforts were focused on breaking any possible nascent alliance between Presbyterians and Anglicans, an alliance that would almost certainly have been successful in encouraging adoption of a general assessment.[13]

During the late autumn of 1784, Madison was successful in injecting discord between the Presbyterians and Anglicans in part because Smith, the author of the November Presbyterian petition, the leading Presbyterian supporter of a general assessment, and a former College of New Jersey classmate of Madison's, was at the same time highly suspicious—one might say paranoid—of Anglican efforts to reassert their preferred position, including their proposals for incorporation. In particular, Smith was deeply concerned about any suggestion that the Episcopal Church, but not the Presbyterian Church, would be incorporated, that the Episcopal clergy would be incorporated separate from their laity, or that in incorporating a church, the legislature would have any say over the church's polity or modes of worship. Smith wrote Madison in June 1784, apparently aware that he was trying Madison's patience, to complain that the Episcopal clergy were seeking "spiritual domination . . . an indefensible remain of Star-chamber tyranny." Smith also complained about the Episcopal request that an act specify that the newly incorporated church be permitted to regulate all spiritual matters of the church, arguing that seeking legislative endorsement of what was a matter of right was "an express attempt to draw the State into an illicit connexion & commerce" with religion.[14]

If Madison had not been skeptical about Smith's concerns in the summer of 1784, he was certainly outraged after the November presbytery petition was received and, knowing Smith's mind, may have worked on his fears, real and imagined. For example, while Smith was correct that the Episcopal clergy framed their 1784 request for incorporation in terms of the "clergy" being incorporated and in a manner that would have largely protected clergy from removal, incorporation of the Episcopal clergy independent of the laity was never a serious possibility in vestry-dominated Virginia. Madison understood this, but whatever the considered unlikelihood of separate incorporation of the clergy, Smith's apprehension seemed to be encouraged by manipulation of legislative language as the incorporation proposal moved through the House of Delegates—one might speculate whether the manipulation was by Episcopal stalwarts or by Madison. After receiving Smith's June letter, Madison's likely tactics were evident in a letter that he wrote to Jefferson stressing the extent of the Episcopal clergy's request, especially its efforts "for re-establishing their independence of the laity." Upon hearing of the apparent Episcopal overreaching, Jefferson wrote gleefully from Paris: "I am glad the *Episcopalians* have again shewn their teeth & fangs. The *dissenters* had almost forgotten them."[15]

When the incorporation bill was finally introduced, it was simply referred to as "A Bill for incorporating the Protestant Episcopal Church." Yet, the inconsistent use of language by the House of Delegates—incorporating the "clergy" on November 17 and December 21 versus incorporating the church on December 11, 13, 17, 18, 20, and 22—may have fed Smith's paranoia.[16]

While the legislation that finally passed made it clear that the assembly was incorporating the church, not the clergy alone, it did assume legislative authority over internal church matters, regulating how Episcopal conventions would be called and how voting in such conventions would take place, exactly the type of legislative interference that Smith feared. Putting a nail in any possible Presbyterian-Episcopal cooperation, by December 24, 1784, when the incorporation proposal passed the General Assembly, it was limited to incorporating only the Episcopal Church. While supporters assumed that "other sects could obtain this privilege if they desired," the damage was done, and any possible Episcopal-Presbyterian alliance was in tatters. Fortuitously, a drafting error in the bill meant that the Episcopal Convention called for in the law would have equal representation from lay and clerical members, even though the assembly had clearly intended to have twice as many lay representatives as clerical; the result: even supporters of the bill were "dissatisfied . . . and will probably concur in a revision if not a repeal of the law." Madison wrote his father that the act "will soon be repealed, and will be a standing lesson to them of the danger of referring religious matters to the legislature."[17]

Passage of the problematic incorporation act not only put many Presbyterians ill at ease, but also assisted Madison by mollifying the most adamant Establishment supporters, weakening their drive for a general assessment. He wrote Jefferson somewhat apologetically that he had voted for the incorporation act because "a negative of the bill too would have doubled the eagerness and the pretexts for a much greater evil, a general assessment, which there is good ground to believe was parried by this partial gratification of its warmest votaries."[18]

Marriage reform also finally passed the assembly in December 1784 with broad support, although vestry reform seemed to fall off the legislative calendar until the following year (potentially further weakening any support for the general assessment among dissenters). The one lingering restriction on dissenting sects was that itinerant preachers were forbidden to perform the marriage service. This may have been a slap at the new Methodist Church which, at a 1784 Christmas conference in Baltimore, was officially breaking its ties with the Episcopal Church just as the Virginia legislature was considering reform; given Methodists' heavy reliance on itinerant preaching, the new law seemed to impose a fairly targeted restriction. Conservatives may have seen this as an opportunity to court Presbyterians and Baptists while not quite abandoning their claim to regulate in matters of religious ceremonies.[19]

Equally important, as the hectic 1784 legislative session approached its denouement, the assembly began to hear from Virginians opposed to any religious assessment, although pro-assessment petitions still dominated. Madison backhandedly recognized as much when he wrote to Jefferson after the session that "[m]any Petitions from below the blue ridge had prayed for such a law [the general assessment]; and though several from the presbyterian laity beyond it were in contrary Stile, the Clergy of that Sect favoured it." As the end of December 1784 approached, Establishment leaders had acquiesced in marriage reform, incorporated the Episcopal Church (expecting to incorporate other churches upon request), accepted the idea of vestry reform, and passed a resolution calling for adoption of a general assessment. While Patrick Henry had been elevated to the governor's office, removing him from the House of Delegates' debates, establishment supporters were still confident of their likely success.[20]

They were mistaken. With the alliance in favor of a general assessment cracking under the pressure of incorporation of the Episcopal Church and Madison's incessant efforts, Madison outmaneuvered assessment proponents with a brilliant delaying tactic. In late December, Madison made one of his infrequent floor speeches to oppose the assessment. In doing so, he directly challenged the underlying assumptions of the assessment's supporters. Not only was "Rel[igion]: no[t] within [the] purview of Civil Authority," but the "True question [is] not—Is Rel[igion]: neces[sar]y.? [But] are Relig[iou]s Estab[lishmen]ts. necess[ar]y. for Religion?" His notes answer the question: "no." On December 24, under Madison's guidance, the House of Delegates agreed 45 to 38 to delay a final vote on the assessment while the proposal was printed—with the names of those voting in favor and against delay—and distributed around the state to gather the views of the people. Later in life, Madison explained the delay: The bill, "being patronized by the most popular talents in the House, seemed likely to obtain a majority of votes. In order to arrest its progress, it was insisted with success that the Bill should be postponed till the ensuing session, and in the meantime [be] printed for public consideration. That the sense of the people might be the better called forth."[21]

Even the vote for delay was not a foregone conclusion, and it was ultimately carried by the votes of the new western (primarily dissenter) counties. (Fortuitously, Jefferson had strongly supported the westward expansion of representation.) One suspects that as the session ended and Madison turned his horse toward his Montpelier plantation, he was increasingly confident that the general assessment effort had passed its high-water mark.[22]

With no spring session of the General Assembly scheduled for 1785, opponents of a general assessment had almost a year to organize. During that period, three streams of opposition gained force. First, the Baptists, who had strangely been publicly silent concerning the proposed general assessment, organized in opposition. As previously noted, the Baptist General Committee had opposed a general assessment during its fall 1784 meeting but failed to convey that opposition to the General Assembly in its formal petition of 1784. With the committee having just been organized to present a coordinated Baptist message to the assembly on matters of general concern, further evidence of the politicization of the Baptists, it would have to do a better job if it was to maintain its members' support. In early 1785, local Baptist meetings and regional associations exhorted their members to make their feelings known. The General Committee met again in August and, making up for lost time, urged its members to protest, suggesting that the assembly be told that an assessment "is believed to be repugnant to the spirit of the Gospel for the Legislature thus to proceed in matters of religion . . . that every person ought to be left entirely free in respect to matters of religion; . . . and that should the Legislature assume the right of taxing the people for the support of the Gospel, it will be destructive to religious liberty." Far from the 1784 call for nondiscrimination, the Spirit of the Gospel resolution was an emphatic demand that government leave religion alone.[23]

For Baptists, this was not only a matter of political wisdom, but a theological matter as well. Even government endorsement of religion interfered with the "free will" offering that God desired and threatened confusion about where a person's ultimate allegiance lies. Having been willing to face social ostracism and large fines in colonial Virginia for refusing to baptize their children, the Baptists were happily willing to forego state funding that might interfere, even indirectly, with a personal faith commitment. Thus, Baptists had previously committed that if an assessment was charged, Baptist ministers would return the money to any citizen who specified that his or her tax payment should go to the Baptists. As the Baptist minister John Leland explained: "Every man must give an account of himself to God, and therefore every man ought to be at liberty to serve God in a way that he can best reconcile to his conscience. If government can answer for individuals at the day of judgment, let men be controlled by it in religious matters; otherwise, let men be free."[24]

The General Committee's recommendation was warmly embraced by Virginia Baptists, with several dozen Baptist congregations using the committee's resolution to form their own petitions. Baptists in Surry, for example, "most earnestly declare[d] against" the assessment, "believing it to be contrary to the Spirit of the Gospel and the [Virginia] Bill of Rights." They instructed the assembly on ecclesiastic history: "[C]ertain it is, that, the Blessed author of our Religion supported and maintained his Gospel in the World for several Hundred Years, not only without aid of civil power, but against all the powers of the Earth. . . . Nor was it the better for the church when Constantine first Established Christianity by human Laws." The Surry petitioners specifically challenged the notion that declension and "baneful" deism were spreading as a result of the lack of an establishment. Baptists in Caroline County were equally skeptical; "how strange . . . to hear it asserted that it [Christianity] must fall, if not established by human Laws." Other churches and groups sent slightly modified versions of this petition to the House, embellishing with their own reasons to oppose a general assessment. Ultimately, the assembly received twenty-nine "Spirit of the Gospel" petitions with almost five thousand signatures. Baptist ministers who previously had suffered active persecution for preaching were among the signatories.[25]

Second, with the new year, rather agitated lay Presbyterians demanded

It would be a mistake, though, to conclude that the evangelical petitioners were less committed than those supporting the Memorial & Remonstrance to a strict separation of church and state. The Baptist "Spirit of the Gospel" and Presbyterian Bethel petitions were clear in this regard. (To report the presbytery's guarded support for a general assessment in 1784 without noting the dramatic reversal in 1785 in an effort to downplay Presbyterian support for separation of church and state, as some historians have done, misconstrues the role of Virginia's Presbyterians.) A strongly worded petition from Accomack County lectured the House that if a legislature was found to have any authority in the area of religion, it would be a "stepping stone" to full establishment, a "snake in the grass," the "first link which Draws after it a chain of horrid consequences, and that by Degrees it will terminate in who shall preach, when they shall preach, where they shall preach, and what they shall preach . . . kindling Smithfield's fires in America." Others were equally adamant and offended by legislative usurpation. Chesterfield citizens scolded that "for the men of the world to undertake to Legislate for his [Jesus's] subjects in matters of Religion is Violating of his Kingly perogative [sic]." Expressly opposing any effort to "unite the Church and State," they insisted that the assembly

> let Jews, Mehometans, and Christians of every Denomination injoy religious liberty, as the decliration of rights has invited them. . . . [T]herefore thrust them not out now by establishing the Christian religion lest thereby we become our own enemys and weaken this infant State[.] it is mens labour in our Manufactories their services by sea and land that Aggrandize our country, and not their creeds.

Their solution was simple: "let the Church of Christ and religion alone." Others responded to the proposed assessment by citing or quoting Jefferson's Bill for Establishing Religious Freedom.[28]

By the time the General Assembly returned to Richmond in the fall of 1785, it was "flooded" with opposition to a general assessment, and the table "almost sank under the weight of the accumulated" petitions. Madison recalled that the assessment was "crushed under" the weight of petitions. Apparently an effort was made by Establishment supporters to resuscitate the general assessment proposal in the Committee of the Whole, but even a vote to return the bill to the House for final action reportedly failed by three votes. Virginians, politicized by the negotiations for religious freedom during the course of the war, rose up to oppose overwhelmingly any government support for religion, even nondiscriminatory support for all (at least all Christian) sects. Continuing his reporting to Jefferson, Madison wrote:

> The steps taken throughout the Country to defeat the Genl. Assessment, had produced all the effect that could have been wished. The table was loaded with petitions & remonstrances from all parts against the interposition of the Legislature in matters of Religion. A General convention of the Presbyterian church prayed expressly that the bill in the Revisal [Jefferson's Bill] might be passed into a law, as the best safeguard short of a constitutional one, for their religious rights.[29]

With the general assessment finally defeated, Madison seized the opportunity to push forward Jefferson's Statute. This battle, too, was hard fought, but with the outpouring of opposition to the general assessment and demands for the broadest possible religious freedom, Madison was clearly in control. In December, a proposal to delete Jefferson's preamble, a ringing declaration of Enlightenment philosophy, was soundly defeated (38–66), and the bill passed with an overwhelming majority (74–20). The more conservative Senate also sought to remove the preamble, but Madison stood firm, and ultimately the bill passed with minor modifications. The Virginia Statute for Establishing Religious Freedom was signed and became law on January 19, 1786.[30]

Madison told Jefferson that the changes to the preamble insisted upon by the Senate were largely stylistic and that, while they "somewhat defaced the composition, it was thought better to agree to [the amendments] than to run further risks, especially as it was getting late in the Session and the House growing thin." For example, the Senate insisted on deleting Jefferson's first phrase: "the opinions and belief of men depend not on their own will, but follow involuntarily the evidence proposed to their minds." This did little to change the meaning, although it did tend to obscure somewhat Jefferson's own religious beliefs. Other changes were dogmatic; for example, members, many committed believers in divine revelation in the Bible, insisted that the General Assembly delete the statement that religion is propagated "by its influence on reason alone"—an Enlightenment doctrine that they did not share. Most significantly, the Senate removed the statement that "the opinions of men are not the object of civil government, nor under its jurisdiction." Citing this change, some have implied that the legislators intended to retain authority to regulate belief, but Madison was probably more accurate when he assured Jefferson in Paris that it merely "defaced the composition." After all, the Statute elsewhere noted "that our civil rights have no dependence on our religious opinions, any more than our opinions in physics and geometry," and "it is time enough for the rightful purposes of civil government for its officers to interfere when principles break out into overt acts against peace and good order."[31]

A more significant proposed edit was the suggestion to add "Jesus Christ" to the preamble, modifying Jefferson's generic (one might say Unitarian or even deistic) "holy author of our religion." Some have too readily dismissed this debate as irrelevant because it related to the preamble rather than the operative language of the Statute. Had this change been made, though, it would support a great deal of argument that the early republic was a "Christian nation." As Madison suggested in a different context, it might "imply and certainly nourish the erronious idea of a *national* religion." While others have mischaracterized the decision to omit "Jesus Christ" as "modestly [holding] back from mentioning the exact name of the 'holy author of our religion,'" Jefferson made clear that far more was at stake.

> Where the preamble declares that coercion is a departure from the plan of the holy author of our religion, an amendment was proposed, by inserting the word "Jesus Christ," ... the insertion was rejected by a great majority, in proof that they meant to comprehend, within the mantle of it's protection, the Jew and the Gentile, the Christian and Mahometan, the Hindoo, and infidel of every denomination.

Madison agreed, reporting that several legislators, "particularly distinguished by their reputed piety and Christian zeal," argued that "the better proof of reverence for that holy name wd be not to profane it by making it a topic of legisl. discussion." Like Jefferson, Madison rightly saw the object of the effort "would have been, to imply a restriction on the liberty defined by the Bill, to those professing his religion only." For Madison, use of Jesus's name to promote a civil bill, "particularly by making his religion the means of abridging the natural and equal rights of all men," would be "in defiance of his own declaration that his kingdom was not of this world."[32]

While the edits to Jefferson's ringing language were limited, the sensitive Jefferson was always troubled by changes to his prose. When he had the Statute translated and reprinted in Europe, for example, he insisted upon using his own, original text, or a hybrid version reflecting only some of the legislative amendments, rather than the version actually adopted (a practice that he also sometimes undertook with the Declaration of Independence). This led to some confusion. Philip Mazzei, for example, in his *Researches on the United States*, published in Paris in 1788, reprints Jefferson's version but fails to note that the text he provides is not the text as adopted. The Jefferson version was also reprinted in America, often without noting that it had been amended. Others in Europe used Jefferson's hybrid formula and made additional stylistic changes. The confusion continued in publications of Jefferson's papers for years. In any case, the changes are relatively limited, and Madison sought to assure Jefferson that, even as amended, the Statute "extinguished for ever the ambitious hope of making laws for the human mind." At least in Virginia, the battle for religious freedom had been won, although skirmishes would continue for years to come.[33]

Several points about the significance of the battle over the general assessment and Jefferson's Statute deserve particular note: First, it is worth pausing on both the source and nature of the opposition to the assessment and growing clamor for adoption of Jefferson's Bill. With the Virginia Experience clearly in mind, William Lee Miller argues that "dissenting Protestantism had more to do, over all, over time, pound for pound, head for head, with the shaping of the American tradition of religious liberty than did the rational Enlightenment." Edwin Gaustad cautions that "though that may be true, it is likewise true that dissenting Protestantism could not by itself have successfully stormed the gates of establishment." They may both be correct. While the effort of evangelical dissenters to stop the assessment and prevent any alliance between church and state was the most decisive politically, it is Madison's Memorial & Remonstrance and Jefferson's statutory language that are remembered and that have played a critical role in defining American religious freedom.[34]

This poses an interesting matter of historic memory. Perhaps the dissenters were simply too numerous and their petitions too diverse to make a compelling and easily retold story. Perhaps history prefers identifiable heroes, famous Founders most of all. Certainly there is evidence that evangelicals themselves lost interest in retelling the story of their role in demanding religious freedom and a strict separation of church and state, and this pattern of targeted forgetfulness may have increased with the arrival of the Second Great Awakening in the early years of the nineteenth century, not to mention battles over church and state in the twentieth. The result, though, is clear: Jefferson and Madison, who unquestionably needed the support of the evangelical dissenters to defeat the assessment and get the Statute adopted, are recalled as the progenitors of American religious freedom.[35]

While both the dissenters and their Enlightenment supporters demanded full religious liberty and a separation of church and state, it is certainly fair to say that the dissenters were more concerned with the pernicious influence of the state on the church, although they joined in the belief that a mixing of religion and government would harm legitimate government. Jefferson was most concerned about the danger that religion posed to republican government, but he, too, was concerned to protect religion (a rational, republican religion) from state interference. As one nineteenth-century religious author rightly explained, "it is thought by some that what this skeptic [Jefferson] meant was not intended by the Christian men who cooperated with him. The history tells another story."[36]

Second, the general assessment proposal provides important context for understanding Madison's Memorial & Remonstrance and later battles for religious freedom. The "establishment" that elicited the wrath of Jefferson, Madison, and the dissenters was not a proposal to benefit one particular sect; rather, it was nondiscriminatory aid to all Christian denominations. While Patrick Henry, for example, might have embraced a narrower definition of an "establishment"—insisting that he was opposed to religious establishments, which he understood to be an exclusive preference for one denomination—that was not the understanding of those who opposed the general assessment.

The more complicated question is whether the limitation of the proposed assessment to Christian sects means that opposition was based upon the provision's discriminatory nature rather than principled opposition to governmental aid to all religion. After all, in recent years, one of the most persistent arguments about the meaning of the First Amendment is that the Founders intended to prevent only preference for one particular sect or denomination, not aid to all religion; if opposition to the general assessment was based only upon the fact that it was limited to Christian sects, such opposition would be consistent with a narrow, "preferentialist" reading of the First Amendment. There are any number of practical, legal, and historic arguments against this "preferentialist" position; in his extended treatment of the issue, Douglas Laycock explains that "the prominence and longevity of the nonpreferential aid theory is remarkable in light of the weak evidence supporting it and the quite strong evidence against it." The issue here, though, is purely a historic one: Can the opposition to the general assessment be understood as objecting only to discrimination in government cooperation with religion?[37]

As a preliminary matter, it is an understatement that there were not a lot of sects in 1785 Virginia that were not Christian. Thus, many at the time, and subsequently, saw the general assessment debate in terms of aid to all religion. This, though, may be too facile.[38]

A related argument is made that the general assessment exempted non-Christians and, thus, could be viewed as wholly nondiscriminatory. George Washington, for example, expressed that erroneous view. In fact, the assessment permitted those who were not members of a Christian sect to designate that their taxes go to "seminaries of learning," but this did not eliminate discrimination: First, those not wanting funds to go to a Christian sect had to pay an "education" tax from which others were, effectively, exempt. Second, at the time, schools were private and almost all were run by ministers; the possibility of funding for teachers under the general assessment bill would have been understood to be a provision for Christian education. Some Supreme Court justices have made a similar, quixotic argument that this minor provision proves that the general assessment was intended to benefit both religious activities and nonreligious activities and, thus, Jefferson and Madison opposed even tangential support for religion in a general funding bill. It would seem, though, that Justice Thomas has the better of that argument: "This provision disposing of undesignated funds hardly transformed the 'Bill . . .' into a truly neutral program that would benefit religious adherents as part of a large class of beneficiaries defined without reference to religion."[39]

This leaves the question of whether opposition was related to the discriminatory nature of the assessment. The historian Robert Cord argues that several of the paragraphs of Madison's Memorial speak to discrimination among sects, and criticizes Leo Pfeffer for his claim that only one paragraph is clearly about the discriminatory aspects of the proposal. Essentially joining Cord's argument, Daniel Dreisbach urges that "it is plausible that if the amendment had passed [replacing 'Christian' with 'Religious'], Madison would have viewed the assessment scheme as nondiscriminatory and, thus, would have dropped his opposition to it." Justice Thomas makes the same general point. Philip Hamburger urges a more subtle form of this argument by noting that Madison wrote to Richard Henry Lee noting concern with the proposal that "comprehends Christians alone" and mentioning that the Hanover Presbytery's November 12, 1784, petition that was understood to support the bill—before the Presbytery emphatically changed its position—opposed an assessment that did not "embrace all Religions."[40]

These arguments range from very weak to just plain wrong. There is no indication that those opposed to the assessment would have supported it had it benefited all religions rather than just Christianity. Certainly the rhetoric was to the contrary. In fact, many proponents argued for the provision on the premise that it was nondiscriminatory, some using a slogan of "Equal Right and Equal Liberty," and this inconsistency was never a focus of argumentation. Edmund Pendleton wrote to Richard Henry Lee that he could see nothing "which can justly alarm any other society." Even when the discriminatory nature of the bill was recognized, there was no suggestion that changing that aspect would result in its adoption. Richard Henry Lee, for example, recognized that the bill should include non-Christians, but continued to support the bill nonetheless. Reportedly a proposal to eliminate the "Christian" limitation in the legislature failed (the proposal to which Daniel Dreisbach refers), but no contemporary suggests that had that amendment been made, the bill would have passed. (Information on this episode is limited, as the *Journal of the House of Delegates* does not mention it.)[41]

While Madison certainly objected to the proposal's discrimination in favor of Christianity, his letter to Richard Henry Lee noted that the assessment was opposed "on the general principle that no Religious Estabts. was within the purview of Civil authority" before turning to the specific, discriminatory "ground on which it was placed." More importantly, the primary thrust of the Memorial & Remonstrance is against any governmental aid to religion. While Robert Cord and Justice Thomas quibble with Leo Pfeffer over which of the fifteen paragraphs speak to discriminatory practices, unless *all* of the paragraphs of the Memorial address only discrimination among sects, Madison is clearly reaching beyond that narrow area. In fact, most of Madison's arguments applied equally to preferential and nonpreferential aid to religion. Similarly, in 1776, Jefferson argued "for discontinuing the establishment of the English church by law, taking away all privilege & pre-eminence of one religious sect over another," but he goes on to demand that disestablishment "totally and eternally restraining the civil magistrate from all pretensions of interposing his authority or exercise in matters of religion." Certainly Jefferson opposed discrimination, but to read his position as only opposition to discrimination is to misread it.[42]

The evangelical petitions were equally expansive and inconsistent with the preferentialist revisionism. While John Blair Smith's November 12, 1784, petition on behalf of the presbytery obliquely supporting an assessment can be read to object to the discriminatory nature of the proposal, the 1785 deluge of Presbyterian petitions in opposition to any assessment are not so limited. The May 1785 petition from the Hanover Presbytery that played a pivotal role in derailing the assessment, for example, spoke generally of "any kind of an Assessment . . . for the support of Religion." The evangelical citizens of Botetourt added: "Civil Government & Religion are, and ought to be, Independent of Each other. The one has for its object a proper Regulation of the External conduct of men . . . ; [the other] our internal or spiritual welfare & is beyond the reach of human laws." Baptist opposition demonstrated a similar breadth. For example, a petition from Orange County Baptists listed seven resolutions against the general assessment: The seventh mentioned its discriminatory nature; several others are worth quoting: "Resolve 1: That no civil Power has, or can have a right to establish such provision as specified in this Bill; it being in our opinion, quite out of the province of any Legislature upon earth. . . . Resolve 3: That the Legislature by such establishment, must in reality assume the prerogative of judging who are, and who are not worthy to receive the public benefice. And of consequence, our religious principles, as well as preachers must be subject to their [illegible], and stand, or fall according to their determination." The central arguments of the dissenters and Madison and Jefferson were that government aid to religion corrupts both church and state and is simply beyond the pale of legislative authority. At least in Virginia, opposition to church/state interaction went well beyond preferentialism.[43]

Third, some have argued that the defeat of the general assessment owed as much to Virginians' opposition to new taxes as to any principled opposition to cooperation between church and state. Certainly, there is a long history of opposition to taxes in Virginia, but the role of such opposition to the defeat of the general assessment appears to be limited. The petitions overwhelmingly denounce any legislative authority over or involvement with religion; a desire to avoid additional taxes is rarely mentioned. Further, there is some disagreement about whether economic conditions at the time would have justified opposition on that basis alone. For example, Madison wrote Jefferson in January 1785 about "[t]he plentiful crops on hand both of corn and tobacco and the price of the latter which is vibrating on this river between 36/ and 40/, seem to enable the Country to bear the burden [of taxes]." In any case, even if one posits that economic factors contributed to the defeat of the general assessment, opposition to church/state cooperation was clearly the dominant factor, and economic issues were not at work in the subsequent adoption of the Virginia Statute. Significantly, the argument that economic factors led to the defeat of the general assessment apparently originated with Hugh Blair Grigsby, but Grigsby offers a highly biased report that mischaracterizes much of the debate, arguing that Virginians really did not oppose the religious tax.[44]

Fourth, while Jefferson's Statute was ultimately adopted with an overwhelming majority, it is worth remembering that the effort to defeat the general assessment and enact the Statute was highly contingent, especially in 1784 (when the majority of petitions supported the assessment as did many of Virginia's most prominent leaders). George Washington noted his view that the majority of people seemed to support an assessment. Nor was the petition campaign as one-sided as many sources suggest. When the General Assembly voted in favor of the assessment on November 11, 1784, eight petitions supported the assessment, and none opposed. After that date, seventy-nine petitions were received in opposition while twenty additional petitions supported it.[45] The fact that the proposal to bring the assessment to the floor of the House for a final reading in 1785 failed by only three votes is an indication of the continued strength of the former Establishment and the highly contested nature of this dispute. At the same time, not only was the final vote in favor of the Statute overwhelming, but it occurred after an extended period of statewide consideration and debate. Madison believed that "the printed Bill has excited great discussion and is likely to prove the sense of the Community to be in favor of the liberty now enjoyed. I have heard of several Counties where the late representatives have been laid aside for voting for the Bill, and not a single one where the reverse has happened." Edmund Pendleton also reported that those supporting an assessment might face electoral difficulties, and one modern commentator suggested that both John Marshall and Philip Barbour likely lost their bids for reelection due to support of the assessment. What is clear is that support for disestablishment, separation of church and state, and free exercise in Virginia was extremely broadly based among both Enlightenment thinkers and evangelicals.[46]

Finally, while most historians focus on Bill 82 of the statutory revision intended to bring Virginia's laws into sync with its new independent status—the Statute for Establishing Religious Freedom—the revisal included other proposed bills on religion, bills 83–86, which arguably contemplated a more active interaction between church and state. Daniel Dreisbach goes so far as to claim that historians seek to "suppress" this information. This, though, is to misapprehend the matter. Historians and lawyers focus on the Virginia Statute in part because Jefferson identified it as one of the most important bills of the revisal and part of his permanent legacy, publishing it throughout Europe and referring to it repeatedly. As discussed in chapters 4 and 5, the Statute for Establishing Religious Freedom played a central part in the development of religious freedom throughout the nation; it has also influenced religious freedom around the world for two centuries. Bills 83–86 are not only not particularly memorable, but are in fact soon forgotten.[47]

Certainly it is true that these additional bills recognized some degree of government "involvement" with religion. The proposed bills would have maintained the property of the formerly established church, protected the Sabbath from disturbers, provided for a governor's declaration of days of thanksgiving, and regulated marriage according to Levitical Law. The significance of these proposals, though, is more complicated. Initially, care must be taken in attributing these laws to Jefferson. Bill 86, suggesting adoption of Levitical Law on marriage, for example, bears the mark of Edmund Pendleton (also a member of the revisal committee). The other bills, even if authored by Jefferson, also are limited. Bill 83, protecting the property of the Anglican Church, was necessary to disentangle the state from a previous Establishment and was part of what Anglicans were promised as they, grudgingly, acceded to disestablishment. While Bill 84 protecting Sabbath worshippers and the peace of the Sabbath is certainly "consistent with Jefferson's lifelong commitment to protecting the citizenry's right to express peacefully religious beliefs and opinions," it goes too far to conclude that "[i]f religious liberty was realized in its richest sense through cooperation between the state and the church, then Jefferson, it would seem, endorsed such a limited union."[48]

Reading the provisions of these laws as a Jeffersonian endorsement of church-state cooperation is strained. Michael Myerson shows that each of these bills was the product of the revisers' assignment to recast prior laws; in most cases, Jefferson and his committee did make efforts to liberalize previous restrictions. Thus, for example, while Bill 85 authorizes the long-standing practice of government proclamations of "Days of Public Fasting and Thanksgiving," this does not change Jefferson's clear and emphatic statements while president that he believed such proclamations both ill-advised and unconstitutional. Steven Green comes to the same conclusion, noting that "only the Sabbath bill was enacted, and that law can be seen simply as extending the long-standing custom of Sunday laws that were enacted in every state." In the end, these laws proposed by the revisal committee certainly do not take anything away from the clear language and intent of the Virginia Statute for Establishing Religious Freedom or Jefferson's lifelong commitment to separation of church and state.[49]

For Virginians, the adoption of the Statute for Establishing Religious Freedom was a major accomplishment, marking the end of the government Establishment and ensuring a robust right to free exercise. In its wake, vestry reform was promptly adopted, ending the civil authority of Anglican vestries, and the rather intrusive 1784 incorporation of the Episcopal Church was repealed. Over the years, the Statute has maintained its unique position in Virginia history and law, with key portions being incorporated into later constitutional revisions in Virginia. Virginia judges have embraced its significance and breadth. For example, in 1846, rejecting religious tests for witnesses in court, tests then relied upon in most states, Virginia's highest court recognized the Statute as

> [d]eclaring to the Christian and the Mahometan, the Jew and the Gentile, the Epicurean and the Platonists, (if any such there be amongst us,) that so long as they keep within its [the law's] pale, all are equally objects of its protection; securing safety to the people, safety to the government, safety to religion; and (leaving reason free to combat error) securing purity of faith and practice far more effectually than by clothing ministers of religion with exclusive temporal privileges; and exposing them to the corrupting influence of wealth and power.

Anson Phelp Stokes and Leo Pfeffer conclude: "The adoption of his [Jefferson's] proposal [the Statute] was of epoch-making significance at home and abroad, as Virginia is believed to have been the first state in the world to provide by self-imposed statute for complete religious freedom and equality."[50]

A very pleased Jefferson wrote to the victorious Madison: "[I]t is comfortable to see the standard of reason at length erected, after so many ages during which the human mind has been held in vassalage by kings, priests and nobles;

and it is honorable for us to have produced the first legislature who has had the courage to declare that the reason of man may be trusted with the formation of his own opinions." Madison came to speak of the Statute in equally trium-phant tones: "This act is a true standard of Religious liberty: its principle the great barrier against usurpations on the rights of conscience. As long as it is respected and no longer, these will be safe."[51]

Yet, the broader significance of the effort remained in doubt. The Statute only applied directly to Virginia, while all of the other new states maintained some form of establishment or, at least, a religious test for political office or suffrage. Both Jefferson and Madison were deeply cognizant of the need to broaden application of the Statute's principles and that an extended battle for religious freedom lay ahead.

4

THE FIRST AMENDMENT
TO THE U.S. CONSTITUTION

A Jeffersonian Compromise

WHILE JEFFERSON'S STATUTE WAS WELL RECEIVED AS A STATEMENT of principle both at home and abroad, the reality in the 1780s was that twelve of the thirteen states had some form of official establishment and/or religious test oath for holding office or voting. While incremental changes were afoot in some new states, the status quo had considerable vitality.

In the years immediately following adoption of the Statute, the national political landscape was dominated by the drafting and ratification of the U.S. Constitution. With the Constitution now having achieved status as legal and cultural scripture, it is difficult to appreciate fully how contingent and precarious its ratification was. Close votes in Massachusetts, Virginia, and New York—each necessary for effective functioning of the union—are important reminders that ratification might have failed.[1]

Two types of concerns took primacy: First, there was a broad outcry for a federal bill of rights, and freedom of religion was at the top of most lists of necessary amendments. Jefferson wrote to the "Father of the Constitution" from Paris to say that the document needed "a bill of rights providing clearly & without aid of sophisms for freedom of religion." Second, a number of antifederalists also sought structural amendments to limit the authority of the federal government. The power of direct taxation was at the center of those structural concerns, but a general foreboding about the threat of distant federal power and its possible interference with state institutions and citizens was also prevalent. As hard-fought battles for ratification were won in state conventions, state after state insisted that after the Constitution was ratified, amendments were needed. Many antifederalists, reluctantly, put their hope in postratification amendments.[2]

A full recitation of the difficulties faced in the adoption of the Bill of Rights is not needed here, and others have covered that topic well. For these purposes, particular consideration needs to be given to the religious freedom clauses of the First Amendment: "Congress shall make no law respecting an establishment of religion, or prohibiting the free exercise thereof."[3]

The Supreme Court has placed Jefferson and Madison and the Virginia struggle for religious liberty at the center of the debates over the religion clauses of the First Amendment. In *Everson v. Board of Education* (1947), the Court explained that the "movement toward this end [religious liberty] reached its dramatic climax in Virginia in 1785–86." The dissenters in that case agreed: "No provision of the Constitution is more closely tied to or given content by its generating history than the religious clause of the First Amendment . . . [including] the long and intensive struggle for religious freedom in America, more especially in Virginia." Viewed thus, Jefferson's Statute for Establishing Religious Freedom was foundational. The Court "recognized that the provisions of the *First Amendment,* in the drafting and adoption of which Madison and Jefferson played such leading roles, had the same objective and were intended to provide the same protection against government intrusion on religious liberty as the Virginia statute." In 1961, Chief Justice Earl Warren similarly explained the matter: "This Court has considered the happenings surrounding the Virginia General Assembly's enactment of 'An act for establishing religious freedom,' . . . written by Thomas Jefferson and sponsored by James Madison, as best reflecting the long and intensive struggle for religious freedom in America, and as particularly relevant in the search for First Amendment meaning." That understanding was broadly embraced by historians.[4]

More recently several justices, joined by a group of historians, have challenged that view. Former Chief Justice Rehnquist claimed that the focus on Jefferson to explain American religious freedom is "mistaken" and that there "is simply no historical foundation" for reliance on the Virginia Experience in understanding the First Amendment and, thus, for privileging a "wall of separation" between church and state.[5]

In spite of decades of courts and historians repeating a Jeffersonian conventional wisdom, to date, neither the historic foundations nor the contrarian's concern have been adequately addressed.

While James Madison had successfully navigated the testy and difficult battle for the Virginia Statute in January 1786, and while he certainly stood at the center of the constitutional debates in Philadelphia in the summer of 1787, religious liberty did not take center stage in Philadelphia as the Constitution was framed. Far from it. Certainly, in several key respects, the Philadelphia Constitution embraced religious freedom. Most notably, Article VI of the Constitution specifies that "no religious Test shall ever be required as a Qualification to any Office or public Trust under the United States," a significant deviation from requirements in most states in 1787. Equally troubling to those who sought an alliance or at least cooperation between church and state, any suggestion of God's providence or call for his assistance was wholly absent from the document. The specified presidential oath, for example, omitted the customary "so help me God." (The tradition that George Washington added "so help me God" to the oath is more myth than fact, although the practice has become the norm in the modern era.) At the same time, though, the Constitution did not include any express protections for religious liberty; in fact, it had no bill of rights at all—a failing that immediately became probably the most common complaint of those opposing ratification of the Constitution and certainly provided their most effective rhetorical tool.[6]

Equally surprising to many, not least of whom Jefferson, James Madison, the champion of liberty in Virginia, initially opposed adoption of any bill of rights. He claimed that it was unnecessary. Since the federal government had been given only enumerated powers and no power to regulate religion, he reasoned that it could neither restrict nor embrace it. Further, Madison argued that a bill of rights would be of little value because "parchment barriers" had been ineffective at preventing states, supported by a determined majority, from interfering with minority rights, a practice that Madison had seen play out in Virginia. Considering the 1784–85 battle over a general assessment, Madison concluded that absent the political support of the Baptists and Presbyterians the legislature would have adopted the assessment, regardless of the Virginia Declaration of Rights. Madison initially concluded that the limited authority of the national government and multiplicity of interests reflected in a popular government of such an extended territory, along with the checks and balances on the various branches of government, would be more effective than a bill of rights at restraining abuse of power. Madison also thought the states far more likely to embrace narrow, parochial interests and interfere with liberty than the federal government.[7]

Perhaps most importantly, as a practical matter, after the Philadelphia Convention completed its draft, Madison initially opposed any discussion of a bill of rights because he recognized that it was a potential trap that could easily prevent adoption of the Constitution, which he believed necessary to the survival of the union. If a bill of rights had to be adopted by a new convention before ratification, as antifederalists were urging, opponents of the Constitution would use the opportunity to seek other substantive changes. The result almost certainly would have been to tie the document up in endless political wrangling.

While many observers complained about the Constitution's lack of a bill of rights, particularly the absence of a guarantee for religious freedom, the exchanges between Madison and Jefferson are especially telling. On October 24, 1787, an exhausted Madison reported the Philadelphia Convention's success in an extended letter to Jefferson in Paris; in that letter Madison mentioned, but paid little heed to, George Mason's concerns about the lack of a bill of rights, concerns that propelled Mason, Madison's colleague in the battle for the Virginia Statute, into opposing ratification. Jefferson received Madison's letter on December 19 and, uncharacteristically, wrote back the next day. The ambassador gave Madison a lukewarm endorsement of the document as a whole, but then launched into problems with the new governmental blueprint:

> I will now add what I do not like. First, the omission of a bill of rights providing clearly and without aid of sophisms for freedom of religion. . . . To say as Mr. [James] Wilson does [and as Madison did, presumably something that Jefferson knew or, at least, suspected] that a bill of rights was not necessary because all is reserved in the case of the general government which is not given . . . is surely a gratis dictum, opposed by strong inference from the body of the instrument, as well as from the omission of the clause of our present confederation which had declared that in express terms. . . . Let me add that a bill of rights is what the people are entitled to against every government on earth, general or particular, and what no just government should refuse, or rest on inferences.

Given the epic battle in Virginia that had been necessary to secure religious freedom, and the fresh memory of the reactionary efforts of supporters of the old Establishment to restore some form of church/state taxation in 1784–85, Jefferson's anxiety is understandable.[8]

Madison, though, was focused on getting the Constitution ratified; his deep concern with the potential collapse of the union is evident in a letter to Jefferson that, fortuitously, he wrote on the same day that Jefferson wrote to him about the necessity of a bill of rights:

> The States seem to be either wholly omitting to provide for the federal Treasury; or to be withdrawing the scanty appropriations made to it. The latter course has been taken by Massachusetts, Virginia and Delaware. The Treasury Board seem to be in despair of maintaining the shadow of Government much longer. Without money, the Offices must be shut up, and the handful of troops on the frontier disbanded, which will probably bring on an Indian war, and make an impression to our disadvantage on the British Garrisons within our limits.

Madison also expressed concern with the growing opposition to ratification in Virginia coming from Patrick Henry, George Mason, and Richard Henry Lee.[9]

Madison finally responded to Jefferson's scolding letter of December 20 in April 1788, explaining that if amendments were required before the Constitution was adopted, "the Constitution, and the Union will be both endangered." In July, after ratification by Virginia was at last achieved, Madison chided his elder colleague that Patrick Henry—Madison's great protagonist in the ratification and general assessment debates and whom Jefferson had vilified for years—had used Jefferson's concerns about the lack of a bill of rights in his near successful effort to block Virginia's ratification and bring down the Constitution. Henry referred to a February 1788 letter from Jefferson to Alexander Donald, a Richmond merchant, in which the ambassador called for a bill of rights "which shall stipulate freedom of religion, freedom of the press, freedom ... against monopolies, trial by juries." Henry upbraided tepid delegates at the Virginia convention that "an illustrious citizen of Virginia, who is now in Paris, ... advises you to reject this Government, till it be amended. ... Living in splendour and dissipation, he thinks yet of Bills of Rights." This reference to Jefferson left Madison seething. Yet, as a result of Henry's efforts, antifederalists extracted commitments from Virginia federalists that amendments would be added to the Constitution; similar commitments had been obtained in Massachusetts and were forthcoming in New York. Madison was deeply suspicious that these efforts posed a continuing danger to the Constitution, and he must have been enormously frustrated with Jefferson. He added in his restrained admonition of the ambassador that Jefferson's concerns had also been used against ratification in the Maryland convention.[10]

Jefferson, receiving Madison's April letter on July 10, and having heard of the success of ratification from other sources, wrote back on July 31, 1788 (before Madison's new missive arrived). In July, Jefferson wrote with more moderation, but he was unrepentant: "I sincerely rejoice at the acceptance of our new constitution by nine states. It is a good canvas, on which some strokes only want retouching. What these are, I think are sufficiently manifest by the general voice from North and South, which calls for a bill of rights."[11]

By October 1788, with ratification secured and commitments to amendments having been made in several key states, Madison began to adjust his own position, explaining to the anxious Jefferson that "[m]y own opinion has always been in favor of a bill of rights; provided it be so framed as not to imply powers not meant to be included in the enumeration [of powers]." Madison was not being disingenuous, but circumstances had changed. Far from risking a defeat of the Constitution, after ratification, Madison recognized that adopting amendments concerning personal liberties would strengthen the Constitution by "separating the well meaning from the designing opponents" of the still very fragile Constitution and undermining continuing calls from Henry and other antifederalists for what would almost certainly have been a disastrous second convention.[12]

Beyond the politics of the situation, over time, Madison also warmed to the necessity of a bill of rights on the merits; he especially grew concerned that the clause granting Congress the authority "[t]o make all Laws which shall be necessary and proper for carrying into Execution" its delegated powers might be used to expand federal power beyond its enumerated bounds. Were this to occur, the need for limits on federal authority over personal liberties would be clear, exactly what many antifederalists had urged. Thus, by the time elections for the new Congress began, Madison had moved decisively beyond his prior position that a bill of rights was unnecessary because the federal government had only enumerated powers—although this argument would continue to be used by some in the congressional debates concerning amendments.[13]

Still, Madison cautioned Jefferson that there was a danger in pursuing a bill of rights, especially as it applied to religious liberty. Madison believed that there was a broad consensus throughout the nation for some form of religious liberty and at least opposition to a narrow establishment. At the Virginia convention he had argued that "a majority of the people are decidedly against any exclusive establishment—I believe it to be so in the other states." He went on, though, to express a broader view of what he understood to be necessary for religious liberty, a view with which Jefferson would readily agree: "There is not a shadow of right in the general government to intermeddle with religion. Its least interference with it, would be a most flagrant usurpation." This broad definition of what was an unacceptable establishment was consistent with the battle against the general assessment and his Memorial & Remonstrance. Madison was concerned that if an express provision on religious liberty was sought for the federal Constitution others would oppose a liberty as expansive as that in the Virginia Statute. "I am sure that the rights of Conscience in particular, if submitted to public definition would be narrowed much more than they are likely ever to be by an assumed power."[14]

For Madison, the danger of federal usurpation initially seemed less than the danger from conservative and reactionary politicians defining religious liberty too narrowly. Madison was particularly concerned that New England representatives would support some church/state entanglement if an amendment was forced upon them, for example restricting religious liberty to Christians or prohibiting only an exclusive establishment. He reminded Jefferson that "one of the objections in New England was that the Constitution by prohibiting religious tests opened a door for Jews, Turks & infidels." And Madison's concern was fed by events in Virginia. While he had defeated Patrick Henry's general assessment proposal after a long and difficult battle, free from the gaze of petitioners who had demanded a strict separation of church and state, Henry had pushed through the Virginia ratification convention a proposal for a constitutional amendment on religious liberty that appeared to endorse just the type of religious assessment that had been soundly defeated in 1785: "no particular religious sect or society ought to be favored or established by law in preference to others." Several of the proposals from other states for religious liberty amendments also endorsed this type of proposal only against preferentialism. Madison's concern was that a narrow federal provision following the Henry model might undermine all that had been accomplished.[15]

Jefferson was undeterred; while offering no specific suggestions on how these real political dangers could be avoided, he argued that "[h]alf a loaf is better than no bread. If we cannot secure all our rights, let us secure what we can." Jefferson was, of course, wrong; Madison, always the careful draftsman and legislative tactician, saw that a narrow provision on religious freedom ("half a loaf") could do more harm than good by endorsing an understanding of disestablishment that would compromise the principle that government had no authority in this area or stand as an impediment to the full participation of all citizens. At a minimum, the exchange made clear that Madison was going to be vigilant against anything short of the broadest possible religious freedom. Jefferson, always the optimist, pressed forward. Importantly, Jefferson built his argument in favor of proceeding regardless of the drafting risk on an important foundation: "In the arguments in favor of a declaration of rights, you omit one which has great weight with me, the legal check which it puts into the hands of the judiciary." Welcoming the Supreme Court's role as constitutional mediator, Jefferson assured his junior partner that a bill of rights "should therefore guard us against their [legislative and executive] abuses of power within the field submitted to them."[16]

Beyond correspondence with Madison, Jefferson's concern about the need for a bill of rights, with religious freedom leading the list, was well known. As already noted, his problematical letter to Alexander Donald, leading with the need for express protection for religious liberty, was used in the Virginia ratification convention. His name and correspondence were also used to bolster demands for a bill of rights in Maryland and North Carolina. In North Carolina, the antifederalist Willie Jones explained that Jefferson wished four states to reject the Constitution "that there might be a certainty of obtaining amendments." (North Carolina did reject the Constitution until amendments were adopted; the lack of a clear protection for religious liberty was central to that decision.)[17]

Jefferson wrote other leaders who would likely have influence in the ratification debates and in the new Congress about his concerns with the lack of a bill of rights, particularly the danger to religious freedom. Given his close friend's involvement in the drafting of the Constitution and initial defense of the absence of a bill of rights, Jefferson wrote to Madison with some restraint, but some of his other letters were less guarded. In November 1787, he complained to William Stephens Smith, John Adams's son-in-law who was returning to New York from diplomatic service in London, that the Philadelphia Convention had been "too much impressed" by Shays's Rebellion in Massachusetts, noting boldly: "[W]hat country can preserve it's liberties if their rulers are not warned from time to time that their people preserve the spirit of resistance? Let them take arms." He concluded at that time that amendments were needed "before the constitution is accepted." On February 2, 1788, undoubtedly influenced by Madison's anxiety for ratification, he wrote Smith with a somewhat moderated position: Nine states should endorse the Constitution while four refused to ratify until a bill of rights was adopted.

> But I own it astonishes me to find such a change wrought in the opinion of our countrymen since I left them, as that threefourths of them should be contented to live under a system which leaves to their governors the power of taking from them the trial by jury ..., freedom of religion, freedom of the press.... This is a degeneracy in the principles of liberty to which I had given four centuries instead of four years.

It was this position that was repeated in the conventions in Virginia, Maryland, and North Carolina. Having been chastened by Madison, no doubt, Jefferson took the opportunity of Massachusetts ratification with its strong request that postratification amendments be promptly adopted to again modify his position and urge acceptance with later amendments, a position on which Madison eventually settled as well. In early 1789, before the first federal Congress was seated, Jefferson wrote Francis Hopkinson, a delegate to the Philadelphia Convention from Pennsylvania, and reiterated that what was needed was a "bill of rights to guard liberty ..., that is to say to secure freedom of religion."[18]

Jefferson was not alone in this concern, of course, and the lack of a bill of rights heralded by Jefferson ultimately became a critical factor in the ratification debates and a major pillar of antifederalist arguments. It is notable that the two states initially to reject ratification—North Carolina and Rhode Island— were Baptist strongholds, and the lack of any express protection for religious freedom was near the top of their concerns. Moreover, many of the leading states that did ratify, including Massachusetts, New York, and Virginia, did so in dangerously close votes, and each, having adopted the Constitution with serious reservations, demanded amendments, including a bill of rights. Without this commitment to amendments, ratification almost certainly would have failed. In almost every case in which a bill of rights was demanded, protection of religious freedom was high on the list of stated concerns.[19]

Many of the advocates of a bill of rights, like Jefferson and Madison, also tended to define religious liberty in broad terms. "Centinel," one of the earliest and leading editorialists for the antifederalists, warned that the Constitution included "no declaration, that all men have a natural and unalienable right to worship Almighty God, according to the dictates of their own consciences ... ; and that no man ought, or of right can be compelled to attend any religious worship, or erect or support any place of worship, or maintain any ministry, contrary to, or against his own free will and consent." An "Old Whig," another leading antifederalist scribbler, wrote: "[I]f a majority of the continental legislature should at any time think fit to establish a form of religion, . . . what is there in the proposed constitution to hinder their doing so? Nothing; for we have no bill of rights, and every thing therefore is in their power and at their discretion." These antifederalist leaders made it clear that even an endorsement of Christianity would be a form of the hated establishment, warning that "when christianity became the established religion, it grew immediately as corrupt in its infancy, as ever it has proved at any period since."[20]

In any case, after ratification was assured, Madison became a leading advocate, and initial draftsman, of the Bill of Rights, and the most able advocate of a Jeffersonian vision of religious freedom who was present for the legislative debates. With the danger to ratification removed, Madison saw amendments guaranteeing rights as a way to mollify many opponents of the Constitution, removing one of the most effective arguments of the antifederalists, and as a way to convince North Carolina and Rhode Island to join the union. He also recognized that by assuring antifederalists of the limits on federal power over individual liberty, a bill of rights would relieve pressure for structural amendments supported by many antifederalists that could have undermined the power of the national government and hobbled the new nation. As the first Congress under the Constitution was distracted by a bevy of pressing matters, Madison urged that "it will be a desirable thing to extinguish from the bosom of every member of the community any apprehensions, that there are those among his countrymen who wish to deprive them of the liberty for which they have valiantly fought and honorably bled." Of course, Madison also wanted the strongest possible protections for religious liberty, and he began to express a concern that, in spite of the enumerated powers doctrine, a willful Congress could use the "necessary and proper" clause to exercise authority in the area of religion. Importantly, in the ensuing congressional debates, Madison endorsed one of Jefferson's main points: "[I]ndependent tribunals of justice will consider themselves in a peculiar manner the guardians of those rights; they will be an impenetrable bulwark against every assumption of power in the legislative or executive; they will be naturally led to resist every encroachment upon rights expressly stipulated for in the constitution by the declaration of rights."[21]

Finally, Madison also felt a sense of obligation to pursue a bill of rights and, in particular, a guarantee of broad religious freedom. He explained that without the promise of amendments, the Constitution "would have been *certainly* rejected.... As an honest man I *feel* my self bound by this consideration." More particularly, the Virginia evangelicals who had demanded religious freedom and a strict separation of church and state played a critical role in election of Madison to the Virginia convention which ratified the Constitution and his subsequent election to the House of Representatives. In each case, his election not only depended upon the evangelical vote, but was specifically contingent upon his commitment to the evangelicals that he would make every effort to protect religious freedom.[22]

In the election for the Virginia ratifying convention, for example, growing opposition to the Constitution by Virginia Baptists made it crucial for Madison to answer their concerns. John Leland, reportedly the most popular minister in Virginia, a Jefferson devotee, and an eloquent advocate of strict separation of church and state, had joined other Baptists in declaring his opposition to the Constitution. Residing in Madison's own Orange County, Leland's influence was extremely important. Madison's father warned his son of the growing risk, both to Madison's election to the Virginia convention and to ratification, and begged him to return to Virginia from the Continental Congress and to campaign. Madison won that election only after hurrying home from New York and personally assuring Leland of his commitment to religious freedom under the Constitution and Leland's throwing his support to Madison. While various sources report Madison's interaction with Leland somewhat differently, the general evangelical/Madison alliance is clear.[23]

Similarly, after a peeved Patrick Henry put an end to Madison's ambition to be one of the first senators from Virginia, when Madison ran for a seat in the House of Representatives he faced a district that had been "gerrymandered" by Henry (before Elbridge Gerry was to receive lasting fame for the same process) and a strong antifederalist opponent in James Monroe—Henry's candidate. Once again, Madison's commitment to evangelical constituents to seek amendments to protect religious liberty proved central to his election. He wrote George Eve, an influential Baptist minister in populous Culpeper County:

> Being informed that reports prevail not only that I am opposed to any amendments whatever to the new federal Constitution; but that I have ceased to be a friend to the rights of Conscience; and inferring . . . that you are disposed to

contradict such reports as far as your knowledge of my sentiments may justify, I am led to trouble you with this communication of them. . . .

I freely own that I have never seen in the Constitution as it now stands those serious dangers which have alarmed many respectable Citizens. Accordingly whilst it remained unratified, . . . I opposed all previous alterations as calculated to throw the States into dangerous contentions. . . . Circumstances are now changed. . . . Under this change of circumstances, it is my sincere opinion that the Constitution ought to be revised, . . . [adding] the most satisfactory provisions for all essential rights, particularly the rights of Conscience in the fullest latitude, the freedom of the press, trials by jury, security against general warrants &c.

It is generally conceded that the renewed support from the previous religious dissenters was crucial for Madison's election. The religious freedom "in the fullest latitude" that Madison committed to obtain was the broad religious freedom—including separation of church and state—sought by the Virginia evangelicals and won locally by his and their efforts in support of the Virginia Statute; anything else would have been inadequate. Notably, Madison not only reported to the evangelicals on his efforts culminating in adoption of the First Amendment but subsequently informed George Washington of the evangelicals' reaction to the amendment, obviously viewing this as central to the political situation.[24]

Thus, Madison became committed to a bill of rights not only because of its general value in protecting liberty and undermining opposition to the Constitution, but very pointedly and specifically because of the need to protect religious freedom, sharing Jefferson's and the evangelicals' conviction on this matter, and political necessity. While prior amendments would have endangered the Constitution, after ratification Madison explained to Jefferson's son-in-law, Thomas Mann Randolph, in a letter obviously intended for public use in the election, that "it is particularly, my opinion, that the clearest and strongest provision ought to be made for all those essential rights of conscience, the freedom of the press, trials by jury, exemption from general warrants, &c." The reluctant convert became the most adamant advocate of a bill of rights.[25]

Once the new federal government was operational, however, there was a serious question as to when (or whether) amendments would be introduced. Federalists who controlled the first Congress were not eager to enter into a complicated debate on a bill of rights once the Constitution was accepted and seemingly more important matters pressed the public business, including taxes, a judiciary, executive departments, etc. James Madison, however, insisted. As with the Virginia Statute for Establishing Religious Freedom, Madison's legislative bullheadedness should not be underestimated. By the end of the first congressional session, the amendments that would become known as the Bill of Rights had been sent to the states for approval. On December 15, 1791, with Virginia's ratification, the Bill of Rights, including the prohibition on Congress's making any "law respecting an establishment of religion, or prohibiting the free exercise thereof" became law.

Hotly contested questions remain: What does that short amendment mean? Who should provide guidance on that question?

In 1879, Chief Justice Morrison Waite, writing on behalf of a unanimous court in *Reynolds v. United States*, turned to Jefferson's language from the Statute's preamble to define the religious freedom protected by the First Amendment: "to suffer the civil magistrate to intrude powers into the field of opinions, and to restrain the profession or propagation of principles on supposition of their ill-tendency, is a dangerous fallacy which at once destroys all religious liberty," what Waite referred to as "the true distinction between what properly belongs to the church and what to the State." Waite went on to note that Jefferson's 1802 Letter to the Danbury Baptists identifying a constitutional "wall of separation" between church and state, "[c]oming . . . from an acknowledged leader of the advocates of the measure [the First Amendment]," deserved to "be accepted almost as an authoritative declaration." Since then, the majority of the Supreme Court has been clear that the "Virginia Experience," including Jefferson's Statute, Madison's Memorial & Remonstrance, and the Letter to the Danbury Baptists, expresses the vision and wisdom at the heart of the First Amendment's protection of religious liberty. Historians have broadly agreed. Based upon the history enunciated in *Reynolds* and later in *Everson v. Board of Education* (1947), Jefferson's Statute has taken center stage in our understanding of the religion clauses of the First Amendment.[26]

Yet, modern critics of the Court's jurisprudence have strongly contested the Jeffersonian-Madisonian history laid out by Chief Justice Waite and the Court in *Reynolds*. These critics claim that, after its adoption, neither the Statute nor Jefferson's 1802 Letter to the Danbury Baptists nor Madison's Memorial played a foundational role in adoption of the First Amendment or the understanding of religious freedom in early America until they were unexpectedly resurrected in 1879 in a serendipitous conspiracy between the historian George Bancroft— a great devotee of Jefferson—and Waite, who happened to be next-door neighbors.[27] In fact, critics note, twelve of thirteen states continued to impose some form of religious test and/or to provide some form of state support for religious establishments even after the First Amendment was adopted.[28] This, they insist, undermines the Court's jurisprudence and brings into question the entire doctrine of a strict separation of church and state under the First Amendment. Jefferson's Statute may well be eloquent, they concede, but it is not seminal.[29]

Of course, the critics are correct that "[n]ot only did the authors of the Constitution possess a diversity of views about the role of religion in the early American legal framework, but there existed in the original thirteen states a diversity of church-state relationships." Building upon that theme, Justice Stevens, in dissent in *Van Orden* (2005), argued that "the widely divergent views espoused by the leaders of our founding era plainly reveal, the historical record of the . . . Establishment Clause is too indeterminate to serve as an interpretive North Star." The historian Ellis West agrees that "the only honest conclusion to be drawn is that the founders were divided over how to protect religious freedom." The natural conclusion, William Lee Miller suggests, is that the First Amendment "was almost surely a compromise between different emphases." The First Amendment "did not represent the triumph of one particular party or specific viewpoint over a clear or entrenched opposition, but rather a consensus of Congress and nation," Thomas Curry concludes.[30]

This "compromise" thesis sounds reasonable, but a careful review of history shows that the real compromise between federalists and antifederalists, between supporters of state religion and evangelicals and their Jeffersonian allies, provided a distinctly Jeffersonian First Amendment.

As a preliminary matter, in evaluating the influence of the Virginia Statute and the Jeffersonian vision of religious liberty on the adoption and meaning of the First Amendment, several important contextual factors need to be considered. First, Virginia was the largest and most populous of the new states; it was also the most politically powerful and influential, for example, providing executive leadership to the new nation for thirty-two of the first thirty-six years and accounting for 10 of the 59 representatives who initially assembled in the House of Representatives (25 percent more representatives than even the largest of the other states), and 19 of 105 by 1790. John Adams made a similar point in 1776 when he wrote to Patrick Henry from the Continental Congress that "[w]e all look up to Virginia for Examples." As a result, given its history of government/church cooperation, Virginia's decision to embrace religious freedom provided an important example for the rest of the nation. Even critics of reliance on the Virginia Experience, both modern and historic, concede the point. Robert Baird noted in the mid-nineteenth century that "the early discussion of the propriety of dissolving the union of church and state in Virginia, after the revolutionary war had broken out, had some effect, probably, on other States placed in similar circumstances." Daniel Dreisbach acknowledges that "the Old Dominion . . . crafted the model that mattered; she set the example other states followed." After all, before the Revolution, no state had a more entrenched establishment nor more aggressively persecuted dissenters; by the first Congress under the Constitution, no state more broadly, and certainly none more eloquently, protected religious freedom. It was natural, then, that Virginia would prove an example and bellwether for religious freedom. Even commentators who attacked the notion of disestablishment understood that Virginia provided the standard. In 1786, in South Carolina, a newspaper editor reprinted a very lengthy attack on Jefferson's Statute from a Philadelphia source, implicitly recognizing the centrality of Jefferson's Statute to a growing local debate on the meaning of religious freedom. A similar pattern applied along the eastern seaboard.[31]

Second, Madison was the original draftsman of the First Amendment and the most important member in the debates leading to adoption of the Bill of Rights, and he was deeply committed to achieving broad religious liberty. Setting aside his impassioned engagement with the prewar religious persecution, his successful campaign to defeat the general assessment including authorship of the Memorial & Remonstrance, and the 1786 adoption of Jefferson's Statute, Madison owed his election to the Virginia ratifying convention and to the House of Representatives to Virginia's evangelicals, and he had committed to defend their interests in religious liberty, including a strict separation of church and state.[32]

A third general reason to see the Virginia commitment to broad religious freedom as seminal is that the two states that initially withheld support for the new Constitution—North Carolina and Rhode Island—were Baptist bastions that based their refusal to accept the Constitution in part on its failure to provide express protection of religious freedom. At the time, Rhode Island was the only other state that protected religious liberty in a form approaching that of the Virginia Statute. Thus, the understanding of the Virginia evangelicals as to the meaning of religious freedom takes on particular significance not only in the adoption of Jefferson's Statute and Madison's Memorial & Remonstrance, but in the specific efforts to amend the Constitution resulting in the Bill of Rights.

These background considerations leave the question of the specific role of Jefferson and Madison and the Virginia Experience in adoption of the First Amendment.

Perhaps the most important fact to understand in seeking to analyze the debates in the first federal Congress and the meaning of the First Amendment is that the Amendment, as adopted, only bound the federal government, not the states. Justice Thomas and other critics of the Jeffersonian interpretation make exactly this point. They are correct: States' rights were at the center of the contemporary understanding of the First Amendment, but not in the way that opponents of a Jeffersonian interpretation suggest.

Looked at in political terms, contrary to the view that differences of opinion led to a vacuous or limited First Amendment compromise, a consensus developed among members of Congress of very different views that what was needed was a very strict restriction on federal power in this area. First, many federalists and antifederalists, particularly those from states with established churches, wanted expressly to limit federal power over religion; they were unsatisfied with the enumerated powers arguments that Madison (and other federalists) had made during the ratification debates. For this group, what was needed was a provision that said the federal government had no authority to interfere with the states, leaving states free to regulate religion as they thought best. Based upon this, in isolation, some critics conclude that the First Amendment is simply a "no jurisdiction" provision. The only "protection" provided against an establishment of religion in this view would be whatever protections, or lack thereof, was provided by the states.

There are several problems with this interpretation, though. Most importantly, other members of Congress needed more. In fact, as Michael Myerson points out, the most vocal demands for a federal religious freedom provision were not coming from those seeking to protect state establishments but, rather, were coming from those—both federalists and antifederalists—from states that had adopted relatively broad religious freedom. These advocates were not seeking to protect state establishments; they wanted a guarantee that the federal government itself would never interfere with broad religious liberty. The Jeffersonians—both evangelicals and rationalists—could support nothing less than a separation of church and state for the federal government in its realm of authority. Other antifederalists were committed to preventing the exercise of expansive federal power against individuals, fearing that a distant government simply could not be trusted and the exercise of power by such a government threatened tyranny. For both of these latter two groups, a consensus around a vacuous provision that said nothing about specific federal authority was impossible.[33]

Further, even those who just wanted the federal government to leave states alone either had no objection to restricting federal authority or favored such restrictions. Moreover, some provision had to address how the national government would act within its own sphere (say the territories, with respect to the military, in the district dedicated to the federal government, etc.). Jefferson had explained this point in a letter to Madison urging the necessity of a bill of rights, including protection for religious freedom: The Constitution "forms us into one nation as to certain objects, and gives us a legislative and executive body for these objects. It should therefore guard us against their abuses of power within the field submitted to them."[34]

Thus, the "compromise" adopted was a provision that very strictly limited federal authority vis-à-vis the states—leaving the states free to protect or regulate religious liberty or religious establishments as they saw fit—while, at the same time, very strictly preventing the federal government from interfering with private rights or directly cooperating with religious institutions in its sphere of authority, consistent with the Jeffersonian vision. No other position, or studied ambiguity, could support the consensus necessary for the First Amendment to be adopted by Congress. Understood in this manner, the Virginia Experience, particularly adoption of Jefferson's Statute and enthusiasm for Madison's Memorial & Remonstrance, played a foundational role in drafting and adoption of the First Amendment and the development of religious freedom.

Looked at from a different perspective, members of Congress were well aware that religious establishments and/or test acts were maintained in a large majority of states, and they had no intention of undermining those provisions in the adoption of the First Amendment. The Founders obviously did not see these state legal regimes as inconsistent with the First Amendment, otherwise, politically, the amendment could never have been adopted. This, though, is not because the substantive language of the First Amendment—"no law respecting an establishment of religion"—was understood to permit establishments and test acts. Quite the contrary; to protect these state regimes, it was essential that the First Amendment apply only to federal action—"Congress shall make no law". Thomas Curry makes a similar point when he explains how Massachusetts's church establishment continued after the First Amendment while Virginia embraced full disestablishment:

> Both states proclaimed equal devotion to the term "rights of conscience," but because all believed that such matters pertained to the states, and that they were making explicit the fact that the federal government had nothing to do with religion, no collision of their differing views as to what constituted a violation of "rights of conscience" took place.[35]

State establishments could be maintained not because those provisions were consistent with the operative terms of the amendment. In fact, if the substance of the First Amendment would not have affected the state regimes, the restriction to Congress would have been unnecessary. Rather, given these state provisions, members of Congress insisted that the states be wholly outside of the jurisdictional scope of the amendment, that it apply only to federal action. This understanding provided the essential conceptual framework for the "compromise" that resulted in the First Amendment: some delegates wanted a very strict restriction on federal authority in the area of religion so that the federal government would not interfere with state establishments (or disestablishments) and state regulation of religion; others, including Madison and Jefferson and their evangelical and Enlightenment supporters (and many antifederalists), wanted to make clear that government could not interfere with private conscience and that government must abstain from acting in the area of religion, particularly as it relates to any alliance with religious institutions. *All* of the various positions wanted the *federal* government, at least, strictly out of the business of regulating religion, prohibited from making an establishment, and separated from religious issues. Arlin Adams and Charles Emmerich rightly speculate that "the final choice of wording may have resulted from a coalition of Founders influenced by different motivations—one faction stressing the danger to religious liberty posed by an alliance between ecclesiastical and civil authority at the national level, and another faction desiring to limit Congress in order to preserve existing state establishments."[36]

Critically, the limitation of the First Amendment to the federal government did not mean that the provision as adopted is *merely* jurisdictional and was substantively vacuous. Language embodying that approach had been tabled—a proposal that the national government should not have "authority to alter, abrogate, or infringe any part of the constitutions of the several states, which provide for the preservation of liberty in matters of religion"—but was not adopted. While that understanding might have been acceptable to those seeking to protect state establishments, it would have been wholly unacceptable to those seeking to oppose establishments or limit direct federal authority over personal liberty, and could have never achieved the consensus necessary for the amendment's adoption. As Donald Drakeman explains, this argument that the First Amendment says nothing substantive about restrictions on federal establishments, and was wholly a jurisdictional provision, would require one to believe "that clever pro-establishment legislators hoodwinked Madison and others in the Congress into thinking that the First Amendment contained restrictions on federal church-state interactions when, in fact, it not only protected established churches in the states but also left Congress free to establish a church at the national level." (Drakeman goes on to conclude that the final provision had to be "noncontroversial" and only a prohibition on a "national church" could satisfy that requirement. Not only could Madison and his supporters not accept such a limited provision, but that is not the type of noncontroversial system that could obtain a consensus.) Irving Brant explains the theoretical appeal of the compromise that was adopted: While Fisher Ames of Massachusetts did not support the Bill of Rights, viewing it as unnecessary, "he would have been ready enough to co-operate in promoting a change which would both attain Madison's objective and relieve the fear of New Englanders that the constitutional amendment might interfere with their established state churches."[37]

Not only was this result the only means to develop a consensus, but this conclusion is also supported by the textual negotiation. When Madison first introduced constitutional amendments into the House of Representatives, he proposed two provisions on religious liberty, one to apply to the federal government, one to apply to the states. The first, for the federal government, was more detailed. Madison's draft provided: "The civil rights of none shall be abridged on account of religious belief or worship, nor shall any national religion be established, nor shall the full and equal rights of conscience be in any manner, or on any pretext infringed." Notably, Madison did not use the language that had been proposed by Virginia (under Patrick Henry's guidance) and other states that would have only prohibited a federal preference for one sect over another. The second provision, intended to apply only to the states, had to be sensitive to their different treatment of church/state issues; as a result, it was drafted to protect a more generic liberty of conscience: "No state shall violate the equal rights of conscience." A certain ambiguity was necessary in this latter case because the various states could not agree with precision on the appropriate level of religious freedom to apply internally and most states maintained test oaths and/or establishments. As a result, Madison proposed a vague term that could be interpreted flexibly later, but that would be understood to provide some level of protection against state interference with religious liberty without imposing the strict limitations that existed in Virginia and were to be placed on the federal government. While one biographer suggests that Madison's state provision on liberty of conscience, "if interpreted in line with his views, would have disestablished state churches throughout the Union," it seems more likely that Madison understood that this general provision, as opposed to the much more detailed federal provision, was subject to differing interpretations. Madison was being coy, not disingenuous. In any case, the greater detail and higher standard applied to the federal government in Madison's proposal was possible *only* because it was not applicable to the states.[38]

Madison's language was modified in the House committee entrusted with developing a set of proposed amendments, but the general structure and intent was maintained. The committee proposed: "No religion shall be established by law, nor shall the equal rights of conscience be infringed," and "No State shall infringe the equal rights of conscience." The more detailed provision concerning restrictions on federal action received most of the attention in the debates. Madison indicated that the intent had not changed from his proposal: "[C]ongress should not establish a religion, and enforce legal observation of it by law, nor compel men to worship God in any manner contrary to their conscience."[39]

Yet, with Madison's "national" language having been deleted, a strong objection was made by Benjamin Huntington of Connecticut (which still had an established religion) that the committee's draft for the federal provision might be used to attack state establishments. Huntington referred sarcastically to the problems that Rhode Island (at the time, a holdout from the federal union) had because it lacked an establishment. Madison immediately said that this was why the "national" language was needed in this clause; apparently all that he had meant with that term was to restrict that particular provision to the federal government, as juxtaposed to the provision applicable to the states. Elbridge Gerry objected to the term "national" as it might suggest a consolidated government (rather than a federal government that left the states with certain sovereign powers), something the antifederalists had alleged during the ratification debate and the federalists had insisted was not the case. The House ultimately adopted language proposed by New Hampshire that addressed this serious problem by making it clear that the more detailed provision that became the First Amendment religion clauses applied only to the federal government— "Congress shall make no law ..." Thus, while Kurt Lash cites Huntington's argument against application of the stricter federal provision to state establishments for the proposition that "had the Establishment Clause been understood to include Madisonian values of separation, it would not have been enacted," it is precisely because the proposal included Madisonian (Jeffersonian) ideas that Huntington spoke up and the limitation of this clause to Congress was added. The substantive meaning of the clause and its impact on state establishments, absent a jurisdictional restriction to the federal government, were clear.[40]

Madison's more general provision applying a constitutional guarantee of liberty of conscience to the states was permitted to remain in the House proposal, although a serious objection was raised by the antifederalist Thomas Tudor Tucker (South Carolina) against any federal interference in state regulation of religion. The language applicable to the states, though, being subject to flexible interpretation, apparently did not initially seem like an excessive threat to a majority of the members of the House. What was reported to the Senate was: "Congress shall make no law establishing religion or prohibiting the free exercise thereof, nor shall the rights of Conscience be infringed," and, separately, "No State shall infringe ... the rights of conscience."[41]

The more conservative Senate suggested a number of changes after an apparently interesting, if not fully reported, debate. First, initially there was an effort, supported by Senator Richard Henry Lee of Virginia, to limit the coverage of the amendment to nondiscrimination among "One Religious Sect or Society in preference to others." (It may be recalled that Lee had been a prominent supporter of the general assessment in Virginia and was elected to the Senate through the good offices of Patrick Henry.) The Senate, though, rejected this narrow language; it simply would not have provided the protection of religious freedom sought. It was just this type of nondiscrimination, "abolishing all distinctions of pre-eminence amongst the different societies or communities of Christians," that was at the heart of the defeated general assessment proposal in Virginia. There can be little question that the drafters knew how to draft a provision providing only for nonpreference among sects if that is what they had meant; not only was such language proposed and defeated in the Senate, but similar language existed in several state constitutions and several state proposals for amendments. The difference was also well understood in the nineteenth century; for example, Robert Baird, in his 1844 tome *Religion in America*, explains the First Amendment thus: "That is to say, the General Government shall not make any law for the support of any particular church, or of all the churches." Robert Cord cites these state provisions expressly prohibiting only a preference for one religion or sect as evidence of the meaning of the First Amendment, but the opposite conclusion seems to be sounder; this approach, while utilized in several states, was rejected at the federal level.[42]

Second, after some debate, the Senate agreed on language for the nascent First Amendment that removed from the first clause (the federal clause) the more general and undefined provision on liberty of conscience but still stated clearly that the proposed restriction applied only to the federal government: "Congress shall make no law establishing articles of faith, or a mode of worship, or prohibiting the free exercise of religion." The Senate's disestablishment language, though, was obviously much narrower than the House proposal.[43]

Third, and most significantly from Madison's perspective, antifederalists in the Senate insisted that no restriction be applied by the federal Constitution to the states' ability to regulate religion. The state provision, even with Madison's general and ambiguous "conscience" language, was rejected.[44]

The House initially rejected the Senate changes to the provisions on religion and demanded a conference, with Madison the chairman of the House conferees. Significantly, the chairman of the Senate conferees was Oliver Ellsworth, also a leader in the constitutional convention and dedicated to a broad form of religious liberty. For example, during the debates over ratification, Ellsworth, writing under the name Landholder, had indicated that "government has no business to meddle with the private opinions of people."[45]

Deeply influenced by the Virginia history of discrimination and persecution, not to mention the Jeffersonian vision that freedom of religion was essential to the development of a young republic, Madison was adamant that preventing states from impairing the liberty of conscience was the "most valuable" of the proposed constitutional amendments. Like Jefferson, he saw government interference in religion as leading to "tyranny over the mind of man" and as beyond the legitimate power of government. Both experience, particularly his recent battle against efforts to reinvigorate the Virginia establishment, and theory, for example his extended republic argument in *Federalist* No. 10, told him that the greater risk lay with the states. Yet, faced with opposition from the Senate, and considerable opposition to imposing restrictions on state religious practices in the House, Madison was forced to recede.[46]

This was the major concession which the House (and Madison) made in the joint House-Senate conference on what was to become the First Amendment. But, in return, the fundamental, strict language on disestablishment adopted by the House was retained; indeed, the conference strengthened the provision by adopting the "respecting" language: "no law respecting an establishment of religion." The final language adopted by the committee was in the handwriting of Oliver Ellsworth, senator from Connecticut and someone who shared a Jeffersonian view of religious liberty. After the conference, the Senate was informed that the House would recede on almost all of its other objections concerning Senate amendments to the proposed constitutional amendments if the language that became the religion clauses of the First Amendment was accepted. The Senate agreed.[47]

Several things can be drawn from this debate. The fact that the First Amendment as adopted only applied to the federal government is critical, though, in understanding the various textual proposals. First, the oft-repeated argument that Madison's use of the term "national religion" in his original proposal suggests that the First Amendment was intended to address only discrimination among sects can be rejected. By its terms, that argument is strained, but in context, Madison had clearly intended to distinguish between a stricter provision affecting the federal government and a more general provision affecting the states, and he initially expressed this with the term "national," language that was removed by the House committee. When a member objected that the reformulation by the committee left open the possible application of the federal clause of the emerging First Amendment to state establishments, Madison reiterated his proposal that this provision should apply only to prevent establishment of a "national religion." This was rejected in favor of the more felicitous language that "Congress shall make no law." Madison accepted this language as equivalent. The context of Madison's suggestion makes it clear that that was all he intended: The more detailed provision (soon to be the First Amendment) applied only to federal action while only a more general "liberty of conscience" was to apply to the states, permitting them to continue their current establishment practices as a general understanding of liberty of conscience developed under this amorphous standard. It is in the same context that Madison explained that "[h]e believed that people feared one sect might obtain a pre-eminence, or two combine together, and establish a religion to which they would compel others to conform. He thought if the word national was introduced, it would point the amendment directly to the object it was intended to prevent," that is, it was a question of federal compulsion. Earlier in the same debate, and elsewhere, repeatedly, and over an extended period, Madison made clear that religious freedom required more than just nondiscrimination among various sects. Even the more conservative Senate rejected language that would have specifically limited the impact of the amendment to nondiscrimination, and the House, led by Madison, rejected Senate language that might have been argued to have the same effect. In fact, in later years, Madison continued to use the "national" language in this context obviously with no intention of narrowing the First Amendment's application to merely nonpreference among sects. For example, he suggested that presidential proclamations of days of prayer and thanksgiving nourish "the erroneous idea of a *national* religion." Clearly, he was not suggesting that this was only true if proclamations were made on behalf of a particular denomination.[48]

Philip Hamburger, attempting to construct an even grander edifice on this locution, argues that Madison's proposal on a "national religion" is evidence that Madison's commitment to broad religious freedom and the strict separation of church and state had substantially waned at the time that he led the battle for the First Amendment. Justice Rehnquist seeks to defend the same argument about Madison's allegedly flagging interest in religious liberty, insisting that the Court and historians are "totally incorrect in suggesting that Madison carried these views"—his arguments in favor of strict separation from the 1785–86 general assessment debate—"onto the floor of the United States House of Representatives." The reason for this strained argument is clear. As Irving Brant explains: "If an establishment of religion covered what he [Madison] said it did in his 'Memorial and Remonstrance,' the amendment insured a total separation of church and state in the federal field."[49]

The historical record does not support the notion that Madison had lost interest in such broad protections. Setting aside the actual limited purpose for which Madison had suggested use of the "national" language, setting aside Madison's other statements in the debate that evidence his commitment to a broad provision, and setting aside that no other evidence is proffered for Madison's alleged retreat from a firmly seated position of principle expressed a few years earlier in the Memorial & Remonstrance and the Virginia Statute, this argument proves far too much. Not only was Madison obviously deeply, personally committed to the broadest possible religious freedom, but his election to Congress was dependent in part on a comparable commitment. Similarly, his subsequent action as Jefferson's secretary of state and as president and his own recollections, notably the "Detached Memorandum" that he wrote in retirement describing the battle for religious freedom, evidence his intent to obtain a strict separation and broad anti-establishment and protection for free exercise. (Efforts to dismiss the Detached Memorandum as a "problematic document, written long after Madison had left public office," are belied by the care that Madison obviously lavished on its preparation, its consistency with his long-held views, and Madison's centrality to development of religious freedom throughout the period.) In no instance, in spite of numerous opportunities, does Madison express the view that religious liberty should only prevent discrimination among denominations. As if to counter future claims of his waning ardor on the point, one year after Congress adopted the First Amendment, Madison went so far as to argue on the floor of Congress that a designation for professional men in the census requiring a separate listing of ministers was inappropriate "as the general government is proscribed from interfering, in any manner whatever, in matters respecting religion." This extreme position is far better evidence of Madison's views. Forrest Church aptly summarizes the point: Madison's Memorial & Remonstrance, "together with Madison's insistence that Jefferson's Statute should guide the Constitution's framers on all matters referring to church-state separation, should leave no doubt regarding Madison's clear intentions with respect to the separation of church and state." As with Jefferson, "to James Madison, . . . freedom of religion was the fundamental item upon which all other forms of civil liberty depend." This view depended upon a strict anti-establishment and separation.[50]

With respect to Madison's initial opposition to a bill of rights, also sometimes cited in an effort to color Madison's position, this was largely political and tactical—stemming from a fear that the antifederalists' proposals to amend the Constitution before its adoption would derail ratification—and, in any case, was reversed by Madison in the face of Jefferson's support for a bill of rights, the evangelicals responsible for his election, and his own principles, not to mention the demands of North Carolina, Rhode Island, and other states for protection against a possible expansive reading of the Constitution and federal authority. By the time of the debates in Congress, Madison expressly recognized that the Bill of Rights was needed to prevent inappropriate exercise of federal power under the "necessary and proper" clause.[51]

A second point can be drawn from the debates: the perceived need to restrict the First Amendment to the federal government speaks to what was understood by the term "establishment." The states embraced a variety of regimes that might have been found infirm had the First Amendment applied to the states. Many of these state regimes were multiple establishments, that is, a system that provided assistance to multiple religious denominations. In fact, Leonard Levy argues that several of the state regimes were so broad as to permit, as a practical matter, essentially any religious group to seek state support. If so, those seeking to restrict the First Amendment to the federal government clearly understood that its rule against "establishments" covered nonpreferential state aid to religion; that is why the amendment had to be restricted to the federal government. On the other hand, even if one recognizes that these various state systems contained explicit or implicit restrictions on aid to Christian (sometimes Protestant) sects, it is still clear that multiple establishments or establishment of Christianity were understood to come within the terms of the prohibitory language. It would make no sense for those making a federalism argument to see "establishment" as limited to exclusive establishments of one sect; if the term was so restricted, there would have been no need to limit the federal provision to Congress—it would have simply been inapplicable to the actual state regimes in place at the time. In fact, if "establishment" in the First Amendment does not include multiple establishments, the restriction would not prevent Congress from regulating (or requiring) multiple "establishments" in the various states.[52]

This leads to the third and more important implication of the debate over the restriction of the First Amendment to the federal government and elimination of Madison's proposed restriction on state regulation of religion. The House insisted that the amendment to become the First Amendment be expressly limited to federal action to prevent any suggestion that it could impair state establishments (or disestablishments), and even Madison's more general provision for the states was rejected precisely because members recognized that they could not easily reach a consensus on what manner of religious freedom to impose on the states and even the somewhat ambiguous requirement of "liberty of conscience" might be read to impair existing state systems. Jefferson recognized this in his Second Inaugural Address, explaining that he left religious exercises "as the constitution found them, under the direction and discipline of state or church authorities." It was far easier to restrict the First Amendment to the federal government recognizing that the standard imposed by its terms was limited in its application. Thus, while it was clear that the terms of the First Amendment would be theoretically inconsistent with some of the state regimes, imposing such terms on the states was avoided. Here, lack of consensus on the appropriate level of religious liberty to impose on the states in the new republic generally does not mean that the federal provision in the First Amendment had to compromise principle or, worse, be vacuous. Logically, once it was clear that the First Amendment would not apply directly to the states, it made no sense to adopt a "least common denominator" approach; after all, those supporting a high standard could not accept a low standard, and those in favor of a lower substantive standard could accept, in fact endorse, a higher standard, so long as it did not apply to their state practices but, rather, restricted only the national government—a general goal at the center of antifederalist complaints. Patrick Henry, for example, as a general matter clearly believed that a state government need only be prohibited from creating a religious preference, but, as Curry notes, this must be understood in a context in which "Henry . . . feared, almost to the point of paranoia, the power of the federal government. . . . There is no evidence that any of the traditionalists who favored having churches established by *state* governments also believed that the federal government should have the power to do so." As William Miller explains: "It certainly does not follow that because a state still had an establishment of religion of some kind or degree that its representatives would favor the same thing at the national level; it might be just otherwise." While some commentators have argued that the relative lack of a record of heated dispute means that a consensus had to develop around a nonsubstantive, essentially meaningless provision, once it was understood that the provision was limited to the federal government, the opposite appears more likely. The result was that the First Amendment was intended as a very strict restriction on the federal government's ability to intervene in the area of religion. In a similar vein, in ratifying the Constitution and the Bill of Rights, the Rhode Island Convention did debate the question of whether a freedom of conscience requirement should be imposed upon all of the states. Ultimately, as the delegate Henry Marchant stated, while he "wishes all men would agree not to establish any Religi[on]—[it is] enough for us to keep it out of the Gen[eral] Gov[ernmen]t." Of course, this leaves to the nineteenth and twentieth centuries the question of constitutional restraints on state actions impacting religion, but a consensus developed that the restrictions on the federal government were, from the start, intended to be strict.[53]

To what, then, should one turn in an effort to understand the contemporary meaning of the First Amendment? Some historians and jurists use this history to suggest that the narrower eighteenth-century understanding of religious liberty utilized by the states that accepted test oaths and had establishments must be read into the First Amendment. John Witte, for example, argues that "the religion clauses bind only the federal government ('Congress'), rendering prevailing state constitutional provisions and the sentiments of their drafters equally vital sources of the original understanding." Similarly, John Jeffries and James Ryan urge that "it seems odd to think that the States would have adopted, with little discussion and less dispute, a constitutional provision condemning their current practices." Yet, it was precisely because the provision condemned the states' practices that it had to be limited to the federal government. Given that the decision to restrict the application of the First Amendment to the federal government was made because of the existence of state constitutional provisions that could not meet its standard, the willingness of the states to adopt a myriad of church/state interactions at the state level in the early republic says nothing about what the First Amendment was substantively meant to restrict at the federal level. After all, the fact that most states still had some form of test oath is hardly evidence that such oaths, expressly prohibited by Article VI, should define Article VI.[54]

Looked at from a different perspective, the fact that Congress insisted that the amendment not apply directly to the states was a recognition that most of those states could not satisfy its requirements. If most states could not meet the standard of the First Amendment, in seeking to understand its breadth it is inappropriate to look at those states' practices and appropriate to give particular attention and credence to the practice in the one state that was certainly understood fully to satisfy its terms—Virginia. As Justice Brennan explained in *Walz v. Tax Commission* (1970): "Although the First Amendment may not have applied to the States during this period, practice in Virginia at the time is nonetheless instructive. The Commonwealth's efforts to separate church from state provided the direct antecedents of the First Amendment." Herein lies another important basis for the focus on Virginia's (and Jefferson's) role in adoption and understanding of the First Amendment.[55]

Jefferson, of course, was not present when the First Amendment was proposed, as Justice Rehnquist was quick to point out. The suggestion is that because Jefferson had not yet returned to New York from Paris at the time Congress acted, his views on religious liberty are irrelevant. Yet, Jefferson's Statute for Establishing Religious Freedom had already received considerable attention throughout the country, and his views were well known. "Widely publicized, Jefferson's Statute encouraged the movement toward complete religious freedom throughout the new nation and the formulation of the First Amendment." The Virginia Experience was already emblematic.[56]

In fact, the important correspondence from Jefferson to Madison and other officials between the conclusion of the Philadelphia Convention and the adoption of the Bill of Rights indicates that Jefferson had deep concerns about the Constitution, and topping his list was the lack of express and broad protection for religious liberty. His concern was expressly debated in at least three state ratification conventions. Madison clearly sought to assuage those concerns. In addition to his commitments to his dissenting constituents, this must have been on Madison's mind as he steered what would become the First Amendment through the Congress, as would have been the most powerful statement of religious freedom in America—Jefferson's Statute. Even by 1800, commentators were noting that Jefferson's vision had a decisive influence on the treatment of religious liberty in the Constitution.

> His [Jefferson's] arguments, irresistibly persuasive arguments, in favour of religious liberty; his observations on the dangerous absurd tendency of civil or legislative interposition respecting religious opinions we may presume, had no little influence in inspiring the framers of our excellent Federal Constitution with a just sense of its importance, and consequently in adopting it as one of its most distinguished principles.

A strong argument then exists for understanding the contemporary meaning of the First Amendment based upon the Virginia Experience, and Jefferson's Statute and Madison's Memorial & Remonstrance, which played important roles in that experience.[57]

As discussed in chapter 5, Jefferson's influence on religious liberty in America would grow further in the nineteenth century.

In interpreting the First Amendment, it must be remembered that the language did not reflect a principle that the members were willing to apply to their states, quite the contrary. Thus, when Jefferson declared in 1802 that the First Amendment demands a "wall of separation" between church and the national government, he might equally have added that the states, on the other hand, were (at that time) not expressly prohibited from protecting or restricting religious liberty as they saw fit, including maintaining a state church (which Massachusetts did, in various forms, until 1833)—although there is little question that Jefferson would have liked to see the other states adopt provisions comparable to those in Virginia.

What the First Amendment did do was apply a broad restriction on the power of the federal government; given the limited jurisdictional nature of the restriction—applying only to the federal government—members of Congress, including conservative members who might otherwise have balked at a strict separation of church and state and antifederalists who wanted to maintain state prerogatives and restrict federal power over personal liberty, were willing to adopt substantive requirements that they would not have agreed, at the time, to apply to their own states. Given this conjunction of events—the limited jurisdiction of the First Amendment, the influence of Virginia generally and especially on this important subject, Madison's seminal role and his commitment to the type of broad Jeffersonian protection for religious freedom sought by his constituents and Jefferson and evidenced in the Statute—a strong case exists for Chief Justice Waite and his Supreme Court progeny who see the foundation for the First Amendment in the Virginia Experience leading to the adoption of the Statute for Establishing Religious Freedom.

Still, this does not wholly answer the important historical question posed by Justices Rehnquist and Thomas concerning the relevance of Jefferson and the Virginia Experience in light of the treatment of religious freedom in the other states. Given the experience in those states, is there reason to believe that the Jeffersonian vision of religious liberty took on a broader significance in the early republic?

5

FROM THE
FIRST AMENDMENT
TO *REYNOLDS*

Jefferson Ascendant

JEFFERSON AND MADISON WERE WELL AWARE THAT THE BATTLE FOR the Virginia Statute for Establishing Religious Freedom and the First Amendment did not end the battle for religious liberty in America. Since the First Amendment applied only to federal action, it had limited direct application in the nineteenth century, an era of relatively narrow federal regulation and a relatively small federal government. While all of the states claimed to protect freedom of conscience in their own way, how they applied that right often fell far short of the Jeffersonian vision, especially in the area of separation of church and state. Jeffersonians expressed a hope that "the sentiments of our beloved President [Jefferson], which have had such genial effect already, . . . will shine & prevail through all these States and all the world till Hierarchy and tyranny be destroyed from the Earth." Yet, some states, notably Massachusetts and Connecticut, retained establishments for many years; others eliminated religious tax assessments but maintained laws promoting religion or conditioning civil rights on religious oaths. A disappointed Madison in retirement implored:

> Ye States of America which retain in your Constitutions or Codes, any aberration from the sacred principle of religious liberty by giving to Caesar what belongs to God, or joining together what God has put asunder, hasten to revise your systems, and make the example of your Country as pure and complete, in what relates to the freedom of the mind and its allegiance to its maker, as in what belongs to the legitimate objects of political and civil institutions.[1]

The diversity of views among the states and the inability of many of them to satisfy a strict disestablishment requirement in 1789 leaves important historic questions: Did Jefferson and Madison, and Jefferson's Statute and the 1802 Letter to Danbury Baptists and Madison's Memorial & Remonstrance, play some additional, significant role in the development of religious freedom in the states by 1879, when a unanimous Supreme Court, in *Reynolds v. United States*, declared them seminal to American notions of religious freedom? Or did the state establishments and test oaths evidence a broad rejection of Jeffersonian principles in the period before the Court acted? After all, if the other states did not intend to be bound by the principles of the Virginia Statute or strict provisions of the First Amendment in 1789, is there reason to believe that they moved in that direction over time, perhaps justifying the Supreme Court's decision to find Jefferson's view of religious freedom essential to American principles of freedom? "It would be valuable to learn," Philip Hamburger writes, "whether his [Jefferson's] words were as influential before 1947 [and the *Everson* decision] as commonly supposed."[2]

In the nineteenth century, the states faced repeated controversies over how broadly religious freedom should be protected. A rich mix of actions by state governments and in the polity generally developed, but even before the Court acted in *Reynolds*, several patterns were evident. First, state constitutions were modified throughout the period, and generally the changes moved the states in the direction of the robust anti-establishment and free exercise approach of the federal Constitution and the Virginia Statute. Second, throughout the debates, Jefferson, Madison, and the Statute increasingly took on iconic proportions; increasingly Americans defined religious freedom against a Jeffersonian norm. Critics of the Court's reliance on Jefferson are fond of pointing out that Madison and he were but two of a plethora of Founders concerned about the meaning of religious liberty and should be seen as "outliers" given their separationist views; Daniel Dreisbach, for example, insists that Jefferson's vision of separation of church and state was "more expansive . . . than virtually all previous interpretations and that held by his contemporaries." Yet, the historic record provides no equivalent focus on any other Founders' views on religious liberty or the views of any other public figure. Over time, far from being outliers, Jefferson and Madison became foundational.[3]

On the other hand, propelled in part by the Second Great Awakening, nineteenth-century evangelicals increasingly defined America as a "Christian nation" (benefiting from a providential manifest destiny) and expected a broad presence of religion in the public sphere. As a result, beyond the very substantial changes the Awakening encouraged in American culture, godly language was often incorporated into state constitutions at the same time or shortly after state establishments or test oaths were eliminated. This "Christian nation" movement, though, certainly did not originate with the Founders and, even at the time, was understood to have a limited legal impact. In fact, the growing cultural significance of the Christian nation idiom, combined with a rising anti-Catholic strain, probably facilitated the diminishing legal significance of religion and acceptance of the principle of separation of church and state, even at the state level. Not until the mid-twentieth century, when church/state issues became federal constitutional concerns, would the conflict between the cultural and legal views lead to a break in the broad evangelical support for a strict separation of church and state.

Influence of the Jeffersonian Vision

Several factors suggest that Jefferson's understanding of religious freedom, including disestablishment and strict separation between church and state, became foundational to Americans' understanding in the nineteenth century. While most of the state constitutions at the time of the First Amendment did not provide religious freedom in a form approaching that of the Virginia Statute, throughout the period from 1786 to 1879 (when the Supreme Court defined American religious freedom in Jeffersonian terms in *Reynolds*), state constitutional provisions relating to religious freedom went through substantial evolution both in the original states and in the new states rapidly joining the growing nation. Almost all of that movement was in the direction of liberalizing religious freedom in a manner more consistent with the federal First Amendment and a Jeffersonian vision. As one of America's leading religious historian notes, "beyond the original thirteen, no new state except Vermont allowed for any sort of an establishment." The ever-popular Baptist preacher John Leland made the point in 1811: "Since the revolution all the old states, except two or three in New England, have established religious liberty upon its true bottom." He goes on to explain his understanding of that "true bottom" in Jeffersonian terms: "Government should be so fixed, that Pagans, Turks, Jews and christians should be equally protected in their rights." (Leland's inclusion of "Pagans" is more evidence that nondiscrimination among religions was not the only issue for the evangelicals who propelled the Virginia Statute to adoption.)[4]

- While Connecticut's 1639 Fundamental Orders were "to mayntayne and prsearue the liberty and purity of the gospell of our Lord Jesus," and voting and office holding were limited to those taking the oath of fidelity, these requirements were eliminated in 1818.

- Delaware's 1792 constitution, adopted six months after ratification of the First Amendment, eliminated a Christian oath requirement for office (expressly prohibiting religious tests) and expanded its 1776 anti-establishment clause from prohibiting preferences for "any one religious sect" to "no man shall or ought to be compelled to attend any religious worship, to contribute to the erection or support of any place of worship, or to the maintenance of any ministry, against his own free will and consent."

- In 1789, Georgia eliminated a 1777 provision requiring legislators to be Protestants. Georgia's 1789 anti-establishment clause was limited to a prohibition on "being obliged to contribute to the support of any religious profession but their own." In 1798, this was expanded to make clear that no man "shall . . . ever be obliged to pay tiths, taxes, or any other rate, for the building or repairing any place of worship, or for the maintenance of any minister or ministry, contrary to what he believes to be right, or hath voluntarily engaged to do." The 1798 constitution still provided that "[n]o one religious society shall ever be established in the State, in preference to another" (Art. IV, § 10), but that limiting language was removed in 1865.

- Maine, in breaking from Massachusetts in 1819, eliminated its religious assessment and Christian oath (although retaining "so help me God").

- Religious freedom was originally limited to Christians in the State of Maryland, and religious assessments were authorized by the 1776 constitution. Religious assessments were made unconstitutional in an 1810 amendment, and the limitation to Christians eliminated in the 1851 constitution. A test oath for office limited to Christians and Jews remained in 1851 but was liberalized (to a belief in God) in 1864.

- Massachusetts removed its Christian oath of office in 1820 (although retaining "so help me God"), and its constitutional religious assessment was repealed in 1833.

- In 1819, by statute, New Hampshire prohibited religious assessment. In 1877, New Hampshire eliminated the requirement that legislators be Protestant.

- Religious liberty was restricted to Protestants in 1776 in New Jersey; the limitation was eliminated in 1844.

+ New York's 1777 constitution required immigrants to "renounce all allegiance" to leaders "ecclesiastical as well as civil" in an effort to prevent Catholic immigration; the provision was deleted from the 1821 constitution.

+ North Carolina's 1776 restriction of offices to Protestants was modified to include Catholics in 1835 before the requirement was eliminated in 1868. North Carolina initially limited the prohibition on establishment to "any one religious church or denomination" before changing its constitution to clarify that "no human authority should, in any case whatever, control or interfere with the right of conscience."

+ Pennsylvania's 1776 requirement that legislators take an oath of their belief in God and in the Old and New Testaments was eliminated in 1790, although the possibility of demanding a belief in God was maintained.

+ The 1663 Rhode Island statute that excluded Catholics from "freemen" was repealed in 1783. (The State of Rhode Island did not adopt a constitution until 1842 [see below].)

+ South Carolina's Anglican establishment was maintained by the 1776 constitution, modified to a Protestant establishment in 1778, before being repealed in 1790. One South Carolina lawyer explained in 1834: "We regard with mortification our own Constitution of 1778, establishing the Protestant as the religion of the State, and rejecting the Catholic and Jew as political outlaws." The 1778 constitution required that oaths of office end with "So help me God," a requirement eliminated in 1790.

+ Vermont's 1786 constitution removes restriction of religious liberty to Protestants and the requirement that they "support" religious worship. The 1793 constitution eliminated a requirement that legislators be Christian.

New Hampshire's proposed constitution of 1779 prohibiting acts "contrary to the laws of God, or against the Protestant religion" was rejected, not simply on that basis, but the fact remains that the 1784 New Hampshire constitution that was adopted included no such limitation. As Steven K. Green notes, "None of these new states considered moving in the opposite direction—toward increasing church-state ties." Certainly none of the new states after 1791 adopted an establishment, and even test oaths were less common. The historian David Sehat focuses on the restrictions that remained as these reformations occurred in state after state, arguing that they evidenced an effort of Christian evangelicals to control "democratic capitalism," but certainly one must first focus on what was changed, and how the changes evidenced a consistent, and Jeffersonian, liberalizing pattern. Interestingly, in 1788, two years after the success of the Virginia Statute in part because of the belated intervention of Virginia's Presbyterians demanding separation of church and state, American Presbyterians amended their own constitution to remove language claiming civil authority's right to convene religious synods.[5]

A number of commentators found Virginian or First Amendment antecedents to this broad constitutional reform movement. Philip Schaff, no friend of Jefferson, explained in the mid-nineteenth century that "after the American Revolution this posture of the State ["entire freedom of faith and conscience"] gradually became general. First, the legislature of Virginia . . . annulled the rights and privileges of the Episcopal establishment, and placed all the dissenting bodies on a perfectly equal footing with it in the eye of the law. Her example was followed by the other colonies, which had established churches." One modern historian, commenting on changes in South Carolina's constitution, explains: "Federal constitutional reform spurred state constitutional reform. The religious clauses of the federal First Amendment and the strong freedom of conscience provisions of Article 8 of the South Carolina Constitution of 1790 were part of the same wave of revisions." The liberalization evident in these constitutional reforms was certainly consistent with a Jeffersonian vision, but the question remains as to whether Jefferson's views, per se, played a significant role in America's expanding understanding of religious freedom.[6]

Beyond the broad influence of Virginia in the early republic, several factors justify a conclusion that Jefferson (and his Statute and Letter to the Danbury Baptists) and Madison (and his Memorial & Remonstrance) provided essential ideological leadership for these reforms and for Americans' developing understanding of religious liberty in the nineteenth century. First, there are some specific references to Jefferson and his Statute in state constitutional debates liberalizing religious freedom. Second, some of the constitutional reforms can be clearly traced to the success of Jeffersonian republicanism in the early nineteenth century even if express reliance on the Statute or Jefferson cannot be identified in debates. Third, and critically, as the state reforms were occurring (and, for example, as Chief Justice Waite and his colleagues on the 1879 Supreme Court were being educated), there was a relatively broad dissemination of the Virginia Statute and Madison's Memorial & Remonstrance and, to a somewhat lesser extent, Jefferson's Letter to the Danbury Baptists as emblematic of American religious freedom and separation of church and state. In an era without electronic databases and with limited library resources, this was both essential and telling. By comparison, while critics of the Jeffersonian view are fond of claiming that other Founders were equally engaged in the debate over religious freedom, no other Founder or commentator enjoyed anything like the broad dissemination and authority of the Jeffersonian vision.

A critical reason to privilege Jefferson's influence in state constitutional reform is that in some instances reformers relied expressly upon his views. In North Carolina, delegates to a constitutional convention in 1835 were excoriated by some of their colleagues for a test oath in the state's earlier constitution. Delegate Weldon Edwards warned his colleagues that "every wise government should keep steadily in view—that *legal* Religion and *political* Liberty are wholly incompatible. That to blend Religion and Politics, would have the effect to open the door wide to a union of Church and State"; then Edwards read into the record the preamble of Jefferson's Statute. He reminded his colleagues that "there never lived a man more devoted to the cause of Liberty or the rights of man" than Jefferson. James Bryan rose and declared that "[i]t would be happy for mankind if religion was permitted to take its own course, and maintain itself by the excellence of its own doctrines. The Divine Author of our Religion never wished for its support by worldly authority"; then, unsatisfied with Edwards's reading of the preamble, he read into the record the entire Statute. (These proceedings were reported in detail in the newspaper.) The new constitution adopted by that convention was somewhat more liberal than its predecessor.[7]

This pattern is also evident in the case of Rhode Island. After the electoral success of the local Jeffersonian Republicans, Rhode Island formally adopted a new constitution in 1842 (having relied upon the seventeenth-century charter before that). Without express comment, the new constitution borrowed the language of Jefferson's Statute. Similarly, Jefferson's language from the Statute was used to define religious liberty in the new West Virginia constitution of 1861–63.[8]

In one interesting case, a delegate to the Louisiana state constitutional convention substantially scrambled the history of the First Amendment, reporting to his colleagues that Jefferson had the First Amendment inserted into the Constitution after Baptists sought to have their religion established. In spite of the confusion, Delegate Wilson's efforts to encourage a liberal state provision on religious liberty in the Jeffersonian tradition were generally successful. Whatever the specific error, there was a broad understanding in constitutional reform that Jefferson stood at the center of the First Amendment and American religious freedom, and that such freedom, as Delegate Cazabat suggested, taught that "when you try, either directly or indirectly, to mix the 'Church' with the 'State,' you are going too far."[9]

A second reason for placing Jefferson and Madison at the center of nineteenth-century constitutional reform and the developing understanding of the principle of religious liberty can be found in the historic context of many reforms. In some cases, even when there is no recorded reference to Jefferson and Madison, state constitutional reform was obviously based upon Jeffersonian views. Republican sources from the period urged that fidelity to Jefferson's ideals required the states to enhance their protection of religious liberty. This movement was particularly evident in previously Puritan New England. In Connecticut, where continued disputes over church/state issues were, perhaps, most contentious, a pamphlet published in 1803 entitled *Republican Notes on Religion* reprinted the Statute and the religion section of Jefferson's *Notes on the State of Virginia*. "By 1818 in Connecticut, the victory of the Jeffersonians in politics made possible the securing of a new constitutional right: No person could be compelled to join, support, or be legally classed with any religious association, and every denomination of Christians would have equal rights and privileges." The centrality of the Virginia experience to reform is also evident in one of the evangelical John Leland's most famous pamphlets—*A Blow at the Root: Being a Fashionable Fast-Day Sermon*—which was reprinted in at least five states while reform was brewing. Leland "did not fail to point out the contrast between the noble language of the statesmen of Virginia on the church-state relationship and 'the little pigmy *shall bes* and *shall not bes* of Massachusetts.'" In Massachusetts,

> when the Republicans (Jeffersonians) were in power, they adopted the Religious Freedom Act of 1811, by which any person who should show a certificate that he belonged to a religious society, either incorporated or unincorporated, other than the regularly established society of the town or parish was exempt from paying taxes for the support of the Establishment. This law led ultimately to the overthrow of the Congregational Establishment in 1833.

Vermont followed an opposite pattern to the same result; while the establishment appeared to have been eliminated in the 1786 constitution, laws permitting religious assessments stayed on the books "until 1807, with the rise of the Democratic-Republican Party in Vermont and an increase in Baptist adherents, . . . the Vermont legislature abolish[ed] all statutory authority for the collection of assessments." In 1842, the *New-Hampshire Patriot and State Gazette* warned that it

> has often pointed out this odious feature in our constitution [officials must be Protestant], . . . and held them up to the view of our people as gross and monstrous violations of our professions of religious and political liberty, of equal rights and privileges to all. . . . [I]f the people of New Hampshire would maintain their reputation as Republicans of the Jefferson school, they must come out boldly, and at once, and by erasing this dark feature from their code of laws, declare that men's speculative opinions, be they orthodox or heretical, *are their own*; that men's religion is a concern between themselves and their Maker; and, that, to encroach upon religious freedom, is to violate the privacy of conscience, and to trample upon those rights, which European despots despise and deny, but which the men of the revolution taught us to cherish and venerate.

In Maryland, a Jeffersonian devotee, Thomas Kennedy, led the battle to remove a provision that restricted public office to Christians. Kentucky's 1792 religion clause, utilizing language from the Pennsylvania constitution that Jefferson had praised, also added the distinctly Jeffersonian "civil rights, privileges, or capacities of any citizen shall in no way be diminished or enlarged, on account of his religious principles." Alabama adopted identical language in 1819.[10]

The Supreme Court explained in *Abington School District v. Schempp* (1963), "the views of Madison and Jefferson, preceded by Roger Williams, came to be incorporated not only in the Federal Constitution but likewise in those of most of our States." It was this statement that particularly elicited Justice Rehnquist's opprobrium, but the evidence supports it. Unfortunately, relatively sparse records (not to mention state pride in not relying expressly on another state's laws) do not provide references to Jefferson and the Virginia Statute as often as his vision likely influenced reform. Many other ideological branches to the Jeffersonian constitutional legacy could be suggested but are harder to identify with certainty.[11]

In that regard, the broad dissemination and use of Jefferson's views is critical. A review of nineteenth-century newspapers available online, for example, shows numerous instances in which the entire Statute or Letter to the Danbury Baptists or Madison's lengthier Memorial & Remonstrance were reprinted or quoted at length with little commentary other than to note their prestigious lineage or to suggest that readers should remember the wisdom of Jefferson and/ or Madison in considering church/state issues. While there were undoubtedly scores of other instances in which local media recognized the importance of these leaders and seminal documents, even based upon those that have been readily located, the geographic and chronological breadth of this dissemination prior to the Supreme Court's 1879 *Reynolds* decision is striking.[12]

Other references to the Statute and the Letter to the Danbury Baptists were common. The popular *Philadelphia Aurora* explained that "Mr. Jefferson (though of that established church) introduced and carried a bill in the [Virginia] legislature by which all religious societies were made equal to and independent of each other." After Jefferson's death, the *Richmond Enquirer* reported on a remembrance from the Louisa County Court that referenced his authorship of "the bill for religious freedom which, of itself, would have immortalized his name," and, while not quoting the Letter to the Danbury Baptists directly, reminded readers that Jefferson "was amongst the foremost in advocating a separation of the two ['church and state'] previously considered inseparable, and permitting man to worship his Creator in his own way." Referring to Jefferson as the "foremost man of the Republic," the *Boston Investigator* in 1855 quoted the Danbury Baptist letter and reminded its readers that "[i]t was the knowledge of [historic religious persecution], that induced the Fathers of the American Republic to expel religion from politics, and to prohibit Congress from proclaiming any religion as a state religion, or from making laws favorable to any form of religion." There was even a note of jingoistic pride when a 1786 newspaper reported with derision the opposition that Jefferson's Statute had evoked from "A Lover of the British Constitution!!!!," a loyalist in Nova Scotia. By midcentury, the *Southern Literary Magazine* could describe the Statute as "embodying principles which lie at the very foundation of our dearest rights, and which are essential to the true prosperity both of Church and State."[13]

In 1801, a Boston newspaper wrongly attributed the Memorial & Remonstrance to "that great Statesman, Patriot and Christian Philosopher Jefferson" before reprinting it in its entirety—the error serving only to cement the obviously pervasive understanding of Jefferson's dominant role and the conflating of Jefferson's vision with American notions of religious freedom. Similarly, an 1832 speaker at Tammany Hall in New York combined portions of the Statute and the Letter to the Danbury Baptists, (mis)quoting Jefferson as teaching that "[t]he legitimate powers of government reach *actions* only, and not opinions. I contemplate with sovereign reverence the *act of the whole American people* . . . building a wall of *separation* between church and state." Even when the details were a bit confused, Jefferson was foundational.[14]

In this same period, the existence of broad religious freedom in America in general and Jefferson's Statute in particular were hailed in Europe as sound reasons for emigration, bringing the Statute and Jefferson to the attention of many an immigrant. One 1792 panegyric reprinted the Statute in whole and, specifically urging emigration to Kentucky, noted that "Kentucky has adopted this liberal and christian plan, since it has become an independent state." Another report of travels in America credited both the Statute and Madison's Memorial & Remonstrance for religious freedom. Speaking of the proposed general assessment in Virginia, that author explained that the Memorial "was in the end so extensively signed by the people of every religious denomination, that the projected measure was entirely abandoned, and the bill establishing religious freedom declared in the charter affixed to the constitution of the states." Here, too, some confusion about the relationship of Jefferson's Statute to the Constitution is evident, but the significance of Jefferson and Madison's roles in obtaining and defining religious freedom is clear.[15]

Even when not quoting the Statute or Letter to the Danbury Baptists directly, Jefferson's influence on religious freedom, and the centrality of a separation of church and state to that freedom, were warmly remembered in the nineteenth century. Some responded to attacks on Jefferson's religion in the 1800 election by heralding his role in establishing religious liberty (rather than seeking to defend his supposed orthodoxy), leading one modern historian to conclude "Jefferson's very election to the presidency was in many ways an early referendum on the constitutional relationship between government and religion." His allies "were able to recast the alternatives as between an 'established church, a religious test, and an order of Priesthood,' on the one hand, and 'Religious liberty, the rights of conscience, no priesthood, truth and Jefferson' on the other." The *Charleston Carolina Gazette* noted that "at the commencement of the revolution, in order more effectually to unite the people in the common cause, an act was passed in the state of Virginia, to dissolve the establishment," and concluded that to this is attributed "the force . . . of a great part of this [religious] odium" against Jefferson. Philip Hamburger characterizes such comments as essentially political (while accepting criticisms by federalist New England clergy as statements of Americans' views). The point here: both supporters and opponents saw Jefferson as progenitor of American concepts of separation of church and state and increasingly a standard for American religious freedom.[16]

A new District of Columbia newspaper reminded readers that "by the piety and exertions of Mr. Jefferson . . . perfect religious liberty and the rights of conscience" were achieved. Wellsboro, Pennsylvania, citizens read in 1843 that "Jefferson lays down the following principles: . . . 'The absolute and lasting severance of church and state.'" Louisianans were told: "Religion is greatly indebted to Mr. Jefferson. . . . It was in a great measure by his early and strenuous exertions, that the complete divorcement of Church and State, was ultimately accomplished." An Illinois paper reminded that the Statute "is certainly the strongest legal barrier that could be erected against a connection between Church and State, so fatal in its tendency to the purity of both." A midcentury New York newspaper also embraced Jefferson on religious freedom: "[T]he work done by Jefferson was enduring. State after State of this Union, and finally the aggregated assembly of the United States, followed the splendid example of the liberality and progress he had established. . . . Religious liberty became the law and principle of the whole United States." Responding to posthumous attacks on Jefferson, the *Workingman's Advocate* lamented the fact that "any individual who enjoys the benefits of our free constitution should dissent from the broad and equal principles upon which that constitution is based—that no 'religious faith' should be recognized, and that, consequently, religious and civil matters should forever be kept distinct and separate." Similar reliance on Jefferson and his role in developing religious freedom was evident in other publications: "It is beyond the jurisdiction of Government to undertake to correct errors of opinion. . . . Jefferson says that 'error of opinion may be safely tolerated when reason is left free to combat it.'" As Jefferson prepared to relinquish public office for the last time, Virginia Baptists wrote to congratulate him: "The heterogenious union of Church and State, was never congenial to our principles. But when we remember that from that source, the persecution and imprisonment of many of our ministers arose, we must declare that this union is as repugnant to our feelings, as to our principles. Your exertions very much contributed to its final dissolution." Perhaps this might not be surprising, but that letter was reprinted by a Boston newspaper emphasizing Jefferson's seminal role. The *Portland (ME) Eastern Argus* similarly reprinted a letter from the Baltimore Baptist Association praising the retiring president for his Statute and adding that "the cause of Religious Freedom is a common cause, and for your efforts in behalf of any part of the community . . . the rest must be impressed with grateful and sympathetic feelings." Other valedictory letters were to the same effect.[17]

Portions of Jefferson's *Notes on the State of Virginia* dealing with religious liberty were also frequently quoted and reprinted. While this source was often used to attack Jefferson's "infidelity"—particularly his comment that "it does me no injury for my neighbour to say there are twenty gods, or no god. It neither picks my pocket nor breaks my leg"—it was also sometimes referred to as the "correct sentiments on the subject of Religious Freedom," with an admonition that "[t]he legitimate powers of government extend to such acts only as are injurious to others." After his death, the inscription on his tomb, with the prominent reference to the Virginia Statute for Establishing Religious Freedom, was also broadly reported and remembered.[18]

In fact, when Jefferson was eulogized there were instances in which his Statute was read at a memorial service without reference to or recitation of the Declaration of Independence. Others stressed equally the importance of the Statute and the Declaration. Reverend Samuel Smith in Baltimore noted Jefferson's particular pride in the "subversion of a dominant religion, commenced by him, and completed by Mr. Madison." An editor in Washington, writing as Jefferson faced his final illness, soliloquized that Jefferson's "*act of religious freedom* has justly procured for him the applause of the world. I consider it one of the most important innovations and changes upon government, that has ever been made." The editor went on to urge that the Statute should be read on every Fourth of July "and would to God, it could be read to every man in South America, and in every other quarter of the world where there still exists a spark of liberty, or a ray of human knowledge."[19]

Significantly, Jeffersonian and Madisonian documents and references tended to surface precisely when constitutional reform or significant church/state issues were agitating in a state. The Memorial & Remonstrance was quoted at length in a Boston newspaper as part of the debate over disestablishment, with the editors' admonition that it was "recommended to the attention of those who hesitate about expunging from our Constitution" religious assessments. Earlier efforts at reform in Massachusetts were accompanied by the publication of the Memorial & Remonstrance with one paper telling its readers that "[t]he pamphlet is peculiarly seasonable at the present time, when the subject of revision of our constitution, so properly and deeply interests the people of Massachusetts." In debates in Connecticut concerning the necessity of an oath for a witness to qualify to testify in court, State Representative Dairchild successfully urged reliance on Jefferson: "He thought the true principle was laid down by Mr. Jefferson, which was—that no man's religious principles should subject him to any civil disabilities. He should prefer the original bill to the amendment, as he had understood it was copied from the laws of Virginia." While New York debated Sunday closing laws, citizens were reminded that "the two great intellects of the Revolution, who framed the basis of our laws, were Madison and Jefferson, of Virginia" and that the New York constitution's provisions on religious freedom were framed in their spirit. When anti-Catholicism led to proposals to inspect nunneries, Philadelphians were reminded of Jefferson's understanding that only "reason" was necessary to combat untruths. Jefferson's legacy of religious freedom was also invoked, for example, in broader political campaigns. The *Aurora* quoted the Statute in opposition to the Sedition Act: Virginians "knew the sublime precept inculcated by the act establishing religious freedom, that 'where discussion is free, error ceases to be dangerous.'" Later, the Statute "penned by the illustrious Jefferson" was made a response to the rising Know-Nothing Party and its anti-Catholicism, and was reprinted and referred to as the "anti–know nothing creed" in Texas.[20]

There was often a recognition that the Statute was aspirational in these local and national debates, and both Jefferson and Madison had recognized as much. Jefferson wrote a Jewish rabbi in 1818: "[M]ore remains to be done. [F]or altho' we are free by the law, we are not so in practice." He explained to another correspondent that "[i]f the freedom of religion, guaranteed to us by law *in theory*, can ever rise *in practice* under the overbearing inquisition of public opinion, truth will prevail over fanaticism." Thus, while David Sehat rightly notes the failure of the principle to address Sunday closing laws that discriminated against Jews and others, the establishment of a Jeffersonian standard against which to judge action is critical (and would find increasing application over time). Its aspirational character did not diminish the drive to build upon its foundation, even while recognizing that state laws might not perfectly conform to the principle. As church/state issues agitated in his state, an Ohio editor urged in 1861 that "it will be well to study it [the Statute] at this day, when men's right to think according to their conscientious scruples, is considered as a great crime." Similarly, when efforts at midcentury to introduce religion into the federal Constitution were unsuccessful, a Boston newspaper suggested that, instead, the Virginia Statute should be printed in "letters of gold" and "widely circulated at the present time, when the Evangelicals are striving to . . . bring about the union of Church and State." By 1870, the Jeffersonian vision was viewed as pervasive and emblematic. A New York paper explained that the Founders "were eminently wise men in making all state theologies, all state religion, all organic connections between religion and the state on any theory or for any purpose, . . . constitutionally impossible. . . . It is this doctrine for which the country is not a little indebted to the mind of Thomas Jefferson."[21]

Even when people attacked Jefferson politically and personally, they recognized that he had played a seminal role in developing and defining religious freedom; that is, American religious freedom was broadly associated with Jefferson well before the Supreme Court took up the matter. An outraged editorialist in South Carolina in 1786 attacked the Virginia Statute by noting that under Jefferson's vision even a Muslim or atheist could hold office; the letter writer—apparently not noticing the winds of change—defended his position by noting that eight of the new states had some form of Christian establishment. Others complained that Jefferson's fight for religious liberty masked antipathy to religion. Robert Baird, in an early history of religion in America, argued that in placing all religions and atheists "on equality, it [the Statute] seemed to degrade Christianity." For Baird, "[i]t was this that made the arch-infidel [Jefferson] chuckle with satisfaction." Still, Baird recognized that Jefferson's influence was important: "On no other point, I am confident, are the evangelical clergy of the United States, of all churches, more fully agreed than in holding that an union of church and state would prove one of the greatest calamities that could be inflicted on us, whatever it might prove in other countries." Of course, there should be no surprise that there were views opposed to Jefferson's vision, but when significant state constitutional reform was occurring or when the role of religion in the public sphere was at issue, it was to Jefferson and to the Statute that the American people turned as a model of perfect religious freedom, including separation of church and state, even when actions sometimes fell short of principle.[22]

Beyond the mass media, other important nineteenth-century sources also attribute American religious freedom to Jeffersonian influence. One of the broadest claims for Jefferson's impact was made by George Bancroft in his magisterial *History of the United States of America from the Discovery of the Continent*. Bancroft concludes that "the preamble to the bill for establishing religious freedom, drawn by Jefferson, expressed the ideas of America." Bancroft reprints much of the Statute and goes on to say "these enunciations of Jefferson on the freedom of conscience expressed [in 1779] the forming convictions of the people of the United States." It is interesting that Bancroft specifically recognizes that the Jeffersonian vision was a "forming" conviction. Of course, Bancroft was one of the most widely read and highly regarded nineteenth-century U.S. historians.[23]

Other noted nineteenth-century histories provided a similar assessment. Richard Hildreth explained that the Statute,

> which the passage was procured by the earnest efforts of Jefferson and Madison, seconded by the Presbyterians, Baptists, and other dissenters from the late Established Church, seemed to them the more imperatively called for in consequence of an attempt the year before, supported by Washington and Henry, and nearly successful, to pass a law in conformity to the ecclesiastical system of New England, compelling all to contribute to the support of some minister.

Robert Howison also quoted the Statute at length and discussed the Memorial & Remonstrance as "one of the best compositions ever produced, even by his [Madison's] great mind" and, long before the Court acted in *Reynolds* (1879), suggested that the antecedents of the First Amendment could be found in Virginia. Burk's history concluded that that Statute was part of a plan "to crush forever the eternal antagonism of artificial aristocracy against the rights and happiness of the people."[24]

Interestingly, Chief Justice Waite, in *Reynolds*, relies in part on Bancroft's conclusion in finding Jefferson's views foundational, itself a significant endorsement of Bancroft's history. There is a twist to this story, though. Bancroft and Waite were, for a time, next-door neighbors, and their correspondence indicates that Waite, while preparing the opinion in *Reynolds*, asked Bancroft for guidance on the origins of the First Amendment and was directed to the Statute and Madison's Memorial. Some point to this correspondence as evidence of an apparent elitist, Jeffersonian conspiracy to redefine the basis of the First Amendment. Yet, how to evaluate this historic fact is more complicated. Bancroft was, after all, one of the most highly acclaimed historians of the era. More-over, Justice Waite did not rely solely upon Bancroft's conclusion but, rather, used it as a stepping-stone to further research that supported Bancroft's sug-gestion and, given the prevalence of Jefferson in the public discourse, perhaps Waite's own perception. Certainly the unanimous *Reynolds* opinion was not unique in finding Jefferson and Madison as foundational. For example, in 1872 the Ohio Supreme Court turned to Madison in upholding a school board deci-sion to ban Bible readings in the public schools, noting that he "had more to do with framing the Constitution of the United States than any other man."[25]

Particularly interesting in this regard is the question: What would an edu-cated mid-nineteenth-century lawyer, state constitutional convention delegate, or judge see as the antecedents of America's religious freedom? Certainly it was well known that America had led the world in the development of religious freedom, but to what source would a nineteenth-century person turn to under-stand the scope and meaning of that protection? The First Amendment itself would be looked to, but that involved only a federal restriction at the time; state constitutions would be considered, and they were changing in the direction of greater protection along Jeffersonian principles. What historical sources, pri-mary and secondary, would they consider? Certainly Bancroft's history would have been relevant and, as noted above, Jefferson's Statute, Madison's Memorial & Remonstrance, and the Letter to the Danbury Baptists were well circulated. While some commentators complain that Jefferson and Madison were not the only Founders engaged on the issue of religious freedom, no one else had any-thing approaching the broad dissemination and influence of the Jeffersonian vision. As several newspapers summarized: "Who but JEFFERSON, could have so clearly defined the inalienable rights of mankind, and the legitimate objects of Government.... What other statesman could have broken down, at once, the connexion between Church and State?"[26]

Interestingly, after the Court's declaration in 1879 of the seminal nature of Jefferson's vision, this view was widely accepted by historians and commen-tators by the time the Supreme Court incorporated the First Amendment into the Fourteenth Amendment in 1940, thus applying its restrictions to the states. The *Los Angeles Times* declared in 1887 that "Virginia came forward and planted the keystone of the arch of American Liberty—the fundamental law guaranteeing religious freedom." A 1926 article in the *Virginia Law Review* explained that "two great Virginians [Jefferson and Madison] are by the unanimous verdict of all impartial students, entitled to the imperishable glory of having furnished the brains, pens and skilled leadership separating church and state and establishing religious freedom as it exists today. Thomas Jefferson drafted the celebrated statute of Virginia for religious freedom." Jefferson's "statute soon became a model for all of the American states and it is in substance embodied as a part of the bill of rights of every one of them. It was the direct and immediate cause of having a similar clause inserted in the first amendment to the Constitution of the United States." An early twentieth-century historian hailed the Statute as "what we proudly cherish and proclaim as the American principle of absolute religious liberty." A well-known clergyman of the same era similarly concluded that the Jefferson principle, "absolute separation of church and state," won "the long fight for religious independence, first in the Statute of Virginia for Religious Freedom, and later, in the First Amendment to the national Constitution." While this later evidence might be viewed as tainted by the Supreme Court's decision in 1879, it certainly is relevant that reliance on Jefferson and Madison for understanding religious liberty and the First Amendment was not viewed as remarkable at the time.[27]

Philip Hamburger, while joining in the view that by the time of *Reynolds* "the separation of church and state had become an almost irresistible dogma of Americanism," questions the wellspring for that doctrine. He finds its antecedents largely in the anti-Catholicism which sought, in part, to prevent public funding of sectarian (read "Catholic") schools. Sarah Barringer Gordon also concludes that Americans shared "an increasingly powerful assumption that separation of church and state was characteristic of American liberty everywhere," but notes the significance of the battle against Mormonism in cementing that view in the nineteenth century. "Only in opposition to Mormon Utah did Americans discover that separation of church and state was a fundamental component of all republican government." Certainly each of these was a factor, but the extent to which the Jeffersonian doctrine pervaded the original understanding of the First Amendment and was viewed as emblematic long before these other developments should not be underestimated.[28]

It is also true that other Founders and historic figures held different views of religious liberty, but the significance of that fact can be questioned. For example, as Daniel Dreisbach explains, the Reverend Jasper Adams, an Episcopal minister and president of the College of Charleston during the early nineteenth century, prepared and published a lengthy sermon on the history of church-state relations challenging Jefferson's vision and engaged in an extensive and historically informative correspondence with American leaders to elicit their views and promote his own. Adams's interesting arguments and history are discussed elsewhere; the point here is that no one in the nineteenth century was relying on Jasper Adams as they worked out the proper breadth of religious freedom and church-state relations. Neither constitutional debates nor court cases relying on Adams have been identified. While Dreisbach argues that "Adams's tract was recognized by contemporaries, as well as by subsequent commentators, as a learned and useful discourse," he cites five instances of Adams's sermon being recognized in the press: Three are in Christian publications; four are announcements of the publication of the sermon (albeit endorsing its views), all from 1833, and one is an extended and detailed thrashing of Adams's arguments in Jeffersonian terms apparently by a noted lawyer and future president of Tulane University. This is not to say that Adams and the Society for the Advancement of Christianity in South Carolina did not make every effort at self-promotion; copies of Adams's sermon were widely distributed. What is lacking is evidence that Adams influenced public understanding of religious liberty, much less state constitutional or legal reform. Dreisbach also tries to make Adams and his supporter, Justice Joseph Story, into contemporaries of the drafters of the First Amendment. But Story, the older of the two, was not yet ten when Congress adopted the Bill of Rights; Adams was not yet born. In fact, Adams's perceived necessity of responding to Jefferson's vision may be more telling.[29]

The record suggests that to understand the public perception of the First Amendment, one might more readily turn to James Madison's response to Adams's inquiry:

> It is true that the New England States have not discontinued establishments of Religion formed under very peculiar circumstances; but they have by successive relaxations advanced towards the prevailing example; and without any evidence of disadvantage either to Religion or good Government.... [T]he existing character [of the community], distinguished as it is by its religious features, and the lapse of time now more than 50 years since the legal support of Religion was withdrawn sufficiently prove that it does not need the support of Govt.... [I]t may not be easy, in every possible case, to trace the line of separation between the rights of religion and the Civil authority with such distinctness as to avoid

collisions & doubts on unessential points. The tendency to a usurpation on one side or the other, or to a corrupting coalition or alliance between them, will be best guarded agst. by an entire abstinance of the Govt. from interference in any way whatever, beyond the necessity of preserving public order, & protecting each sect agst. trespasses on its legal rights by others.

Jasper Adams simply did not engage the American mind the way that Jefferson's Statute and the Letter to Danbury Baptists and Madison's Memorial did. No one did. If one is looking for the impetus for the constitutional reform of the nineteenth century and for blossoming American understanding of religious liberty and the proper role of church/state relations, the broad and deep appreciation for the role of Jefferson and Madison is decisive.[30]

This pattern of seeking to minimize the influence of Jefferson and Madison by relying on alternative nineteenth-century authorities has also been pursued in the courts. A favorite source is the venerable Justice Joseph Story's *Commentaries on the Constitution*, which claimed that the First Amendment was intended only to protect against preference for one Christian sect over another. Story, a conservative scion of Massachusetts, expressly opposed Jefferson's views on the breadth of religious freedom. Perhaps it is not surprising that his *Commentaries* would adopt such a narrow view; they were first published in 1833 when the battle over Massachusetts's establishment was active—pitting old-style New England federalists and conservative allies against rising Jeffersonian Republicans. As a general matter, Story was hardly an advocate for broad toleration and argued for a preferred legal position for Christianity under the Constitution. He insisted that "[t]he real object of the [First] amendment was, *not to countenance, much less to advance Mahometanism, or Judaism, or infidelity, by prostrating Christianity; but to exclude all rivalry among Christian sects, and to prevent any national ecclesiastical establishment.*" (Justice Burger, in *Lynch* (1984), excluded from this quote the highlighted language.) Yet critics' focus on Story begs the question of who better reflects the understanding of religious liberty at the Founding and in the nineteenth century and who was relied upon as state constitutional reform moved unstoppably in a Jeffersonian direction.[31]

Not only was Story not involved in the Founding, but even in his time he seemed out of touch with the general view of religious freedom that was being propelled by the Jeffersonian vision. For example, his *Commentaries* defended Massachusetts's establishment as a "pointed affirmation" of the proper relationships between church and state just as Massachusetts's citizens rose up by overwhelming margins to end the tax-supported establishment, the last one in the country. He also ignored the trend in nineteenth-century disestablishment.

> [E]very American colony, from its foundation down to the revolution, with the exception of Rhode Island ... did openly, by the whole course of its laws and institutions, support and sustain, in some form, the Christian religion; ... And this has continued to be the case in some of the states down to the present period, without the slightest suspicion, that it was against the principles of public law, or republican liberty.

Jasper Adams made a similar argument divorced from the reality of the changes that were occurring across the country: "It is the duty of Congress, then, to permit the Christian religion to remain in the same state in which it was, at the time the Constitution was adopted," including the continuance of establishments and test oaths.[32]

Story's and Adams's cramped view can be juxtaposed to the Jeffersonian analysis of St. George Tucker, an early American jurist and actual contemporary of the constitutional debates who prepared an American edition of *Blackstone's Commentaries* in which he explained that the U.S. Constitution guaranteed that "every honest and peaceable man, whatever is his faith, be protected there [in the United States]; and find an effectual defence against the attacks of bigotry and intolerance. In the United States may religion flourish!" Tucker, relying on the First Amendment, the Virginia Declaration of Rights, and Jefferson's Statute, explained that public officials can help religion only by example: "They cannot, as public men, give it any other assistance. All, besides, that has been called a public leading in religion, has done it an essential injury, and produced some of the worst consequences." Even in the nineteenth century, commentators recognized that "the learned Justice [Story] here [church/state issues] was in opposition to the men who controlled formation of the Union and the changes of State Constitutions. . . . The statesmen whom Jefferson represented were directly at variance with the ideas of Justice Story, as was also that party of the Church which favored separation."[33]

Other nineteenth-century sources relied upon in an effort to diminish the influence of the Jeffersonian view are, at best, selectively cited by critics. Thus, Justice Rehnquist points out that the early constitutional scholar Thomas Cooley supported official "solemn recognition of superintending Providence in public transactions," for example, in thanksgiving proclamations and the use of chaplains (topics taken up in chapter 6), one page before Rehnquist argues that the Establishment Clause was intended only to prohibit "preference" for one sect over another. Yet, he omits Cooley's more important statement on the scope of the First Amendment and religious liberty:

> [T]he general voice has been to make all persons equal before the law, and to leave questions of religious belief and religious worship to be questions between every man and his Maker, which human tribunals are not to take cognizance of, so long as the public order is not disturbed.... The legislatures have not been left at liberty to effect a union of Church and State, or to establish preferences by law in favor of any one religious denomination or mode of worship.... Not only is no one denomination to be favored at the expense of the rest, but all support of religious instruction must be entirely voluntary.

Cooley (quoted as a nineteenth-century First Amendment authority on page 105 of the *Wallace* [1985] dissent) emphatically rejects the preferentialist doctrine that Rehnquist insists (on page 106) is "well-accepted" in the nineteenth century. Similarly, Justice Story, when not directly responding to Jefferson, is not as "accommodationist" as critics suggest. Elsewhere Story noted that the Constitution's prohibition of test acts "had a higher object; to cut off forever every pretence of any alliance between church and state in the national government." In the end, one is left with a contest between the vision of Jefferson and Madison and the views of reactionary opponents who had limited impact in their own times.[34]

Beyond the state constitutional movement toward a Jeffersonian understanding of religious liberty, and the very substantial influence that Jefferson had on constitutional reform and commentary, one might also look for the influence of Jefferson and the Virginia Statute in other nineteenth-century state legal developments. After all, the Statute, Memorial & Remonstrance, and Letter to the Danbury Baptists were often reprinted precisely when state legal reforms were in the works. Here, though, the picture becomes more complicated.

On the one hand, the nineteenth century witnessed changes in state statutes and court decisions in a range of areas relating to religious freedom and separation of church and state. Steven Green has documented at great length changes in blasphemy convictions, restrictions on witnesses' oaths, Sunday closing laws, and a host of other areas that invited legal reliance on a Christian foundation. Green demonstrates that these laws matured throughout the nineteenth century such that, in legislatures and courts, they were either diminished or increasingly justified on a secular regulatory basis. For example, Sunday closing laws became a labor regulation, providing a day of rest, rather than a means of enforcing Christian conformity. Green does not consider the extent to which these developments in state courts and legislatures were specifically based on a Jeffersonian vision, although the prevalence of that vision in the constitutional debates and common discourse suggests that if one looked, substantial evidence would be found.[35]

On the other hand, David Sehat sees the continued existence of these laws at all as evidence of the limited impact of the Jeffersonian principle in this period. While constitutions eliminated formal establishments, an effective "moral establishment" remained; fundamental reform had to await the mid-twentieth century. Sehat does an excellent job in documenting and explaining such deviations from principle and developments in the twentieth century, but several points should be kept in mind. First, and foremost, principle matters. Jefferson recognized the failure to apply the theory of religious freedom fully in the early nineteenth century, but he also saw that establishing the principle was critical. In the twentieth century, when many municipal laws based on religion were addressed, it was the principle that Jefferson championed and that became an American principle in the late eighteenth and nineteenth centuries that was crucial in addressing Sehat's "moral establishment." Justice Blackmun, writing for the Court in 1989, explained: "The history of this Nation, it is perhaps sad to say, contains numerous examples of official acts that endorsed Christianity specifically.... [B]ut this heritage of official discrimination against non-Christians has no place in the jurisprudence of the Establishment Clause." Second, while limits on the application of religious freedom deserve close attention, a focus on troubling municipal laws should not obscure the changes and progress that were made. Finally, Sehat's focus on laws seeking to enforce "morality" can be overly broad for these purposes. There is a fundamental difference between a law that prohibits business only on the Christian Sabbath, discriminating against Jews and other sabbatarians, and a law that prohibits the sale of alcohol, even if the latter was supported by Christian crusaders. Abolition provides an even more powerful example. It is hardly surprising that many necessary and meritorious laws intended to prevent harm to members of society would regulate "morality," whatever the stated or unstated intent of legislators. (Some cases may prove difficult: For example, does a prohibition of polygamy address legitimate concerns for women and children or, solely, a religious bias?) In any case, as more recent history demonstrates, establishment of the Jeffersonian principles has had, and continues to have, important effects both in the courts and in the broader polity.[36]

Christian Nation

At the same time that many of the states were amending their constitutions to make them more consistent with a Jeffersonian vision of religious liberty and that vision was becoming emblematic for understanding the principle of American religious freedom, developments in the broader culture were reemphasizing the centrality of religious experience. Early in the nineteenth century, the Second Great Awakening led to an explosion of evangelism, church membership, and new religious sects. Increasingly, religious convictions were playing a critical role in encouraging broad social reform, from the temperance movement to abolitionism. Not surprisingly, the use of religious language in the public square exploded, including efforts to identify the United States more formally as a "Christian nation." While the Awakening certainly had enormous implications for American culture, the question here is how this cultural upwelling affected constitutional law and the American understanding of religious freedom.[37]

The federal Constitution contains no direct recognition of God much less obeisance to divine providence. Even the preamble proclaims that authority came from "the People," rather than a traditional notion of civil authority descending from God. While Jefferson (and Madison) believed that rights are the gift of heaven, that is a very different matter than their being the source of legal authority in a social compact. The omission was hardly happenstance. Luther Martin, a Maryland delegate to the Philadelphia Convention, noted ruefully that "in a Christian country, it would be at *least decent* to hold out some distinction between the professors of Christianity and downright infidelity or paganism." Martin's complaint, though, makes clear that the Constitution gave no such consideration to Christianity or religion, a complaint repeated throughout the ratification process. The only significant reference to religion in the original document is the provision in Article VI specifying that no test oath will ever be required for office, a provision one antifederalist declared "is by many thought dangerous and impolitic. . . . pagans, deists, and Mahometans might obtain offices among us." Other sources understood that this lack of verbiage was a fundamental recognition that the governmental sphere was separate from the religious.

> This clause [Art. VI, test clause] is not introduced merely for the purpose of satisfying the scruples of many respectable persons, who feel an invincible repugnance to any religious test or affirmation. It had a higher object; to cut off forever every pretence of any alliance between church and state in the national government. The framers of the constitution were fully sensible of the dangers from this source, marked out in the history of other ages and countries, and not wholly unknown to our own. They knew that bigotry was unceasingly vigilant in its stratagems to secure to itself an exclusive ascendency over the human mind; and that intolerance was ever ready to arm itself with all the terrors of the civil power to exterminate those who doubted its dogmas, or resisted its infallibility.

The result—as several historians have termed it—a "Godless Constitution."[38]

One might try to hang on threads: The Constitution is dated "in the Year of our Lord," and some argue that use of that language suggests an obeisance to Christianity. Setting aside the limited significance of a passing reference in a traditional dating device, this language was apparently added by a clerk after the delegates had agreed to and voted on the text. Similarly, "the 'Sunday excepted' and the 'oath and affirmation' provisions demonstrate a governmental respect for religious practices and an awareness that the vast majority of American citizens were Christians." They hardly make the Constitution, or the nation, in some formal or legal sense "Christian." "The 'no religious test' clause, presidential oath, and Preamble . . . signify[ ] that regardless of the individual religious beliefs of most citizens, the American government was not to be defined by even the broadest religious conception."[39]

Some urge more fundamentally that, whatever the lack of religious language in the constitutions of the early republic, America's founding principles developed based upon Christian doctrines, for example the inherent value and equality of human life. The nineteenth-century historian Philip Schaff, having noted the absence of any mention of the deity in the Constitution, argued: "We may go further and say that the Constitution not only contains nothing which is irreligious or unchristian, but is Christian in substance, though not in form.

It is pervaded by the spirit of justice and humanity, which are Christian. The First Amendment could not have originated in any pagan or Mohammedan country, but presupposes Christian civilization and culture." Others have made similar arguments, claiming, for example, that the origins of American constitutional fixation on checks and balances lies in Calvinistic assumptions of human sinfulness and that the contract theory of constitutionalism is a form of the Calvinist compact. Of course, intellectual antecedents of any complex ideas are notoriously difficult to trace, and caution is advisable. As others show, these claims were largely the product of the nineteenth century, accelerating after the Second Great Awakening. Still, one might readily accept that in some sense Christian doctrines contributed significantly to the development of the American mind and, thus, the American system. Yet, the legal significance of that Christianity was another matter. As a North Carolina court explained at the beginning of the twentieth century: "The beautiful and divine precepts of the Nazarene do influence the conduct of our people and individuals, and are felt in legislation and in every department of activity. They profoundly impress and shape our civilization. But it is by this influence that it acts, and not because it is a part of the organic law, which expressly denies religion any place in the supervision or control of secular affairs." But for the reference to divinity, Jefferson might have said the same.[40]

Some early apologists sought to minimize the significance of the omission of godly language from the Constitution. Echoing, probably unintentionally, Jefferson's observation in the Statute that "civil rights have no dependence on our religious opinions, any more than our opinions in physics and geometry," Schaff explained that "the absence of the names of God and Christ, in a purely political and legal document, no more proves denial or irreverence than the absence of those names in a mathematical treatise, or the statutes of a bank or railroad corporation." This, though, is to confirm the legal and constitutional point while missing the extent to which this evidenced a change from prior practice and how the issue would develop in the nineteenth century.[41]

The pervasiveness of religion, particularly a generic Protestant Christianity, in early American culture was not in dispute. Nor is the cultural significance of that religion at issue. Looked at in Jeffersonian terms, in excluding test oaths and omitting any reference to God, the Constitution's framers were not seeking to eliminate or prejudice what occurred on the "other," private side of the wall. Jefferson expected a vibrant, rational religion to encourage the development of the republic. While less expected by the sage, the voluntary principle that he espoused launched a cacophony of nineteenth-century religions, and American culture was permeated by their noise and color. As Peter Onuf explains:

> In the founding era, Jefferson and his fellow revolutionaries campaigned for the formal separation of church and state in order to uproot and demolish the old regime. Far from banishing religion from the "public square," this constitutional separation unleashed a tremendous outburst of religious energy that authorized a providential conception of America's role in world history: the new nation's rising and expansive power was inextricably linked with the progress of Christian civilization.

While developments failed to comport with Jefferson's expectations, in some sense, he might not have been entirely displeased: Not only did many of the emerging religions have a democratic polity, but some sought to avoid dogmatism, and many of the new sects, while proclaiming the Christianity of the American people and nation, were strong advocates of separation of church and state.[42]

What is at issue here, though, is the constitutional regime and its relationship to American concepts of religious liberty. In fact, to note the continuing, indeed, expanding, significance of religion in culture as a response to its omission in the Constitution may be to highlight the significance of the change made by this omission. Colonial charters, certainly, were peppered with references to colonists' and Britain's godly missions. The Articles of Confederation noted the guidance of the "Great Governor of the World." Yet, the state constitutions drafted in the Revolutionary era tended to omit such language or, at most, refer to God in Enlightenment terms. The change owed much both to the deep-seated antipathy to British notions of the divine right of kings and to Enlightenment rationalism. Even these references tended to disappear in the waning years of the eighteenth century. Intentional decisions were made not to tie the nation, at least not formally and legally, to Christianity or even religion generally, even while Christianity blossomed in the culture.[43]

It was also the case that most eighteenth-century leaders believed that religion, specifically the Christian religion, would encourage virtue and that virtue was essential for the proper functioning of the republic. George Washington famously expressed this widely held belief in his Farewell Address, noting:

Of all the dispositions and habits which lead to political prosperity, religion and morality are indispensable supports. In vain would that man claim the tribute of patriotism, who should labor to subvert these great pillars of human happiness, these firmest props of the duties of men and citizens.... And let us with caution indulge the supposition that morality can be maintained without religion.... [R]eason and experience both forbid us to expect that national morality can prevail in exclusion of religious principle.

The Northwest Ordinance made much the same point in stating that "religion, morality, and knowledge, being necessary to good government and the happiness of mankind, schools and the means of education shall forever be encouraged." Madison and Jefferson did not disagree with the role of religion in promoting virtue and the republic. In fact, Jefferson claimed that "the Christian religion when divested of the rags in which they [the clergy] have inveloped it, and brought to the original purity & simplicity of it's benevolent institutor, is a religion of all others most friendly to liberty, science, & the freest expression of the human mind."[44]

This, though, is far from any official recognition of religion or Christianity, much less an endorsement of church/state entanglement or governmental aid. Jefferson and Madison reasoned that while religion would promote the virtue necessary for effective republican citizenship, government was not needed to promote religion; indeed, it tended to undermine true religion. Both the Statute and Memorial & Remonstrance make this point, as did the Virginia dissenters. Government, too, would benefit from the formal separation. Writing to Jasper Adams in 1832, Madison was confident in asserting that "it will scarcely be contended that Government has suffered by the exemption of Religion from its cognizance, or its pecuniary aid." The same was true of the language in the Northwest Ordinance; the Ohio Supreme Court, in an 1872 case upholding Cincinnati's decision to ban Bible reading from public schools, explained that the language from the Northwest Ordinance neither demanded nor even authorized government action directly promoting religion: "[T]rue 'religion' and 'morality' are aided and promoted by the increase and diffusion of 'knowledge,'... and that all three—religion, morality, and knowledge—are essential to good government.... The truth is that these are matters left to legislative discretion, subject to the limitations on legislative power, regarding religious freedom, contained in the bill of rights." In fact, Washington deleted from a draft of the Farewell Address Alexander Hamilton's suggestion that he ask, "Does it [national morality] not require the aid of a generally received and divinely authoritative Religion?" Thus, while Vincent Muñoz correctly relates that "like many, if not most, leaders of the founding generation, Washington believed a pious citizenry was indispensable to republican government," this does not justify his conclusion that Washington believed "that civil government could and should endorse religion"; it certainly does not mean that Washington supported the "propriety of government support" for religion. Those who excluded any reference to God from the Constitution did not abandon or renounce the advantages of religion; they believed that they could be obtained without government endorsement. Jeffersonians believed that government involvement would be positively harmful to both religion and government.[45]

A separate question was the use of religion in politics. At the same time that religious terms and limitations were being expunged from constitutions, there was no question that private citizens could generally act on their religious beliefs, including acting publicly and politically, as they thought appropriate; this was implicit in free exercise. This issue manifested itself in a number of ways. First, there was the matter of how voters might act. The Reverend Ezra Stiles Ely of Connecticut explained early in the nineteenth century: "We are a Christian nation: we have a right to demand that all our rulers in their conduct shall conform to Christian morality; and if they do not, it is the duty and privilege of Christian freemen to make a new and better election." Jefferson, philosophically opposed to religiously motivated politics and highly suspicious of politicians who flaunted their religion, would have disapproved of Ely's methods, but he did not question the "privilege" of people in a republic to vote their personal preferences, including religion. While religious invocations in the election of 1800 sorely tried Jefferson, his lack of response to the assaults is telling. One Jeffersonian expressed shock at that vicious campaign, particularly in light of "how anxious the founders of our government were to shut the door against religious disputes, and to prevent them from ever mingling in our political concerns." There was no effort, though, to regulate such disputes.[46]

Further, there were perennial issues surrounding the participation of ministers in politics. Given his fear of priestcraft, Jefferson initially insisted that ministers be prohibited from running for political office, and this view initially triumphed in a number of states. Eventually though, under the influence of Madison and time, Jefferson accepted the fact that to deny ministers a right to participate in the polity was to interfere with their free exercise of religion. Commenting on a draft constitution for Kentucky in 1800, he conceded: "I observe . . . an abridgement of the right of being elected, which after 17. years more of experience & reflection, I do not approve. [I]t is the incapacitation of a clergyman from being elected." His initial exception for ministers' participation in politics tends to prove the broader rule: It was certainly understood that Christians would participate in the polity and might well choose to make political decisions based upon religious criteria, even if Jefferson would see that as ill-advised.[47]

Make no mistake, Jefferson continued to be opposed to the use of politics in religion or religion in politics. He believed that a minister's congregation should view preaching on politics as a breach of contract for which the minister should be fired. He also did not deviate from his deep concern about hypocrisy among politicians who wore religion on their sleeves, seeking to live by his advice that "it is in our lives, and not from our words, that our religion must be read. By the same test, the world must judge me."[48]

Yet, while Christianity permeated the culture and, initially, a number of municipal laws and was invoked in political campaigns, the lack of any official, legal recognition in the Constitution and at the founding is still striking. For Jefferson and Madison, any official recognition would bring with it great danger, both to government and to religion. Madison's Memorial & Remonstrance was a paean against any such effort. For Jeffersonians, Christianity not only needed no government recognition or support, but it would suffer from it.

> [F]or every page of it [Christianity] disavows a dependence on the powers of this world: . . . for it is known that this Religion both existed and flourished, not only without the support of human laws, but in spite of every opposition from them, . . . Nay, it is a contradiction in terms; for a Religion not invented by human policy, must have pre-existed and been supported, before it was established by human policy. It is moreover to weaken in those who profess this Religion a pious confidence in its innate excellence and the patronage of its Author; and to foster in those who still reject it, a suspicion that its friends are too conscious of its fallacies to trust it to its own merits.

Similar sentiments were expressed in the Baptist "Spirit of the Gospel" petitions from 1785. This view was reflected in the 1796 U.S. treaty with Tripoli, which specified that "the Government of the United States of America is not, in any sense, founded on the Christian religion; as it has in itself no character of enmity against the laws, religion, or tranquility, of Mussulmen." Judge Jeremiah S. Black of Pennsylvania (also the U.S. attorney general and a Supreme Court appointee) explained:

> The manifest object of the men who framed the institutions of this country, was to have a *State without religion*, and a *Church without politics*—that is to say, they meant that one should never be used as an engine for any purpose of the other. . . . Our fathers seem to have been perfectly sincere in their belief that the members of the Church would be more patriotic, and the citizens of the State more religious, by keeping their respective functions entirely separate. For that reason they built a wall of complete and perfect partition between the two.

John Leland, a leading Baptist minister and a firm Jeffersonian, made the same point in 1811: "Let christianity stand upon its own basis, it is the greatest blessing that ever was among men; but incorporate it into the civil code and it becomes the mother of cruelties." In 1872, the Ohio Supreme Court spoke in evangelical tones in holding that "*Legal* Christianity is a solecism, a contradiction in terms."[49]

One example of this distinction in the cultural and legal reality was that while no one doubted the predominance of Christianity in American culture, evangelical religious dissenters and their Enlightenment supporters in the early republic made it clear that the polity would be equally open to all people: Christians, Jews, Muslims, Hindus, or pagans. Jefferson happily reported that the Statute "meant to comprehend within the mantle of its protection the Jew and the Gentile, the Christian and Mahometan, the Hindoo and infidel of every denomination." Jefferson's evangelical allies agreed. Some newspaper editors cited with pride the vote to exclude the phrase "Jesus Christ" from the Statute. George Washington, too, while arguably not as committed as Jefferson and Madison to broadly defined separation of church and state, assured the Jewish community of Newport that they would not be prosecuted for breach of Christian requirements: "All possess alike liberty of conscience and immunities of citizenship." It was just this fact, ruefully acknowledged, that led to complaints about Article VI of the Constitution.[50]

This pointed lack of Christian or godly language in early constitutions makes all the more interesting the movement during the nineteenth century to incorporate such language into constitutions, often at the same time that state constitutions were being amended to provide clearer and broader protections for religious freedom.[51]

The effort to express some official institutional fealty to God was often made through amendments to the preambles of state constitutions. Beginning with Maine in 1819, the pattern of amendments was broadly based. By 1848, the practice began to blossom as delegates to the Illinois constitutional convention expressed gratitude "to Almighty God for the civil, political, and religious liberty which He hath so long permitted us to enjoy, and looking to Him for a blessing upon our endeavors." Similar language was used in Indiana in 1851 ("grateful to Almighty God for the free exercise of the right to choose our own form of government"), in Iowa in 1857 ("grateful to the Supreme Being for the blessings hitherto enjoyed, and feeling our dependence on Him for a continuation of those blessings"), and in Kansas in 1858 ("grateful to Almighty God for our freedom"). Such godly language permeated nineteenth-century state constitutional conventions.[52]

The change from the eighteenth-century pattern is telling. Pennsylvania, which included an invocation of the deity in its 1776 constitution, removed it in 1790 before reinstating it in 1873. Similarly, while Vermont included such language in 1777, the 1793 constitution deleted it. Of course, even in the mid-nineteenth century, support for such changes was not universal, and in some notable instances the trend was opposed. California, for example, after debating the matter, rejected introduction of such language into its constitution. It is also noteworthy that constitutional references were rarely expressly "Christian," a change from the era before the Philadelphia Convention. In fact, in some cases, while preambulatory language recognizing God was added, a reference to Christianity was expressly rejected. One Illinois delegate made clear that "though the great body of our people are believers in the Christian religion, in some form or other, this is no more, under the fundamental laws, a Christian than it is a Mohammedan government."[53]

Setting aside the exclusion of such language from the federal Constitution, several points should be made about these efforts officially to label individual states as godly. First, there is a striking willingness of constitutional conventions in the nineteenth century to insert this type of religious language into preambles at the same time that they were incorporating very broad protections for religious liberty and separation of church and state into their constitutional texts. Maine, for example, when it broke away from Massachusetts and drafted its first constitution, "acknowledge[d] with grateful hearts the goodness of the Sovereign Ruler of the Universe in affording us an opportunity, so favorable to the design; and imploring His aid and direction in its accomplishment" at the same time it eliminated the Massachusetts establishment. Rhode Island provided a preamble reciting its gratitude to God when it incorporated language from Jefferson's Statute into its new constitution specifying "that no person shall be compelled to frequent or to support any religious worship, place, or ministry whatever, . . . nor enforced, restrained, molested, or burdened in body or goods; nor disqualified from holding any office; nor otherwise suffer on account of such person's religious belief." Some of this apparent conflict seems to be an intentional effort to satisfy a political demand for recognition of religion while not impeding religious liberty; a number of state convention delegates mentioned their view that the language of a preamble was entirely hortatory with no substantive impact. In debates in Illinois, a supporter of inserting such language specifically urged that it would have no effect on the rights recorded in the state's bill of rights. Of course, the issue here is not whether preambles can, as a matter of legal theory, be so easily dismissed. The point is that there was a specific recognition of those advocating such language that it should not change the operative provisions of state bills of rights. While he certainly would have used the most inclusive language possible, Jefferson's own invocation of God in both the Statute and the Declaration demonstrate that he was not immune to such an approach.[54]

An interesting parallel occurs with respect to declarations in nineteenth-century court cases that the United States, or a given state, was a "Christian nation." The *Ruggles* blasphemy case in New York has oft been cited for the notion that, whatever the terms of the Constitution, this is a "Christian nation." What the court said in that proceeding was that "we are a christian people"; yet, at a New York constitutional convention, the author of that opinion was at pains to minimize its legal significance. Chancellor Kent explained that "he never intended to declare Christianity the legal religion of the state, because that would be considering Christianity as the established religion, and make it a civil or political institution. . . . But Christianity was, *in fact*, the religion of the people of this state, and that fact was the principle of the decision." Thus, the defendants "were indicted on the same principle as the act of wantonly going naked, or committing impure and indecent acts in the public streets." While Christianity was nominally declared part of the "common law" in a number of states, a broad pattern of minimizing the legal significance of such declarations followed. Delaware Chief Justice John Clayton, for example, backpedaled from the proposition much as had Chancellor Kent: "The maxim did not mean that Christian principles were essential to the common law; rather, the phrase merely meant that the law recognized, or gave judicial notice of the fact that Christianity was 'the prevailing religion of the people.'" Justice David Brewer, author of the 1892 *Holy Trinity* Supreme Court opinion that stated in passing that the United States was a "Christian nation," makes much the same point in Jeffersonian terms: If ministers seek to obtain some particular authority in civil matters as a result of their position, "Brewer asserted, the average citizen is justified in telling him to 'go back to your pulpit and leave matters of education and business and legislation to those who are trained therefore.'" As Green documents at length, the nineteenth century saw a consistent and dramatic draining of such religious language from state laws and court decisions concerning blasphemy, oaths, Sunday closing laws, and the like. American culture would be Christian, and Christian rhetoric expanded in the nineteenth century, but America's law would emphatically not be so constricted.[55]

Second, whatever the meaning of this effort to label the United States or individual states a "Christian nation," it cannot be attributed to the Founders or the U.S. Constitution. This language was almost entirely absent in earlier constitutions and was removed in the eighteenth century in several constitutions in which it did appear.

Third, by 1863, with the Civil War raging and each side seeking divine intervention and claiming divine inspiration, the National Reform movement sought to declare the United States officially a "Christian nation" by securing an amendment to the federal Constitution to "declare the nation's allegiance to Jesus Christ." This effort failed. Efforts to introduce expressly the phrase "separation of church and state" into the Constitution also came to naught, but those efforts were largely responsive to the failed "Christian nation" effort.[56]

Fourth, arguably, and ironically, the growing cultural weight of Christianity and significance of the "Christian nation" idiom in public rhetoric probably facilitated the diminishing constitutional and legal significance of religion, even at the state level. The dominance of Christianity in the public discourse tended to obviate any need for inserting Christianity into legal documents (other than, perhaps, a generic declaration in constitutional preambles). Moreover, in the nineteenth century, Protestant Americans were finding other reasons to resist any overt church/state cooperation. For example, southern slave owners sought to depoliticize ministers, some of who had a propensity to denounce slavery as a moral abomination. One commentator concluded that "it was this interpretation of freedom of conscience and the separation of church and state, not that of Leland and Barrow [persecuted Baptist ministers], that gained sway in Virginia at the beginning of the nineteenth century, and it was this interpretation that persisted." Similarly, an influx of Catholic immigrants stirred anti-Catholicism, and Catholic demands that public schools either not use the Protestant King James Bible or that public funds be made equally available to Catholic schools often elicited a sharp reaction. These efforts to ban the use of public funds for sectarian education, so-called Blaine Amendments, were often supported on the grounds of separating church from state. President Ulysses Grant advised: "Leave the matter of religion to the family altar, the church, and the private school, supported entirely by private contributions. Keep the church and the state forever separate." James Garfield agreed: "The separation of the Church and State in everything relating to taxation should be absolute." Teddy Roosevelt added that it is "not our business to have the Protestant Bible or the Catholic Vulgate or the Talmud read in those [public] schools." By the end of the century, Blaine Amendments had been adopted by more than half of the states; many were required as a condition for a new state being admitted to the union. This movement was central to Philip Hamburger's suggestion that anti-Catholicism played a critical role in the development of separation of church and state. Another example of how a pervasive public Christianity contributed to support of a Jeffersonian separation can be found in attacks on church/state cooperation in Mormon Utah; Americans rallied to defending the separation of church and state when faced with polygamist protagonists who combined the two. Henry Ward Beecher, a famous Congregationalist preacher, defended his attack on the Mormon Church by noting that "it is a union of church and state, which we fear, and to prevent which we lift up our voice: a union which never existed without corrupting the church and enslaving the people, by making the ministry independent of them and dependent on the state." Yet, while these various nineteenth-century interests—protecting slavery, anti-Catholicism, anti-Mormonism—undoubtedly played a role in strengthening the doctrine of strict separation of church and state in some circles, the principle of Jeffersonian religious freedom clearly had earlier antecedents and was ascendant long before an influx of Catholic immigrants, antislavery preachers, or Mormons. In fact, as noted earlier, Jefferson's Statute was cited as an appropriate response to the anti-Catholicism of the Know-Nothing Party. In any case, by the time the Court acted in *Reynolds*, Americans defined the Jeffersonian principle of a fundamental separation of church and state as essential to republican government, even while that understanding was buttressed by more parochial concerns.[57]

While recognizing the extent to which constitutions and the law were being separated from any direct reliance on or preference for religion, one should not confuse this with a parallel separation in the cultural realm. As others have documented extensively, the "voluntary principle" that justified disestablishment also became a primary factor in encouraging religiously based social movements with broad-ranging impact. Moreover, the increasing reliance on language of Christian nationhood also had long-term implications. Steven Green explains that while, "as legal authority, the [Christian nation] maxim was relatively ineffective . . . , the significance of the maxim was not whether it was legally determinative but in how it reinforced a narrow view of disestablishment and legitimized popular belief about the government's role in promoting religion." The use of this idiom in the cultural wars of the modern era is well known. Still, the legal pattern is clear. The nineteenth century saw an increasing reliance on a Jeffersonian vision to define religious liberty, especially in terms of constitutional reform, while, at the same time, an increased willingness privately to declare the country a "Christian nation," so long as that did not interfere with the rights of religious freedom. More serious conflict between these cultural and legal trends would have to await the twentieth century.[58]

This was the state of affairs when, in 1879, a unanimous Supreme Court concluded that Jefferson's Statute, passed with the assistance of the Memorial & Remonstrance, defined religious freedom. Waite's opinion in *Reynolds v. United States* quotes the Statute, the Memorial, and the Letter to the Danbury Baptists extensively, saying of the latter that "it may be accepted almost as an authoritative declaration of the scope and effect of the [First] amendment thus secured." The Court also found the Virginia Experience seminal in the development of the First Amendment. As one commentator explained: "Virginia's legislative act gained much greater influence than one should have expected from the statute of a member state of this Union. This is due to the fact that this law, more precisely than others, reflects and contains this outstanding philosophical principle [religious freedom] of the Founding Fathers of the Nation."[59]

The twentieth-century Supreme Court built on this history when it, too, found Jefferson and Madison seminal. From a historic perspective, the Court's majority has been correct to find the foundations for the First Amendment and American religious freedom in the Virginia Experience and, particularly, the extraordinary work of Jefferson and Madison.

Yet, as a practical matter, what precipitated modern cultural warfare was not that interpretation of the First Amendment per se, but its extension to apply to each of the states, making it far more likely to come into conflict with a pervasive religious culture. This constitutionalization of religious freedom, then, led to a new challenge to the relevance of Jefferson and Madison and requires a more careful consideration of some of Jefferson's (and Madison's) particular practices concerning religion and church/state relations.

6

FEDERAL CONTROL

Jefferson's Vision in Our Times

RELIGIOUS LIBERTY AND JEFFERSON'S AND MADISON'S VIEWS ON THE same were active topics in the political discourse in the states throughout the nineteenth century. On the other hand, after adoption of the First Amendment, applicable only to the federal government, its religion clauses appeared to slumber judicially for the better part of 150 years. This was not entirely unexpected; most relevant treatment of religion and religious freedom occurred at the state level and was not directly affected by the First Amendment. It was not until 1940, in *Cantwell v. Connecticut,* that the Supreme Court concluded that the First Amendment's protection of religious freedom applied equally to the states. As a result, for the past three-quarters of a century, the courts have faced a veritable blizzard of litigation concerning the scope of the religion clauses as questions of religious liberty appear to have been largely constitutionalized. This was a change that neither Jefferson nor Madison could have foreseen.

This raises a question: Since the Establishment Clause only applied to the federal government when adopted, and was intended to leave the states free to regulate religion as they saw fit, should it now be applied to the states? Since application of the First Amendment to the states drove the explosion in First Amendment jurisprudence in the twentieth century, this is a good place to start.

Initially, though, the application of the First Amendment to the states seemed largely noncontroversial, as did the reliance on a Jeffersonian vision. At midcentury the Supreme Court suggested a continuing, if not strengthened, vitality for the Virginia Statute as a Rosetta Stone for understanding the First Amendment, referring to Jefferson's and Madison's writings and the Virginia Experience as the "warp and woof of our constitutional tradition" and the Statute as "particularly relevant in the search for First Amendment mean-ing." This view was virtually unanimous on the Court in the 1940s and 1950s, and twentieth-century historians broadly agreed. Beyond the courts, Jefferson's "wall of separation between church and state" was largely absorbed into the cultural fabric.[1]

Yet, beginning in the 1950s and 1960s, many evangelical Christians, tradi-tionally some of the strongest supporters of a strict separation between church and state and the Jeffersonian ideal, started to question that approach. The causes of this change were myriad but paralleled the apparent growth in the Supreme Court's reach, particular *Brown v. Board of Education* in 1954 and the school prayer cases in the early 1960s. Reflecting that same unease, in the past thirty years the conservative wing of the Court has sought to narrow the separation between church and state and broaden government "accommoda-tion" of religion. In doing so, several justices have launched an open attack on the Court's (and historians') reliance on Jefferson and Madison and the Vir-ginia Experience. These critics ask why Jefferson's views should be privileged rather than the views of other Founders who had a more robust notion of the permissible cooperation between church and state. These concerns will be con-sidered briefly here—briefly because many are addressed in earlier chapters.

This leaves the problem of application of Jeffersonian principles to a host of modern issues that even the most erudite of eighteenth-century minds could not have predicted. Such application is always complicated by context and changes in law, society, and technology, and this work presents neither the time nor the place for an exhaustive review of recent religious freedom cases and an evaluation of how Jefferson might view such issues through the mist of time. Still, a survey of Jefferson's and Madison's actions concerning several controversies in their own time is essential to a fair understanding of how rich and nuanced their views were and can provide a useful backdrop for appreciat-ing how extensively Jefferson still speaks to us today on the issue of religious freedom. He was certainly emphatic that government should neither encourage nor endorse religion, but he never sought to purge religion (private religion) from the public square.

Incorporation

The First Amendment, when adopted, applied only to the federal government.[2] In fact, as previously noted, the religion clauses were crafted in part to ensure that states could continue to regulate religion as they saw fit, accommodating or restricting religion free from federal interference. After all, in 1791, when the amendment was adopted, all but one of the new states had some form of establishment or test oath and certainly most did not apply religious freedom in anything like a Jeffersonian sense. While the states may have modified their practices throughout the nineteenth century, they did so of their own accord, and, some argue, nothing should prevent the states from again modifying their legal regimes to permit a much closer interaction of government and religion, to discriminate in favor (or against) religion (or religions), or to restrict free exercise. If the amendment's original intent was to restrict the federal government, and to leave the state governments free to act as they saw best, why should it now restrict the states?

The simple answer is that amendments to the Constitution after the Civil War were intended to ensure that the states could no longer violate the basic rights of citizens. The Fourteenth Amendment, adopted in 1868, mandates that states not "abridge the privileges or immunities of citizens of the United States" nor "deprive any person of life, liberty, or property, without due process of law; nor deny to any person within [their] jurisdiction the equal protection of the laws." While that amendment was precipitated by slavery, it applies broadly to all citizens.

The question, then, is whether the rights inherent in the First Amendment's religion clauses fall within the Fourteenth Amendment's protections against abuse by the states. Others have made a strong case that the Fourteenth Amendment was intended to apply all of the Bill of Rights to the states immediately.[3] The Supreme Court, though, rejected that view in the *Slaughter-House Cases* in 1873, limiting the scope of the Civil War amendments and, not coincidentally, undermining an aggressive Reconstruction and effectively protecting segregation. Instead, since at least *Gitlow v. New York* (1925), the Supreme Court has found that "fundamental personal rights and 'liberties' [are] protected by the due process clause of the Fourteenth Amendment from impairment by the States," thereby "incorporating" those rights into the Fourteenth Amendment. Since the Bill of Rights does not specify which rights are fundamental, the Supreme Court, on a case-by-case basis, has decided whether particular portions of the Bill of Rights are "incorporated" into the Due Process Clause based upon the Court's judgment of whether they are fundamental to the "ordered liberty" expected in the American system. There is a voluminous literature on the question of incorporation of the Bill of Rights that will not be rehearsed here. Instead, several particular issues relating to incorporation of the First Amendment's religion clauses will be considered.[4]

In 1940, in *Cantwell v. Connecticut*, a case recognizing the right of Jehovah's Witnesses to canvas door to door, the Court incorporated the Free Exercise Clause of the First Amendment into the Fourteenth, thereby preventing states from "prohibiting the free exercise" of religion. In 1947, in *Everson v. Board of Education*, a case involving tax-supported bus transportation to private schools, the Establishment Clause was incorporated. Incorporation of the religious liberty protections of the First Amendment into the Fourteenth Amendment, making them applicable to the states, led to an explosion both of religious freedom and of litigation, in particular church/state disputes. (In a similar vein, much of modern civil rights practice has developed because most of the key provisions of the Bill of Rights have been "incorporated" over the latter half of the twentieth century.)[5]

While the incorporation of the religion clauses of the First Amendment has been settled law since the 1940s, Justice Thomas and several academics have been vocal in challenging that view, at least as it applies to the Establishment Clause. Their objections fall into essentially three closely related arguments: First, noting that the Establishment Clause was initially intended to protect the states, the argument is made that it cannot now be applied against them. Thomas urges the Court to "acknowledge that the Establishment Clause is a federalism provision, which, for this reason, resists incorporation" and that it is "best understood" to "protect[. . .] state establishments."[6] Second, convinced that the Establishment Clause was entirely jurisdictional, that is, *all* that it did was specify that the states controlled this issue, those opposing incorporation urge that it can have no substantive impact. In this view, incorporation of the clause is not only inappropriate, but meaningless—essentially telling the states that the states are responsible for issues of establishment. Third, it is argued that the Fourteenth Amendment was intended to apply only private rights against the states. Since the Establishment Clause "does not protect any individual right," it should not be incorporated. The Free Exercise Clause, "paradigmatically about citizen rights, not state rights," can be incorporated in this understanding.[7]

Thus, for Akhil Amar, the Establishment Clause is "a pure federalism provision. . . . [T]he clause was utterly agnostic on the substantive issue of establishment; it simply mandated that the issue be decided state by state and that Congress keep its hands off, that Congress make no law 'respecting' the vexed question." Justice Thomas concludes, "the States may pass laws that include or touch on religious matters," presumably including establishments or integrating church and state, "so long as these laws do not impede free exercise rights or any other individual religious liberty interest."[8]

Justice Thomas notes the irony that incorporating the Establishment Clause into the Fourteenth Amendment "prohibit[s] precisely what the Establishment Clause was intended to protect—*state* establishment of religion." Amar seems similarly exercised: "[T]o apply the clause against a state government is precisely to eliminate its right to choose whether to establish a religion—a right explicitly confirmed by the establishment clause itself!"[9]

Justice Thomas's colleagues on the Court have shown little proclivity to revisit the issue of incorporation, but it deserves careful consideration. First, Justice Thomas is certainly correct that the compromise that led to the First Amendment was joined by members of Congress who wanted to ensure that the federal government could not control state religious establishments and that states were left free to regulate religion as they thought best. This, though, is hardly unique to the religion clauses of the First Amendment, and certainly not to the Establishment Clause. The same could be said of all of the provisions of the Bill of Rights. States were left free to have jury trials or not, to conduct unreasonable searches and seizures, to impose cruel and unusual punishments, etc. Still, one might argue that while the entire Bill of Rights is implicitly a restriction only on the federal government, the First Amendment is expressly limited to "Congress shall make no law." Yet, this proves too much; the same logic would mean that free speech, assembly, and petitioning could be controlled by the states. Similarly, while the Establishment Clause was adopted with a specific intent of permitting states to continue to regulate in this area, the same was true in the area of speech; for example, libel and sedition were regulated by the states, and the Founders understood that state regulation in this area would continue. Even more to the point, while Madison sought to impose a federal constitutional requirement on the states to protect liberty of conscience, that provision was rejected on federalist grounds. While the Free Exercise clause bound the federal government, Congress intended equally that states be permitted to regulate free exercise as they saw fit. Thus, the federalist argument against incorporation of the Establishment Clause applies with equal force to the Free Exercise Clause, a result that Justice Thomas rightly eschews.[10]

Second, the real essence of Thomas's and Amar's argument is that *all* that the First Amendment was intended to do was to keep the federal government from controlling state establishments. That is, it is entirely jurisdictional; thus, to apply it as a substantive restraint on church/state cooperation in the states, the argument goes, is ahistorical. As Amar characterizes the issue, the First Amendment was "utterly agnostic" on the substantive question of establishment. If true, the same "nonsubstantive" interpretation would apply to the federal government.[11]

On its face, this view is inconsistent with the amendment's terms and is too pinched a view of the history of the First Amendment. The amendment did have an important jurisdictional element, but it also created rights against federal action in the area of church/state relations. Congress was not only told to leave the states alone to establish or disestablish as they wished, but it was also told that it could not pass federal laws relating to establishment—that is, it could not create an establishment, for example in the military, the territories, the District of Columbia, by treaty, in dealing with Native Americans, for the legislative and executive branches, or through the use of the "necessary and proper" clause—something that especially concerned Madison and many antifederalists. Thus, while some commentators point to Jefferson's alleged funding of Indian missions in the Northwest Territory as evidence that he did not believe in a strict separation of church and state, an issue discussed further below, this is an obvious example of substantive application of the Establishment Clause beyond mere states' rights—Congress cannot establish a religion for Native Americans or in the territories.[12]

The debates over the text of the amendment would have been meaningless if all that it was intended to do was to leave the matter to the states. Certainly Madison's description of the provision during the debate was substantive: "Congress should not establish a religion, and enforce the legal observation of it by law, nor compel men to worship God in any manner contrary to their conscience." It is true that Madison had originally urged, when ratification of the Constitution was in doubt, that no amendment was needed because the federal government wholly lacked authority in this area, and this position is sometimes cited to support the "no substance" view. However, Madison abandoned that position (under pressure from Jefferson and evangelical constituents not to mention his own reflection) and after ratification wholeheartedly supported amendments, noting in the debates that the argument that the government lacked authority could not be relied upon in part because the "necessary and proper" clause might be found to expand federal authority into the area of religion. The antifederalists demanding amendments did so precisely because they rejected the "no authority" argument. Certainly a "no substance" provision might have been adopted; for example, Pennsylvania proposed just such a limited religious liberty amendment—"neither the legislative, executive nor judicial powers of the United States shall have authority to alter, abrogate, or infringe any part of the constitution of the several states, which provide for the preservation of liberty in matters of religion"—but that approach was not adopted.[13]

Neither Jefferson nor Madison, nor their supporters, nor the states and antifederalists demanding constitutional protection for religious liberty could have embraced the amendment if it included no substantive constraint on the federal government. The complaint of "Centinel II" during the ratification debates is indicative: "[T]here is no declaration [in the Constitution], . . . that no man ought, or of right can be compelled to attend any religious worship, or erect or support any place of worship, or maintain any ministry, contrary to, or against his own free will and consent." While federalism concerns were central to the First Amendment compromise, the better understanding of those concerns is that the amendment was a very strict substantive provision applicable only to the federal government.[14]

Akhil Amar seeks to buttress his argument by urging that there was a parallel in the construction of the amendment that supports the view that it was indifferent to establishments: "The establishment clause did more than prohibit Congress from establishing a national church. Its mandate . . . also prohibited the national legislature from interfering with, or trying to *dis*-establish, churches established by state and local governments." Others make the same symmetry argument: Kurt Lash explains that under the Establishment Clause, the "federal government could neither establish religion at the federal level, nor *disestablish* religion in the states. The Clause made no statement regarding the merits of religious establishments as such." Thus, for nonincorporationists, "[u]nder the federal Establishment Clause, religious establishments were neither good nor bad—they were simply a matter left to the states."[15]

Not only is this argument inconsistent with the broad and heated demands for a Bill of Rights protecting religious liberty, but it is based upon a false pretense of balance. After all, the federal government was prohibited not only from disestablishing state religions, but it was also prohibited from establishing religions in the states; with respect to the states, there is a parallel and a balance. For federal authority, the clause was not balanced at all. With no federal establishment in existence, the federal government was specifically and forcefully prohibited from creating one. Contrary to the argument that the First Amendment is neutral on the merits of establishments, it speaks emphatically to reject a federal establishment.

Third, Justice Thomas argues in *Zelman* (2002) that the Establishment Clause "protected States, and by extension their citizens," from federal establishment, implying that citizens received no rights from the Establishment Clause directly that might be incorporated into the Fourteenth Amendment. Assuming for the sake of argument that the Fourteenth Amendment can incorporate only personal rights, the historic understanding of the Establishment Clause by those insisting upon its necessity was that it did create individual rights. Protecting individuals from government establishment was at the heart of what dissenters had sought in Virginia, and they and their allies, not to mention the antifederalists, sought similar protections against the federal government. Certainly Jefferson saw the Establishment Clause as creating personal liberty. Any establishment would "compel a man to furnish contributions of money for the propagation of opinions which he disbelieves, . . . that to suffer the civil magistrate to intrude his powers into the field of opinion . . . is a dangerous fallacy, which at once destroys all religious liberty." As he made clear in his Letter to the Danbury Baptists, prohibiting an establishment was part of protecting personal "rights of conscience."[16]

This understanding was not limited to Jefferson, and the drive for a religion clause in a Bill of Rights was quintessentially about protecting people's rights from the federal government, not only states' rights. William Tennent, the famous eighteenth-century Presbyterian minister, insisted that "all religious establishments . . . *are an infringement of religious liberty* . . . [and] interfere with the rights of private judgment and conscience." Justice Brennan, concurring in *Abington* (1963), explained the "fallacy" in the argument that the Establishment Clause does not guarantee individual liberty: "[I]t underestimates the role of the Establishment Clause as co-guarantor, with the Free Exercise Clause, of religious liberty. . . . The Free Exercise Clause 'was not the full extent of the Amendment's guarantee of freedom from governmental intrusion in matters of faith.'" Even those who wanted to restrict the reach of the First Amendment in order to protect states' rights did not oppose a substantive provision protecting individual freedom applied to the federal government.[17]

A number of other arguments are sometimes made to buttress the non-incorporation position. For example, it is urged that during debates over the Fourteenth Amendment, some members of Congress mentioned the other, political rights of the First Amendment, but not the Establishment Clause. True enough, but other members specifically mentioned the religion clauses. John Bingham (Republican), the author of the first clause of the Fourteenth Amendment, read the entirety of the first eight amendments of the Bill of Rights into the record. After adoption, Senator Thomas Norwood (Democrat) also said that the religion clauses were included. Other members noted that the South's use of state-supported religion to perpetuate slavery gave more than adequate justification for incorporation of these clauses; in an 1864 speech, Senator (and future Vice President) Henry Wilson read the First Amendment into the record and said "southern states had trampled on these 'great rights,' which were 'essential to liberty.'"[18]

A similar argument is made that the Fourteenth Amendment could not have intended to incorporate the Establishment Clause because the clause's specific language was repeated in the Blaine Amendment (barring use of government funds by sectarian schools), which fell just short of the requisite two-thirds congressional majority for its submission to the states; if the Fourteenth Amendment (1868) incorporated the Establishment Clause, the argument goes, there would have been no reason to repeat it in the Blaine Amendment (1875). This, though, is to prove too much, and on a thin reed of inaction. After all, the Blaine Amendment also repeated the Free Exercise Clause, incorporation of which is generally conceded. Moreover, since the Blaine Amendment was introduced after the *Slaughter-House Cases* (1873), it would make sense to seek to clarify the application of the Establishment Clause to the states. Senator Morton urged just this point. Interestingly, at least one senator opposed Blaine because, he concluded, states already could not "pass any law respecting religion or prohibiting the free exercise thereof."[19]

Several other observations on incorporation are in order. First, objections based upon early understandings of federalism must be taken with considerable caution. The fact is that not only were the southern states that sought to protect slavery behind a veneer of states' rights thoroughly beaten in a devastating war, but that loss had institutional implications that, in an organic manner, changed the Constitution in terms of federal relations. The postwar amendments were understood, at least in some manner, to alter the previous balance in state/federal power in the area of citizens' rights. (It is ironic that those who most vehemently insist that the Civil War was about states' rights are often the most unwilling to concede that the South's loss resulted in a structural change in, and limitation to, those states' rights.) Thus, Justice Thomas's argument that states in the early republic had constitutional authority to mix church and state and support religion is largely irrelevant. Early nineteenth-century notions of states' rights, at least in their full breadth, were swept away at Appomattox. The post–Civil War amendments were precisely about making the states protect rights that they had previously legally refused to protect based on the shield of federalism. Thus, it is incorporation that demanded integration of education in *Brown v. Board of Education* in the face of "massive resistance" by the states. An imposition on state sovereignty? A violation of the federalism intended by the Founders? Of course, but equally a reasonable (indeed, overdue) outcome from the Civil War amendments.

Second, to transpose a twentieth-century issue into eighteenth-century terms, in the abstract one might argue that Jefferson and a mature Madison would have opposed the dramatic growth in federal power over the states resulting from incorporation. The "Revolution of 1800" by which Jefferson became president and his Democratic-Republican Party assumed dominance in Congress can be described as an effort to circumscribe federal power and to ensure a dominant role for states in domestic matters. Yet, neither Jefferson nor Madison could possibly have anticipated the incorporation debate in the aftermath of a cataclysmic Civil War brought on by the unwillingness of some states to protect individual liberties and the demands of other states that the federal government take a more active role. Nor could they have anticipated what members of the Court have called in this context a "pervasive public sector." Simply to transpose the question to the eighteenth century is a largely vacuous exercise.[20]

Moreover, while Jefferson and Madison generally advocated limitation on the federal authority to control the states, in this important area, they both would have welcomed expansion of religious freedoms. Madison initially sought a provision in the Bill of Rights that would have required the states to protect "rights of conscience," and was deeply disturbed when the more conservative Senate deleted that provision. Later, Madison expressly urged the states to incorporate the protections of the Virginia Statute into their own law. After all, as the Statute makes clear, Jefferson and Madison saw these rights as "the natural rights of mankind," rights with which governments (state or federal) were simply incompetent to interfere. Thus, while Jefferson's 1808 letter to the Reverend Samuel Miller notes that "no power to prescribe any religious exercise, or to assume authority in religious discipline, has been delegated to the general [federal] government. It must then rest with the states," he goes on to qualify that statement by noting "as far as it can be in any human authority." For Jefferson and Madison, states cannot, properly, violate natural rights regardless of whether or not the First Amendment is incorporated in the Fourteenth.[21]

Third, nor can one object too strongly on Jeffersonian grounds to the fact that the judiciary has led the way in incorporation and expansion of religious freedom. Jefferson, while certainly concerned about judicial overstepping, specifically urged the importance of a bill of rights on Madison in part by noting that it would provide the courts with the authority to police the legislative and executive branches to protect the rights of the people. Madison, having warned Jefferson that "the invasion of private rights is *chiefly* to be apprehended, not from acts of Government contrary to the sense of its constituents, but from acts in which the Government is the mere instrument of the major number of the constituents," welcomed the role of the judiciary in policing the tyranny of the majority against the minority's rights of conscience.[22]

Fourth, one should be wary of claims from a particular political perspective calling for serious limits on the doctrine of incorporation. The doctrine provides expansive protection to a broad set of rights for all citizens. Thus, some of those who complain bitterly about Supreme Court decisions defining the scope of the religion clauses of the First Amendment in light of incorporation fully support the same doctrine when, for example, it comes to application of the Second Amendment's protections for gun ownership against state and municipal restrictions. Surely if the Fourteenth Amendment is intended to protect citizens' rights to keep and bear arms against overly intrusive state practices, then it equally can be found to protect citizens' rights to a separation of church and state.[23]

This leaves an important caveat to the entire modern "incorporation" debate: Justice Thomas has called for a far-reaching and long overdue reconsideration of the meaning of the Fourteenth Amendment, not just in religion clause cases, but in incorporation of the Bill of Rights generally. For example, in *McDonald v. City of Chicago* (2010), Thomas wrote that the Court's practice of incorporating rights through the Fourteenth Amendment's Due Process Clause is a "legal fiction" brought about by "this Court's marginalization of the [Privileges and Immunities] Clause" in the *Slaughter-House Cases* (1873). In Thomas's view, rather than simply incorporating ill-defined fundamental rights under the stretched rubric of "due process," the Court should seek to identify the "privileges and immunities" of the citizens of the United States. Such an approach makes eminent sense, and the Court should take up Justice Thomas's well-founded challenge. Still, a fair review of the "privileges and immunities" of citizens would include a robust understanding, a Jeffersonian understanding, of religious freedom.[24]

In any case, the issue of incorporation should not distract from the fundamental question of the meaning of the First Amendment. Even if the First Amendment did not apply to the states, that would not change the fact that it applies to the federal government, a government of dramatically expanded scope and powers. Moreover, even with respect to the states, many adopted a Jeffersonian vision of religious liberty in the nineteenth century; thus, the Statute and Jefferson should inform application of their state constitutional protections as well, many of which arguably provide for an even stricter separation of church and state than the First Amendment.

Challenges to a Jeffersonian Vision

After incorporation of the First Amendment's religion clauses into the Fourteenth Amendment in the mid-twentieth century, there was remarkably broad agreement on the Supreme Court and among academics that the understanding of those provisions should be based upon the robust Jeffersonian vision and the Virginia Experience. In *Everson* (1947), for example, the majority wrote that:

> The "establishment of religion" clause of the *First Amendment* means at least this: Neither a state nor the Federal Government can set up a church. Neither can pass laws which aid one religion, aid all religions, or prefer one religion over another. . . . No tax in any amount, large or small, can be levied to support any religious activities or institutions, whatever they may be called, or whatever form they may adopt to teach or practice religion.

What is notable is that the dissent was even more adamant. The First Amendment "was to create a complete and permanent separation of the spheres of religious activity and civil authority." The near unanimity on the centrality of the Jeffersonian vision was maintained in *McCollum* (1948) (8–1 striking down release time for religious study: the wall "must be kept high and impregnable") and into the far more controversial decisions of *Engel v. Vitale* (1962) (6–1 striking down official school prayer: First Amendment's "first and most immediate purpose rested on the belief that a union of government and religion tends to destroy government and to degrade religion") and *Abington* (1963) (8–1 striking official school Bible reading: quoting *Everson* dissent "the object . . . was to create a complete and permanent separation of the spheres of religious activity and civil authority by comprehensively forbidding every form of public aid or support for religion").[25]

Yet, in the period from the mid-1950s through the 1970s, the broad consensus for separation of church and state, particularly among evangelicals, began to unravel. The reasons are myriad. Some date the change to the forced integration of schools after *Brown v. Board of Education* (1954). With many seeking desperately to maintain segregation, a profusion of private "Christian" schools were founded; as a result, prohibiting government funding of private sectarian education became far less compelling to some evangelicals, and they defected "from the separationist coalition." Thus, "[b]y the late 1970s, [Jerry] Falwell and other leaders of the religious right began to flip on church-state separation; where they once had argued that financial aid to religious schools violated the Establishment Clause, they now clamored for increased government assistance." At the same time, John F. Kennedy's election seriously eroded the apparent virulence of the "Catholic threat" that had been a part of Protestant opposition to funding of sectarian schools and support for separation of church and state since the nineteenth century.[26]

Sarah Barringer Gordon, on the other hand, dates the demise of the Enlightenment/evangelical alliance in favor of a strict separation of church and state to the school prayer and Bible-reading cases of the early 1960s. The implications of a strict separation in a world with an increasingly pervasive public sector and in which the First Amendment's provisions would apply directly to the states appeared to threaten serious decline of civil religion for many Christians. *Roe v. Wade* (1973) also dramatically increased the apparent threat of government secularism for some. Others suggest that the growth of fundamentalism in society played a part.[27]

Likely all of these factors had some influence. What was clear, though, was that the virtual consensus among academics and evangelical Protestants for a strict separation between church and state on Jeffersonian principles began to crack.

Critics quickly recognized that the Jeffersonian understanding of religious liberty and reliance on the Virginia Experience was part of the problem. If a more accommodationist view of disestablishment was adopted, incorporation would not pose such a problem and the federal government would be free to assist religion so long as it did not act in an overtly sectarian manner. Thus, as many evangelicals abandoned the Jeffersonian vision, a growing discordant note from some Supreme Court justices and historians questioned whether our historic understanding of the First Amendment should be based upon the vision evident in the Statute, the Letter to the Danbury Baptists, and Madison's Memorial & Remonstrance. Former Chief Justice Rehnquist led this effort at revision, and his objections were joined, for example, by former president Ronald Reagan; his education secretary, William Bennett; and the newspaper columnists George Will and James Kirkpatrick, not to mention a number of historians.[28]

The fundamental historic objection to reliance on Jefferson and Madison is that their views were not representative of the Founders, that establishments and test oaths were the norm, and that Virginia was the outlier. Daniel Dreisbach writes that Jefferson's and Madison's "views on church-state relations are among the least representative of the founders." At best, the critics argue, the First Amendment was a compromise between the view of the Enlightenment rationalists seeking separation between church and state and proto-accommodationists.[29]

These objections miss the mark. As previously shown, the First Amendment "compromise" was between those who wanted to prevent the federal government from interfering with state establishments, but were more than happy to restrict federal authority severely, those who wanted to keep a distant federal government out of peoples' lives, and supporters of Jefferson and Madison who wanted to prevent government interference in religion (sometimes overlapping groups). The result was not a weak provision with a hobbled separation of church and state but a very strong Jeffersonian provision, limited in its jurisdiction to the federal government. No other compromise was practical. As is often the case in politics, the result was that each group got what it most needed while not interfering in the others' fundamental goals.

The focus on Jefferson and Madison as outliers also ignores the fact that a broad group of early evangelicals were as adamant as Jefferson in their search for separation of church and state. Moreover, even if Jefferson and Madison might be characterized as outliers on religious liberty in 1789, their vision of religious freedom became increasingly paradigmatic for America as the eighteenth century concluded and the nineteenth began. As the Court in *Abington* noted, Jefferson's and Madison's views were adopted in state constitutions. Rehnquist attacked this conclusion as "demonstrably incorrect" because state establishments and test oaths existed in 1791 when the First Amendment was adopted, but that misses the point. While the states were free to treat religion as they thought best in 1791 (although many were already moving in a Jeffersonian direction), Jefferson's and Madison's vision of religious liberty was a bellwether upon which the citizens and states increasingly relied as they rejected establishments and test oaths and adopted state constitutional reforms reflecting that vision. By the time of the Fourteenth Amendment, the Jeffersonian vision was the essence of American religious freedom.[30]

Justice Rehnquist also insisted that nothing in the debates surrounding adoption of the First Amendment suggested that the government was to be neutral vis-à-vis religion and irreligion; rather, he concludes that the concern was only with discrimination among religions, that is, preferentialism. In a similar vein, Robert Cord argues that Madison only advocated that government could not prefer one sect over another, citing various paragraphs from the Memorial & Remonstrance that sound against discrimination in the area of religion. Justice Thomas joined this argument in *Rosenberger* (1995). As noted earlier, this view is clearly inconsistent with the foundational Virginia experience. As the *Everson* dissent explained, "Madison's entire thesis, as reflected throughout the Remonstrance and in his other writings, as well as in his opposition to the final form of the Assessment Bill, . . . was altogether incompatible with acceptance of general and 'nondiscriminatory' support." Similarly, Jefferson wrote that his goal in disestablishment was "for discontinuing the establishment of the English church by law, taking away all privilege & pre-eminence of one religious sect over another," but he goes on to say "& totally and eternally restraining the civil magistrate from all pretensions of interposing his authority or exercise in matters of religion." The eighteenth-century evangelicals who were politically essential to the defeat of the general assessment and adoption of the Virginia Statute had equally broad notions of religious liberty.[31]

Setting aside the history of the Virginia general assessment and adoption of the Statute for Establishing Religious Freedom, Rehnquist simply ignored in-convenient facts. While engaging in what appears to be an exhaustive recitation of legislative debates on the First Amendment, Rehnquist omitted the fact that the Senate considered and rejected proposals that the Bill of Rights only pro-hibit Congress from supporting "One Religious Sect or Society in preference to others." Rehnquist ignored the relevant statements in Cooley's constitutional treatise. Rehnquist also relied on an early version of Webster's dictionary in an effort to justify a relatively narrow definition of "establishment" that, he argued, limits the First Amendment provision to particular preference for one sect or denomination, but ignored Madison's definition of establishment in the Me-morial & Remonstrance and the dissenters' in their petitions that make clear that an establishment entails not just a preference for one or several sects, but for religion generally. In fact, Oliver Ellsworth, a member of the Philadelphia Convention, important scribe in support of ratification, and the head of the Senate's conference committee on the First Amendment who penned the ac-tual words, included within the term "establishment" even a test oath, banned by Article VI.[32]

The preferentialist argument of Justices Rehnquist and Thomas and a group of academics also suffers from definitional and practical problems, par-ticularly given the reality of modern America. To some extent the preferen-tialist argument responds to the idea that the Court is protecting irreligion (favoring irreligion to religion), something that they view as an anathema and that would raise serious constitutional problems. This is arguably an issue of definition. Arlin Adams and Charles Emmerich rightly note that "the Court's use of nonreligion is more properly understood as connoting the right of an individual to believe or not to believe in religious matters."[33]

On a practical level, even in 1789, a true preferentialist position would have been untenable in implementation. Madison made that point in his Detached Memoranda:

> The idea also of a union of all [sects] who form one nation under one Gov-ernment in acts of devotion to the God of all is an imposing idea. But reason and the principles of the Christian religion require that if all the individuals composing a nation were of the same precise creed and wished to unite in a uni-versal act of religion at the same time, the union ought to be effected thro' the intervention of their religious not of their political representatives. In a nation composed of various sects, some alienated widely from others, and where no

agreement could take place thro' the former [their religious representatives], the interposition of the latter [political representatives] is doubly wrong.

Historic change heightens the power of those conclusions. While preferential-ism might have seemed practical in defined regions in the eighteenth century when several states nominally adopted that model for a period of time, today it would be wholly impractical for legislators or jurists to seek to limit any gov-ernment support to "all religions." One need look no further than Pat Robert-son's indignant complaint that government money might go to the Church of Scientology or the Unification Church. How much more politically problem-atic support for Hinduism, Tao, Buddhism, or Wicca? As the Court said in *Torcaso* (1961), a government could not prefer "those religions based on a belief in the existence of God as against those religions founded on different beliefs." Today, "with more than two hundred sects in the United States, over eighty of them having more than fifty thousand members each, it is not easy to envisage a strictly nonsectarian exercise. One man's piety is another's idolatry."[34]

While some have attempted to limit the preferentialist argument to Chris-tian religions or monotheism, such arguments have even less textual or his-toric support and are even more problematic in our modern society in which nonmonotheists, not to mention atheists and agnostics, play an increasing role. Even government decisions on what are "Christian" sects would be problem-atic, as recent events demonstrate. Historically, Madison's and Jefferson's evan-gelical supporters rejected just such an approach in Virginia.[35]

Beyond the allegation that Jefferson and Madison were outliers or that the First Amendment was intended only to prohibit preferentialism, a third objec-tion to the conventional history is that Jefferson and Madison may not have re-ally intended a strict separation of church and state, at least as it has come to be understood. The argument that Madison had abandoned a strict separationist view in 1789 (apparently to readopt it later in life) was addressed earlier. Yet, any number of actions taken by Jefferson and Madison are raised in an effort to demonstrate the point: Jefferson attended church services in the House of Representatives; Madison issued calls for thanksgiving and prayer while presi-dent; a Jeffersonian treaty provided for ministers on Indian reservations; Madi-son was on the committee that approved legislative chaplains, etc. Thus, the argument goes, even if a Jeffersonian vision is central to our legacy of religious liberty, modern Court decisions have turned the vision into a mirage.[36]

Here, the critics arguably hit closer to the mark. Jefferson wanted a secular government but never sought a secular society nor expected public officials to have a purely secular life. "Our problem," Paul Kauper explains, "is that we constantly fail to differentiate between secularlism as a term that describes the essentially secular character of our culture and its institutions, such as government and law, and secularism as a philosophy that rests on the notion that any belief in God is irrelevant to life and that man can by his own efforts achieve his own salvation or at least that he must be content to operate wholly within the framework of his own aspirations and resources." Efforts to co-opt Jefferson's separationism to demand a wholly secular polity are ill-founded, but courts and commentators have on occasion reached that extreme.[37]

Before considering Jefferson's and Madison's actions that suggest a more nuanced understanding of what separation of church and state requires, one might start by asking what is the significance of some political actions that are arguably inconsistent with clearly stated principles. Should the Founders be held to a greater than human standard or their principles rejected? Madison, for example, sat on the committee that approved a congressional chaplain, but he was later emphatic that Congress's decision to pay for chaplains was a violation of the First Amendment. He expressly cautioned against making much of this "exception" and apparent inconsistency:

> Rather than let this step beyond the landmarks of power have the effect of a legitimate precedent, it will be better to apply to it the legal aphorism, *de minimis non curate lex* [the law does not concern itself with trifles]: or to class it *"cum maculis quas aut incuria fudit, aut humana parum cavit natura"* [faults proceeding either from negligence or from the imperfection of our nature].

Madison's admonition on minor exceptions is sometimes misapplied to suggest that minor breaches of the wall of separation should simply be ignored. Madison's point was exactly the opposite: While some political deviations from principle are inevitable, these should not become precedent for future violations.[38]

Others have made similar points. The historian Thomas Curry observes that bills 83–86 of the Virginia statutory revisal can be seen in this light: "Congress, after all, sometimes breaches the limits of the Constitution." "[L]egislators sometimes vote for measures that they could be fairly certain would be declared unconstitutional, and that may not even represent their own views about how the Constitution should be interpreted." As Justice Souter explained:

[I]ndividual Acts of Congress, especially when they are few and far between, scarcely serve as an authoritative guide to the meaning of the Religion Clauses, for "like other politicians [members of the early Congresses] could raise constitutional ideals one day and turn their backs on them the next. . . . [T]en years after proposing the First Amendment, Congress passed the Alien and Sedition Acts, measures patently unconstitutional by modern standards."

For example, while Jefferson successfully ensured that the University of Virginia would not be a religious school and that attendance at religious worship would not be mandatory, he was forced, as a compromise, to suggest that ministers might hold services on campus or build sectarian schools there. As Curry states, "that Americans during the revolutionary period did not always carry their principles into practice either in Church-State or other matters did not negate those principles." While interpretations of the Founders that are inconsistent with pervasive or major exceptions should be seriously questioned, some flexibility in analysis is needed.[39]

In a similar vein, Daniel Dreisbach argues that Madison abandoned Jefferson's "wall of separation" for a less "rigid" and "more subtle" line of separation. Dreisbach is referring to Madison's admonition to Jasper Adams that "it may not be easy, in every possible case, to trace the line of separation between the rights of religion and Civil authority." Sydney Mead also suggests that Madison's "line"—a point that is "constantly moving, and even zig-zagging"—is "more accurate terminology" than Jefferson's "wall," which "conjures up the image of something quite tangible and solid." This close reading is perhaps more than the terms can bear. That Jefferson, the quintessential architect, should use a three-dimensional metaphor while Madison, the consummate careful draftsman, should use a two-dimensional metaphor, is thin gruel on which to seek to undermine the latter's commitment to Jeffersonian separation of church and state. Michael Myerson makes a more subtle and reasonable argument when he notes that Madison's "line" was delineating "religion and Civil authority" rather than a more particular delineation of church and state. Whatever metaphor one chooses, both Jefferson and Madison certainly believed that government had no business supporting religion and wanted institutional religion not to interfere in government.[40]

A parallel argument seeking to temper Jefferson's views is that his Letter to the Danbury Baptists insisting upon a "wall of separation between church and state" was merely a "short note of courtesy," a political missive issued in a fit of pique against New England federalist ministers who had opposed Jefferson's election of no constitutional significance. As noted in chapter 1, though, this attempt at revisionism by James Hutson mischaracterizes both the letter and Jefferson's dedication to the principle. That the 1802 letter was edited in an effort to minimize unnecessary political turbulence in New England, as Hutson shows, is hardly proof that Jefferson, in the part of the letter that was retained, was not making a solid and deeply felt point of principle, a fact that he noted expressly in the contemporaneous letter to his attorney general, Levi Lincoln. The effort to dismiss the letter as irrelevant is also belied by the letter's propagation and use in the nineteenth century. As the unanimous Court stated in 1879: "Coming as [it] does from an acknowledged leader of the advocates of the measure, it may be accepted almost as an authoritative declaration of the scope and effect of the amendment thus secured."[41]

In the end, the historical arguments for reliance on the Statute and a Jeffersonian vision of religious freedom are strong. Difficulty remains, however, in applying that vision to complex problems in the twenty-first century. In fact, various actions of Jefferson and Madison support the point that modern secularists can seek to go beyond the Jeffersonian vision in purging the public (private) landscape of religious idiom. Objections to a Jeffersonian vision have been precipitated, in part, by the false dichotomy that has been created between a strict separation of church and state and the practices of a religious people. Both Jefferson and Madison recognized that their vision of religious liberty would not, indeed should not, interfere with a vibrant religion in the public square.

Jefferson in Practice: A Neighborly Wall

Recognizing Jefferson's central role in the development of American religious freedom does not mean that modern questions about complex issues can be easily resolved. While Jefferson was certainly a strong advocate of a strict separation between church and state, he would have rejected the idea of a dichotomy between a wholly secular country and a formally "Christian nation." He worked assiduously to prevent religion from interfering in governmental affairs and government from interfering in religion, but he welcomed the role of a vibrant (for him, rational) religion in the polity. In fact, some of the objections to reliance on a Jeffersonian vision may originate in a misunderstanding concerning his perspective. Analysis of that perspective requires not only careful review of the principles that Jefferson and Madison espoused, but some consideration of how they applied those principles in difficult circumstances.

Proclamations/Public Prayer

In 1774, Jefferson, as a member of the Virginia House of Burgesses, was famously involved in drafting a proclamation for a day of fasting and prayer in support of the people of Massachusetts suffering from the British Coercive Acts issued in response to the Boston Tea Party. Commentators sometimes point to this incident as evidence that Jefferson supported government prayer proclamations or, more broadly, did not support strict separation. Moreover, in both of his inaugural addresses, Jefferson made a religious invocation and offered a prayer. Yet, there is little question that a mature Jefferson opposed government religious proclamations. To understand his views, these facts must be reconciled.[42]

Defending his decision to flout tradition and to refuse to issue religious proclamations as president,[43] Jefferson explained in his Second Inaugural Address:

> In matters of religion I have considered that its free exercise is placed by the constitution independent of the powers of the general government. I have therefore undertaken, on no occasion, to prescribe the religious exercises suited to it; but have left them, as the constitution found them, under the direction and discipline of the church or state authorities acknowledged by the several religious societies.

Jefferson made it clear that this was not merely a matter of federalism. Responding to a request for a proclamation during a period of national strife, he lectured his correspondent:

> This [my refusal to issue proclamations] results not only from the provision that no law shall be made respecting the establishment, or free exercise, of religion, but from that also which reserves to the states the powers not delegated to the U.S. . . . But it is only proposed that I should *recommend*, not prescribe a day of fasting & prayer. That is, that I should *indirectly* assume to the U.S. an authority over religious exercises which the Constitution has directly precluded

them from. It must be meant too that this recommendation is to carry some authority, and to be sanctioned by some penalty on those who disregard it; not indeed of fine and imprisonment, but of some degree of proscription perhaps in public opinion.... I do not believe it is for the interest of religion to invite the civil magistrate to direct it's exercises, it's discipline, or it's doctrines.... Fasting & prayer are religious exercises.... Every religious society has a right to determine for itself the times for these exercises, & the objects proper for them, ... and this right can never be safer than in their own hands, where the constitution has deposited it.

Madison, too, objected to the idea that an official proclamation could be viewed as wholly voluntary: "An *advisory* government is a contradiction in terms." Clearly, for Jefferson, official prayer proclamations violated the law "respecting an establishment" of religion.[44]

Beyond the constitutional restraint, the primary problem with government religious declarations was the fatal effort to gain government endorsement, to infuse religious opinion with government authority, discouraging free inquiry and choice, in essence, "priestcraft." The endorsement was inappropriate whether or not there was a legal penalty; Jefferson was equally concerned with government action resulting in "some degree of proscription perhaps in public opinion." The principle in the preamble to the Statute applied: "[T]he impious presumption of legislators and rulers ... who ... have assumed dominion over the faith of others, setting up their own opinions and modes of thinking as the only true and infallible, and as such endeavoring to impose them on others, hath established false religions over the greater part of the world." Virginia's eighteenth-century evangelicals rejected government actions encouraging religious activity on similar grounds; God desired only a free will offering of the individual and the individual had to be entirely responsible for that decision. Madison made the point expressly: The absence of government endorsement would "attract to the divine altar those freewill offerings of humble supplication, thanksgiving, and praise which alone can be acceptable to Him whom no hypocrisy can deceive and no forced sacrifices propitiate."[45]

Madison, though, also struggled with proclamations. During his administration, Congress asked for prayer proclamations at a time when the country faced the crisis of the War of 1812, a political crisis of confidence was almost overwhelming Madison, and dissolution of the union seemed a real possibility.

Even then, Madison was uneasy with the exercise. In 1813, he acquiesced to one declaration noting that Congress "signified a request" for a day of prayer, but he still moved cautiously, issuing "this my Proclamation, recommending to all, who shall be piously disposed. . . . guided only by their free choice." Later he explained: "I was always careful to make the Proclamations absolutely indiscriminate, and merely recommendatory; or rather mere *designations* of a day, on which all who thought proper might *unite* in consecrating it to religious purposes, according to their own faith & forms." Still, after the crisis passed, Madison regretted having issued even these qualified proclamations, viewing them as exceeding constitutional bounds. Government religious proclamations "seem to imply and certainly nourish the erroneous idea of a *national* religion." In addition to the problem of endorsement, Madison was concerned with the use (abuse) of religion to support political institutions (again, "priestcraft").[46]

Yet, while emphatically eschewing official religious proclamations, both of Jefferson's inaugural addresses invoked divine blessing. On March 4, 1801, he publicly declared that the nation was "enlightened by a benign religion, professed indeed and practised in various forms, yet all of them inculcating honesty, truth, temperance, gratitude and the love of man, acknowledging and adoring an overruling providence, which by all its dispensations proves that it delights in the happiness of man here, and his greater happiness hereafter." He concluded with the hope that the "Infinite Power, which rules the destinies of the universe, lead our councils to what is best, and give them a favorable issue for your peace and prosperity." Interestingly, having characterized Jefferson as the "arch-infidel," federalist newspapers did not know what to make of this language; some simply edited it out, so much the easier to write of the danger Jefferson posed to religion. Yet, four years later, he reminded his listeners that

> I shall need, too, the favor of that Being in whose hands we are, . . . who has covered our infancy with his providence, and our riper years with his wisdom and power; and to whose goodness I ask you to join with me in supplications, that he will so enlighten the minds of your servants, guide their councils, and prosper their measures, that whatsoever they do, shall result in your good, and shall secure to you the peace, friendship, and approbation of all nations.[47]

On this basis, Daniel Dreisbach argues that Jefferson used "rhetoric in official utterances that, in terms of religious content, was virtually indistinguishable" from thanksgiving proclamations. Jefferson obviously did not see it that way, expressly rejecting religious proclamations as unconstitutional and ill-advised. One must distinguish the official proclamations that Jefferson adamantly refused to issue from the acceptable public invocations in his inaugural addresses.[48]

Three factors seem to be important: First, Jefferson's invocations were made at voluntary, ceremonial events, not official or mandatory exercises. No one was required to be present for his invocations nor in the least disadvantaged by not attending. Second, the invocations were made in his individual capacity; he had not officially been assigned to pray, with the commensurate suggestion that the prayer was with the approval of the state, as it would be in the case of an official proclamation. As Madison explained: "In their individual capacities, as distinct from their official station, [officials] . . . might unite in recommendations of any sort whatever; in the same manner as any other individuals might do. But then their recommendations ought to express the true character from which they emanate." Similarly, even while holding office, Jefferson attended church and contributed to many churches in his private capacity. Noting Jefferson's private actions, one early nineteenth-century supporter advised those seeking greater public support for religion that denominations "will find their only safety in perfect religious freedom, in the government's not interposing at all in religious matters, but in its *letting those matters alone*. . . . And they ought to bless God for the illustrious example which Mr. Jefferson is setting on this subject, in disclaiming a right to intermeddle with religion *in his capacity as chief magistrate*." Third, as a corollary, no one was being told to pray or even officially called to prayer; there is no semblance of "assum[ing] authority in religious discipline." As Jefferson said, no one was being "prescribe[d]" to pray. Certainly, there was no suggestion of a "proscription perhaps in public opinion" against those who declined to pray.[49]

A fourth factor worth noting is that when Jefferson did invoke religious language in public, as with Washington and Madison, he always used the broadest possible language and never used language that would limit the scope of prayer to Christians. Of course, Jefferson would be the first to agree that an official making a private prayer, even if in public, can pray as he or she thinks best; the point is that Jefferson realized that sectarian prayer by the chief executive, even a broadly Christian prayer, would tend to divide the American people and was ill-advised.

Madison also likely spoke for Jefferson when he noted that public, official calls to prayer were subject to easy and gross abuse: "[T]he last and not the least objection is the liability of the practice to the subserviency to political views; to the scandal of religion, as well as the increase of party animosities." The Court in *Engel* (1962) properly quoted Madison's Memorial & Remonstrance in concluding that for the Founders "religion is too personal, too sacred, too holy, to permit its 'unhallowed perversion' by a civil magistrate."[50]

Jefferson would have viewed as an object lesson Alexander Hamilton's express support of the use of religious proclamations for political purposes. In a cabinet dispute with Edmund Randolph, Washington's attorney general, over the content of a proclamation, Hamilton dismissed Randolph's plea that "this proclamation ought to savour as much as possible of religion; and not too much of having a political object." Hamilton insisted that "a proclamation by a Government which is a national act, naturally embraces objects which are political." Here, Jefferson would have agreed with Hamilton, but this use of religion for political purposes would serve only to confirm Jefferson's objections to such proclamations on both legal and policy grounds. Thus, for Jefferson, public prayer by an official was not prohibited, but official prayer was both prohibited and a dangerous tool.[51]

What then of Jefferson's 1774 call for a day of fasting and prayer? Or of the inclusion of a statute permitting thanksgiving proclamations in the proposed revisal of Virginia's colonial laws? Of course, neither the Statute nor the First Amendment applied in 1774 or 1779, nor had Jefferson's religious views fully matured. Moreover, Jefferson later suggested that the 1774 proclamation was "cooked up" as a way to unite the people of Virginia in the Revolutionary cause, hardly an endorsement of the appropriateness of government religious practice. Similarly, while the proposed revisal of Virginia's colonial laws that Jefferson helped to craft provided the governor authority to proclaim days of fasting and thanksgiving, it was intended to liberalize and conform colonial laws and was, in any case, the product of a committee. Neither can be seen as defining Jefferson's mature, clearly expressed position.[52]

University of Virginia and Public Spaces

Perhaps the best means to understand Jefferson's views on the role of religion in government institutions or on government property is to consider his treatment of religion at his beloved creation, the University of Virginia (UVA)—

itself a Jeffersonian monument to freedom of the mind. The particular concern that Jefferson paid to all aspects of UVA is evident in the fact that it is listed as one of the three accomplishments that Jefferson asked to be recorded on a memorial. It is a fitting canvas on which to read Jefferson's views.

In the early nineteenth century, educational institutions were almost universally associated with some religious denomination, and UVA was only the second truly state-created college (after the University of North Carolina—a point of pride for UNC). Given its public character, Jefferson fought strenuously to keep religion out of UVA, particularly opposing the appointment of any professor of divinity. For Jefferson, this was an easy matter: To use state funds to pay a professor who would be teaching religious doctrines would create an ostensibly state-approved minister and religion; it was priestcraft. A professor of ethics would be responsible for teaching religion as an academic matter, included as part of Hebrew, Greek, Latin, history, moral philosophy, and ethics.[53]

This position was heavily criticized at the time, but Jefferson was adamant. Yet, criticism grew as opponents argued that the effect of Jefferson's plan would be not just to prevent any state-sponsored religious teachings but to deny students access to religious exercises. Jefferson wrote to Dr. Thomas Cooper, a deist whose selection as a professor for UVA had created a firestorm of criticism (a firestorm that ultimately prevented Cooper from taking the position), that the claim was being made that UVA was not simply an institution with no religion, "but against all religion." (In modern terms, Jefferson faced a claim that his "neutrality," de facto, amounted to "hostility.") The problem was serious, and opposition was contributing to delays in opening the school. Some compromise was necessary; Jefferson wrote in 1822 that "[o]ccasion was taken at the last meeting of the Visitors, to bring forward an idea that might silence this calumny, which weighed on the minds of some honest friends to the institution." Jefferson reluctantly accepted a proposal to permit private religious schools on university grounds, explaining to a state board:

> It was not, however, to be understood that instruction in religious opinion and duties was meant to be precluded by the public authorities, as indifferent to the interests of society. . . . But it was thought that this want, and the entrustment to each society of instruction in its own doctrine, were evils of less danger than a permission to the public authorities to dictate modes or principles of

religious instruction, or than opportunities furnished them by giving countenance or ascendancy to any one sect over another. . . . It has, therefore, been in
contemplation, and suggested by some pious individuals, . . . to establish their
religious schools on the confines of the University, . . . enabling the students of
the University to attend religious exercises with the professor of their particular sect, either in the rooms of the building still to be erected, and destined to
that purpose under impartial regulation, . . . or in the lecturing room of such
professor. . . . But always understanding that these schools shall be independent
of the University.

Jefferson concluded that "such an arrangement would complete the circle of
useful sciences embraced by this institution, and would fill the chasm now
existing, on principles which would leave inviolate the constitutional freedom
of religion, the most unalienable and sacred of all human rights." Thus, Jefferson, albeit somewhat reluctantly, endorsed nondiscriminatory, "impartial"
access of religious bodies (and others) to public facilities when private facilities
were lacking and public facilities were not otherwise in use.[54]

The story does not end there, though. It appears that Jefferson hoped that
the legislature would not require this accommodation; the minutes of the board
note that "the idea will be relinquished on any surmise of disapprobation which
they [legislators] might think proper to express." Having won the battle not to
fund a public minister, Jefferson, somewhat grudgingly, accepted the political
necessity of this compromise for neutral use of public facilities hoping that it
would not be necessary. He recognized that political reality meant that "we cannot always do what is absolutely best."[55]

The scope of Jefferson's compromise was limited, and having been forced
to make the compromise, Jefferson tried to further limit its application. For
example, he initially recognized that denominations might locate their schools
on grounds and that "it is supposed probable, that a building . . . may be called
for in time, in which may be rooms for religious worship, under such impartial regulations as the Visitors shall prescribe, for public examinations, . . . and
other associated purposes." Yet, when the legislature failed specifically to sanction the use of a room for public activities including worship, as likely through
oversight as intention, he declined a request to have a sermon preached at the
university. Jefferson was emphatic, while the Rockfish report recognized "that
a building larger than the Pavilions might be called for in time, in which might

be rooms for a library, for public examinations, and for religious worship *under such impartial regulations as the Visitors should prescribe*, the legislature neither sanctioned nor rejected this proposition." He concluded, "the buildings of the Univ. belong to the State, that they were erected for the purposes of an University and that the Visitors, to whose care they are comm^d. for these purposes, have no right to permit their application to any other." Madison also described the compromise in narrow terms, seeking to restrict denominations to building adjacent to grounds, "so *near* that the Students of the University may respectively attend the religious exercises in them." The Visitors were authorized "to open the public rooms for Religious uses, under *impartial* regulations, (a task that may occasionally involve some difficulties) and admitting the establishment of Theological Seminaries by the respective sects contiguous to the precincts of the University." This—nondiscriminatory use of a public building for public exercises, religious and otherwise—was something that Jefferson could accept as consistent with his Statute. Still, he continued to work to limit the access of religious ministers to the public facilities of the university to avoid any appearance of endorsement. A religious sermon at UVA had to await Jefferson's absence.[56]

Jefferson's attendance at church services in the House of Representatives while he was president was in a similar vein. Washington, D.C., was, of course, a young and forming city during the first years of Jefferson's presidency. At the time, there were only two churches in the District: a small Catholic church built to accommodate some Irish workmen and an Episcopal church meeting in an old tobacco barn (which Jefferson frequently attended). With the House of Representatives being one of the few usable large buildings in the District, it was an obvious place for other Protestant services. These meetings were not joint sessions of Congress (as sometimes claimed); they had no official status, and use of the facilities was apparently simply authorized by the House leadership. Nor is there any evidence that Jefferson ordered the Marine Band to play at the services, an oft-repeated claim, although members of the band did on occasion provide both religious and nonreligious music. (James Hutson stated that "Jefferson permitted executive branch employees under his direct control, members of the Marine Band, to participate." Other than Jefferson's episodic attendance, there is no evidence of his involvement or evidence that the Marines appeared in an official capacity. The only contemporaneous reference to Marine Band participation is from the recollections of Margaret Bayard

Smith, although she reported that the "musick was as little in union with devotional feelings, as the place." The practice, which Smith described as "ridiculous," was "after a while ... discontinued.")[57]

Still, the fundamental point remains: Jefferson attended church services in a government building without apparent objection (although he reportedly waited to do so until the Baptist minister and devoted Jeffersonian, John Leland, was preaching). Speaking of Jefferson's attendance, Manasseh Cutler, a Massachusetts federalist minister, noted the political nature of the gatherings, but acknowledged that "although this [Jefferson's attendance] is no kind of evidence of any regard to religion, it goes far to prove that the idea of bearing down and overturning our religious institutions ... has been given up." Of course, Jefferson never intended "bearing down and overturning ... religious institutions," but the point is well taken: Jefferson did not attempt to purge the public square of religious activity, even on government property, carried on without government endorsement and with no apparent governmental favoritism.[58]

Thus, while opposing any appearance of endorsement, Jefferson was willing to accept nondiscriminatory access to public facilities when not being used for governmental purposes. For example, in 1822, he noted with some pride the practice in Charlottesville: "We have four sects, but without either church or meeting-house. The court-house is our common temple, one Sunday in the month to each. . . . and all mix in society in perfect harmony." His use of the term "impartial regulations" for private access to public facilities presaged the use of the term "neutral" access by religious and nonreligious organizations while avoiding any government "endorsement" of religion. As the Court explained in *County of Allegheny* (1989): "Whether the key word is 'endorsement,' 'favoritism,' or 'promotion,' the essential principle remains the same. The Establishment Clause, at the very least, prohibits government from appearing to take a position on questions of religious belief or from 'making adherence to a religion relevant in any way to a person's standing in the political community.'" As Jefferson put it: "[O]ur civil rights have no dependence on our religious opinions." At the same time, if government property is opened to some private uses, Jefferson would add that the "civil magistrate" must not "restrain the profession or propagation of principles on supposition of their ill tendency."[59]

A modern twist on this issue was presented in a case involving Mr. Jefferson's university. In *Rosenberger v. Rector and Visitors of the University of Virginia* (1995), the Court struck down UVA's allocation of student fees to a broad array of activities about campus, from student publications to athletic clubs, when UVA refused to fund a publication based upon its religious affiliation. The Court reached a similar conclusion in dealing with access of private and student organizations to state university facilities. This is not a case of "nondiscriminatory" support for different religions by government as it was understood in the general assessment debate, something that both Jefferson and Madison vehemently opposed. This was general, nondiscriminatory ("impartial") support to a broad range of secular and sectarian activities in which religious activities could not constitutionally be singled out as unworthy.[60]

Jefferson's position on use of government facilities for religious purposes, both as it related to UVA and in the case of his attendance at church services in the House of Representatives, has often been seriously overstated. Based in part on the Report of the Board of Visitors, Justice Reed, dissenting in *McCollum* (1948), suggested that Jefferson and Madison were only concerned about financial "aid" to religion and not other church-state interactions or use of property:

> It is clear from its historical setting and its language that the [Memorial &] Remonstrance was a protest against an effort by Virginia to support Christian sects by taxation. . . . Thus, Mr. Madison's approval of Mr. Jefferson's report as Rector gives, in my opinion, a clearer indication of his views on the constitutionality of religious education in public schools than his general statements on a different subject. . . . "[A]id" must be understood as a purposeful assistance directly to the church itself or a religious group or organization.

Others make a similar error. Ian Bartrum, citing Reed, concludes that Jefferson planned a significant role for religion in UVA's classrooms. Reed, though, not only understated the terms of the Memorial & Remonstrance—which applies to church-state interactions that go well beyond financial support—but overstated Jefferson's concessions concerning UVA, not to mention ignoring the functional equivalence of financial aid and use of facilities.[61]

Chaplains and Missionaries

Paid chaplains have a long historic pedigree and were authorized by the first Congress only three days before Congress endorsed the First Amendment. Critics of a strict separation point to the fact that Madison was on the committee that set rules for congressional chaplains. It was largely on this historic basis that the Supreme Court effectively created an exception to Establishment Clause doctrine to sanction paid legislative chaplains in *Marsh v. Chambers* (1983).[62]

Similarly, critics note that Jefferson signed a treaty providing missionaries to the Kaskaskia Indians. For Donald Drakeman, Jefferson simply acted inconsistently: "Is our Jeffersonian muse the 'wall of separation' letter or the treaty funding Christian missions to Native Americans?" But a proper understanding of Jefferson must encompass all these facts.[63]

Madison was on the committee in the first federal Congress that endorsed legislative chaplains, and he likely recognized that chaplains were a political inevitability. Later, though, he said that he had opposed the effort. "The Constitution of the U.S. forbids everything like an establishment of a national religion. The law appointing Chaplains establishes a religious worship for the national representatives, to be performed by ministers of religion, . . . and those are to be paid out of the national taxes." Madison saw the danger not only in the violation of an abstract principle, but "he doubted . . . whether in their [chaplains'] appointments, more heed was not given to the temporal interest of the shepherds than the spiritual interests of the flock." Such use of religion for political ends also elicited Jefferson's ire.[64]

In fact, Jefferson might note with a bemused smile the contradictions and complexities that have followed the *Marsh* decision. While the Court authorized legislative chaplains, it recognized that chaplaincies might violate the Establishment Clause if adopted with an "impermissible motive" or if their official prayers "proselytize or advance any one, or disparage any other, faith or belief." The result has been a hodgepodge of cases in which courts have: permitted a county board to limit those that pray to a Judeo-Christian tradition, rejecting a Wiccan priestess; allowed sectarian prayers when a rotating process did not discriminate among those selected; struck down well-established rotating invocations because the legislature continued to appoint chaplains who used their prayers for sectarian proselytizing; struck down town council members' Christian invocations when those not participating were effectively discriminated against or a county board's invocation that, while nominally rotating, consistently proselytized for Christianity. In one case, a court upheld the right of a city council to reject a prayer based on content when a minister intended to mock governmental prayer:

We pray that you prevent self-righteous politicians from mis-using the name of God in conducting government meetings; and that you lead them away from the hypocritical and blasphemous deception of the public, attempting to make the people believe that bureaucrats' decisions and actions have thy stamp of approval if prayers are offered at the beginning of government meetings.

Jefferson and Madison likely would have approved of the prayer.[65]

For Jefferson, the courts' efforts to control aspects of the preaching of ministers who are receiving some form of government support or endorsement would demonstrate the real problem. The notion that government would intervene to prevent a minister from proselytizing his own beliefs would be an anathema to the man dedicated to personal liberty and thought. Such controls result in government officials choosing what is orthodox in violation of Jefferson's Statute:

[T]he proscribing any citizen as unworthy the public confidence by laying upon him an incapacity of being called to offices of trust and emolument, unless he profess or renounce this or that religious opinion, is depriving him injuriously of those privileges and advantages to which … he has a natural right; that it tends also to corrupt the principles of that very religion it is meant to encourage, by bribing, with a monopoly of worldly honours and emoluments, those who will externally profess and conform to it; … that to suffer the civil magistrate to … restrain the profession or propagation of principles on supposition of their ill tendency is a dangerous fallacy, which at once destroys all religious liberty.

Dissenters well understood this during the disestablishment fight in Virginia.

If, therefore, the State provides a support for preachers of the gospel, … they must certainly, when they preach, act as officers of the State, and ought to account thereto, not only as members of civil society, but also as preachers. The consequence of this is, that those whom the State employs in its service, it has a right to regulate and dictate to; it may judge and determine who shall preach, when they shall preach, and what they shall preach.

The fault lies not in the decision to demand that public funds or official positions be used in a manner that neither promotes nor disparages one religion or all religions, but the decision to permit official government preaching in the first place.[66]

Interestingly, Madison proposed an alternative to government chaplains for legislators who wished to begin their day with prayer: They should simply raise private funds to hire an unofficial chaplain, rather than asking the government to fund or endorse their religious activity. The resulting chaplain would not be a government official and would not be subject to content oversight by the government.

> If Religion consist in voluntary acts of individuals, singly or voluntarily associated, and it be proper that public functionaries, as well as their constituents should discharge their religious duties, let them, like their constituents, do so at their own expense. How small a contribution from each member of Congress would suffice for the purpose! How just would it be in its principle! How noble in its exemplary sacrifice to the genius of the Constitution; and the divine right of conscience!

This, too, Jefferson would have endorsed. Notice, however, what was not at issue: Madison did not question the right of members to invoke a (nonofficial) prayer at the beginning of a session of Congress, presumably in the halls of Congress. Jefferson, given his sensitivity in this area, would have probably discountenanced such a practice, but would likely agree with Madison that it does not violate the Constitution so long as there is no government funding or official endorsement, no advantage or disadvantage to participation (other than any spiritual advantages), and members are free to make other invocations. (In application, avoiding an apparent endorsement may sometimes require great care.)[67]

Military and prison chaplains present a different issue. Madison understood that in the military, when government takes people away from their normal access to religious services, a potential conflict between prohibiting establishment and permitting free exercise might be presented. Still, Madison concluded that while "the object of this establishment is seducing; the motive to it is laudable," military chaplains should not be government-paid officials. He suggested that religiously motivated officers simply lead prayers on their own time or local ministers meet troops' needs. This, though, is certainly an area in which developments over several centuries would inform Jefferson's and Madison's thinking (not to mention the theological problems with lay ministers for some denominations). Madison recognized that "navies with insulated crews may be less within the scope of these reflections" against paid chaplains. Given the nature of modern military service, including prolonged deployments away from one's local community and security-restricted access to facilities, some government system is likely inevitable. Prison chaplains are of a similar sort.[68]

Certainly Jefferson and Madison would have insisted that any provision of chaplaincy services be done on a nondiscriminatory basis so to avoid any suggestion that the government is endorsing a particular religious message. Here, too, times have changed. Madison speculated that a Catholic priest could never be a congressional chaplain, but history has proven him wrong (although mainline Protestant denominations have predominated). The presence of Buddhist and Muslim chaplains in the military, and Wiccan services on military bases, owe much to the Jeffersonian vision.[69]

In any case, it was speaking specifically about Congress's decision to fund chaplains that Madison declared: "Rather than let this step beyond the landmarks of power have the effect of a legitimate precedent, it will be better to apply to it the legal aphorism, *de minimis non curate lex* [the law does not concern itself with trifles]."[70]

In a similar vein, it is often noted that Jefferson signed a treaty with the Kaskaskia Indians providing for payment of a missionary. Daniel Dreisbach, for example, argues that Jefferson's and Madison's support for chaplains and an Indian missionary proves that "many of the founding fathers, including Jefferson and Madison, did not interpret the No Establishment clause to prohibit federal assistance to religion as long as it did not discriminate in favor of one religious group against another." Robert Cord concludes that the Kaskaskia Treaty shows that the First Amendment was intended only to ensure that "one religion, religious sect, or religious tradition [would not] be placed in a legally preferred position."[71]

The facts suggest a different conclusion: In an 1803 treaty, the Kaskaskia Indians agreed to cede a vast tract of land; among the payments that they sought in return was an agreement that the United States would pay for a Catholic missionary for seven years. (The Kaskaskia had been converted by French missionaries, and many had been Catholic for generations.) In essence, the government owed the Indians money for land and the Indians chose to have some funds—their funds—dedicated to payment of missionaries; Jefferson agreed. Cord recognizes the significance of this fact, but argues that Jefferson could have changed the treaty to give the Indians the money for their own dispersal. Yet, given the state of communications, this could not have been done in any practical or timely manner. In any case, this does not change the fact that the funds actually paid belonged to the Indians, and the Kaskaskias may have wanted to discourage any diversion of funds to other uses, a significant problem in a loose polity.[72]

As various courts have observed, when the government holds private funds as a trustee, and the private beneficiary directs use of the funds, normal restraints on government spending are inapplicable. "[T]he Court distinguished sharply between appropriations from public funds for the support of religious education and appropriation from funds held in trust by the Government essentially as trustee for private individuals, Indian wards, as beneficial owners."[73]

It is noteworthy that, in spite of the very narrow and special circumstances of the Kaskaskia Treaty, this expenditure was considered to be very sensitive. Madison, Jefferson's secretary of state, suggested that they avoid publicly discussing the expenditure so as not even to suggest "a principle, not according with the exemption of Religion from Civil power." As a result, Jefferson's message to Congress accompanying the treaty did not mention this provision expressly, referring only to the government providing "other articles of their [the Kaskaskias'] choice." It may also be noted that this treaty was the exception among several score of early Indian treaties signed by Jefferson.[74]

Cord and Dreisbach seek to make even more of this unique episode by claiming that the Kaskaskia Treaty shows that the First Amendment was intended only to prohibit discrimination among sects. Yet, since the treaty specifically provided funding for a *Catholic* missionary, and no other missionaries were funded during Jefferson's presidency, if this is government aid to religion, it is exclusive, preferential aid. Turning this into an argument for nonpreferentialism requires a mighty twist.

Government Contacts/Contracts

During his presidency, Madison vetoed legislation that provided for government/church cooperation, including a bill giving a small piece of land to a Baptist church and another bill incorporating the Episcopal Church in Washington. The latter, in particular, is sometimes held up in an effort to demonstrate that virtually any church/state cooperation is prohibited. Yet, considered carefully, these vetoes, and Jefferson's action on a similar bill, suggest a useful distinction between appropriate and inappropriate government interaction with religious entities.

In February 1811, after a surveying error, apparently no fault of the Baptists, resulted in a Mississippi Baptist church being located on government property, Congress agreed to give the church a five-acre parcel to eliminate the considerable expense of moving the building. Madison vetoed the law, explaining that the bill "comprises a principle and precedent, for the appropriation of funds of the United States, for the use and support of religious societies; contrary to" the First Amendment. Reminded of the establishment issue, an effort to overturn the veto failed miserably: 33–55. Madison explained himself in a subsequent letter to a group of North Carolina Baptists: He "always regarded the practical distinction between Religion and Civil Government as essential to the purity of both and as guaranteed by the Constitution." He congratulated the Baptists that "none has been more vigilant or constant in maintain[in]g that distinction, than the Society of which you make a part, and it is an honorable proof of your sincerity & integrity, that you are as ready to do so, in a case favoring the interest of your brethren, as in other cases."[75]

This episode is often cited as evidence of Madison's commitment to a strict separation of church and state. Yet, to stop there is to miss the essence of the issue. While vehemently opposed to any aid targeted to a particular church or even religion generally, Madison certainly had no objections to the federal government entering into a nondiscriminatory commercial contract with the church for the sale of the land. Madison pointed out that the application of the Mississippi meeting house to Congress "does not appear to have contemplated a grant of the Land in question, but on terms that might be equitable to the public as well as to themselves." A commercial contract was not the "aid" prohibited by the First Amendment. The essence of the forbidden relationship is some special care or consideration for religion. Neutral, commercial treatment of religious institutions would not run afoul of the prohibition.[76]

Similarly instructive, Madison vetoed incorporation of the Episcopal Church in Washington for much the same reason that he opposed the 1784 incorporation of the Episcopal Church in Virginia: The bill regulated the church's internal polity and gave it responsibility for poor relief. With respect to the latter, Madison surely remembered that Virginia's religious dissenters vehemently objected when Anglican vestries had authority over welfare and orphans and, reportedly, used that authority in a discriminatory manner. The problem for Madison may not have been a generic involvement of a religious organization in providing a social service, but in the exclusivity of the authorization to the Episcopal Church, which might be seen as "a precedent for giving to religious societies, as such, a legal agency in carrying into effect a public and civic duty." In such circumstances, Christopher L. Eisgruber and Lawrence G. Sager suggest that government must not discriminate in favor, or against, religious organizations and that neutrality must be something more than theoretical; a real secular alternative source of services must be available. While Madison's veto might be seen as rejecting any provision of social services by a religious organization, it may equally be seen as requiring neutrality.[77]

The bill's regulation of the internal doctrine and polity of the church—providing for who could vote, how internal decisions would be made, how vacancies would be filled, etc.—was even worse. "In short, Madison did not say Congress could never incorporate a religious organization; he faulted the bill for regulating the church's internal affairs and for entrusting it with governmental authority." By comparison, Jefferson had signed a bill incorporating a church in the District of Columbia, but it did not include such restrictive measures. Critics, both contemporary and modern, have suggested an inconsistency. Josiah Quincy, for example, urged overriding Madison's veto by arguing that Jefferson had signed a bill "in every material respect" the same as that Madison vetoed. That, though, is to ignore the very substantial differences. (The effort to overturn this veto failed 29–74.)[78]

Free Exercise and the Law

Finally, Jefferson had well-developed views on the question of whether the free exercise of religion could justify exemption from a facially neutral law, that is, one that does not by its terms discriminate against religion. He disapproved. In the nineteenth century, the Court agreed: "However free the exercise of religion may be, it must be subordinate to the criminal laws of the country, passed with reference to actions regarded by general consent as properly the subjects of punitive legislation." The modern Court, initially, was sympathetic to such claims for exemption, ruling in *Sherbert* (1963) that a person who refused to work on Saturday, based upon their religious convictions, could not on that basis be denied unemployment benefits. Arguably *Holy Trinity* (1892), in which an immigration law was held not to apply to a New York church's decision to hire a minister abroad, could also be seen as such a case (albeit the Court's explanation for that decision is far from clear). More recently, though, the Court has withdrawn its support for such exceptions and essentially held that facially

neutral laws should be enforced even if they incidentally burden religious practices. Like the Virginia Statute, the Court "affirmed freedom of belief as an absolute liberty, but recognized that conduct, while it may also be comprehended
by the Free Exercise Clause, 'remains subject to regulation for the protection of
society.'"[79]

Jefferson's position was consistent with the recent trend. "The declaration
that religious faith shall be unpunished," he made clear, "does not give immunity
to criminal acts dictated by religious error." Presumably the same would hold
true for regulatory acts within the legitimate power of government. Recognizing the broad sensitivity of this issue, Jefferson explained his position in some
detail:

> [W]hatsoever is lawful in the Commonwealth, . . . cannot be forbidden to him
> for religious uses; & whatsoever is prejudicial to the commonwealth in their
> ordinary uses & therefore prohibited by the laws, ought not to be permitted
> to churches in their sacred rites. [F]or instance, it is unlawful in the ordinary
> course of things or in a private house to murder a child. [I]t should not be
> permitted any sect then to sacrifice children: [I]t is ordinarily lawful (or tempo-
> rarily lawful) to kill calves or lambs. [T]hey may therefore be religiously sacri-
> ficed. [B]ut if the good of the State required a temporary suspension of killing
> lambs (as during a siege); sacrifices of them may then be rightfully suspended
> also. . . . [I]f any thing pass in a religious meeting seditiously & contrary to the
> public peace, let it be punished in the same manner & no [sic] otherwise than as
> if it had happened in a fair or market.[80]

At the same time, Jefferson recognized that free exercise must mean that
discrimination based upon one's religion, or religious exercise, was impermissible. These two principles come together when a law that is facially neutral
is, in fact, used to discriminate against religion or a religious minority. For example, in *Sherbert*, the law exempted those who refused to work on a Sunday,
but not those who had other holy days. Jefferson would have been sensitive
to prevent such practices, including the use of seemingly neutral laws to discriminate in fact. After all, in pre-Revolutionary Virginia, dissenting ministers
were often arrested for "disturbing the peace" by preaching; while the law was
facially neutral, neither Jefferson nor Madison would have countenanced its use
in that manner. More broadly, this is an area in which the massive expansion of

government functions, and its increasing influence on the personal lives of its citizens might well color Jefferson's perspective.[81]

In ways that he could never have anticipated, Madison's desire to impose federal restrictions on the ability of the states to violate religious liberty has been achieved. The protections of the religion clauses of the First Amendment have been incorporated into the Fourteenth Amendment as fundamental to the ordered liberty that all U.S. citizens enjoy. To seek to fathom Jefferson's and Madison's views on incorporation per se is a fool's errand. They could not have foreseen the Civil War and its consequences. At the same time, historic objections to incorporation based upon federalism are anachronistic.

Similarly, arguments that seek to minimize the significance of the Jeffersonian vision of religious freedom—either in the Founding, the drafting of the First Amendment, or in its development in the nineteenth century—tend to avoid the historic evidence.

This, though, does not answer complex modern questions about the breadth of religious freedom and the scope of the separation of church and state. Justice Brennan was correct that what is needed is a close consideration of the problems that the First Amendment was intended to address, "whether the practices . . . challenged threaten those consequences which the Framers deeply feared; whether, in short, they tend to promote the type of interdependence between religion and state which the First Amendment was designed to prevent."[82]

At the same time, our understanding can be informed by specific issues with which Jefferson and Madison grappled. Of course, as Donald Drakeman notes, "writers on all sides of this debate tend to encourage their readers to see this controversy as resolvable by a dedicated and objective review of the facts ('true facts' versus 'false facts,' as it were) rather than what it is, which is a bitter dispute over which of the largely undisputed facts are the most important ones for interpreting the establishment clause."[83] Yet, not all versions of the facts are created equal, and a careful review suggests that some circumstances must be viewed with caution. The decision to permit funds to be used for a Kaskaskia missionary, a fact that Jefferson and Madison saw as troubling even if very limited, is hardly the same as an express decision to refuse to issue a thanksgiving proclamation on principle or a proposal to permit direct funding of religious activity. Considered carefully, both Madison and Jefferson evidenced remarkable consistency in their insistence on a strict separation of church and state while maintaining a vibrant public square for religion.

More generally, this discussion begs the question of how and why we should rely on Jefferson (or other Founders) at all in seeking to answer modern questions.

7

JEFFERSON'S
ENDURING LEGACY

THERE IS A CERTAIN INCONGRUITY IN THE EFFORT TO SEEK JEFFER-
son's views in the midst of modern controversy. After all, Jefferson was adamant
that the world is for the living; he was so insistent upon this that he would have
had each generation draft its own constitution. Jefferson would advise that a
fixation on the Founders' views is fundamentally misguided.

Religious liberty, though, was different for Jefferson; protecting religious
freedom was essential to both reason and republicanism. It was a natural right.
Understanding its source, and the Founders' passion for its protection, speaks
to that fundamental nature. This must explain, in part, the remarkable consensus at the Supreme Court that our understanding of the First Amendment's
religion clauses should be particularly driven by history, making Jefferson's
legacy all the more important.

Others have objected that fair-sounding Jeffersonian principles mask a social and legal reality in which religious liberty is a "myth." This, though, is to
miss the significant changes that those principles have compelled and the attention that they continue to compel.

More troubling, that legacy has been twisted by modern efforts, on both
right and left, to define a strict dichotomy between a wholly secular nation and
a "Christian nation," a dichotomy that Jefferson certainly would have rejected.
Efforts to confuse our secular government with a secular citizenry have distorted more than they have informed.

Jefferson's legacy is a fundamentally secular government and a vibrant private religious realm bounded only by an expansive voluntary principle. The
result has been a remarkably active U.S. religious community, an increasingly

rich and diverse polity, and an international intellectual debt to the United States, and Jefferson, for freedom of religion. Arguments about the meaning of religious freedom for Jefferson, and how Jeffersonian liberty can be applied today will certainly continue. That legacy, though, provides an exceptionally rich intellectual, political, and religious heritage.

It is ironic that Jefferson, more than any other Founder, seems a ready participant in modern policy and constitutional debates. After all, it was Jefferson, more than any of the other Founding Fathers, who was deeply suspicious of the power of historical legacy in defining laws or status. Beyond his well-known assault on primogeniture and entail, it was Jefferson who suggested that laws should last only nineteen years, for one generation (dissuaded only in part when the ever-practical Madison explained the insurmountable problems with such an approach). It was Jefferson who warned:

> Some men look at constitutions with sanctimonious reverence, and deem them like the ark of the covenant, too sacred to be touched. They ascribe to the men of the proceeding age a wisdom more than human, and suppose what they did to be beyond amendment.... But ... laws and institutions must go hand in hand with the progress of the human mind. As that becomes more developed, more enlightened, as new discoveries are made, new truths disclosed, and manners and opinions change with the change of circumstances, institutions must advance also, and keep pace with the times.

Jefferson's commitment to reason, empiricism, and the Enlightenment fed his suspicion of overreliance on sclerotic historic precedent. In one of the reports on UVA, he worried that excessive deference to the past fed "the preposterous idea that they [students] are to look backward for better things, and not forward." He reminded even devotees who came seeking the sage's wisdom that the past "was very like the present, but without the experience of the present." Jack Rakove spoke for Jefferson when he pointed out that the Founders, generally empiricists, "would not have denied themselves the benefits of testing their original ideas and hopes against the intervening experience that we have accrued since 1789."[1]

For Jefferson, though, religious liberty was different; it was foundational for a republic. Government was not safe, religion was not safe, ... the mind was not safe, without religious freedom. History demonstrated that an alliance between church and state would inevitably create a domineering priesthood (aided by the sanction of government) and an aristocracy (aided by the sanction of priestcraft), both an anathema to the free inquiry and rational debate that he revered and that were essential for a republic. Paradoxically, the whole idea of republican majoritarianism would be at risk without careful protection of religious freedom and free inquiry, including separation of church and state and protecting against the legal dominance of a majoritarian religion. Thus, while Jefferson recognized that neither he nor any legislature or group of persons had "power to restrain the acts of succeeding Assemblies, . . . yet," he opined, "we are free to declare, and do declare, that the rights hereby asserted [in the Virginia Statute] are of the natural rights of mankind, and that if any act shall be hereafter passed to repeal the present or to narrow its operation, such act will be an infringement of natural right." For Jefferson, then, the First Amendment had a particular importance: "No provision in our Constitution ought to be dearer to man than that which protects the rights of conscience against the enterprises of the civil authority."[2]

Thus, when Jefferson asked that his tombstone mention the Declaration of Independence, the Statute for Establishing Religious Freedom, and his founding of the University of Virginia, and "not a word more," ignoring his numerous public offices and his deep commitment to family, he was not being obtuse. Each of these things is a living legacy of, and foundation for, the essential elements of republicanism and reason: political freedom, religious freedom, and academic freedom.[3]

Given the nature of religious liberty and the threats to it, Jefferson, then, would hardly object to our continued invocation of the Statute and, more importantly, the principles that underlay it. Here, he would be pleased to have Madison speak for him: the Statute "is a true standard of Religious liberty: . . . As long as it is respected and no longer, these [rights] will be safe."[4]

Of course, the legal issue of originalism, whether we should turn to the Founders for understanding the Constitution at all, remains controversial. Volumes have been written and conferences filled with the merits, methods, and problems of an "originalist" approach, and this work will not end that dispute. Several particular observations, though, are in order. First, from across the political and judicial spectrum, there has been a remarkable consensus that the First Amendment's religion clauses must be understood in their historical context. Second, in key respects there is broad agreement that looking at an original understanding can at least provide some agreed baseline on which analysis can build; "for better or worse, the Revolutionary era provides Americans with the one set of consensual political symbols that come closest to universal acceptance." The issue is to whom should we turn for a contemporaneous understanding—the draftsmen, all the Founders, ratifiers—and whether contemporaneous actions or the principles on which constitutional provisions were formed should control. However one might answer those questions in other circumstances, for the religion clauses of the First Amendment, a Jeffersonian vision is at the center of the original understanding; other voices cannot fill that role.[5]

Supreme Court justices from across the political spectrum, repeatedly, have said that no section of the Constitution should be more carefully defined by its history than the religion clauses of the First Amendment. The four dissenters in *Everson* (1947) made clear that "no provision of the Constitution is more closely tied to or given content by its generating history than the religious clause of the First Amendment ... [including] the long and intensive struggle for religious freedom in America, more especially in Virginia." Justice Rehnquist, in dissent in *Wallace* (1985), took the position that "the true meaning of the Establishment Clause can only be seen in its history." Justice Scalia has made similar broad claims about the unique importance of history in understanding the First Amendment: "Justice Holmes' aphorism that 'a page of history is worth a volume of logic,' ... applies with particular force to our Establishment Clause jurisprudence."[6]

While judges and commentators generally join a harmonious chorus on the importance of history to this inquiry, none provides a particular explanation for why history is uniquely important in understanding the religion clauses of the First Amendment, as opposed to, for example, search and seizure, gun rights, or trial by jury, each of which has a rich historic record from which to draw. Perhaps the reason harks back to the exceptional nature of the American experience of religious freedom. Not only did many settlers come to these shores, in part, to enjoy religious freedom (admittedly defined very differently over time and place), but the United States was the first nation to adopt religious freedom for all people and demand a separation of church and state, a point that was evident even during the Founding. Tench Coxe, the political gadfly who often found himself in the thick of early American politics, explained the unique nature of American religious freedom:

In Italy, Spain and Portugal, no protestant can hold a public trust. In England every Presbyterian, and other person not of their established church, is incapable of holding an office. No such impious deprivation of the rights of men can take place under the new Federal constitution. The [Philadelphia] convention has the honor of proposing the first public act [prohibition of test oaths], by which any nation has ever divested itself of a power, every exercise of which is a trespass on the Majesty of Heaven.

Coxe might have added that similar restraints still existed in many of the states, but they were inconsistent with constitutional principles and would soon fade under their pressure and the heterogeneity of the American people.[7]

The break with history was dramatic—no state provides clearer evidence of that break than Virginia. Given the pervasiveness of religious intolerance and persecution and alliances between church and state at the time of America's Founding, understanding the American experience of religious liberty, and the meaning attached to it even today, must start with history.

The conclusion that history is so central to understanding in this particular area seems also to be justified looking forward from ratification. The changes that resulted over time were no less revolutionary. Beyond the development of constitutional doctrine based on a Jeffersonian vision, contrary to the fears of federalist ministers in New England and their judicial ally Joseph Story, the voluntary principle did not spell the end of the American republic or the end of American religion, quite the contrary. Freed from the restraints of government intervention (Jefferson and his evangelical supporters would say meddling), religious activity exploded. Not only did the Second Great Awakening witness the birth of myriad new sects and denominations, but American religiosity seemed to experience broad and prolonged growth for two centuries, resulting in the "most openly and professedly religious culture" among modern, democratic states. While other nations sought to promote religion through government aid and endorsement, American religion, independent of government, dramatically outpaced that of any other developed democracy. Today, while Americans attend church, English congregants—a diminishing group— must pray for the civil head of the church, Queen Elizabeth. While Americans fill the airwaves with religious music and prayers on private programs, Italy's government places crucifixes in public schools. While Americans contribute to church missions, many Germans still pay church taxes. In the United States, the First Amendment and separation of church and state serve the purpose of "preserving religious liberty to the fullest extent possible in a pluralistic society." Those who wish to constrain Jeffersonian religious liberty should carefully consider the history of how it has served the nation, and religion; perhaps this, too, is part of the reason for the consensus on the centrality of First Amendment history.[8]

Yet, recognizing the centrality of the historic development of religious freedom in America, the question remains: To whom or what should we turn for that understanding: the draftsman of a constitutional provision, all the Founders, or those who ratified the Constitution? Do we look to particular actions at the Founding or the principles the Founders embraced?

In fact, much of the criticism of originalism starts by noting that it is impossible to speak rationally about the views of the "Founders"—a broad group of persons who had widely divergent views on many constitutional issues. Making the same objection, critics of the Jeffersonian vision note that Jefferson and Madison were not the only participants in First Amendment debates. The "new originalism," which seeks to focus on the understanding of the ratifiers rather than the members of the Philadelphia Convention, presents similar difficulties. In fact, not only are there many more ratifiers, but when dealing with the Bill of Rights, the ratification debates are especially thin. Justice Scalia would focus on actions at the Founding, rather than the views of individuals, but that, too, poses problems. As a preliminary matter, there is the question of whose actions: In the case of the First Amendment, at the time of adoption the various states generally could not satisfy its requirements, and their actions cannot be relied upon to understand its breadth. With respect to federal practice, as Madison was quick to note, political actions "are frequently of a character entitled to little respect, and that those of Congress are sometimes liable to peculiar distrust."[9]

However one addresses these concerns as a general matter, in the case of religious freedom, the Jeffersonian vision is the historic foundation. With respect to the first issue, the question is not what the "Founders" thought collectively—admittedly often an unknowable concept. Rather, the question is whether a particular Founder or Founders were so engaged in the drafting, adoption, or definition of a particular provision that their understanding should be privileged.

Not only was the Jeffersonian vision embodied in the Virginia Experience central to the objections about the lack of religious freedom that were ultimately expressed in the First Amendment, not only was it the only view that could develop a consensus in Congress (admittedly limited in its impact to the federal government), but that vision of religious freedom was gaining popular sway at the time and became the dominant principle in the early nineteenth century. The Jeffersonian vision became a bellwether against which practices were judged, and no other Founder or view played anything like the foundational role of Jefferson. By the time the Fourteenth Amendment was adopted, the Jeffersonian vision defined religious freedom, even if not always followed perfectly in practice.

Equally important, reliance on historic actions without consideration of context or principle can often be vacuous or subject to easy manipulation and misunderstanding, as is evident from the discussion of Jefferson's and Madison's actions in the previous chapter. Equally, two-hundred-year-old actions, uninformed by principle, may be unhelpful in addressing modern issues. For example, while Justice Scalia urges that original understanding should be based on experience at the Founding, he concedes that modern means of communication that could not have been contemplated at the time deserve First Amendment protection. More pointedly, analysis of original intent based only on actions is subject to the objection that "a structurally identical argument was made on behalf of laws mandating segregated schools, or prohibiting interracial marriage: the Framers knew and approved of such laws, therefore the Fourteenth Amendment, whatever it means, cannot prohibit that." Justice Scalia rightly abjures such an interpretation, but this goes to demonstrate that an honest reliance on the history of the First Amendment and religious freedom requires a much more encompassing understanding of the principles at issue, the Jeffersonian vision. As Justice Brennan explained in *Abington* (1963):

> The specific question before us has, for example, aroused vigorous dispute whether the architects of the First Amendment—James Madison and Thomas Jefferson particularly—understood the prohibition against any "law respecting an establishment of religion" to reach devotional exercises in the public schools.... A more fruitful inquiry, it seems to me, is whether the practices here challenged threaten those consequences which the Framers deeply feared; whether, in short, they tend to promote the type of interdependence between religion and state which the First Amendment was designed to prevent.

Or, as Andrew Koppelman puts it, we should ask, "Why did the Framers think establishment of religion is a bad thing?" Jefferson made much the same point when he said that future interpreters should turn to the "spirit manifested" at the time a proposition was adopted. Madison also warned against defining constitutional protections by focusing on political actions that violated principles, noting his own failures in this regard.[10]

Several caveats are in order. First, there is an objection that the lack of clarity of any "original intent" undermines the argument that it provides an agreed baseline or principle on which understanding can be built. Rakove, for example, stated skeptically that originalism "rests on the belief—or legal fiction—that most clauses of the Constitution possessed a clear meaning at their inception." The objection is overstated. People can disagree considerably on what the original meaning is. That is to be expected, but it does not mean that no sound basis for understanding, or at least a basis for reasonable discourse, can be established. Disagreement on exactly how Jefferson and Madison would understand religious liberty is likely, but it is still very significant that it was a Jeffersonian vision that held sway. One can reject the idea that any interpretation is acceptable or that any quote or comment from any person 220 years ago, without context and understanding, should be given great weight. This is why historians have an important role to play in seeking a better understanding of the origins and meaning of the Constitution.[11]

Second, original intent is not usually the end of the question. Much has changed since 1787. More broadly, if the Bill of Rights is understood as defining principles, application of even the original understanding of those principles to a modern dispute may be complex and requires an appropriate consideration of the context of history and modern facts. At the end of the day, Jefferson was right—law is for the living. Courts must make complicated decisions resolving very specific cases and controversies in light of the Constitution, precedent, law, custom, practicality, and cultural understanding. Madison explained what should be obvious: Constitutional provisions are "more or less obscure and equivocal, until their meaning be . . . ascertained by a series of particular discussions and adjudications." Nonetheless, an original understanding can provide a foundation on which to build—and in the area of religious freedom, the Jeffersonian vision is the proper foundation for that understanding.[12]

This leaves historians' objections to original intent—all too often an apparent consensus of derision for the very concept cloaked in an inflated claim of objectivity. Yet, the refusal of some historians to engage originalism ignores the real significance of the debate and, too often, leaves the field to "quack" history. As Mark DeWolfe Howe notes, "superficial and purposive interpretations of the past . . . dishonor[ ] the arts of the historian and degraded the talents of the lawyer." This, though, is not a reason for historians to abandon the field; rather, they must confront more fully questions of originalism.[13]

Gordon Wood's extended book review of Jill Lepore's *The Whites of Their Eyes* provides an interesting backdrop to this discussion. Wood, while certainly not disagreeing with many of Lepore's criticisms of revisionist history by members of the Tea Party, takes issue with her derisive attitude toward the idea of originalism that motivates many members of the Tea Party. "She [Lepore] believes that the jurisprudential theory of originalism is all part of the 'kooky' thinking of the Tea Party." Wood's response to that view: "No Thanks."[14]

Yet, Wood's approach to originalism seems only marginally more open to the concept than Lepore's. His argument seems to be an admonition to a historian that lawyers, a strange and at times benighted lot, find originalism valuable and, therefore, it cannot be wholly dismissed: "Originalism may not be good history, but it is a philosophy of legal and constitutional interpretation that has engaged some of the best minds in the country's law schools over the past three decades or so."[15]

This presents a false dichotomy between historians' disdain for originalism and lawyers' embrace and misses the more fundamental question for historians. The issue is not originalism versus no originalism. Certainly Wood is correct that the reality is that the law will consider originalism; in the case of religious liberty, the virtual unanimity from the Supreme Court about the unique importance of history to our understanding is clear. Yet, properly understood, originalism also speaks in a historic voice. The real issue is good versus bad originalism, and historians need to take ownership of that discourse.

Here, one cannot declare Jefferson as central to the meaning of the First Amendment, nor, even, as a supporter of strict separation, without addressing the history of the development of the amendment and his views on religion and religious freedom, including, for example, the role of evangelicals in the battle for religious freedom, the use of public buildings for religious purposes, or treatment of religion in proclamations and public speeches. A more fulsome, more historical analysis of originalism provides a far richer picture. That picture, though, leaves Jefferson and his vision at the center of the truly exceptional American doctrine of religious freedom.

David Sehat, in *The Myth of American Religious Freedom*, raises a more fundamental objection to that history. Sehat argues that whatever the constitutional and Jeffersonian rhetoric, legal and social systems in the nineteenth and twentieth centuries were often dominated by a religious, indeed Christian, reality, Tocqueville's "moral empire." He goes on to suggest that the "myth" has been used by conservatives to argue that such Christian legal and social systems must be consistent with the original understanding of Jeffersonian religious liberty, an argument that others have been reticent to challenge so as not to draw into question the myth itself.[16]

Certainly Sehat is correct about the reality of legal and social systems during this period, and that reality has had, and continues to have, serious consequences. Yet, to focus solely on the shortcomings misses several key points. First, while laws were deeply influenced by religion throughout that period, that influence was also waning under the pressure of Jeffersonian principles of religious freedom and that movement continued powerfully into the twentieth century. The *Everson* Court spoke to this issue:

> These words of the *First Amendment* reflected in the minds of early Americans a vivid mental picture of conditions and practices which they fervently wished to stamp out in order to preserve liberty for themselves and for their posterity. Doubtless the goal has not been entirely reached; but so far has the Nation moved toward it that the expression "law respecting an establishment of religion," probably does not so vividly remind present-day Americans of the evils, fears, and political problems that caused that expression to be written into our *Bill of Rights*.[17]

Second, while social pressure can have serious consequences, there is still an enormous difference between social pressure and legal/governmental pressure. Jefferson sought to purge religion from government, but not from society. Certainly Jefferson wanted people to think for themselves, especially on issues relating to religion and republicanism, but he believed if the government was removed from the equation—providing an unbiased forum for discussion, truth would prevail. Social pressures may be inevitable; they existed in the eighteenth century as much as the twenty-first. Once the additional sanction of government was removed, though, and free exercise was not legally impaired, Jefferson believed that a free society would not be threatened.

In any case, what should not be missed is the significance of the underlying Jeffersonian principle. Jefferson's friend Philip Mazzei made a penetrating observation in that regard:

Although religious liberty is on a better footing everywhere [in America] than in Europe, each state could improve it.... [I]n Massachusetts, New Hampshire, and South Carolina, Protestantism is favored. In Massachusetts non-Christians cannot be representatives, and they are excluded from other posts in Maryland and Delaware. Catholics cannot fill some positions in New Hampshire, New Jersey, North Carolina, and Georgia. The Pennsylvania constitution excludes non-Christians, although the second [third] article of its Declaration of Rights states that "all men have a natural and indefeasible right to worship Almighty God according to the dictates of their own consciences." This proves that although reason triumphed theoretically, it was often forced to yield to prejudice.

Jefferson and Madison, too, complained about the failure to implement the principle of religious freedom in its full breadth. Establishing the principle, though, was central to the progress that had been made and would continue to be made throughout the nineteenth and twentieth centuries, and it is central for moving forward.[18]

This concern might be expressed even more forcefully in the context of the Jeffersonian principle that "all men are created equal" and the failure to implement that principle in legal or social action. The principle, though, is still important. Abraham Lincoln, a president who had to live with painful real-world compromises, explained Jefferson's centrality to the American creed and vision:

> All honor to Jefferson—to the man who, in the concrete pressure of a struggle for national independence by a single people, had the coolness, forecast, and capacity to introduce into a merely revolutionary document, an abstract truth, applicable to all men and all times, and so to embalm it there, that to-day and in all coming days, it shall be a rebuke and a stumbling-block to the very harbingers of re-appearing tyranny and oppression.

Lincoln, recognizing that Jefferson had stated an abstract truth, was well aware that the truth had not set itself fully into the body politic and that Jefferson, himself, failed to live that truth. This, though, for Lincoln, did not diminish or weaken the truth. In many respects, this inability fully to live up to the ideals on which the nation was founded should be viewed less as a failure than as a mark of the greatness of the principles. What we aspire to as a nation more frames who we are as a people than our historic failures, although those failures must be recognized and owned. America's greatness lies in its promise, not in its history. Here, Jefferson speaks most forcefully.[19]

Nor should the fruit that has been born from the principle, some in remarkable ways, be gainsaid. As William Lee Miller points out, Jeffersonian freedom of religion had an important part to play in bringing to the shores of this distinctly Protestant, Christian nation a large Jewish population—likely the largest Jewish population in the world—a vast Catholic population, and, now, Eastern, Middle Eastern, and African populations as well. Few would doubt that these earlier waves of immigration have strengthened and defined our nation in innumerable ways, and there is little cause to doubt that the latter will as well. Here, Jefferson and the Statute stand in appropriate relief.[20]

Unfortunately, Jeffersonian principles have frequently been ignored or distorted. Too often modern debates about the role of religion and religious freedom tend to present a false dichotomy based on the alternatives of a "Christian" or "secular" nation, with both sides often claiming a Jefferson provenance. He certainly would have rejected any such dichotomy. Jefferson expected separation; yet he did not bespeak a secular nation but, rather, a secular government. "Two misconceptions have obscured the meaning of separation: that it requires a secular society, and that it demands the exclusion of religion from political discourse." Critical distinctions—between government and private action, a "public square" and public property, government endorsement and neutrality—are too often ignored or swept aside, leaving advocates jousting with ghosts. Confusion in this regard, some apparently intentional, threatens great mischief.[21]

Jefferson never suggested that refusing to endorse religion officially means purging the public square of religious symbols. Private speech and action—even in a political context—are free to endorse religion, although Jefferson clearly saw the use of religion for such political purposes as ill-advised in light of the divisiveness and hypocrisy that it generated. Jefferson likely would have embraced Pittsburgh's solution to a court case in which its display of a Christmas crèche in a government building was found unconstitutional: A larger crèche was displayed in a private, but very public, location. Nor do all presentations of religion on government ground constitute an endorsement. Jefferson recognized that teaching religion as an academic subject in a public institution is acceptable, and he participated in religious services in public buildings. What

Jefferson insisted upon was "impartial regulations," what modern courts have called "neutrality," even between religion and no religion, and that there be no government endorsement resulting even in "some degree of proscription perhaps in public opinion" against those who do not share the favored religion. Those principles, even when jostled and bruised in complex modern disputes, are well worth remembering.

It is of some significance that Jefferson is reportedly the most often cited of the Founding Fathers. Jefferson intrigues us and has been at the center of political discussions for more than two hundred years. An 1840 editorialist might have been speaking for us when he noted that "whatever may be thought of the character and public measure of Mr. Jefferson, it must be admitted by all that he filled a larger space in the public eye, and exerted a more important influence upon the destinies of his country, than any other man of his time, except Washington." The dean of modern Jefferson scholars, Merrill Peterson, declared that "everyman was his own Jeffersonian." Echoing the words of Jefferson's First Inaugural Address, we might today declare, "we are all Jeffersonians," liberal/conservative, young/old, Democrat/Republican, freethinker/evangelical . . . [22]

Whatever Jefferson's other shortcomings or inconsistencies, in the realm of religious liberty, he spoke with an exceptionally strong and consistent voice. If the Declaration of Independence was to be the United States' mission statement, the Statute was to be its creed. Upon hearing of the adoption of the Virginia Statute, he proudly wrote to Madison that "it is honorable for us, to have produced the first legislature who has had the courage to declare, that the reason of man may be trusted with the formation of his own opinions." More than two hundred years later, Jefferson still defines American religious freedom. The result: a government that is officially secular and a religion that is more vibrant than that of any other developed democracy.[23]

Equally important, the American/Jeffersonian principle has provided a beacon for others to emulate. As one leading historian explained: "The greatest single contribution made by America to contemporary civilization is the evolution and successful launching of the uniquely American experiment of religious freedom and the separation of church and state." Other historians are more specific, concluding that Jefferson's Statute is the "greatest distinctive contribution of America to the sum of Western Christianized Civilization," a cornerstone of the development of liberal democracy for the past two hundred years. One need look no further than the United Nations Covenant on Civil and Political Rights, which speaks of religious freedom in a distinctly American accent. While establishments continue in many countries, and while America seems to grapple with the boundaries of Jefferson's wall, the shift in treatment of religion since the eighteenth century, particularly religious dissent, is remarkable, and Jefferson was correct in identifying its American antecedents. The rhetoric of American religious decline misses the genius of Jefferson's vision and the world that it has wrought.[24]

Looking at the American religious freedom that he played a central role in creating, he spoke for history when he stated:

> We have solved, by fair experiment, the great & interesting question Whether freedom of religion is compatible with order in government, and obedience to the laws. & we have experienced the quiet as well as the comfort which results from leaving every one to profess freely & openly those principles of religion which are the inductions of his own reason. & the serious convictions of his own inquiries.

Jefferson saw this as one of his most important legacies. We should be pleased that it is a central part of our heritage.[25]

Documentary Appendix

VIRGINIA STATUTE FOR ESTABLISHING RELIGIOUS FREEDOM
(original and edited versions)

Well aware that the opinions and belief of men depend not on their own will, but follow involuntarily the evidence proposed to their minds; that [Whereas,] Almighty God hath created the mind free, *and manifested his supreme will that free it shall remain by making it altogether insusceptible of restraint;* that all attempts to influence it by temporal punishments, or burthens, or by civil incapacitations, tend only to beget habits of hypocrisy and meanness, and are a departure from the plan of the holy author of our religion, who being lord both of body and mind, yet chose not to propagate it by coercions on either, as was in his Almighty power to do, *but to extend it by its influence on reason alone,* that the impious presumption of legislators and rulers, civil as well as ecclesiastical, who, being themselves but fallible and uninspired men, have assumed dominion over the faith of others, setting up their own opinions and modes of thinking as the only true and infallible, and as such endeavoring to impose them on others, hath established and maintained false religions over the greatest part of the world through all time: That to compel a man to furnish contributions of money for the propagation of opinions which he disbelieves *and abhors,* is sinful and tyrannical; that even the forcing him to support this or that teacher of his own religious persuasion, is depriving him of the comfortable liberty of giving his contributions to the particular pastor whose morals he would make his pattern, and whose powers he feels most persuasive to righteousness; and is withdrawing from the ministry those temporal[ry] rewards, which proceeding from an approbation of their personal conduct, are an additional incitement to earnest and unremitting labours for the instruction of mankind; that our civil rights have no dependence on our religious opinions, any more than our opinions in physics or geometry; that therefore the proscribing any citizen as unworthy the public confidence by laying upon him an incapacity of being called to offices of trust and emolument, unless he profess or renounce this or that religious opinion, is depriving him injuriously of those privileges and advantages to which, in common with his fellow citizens, he has a natural right; that it tends *also* [only] to corrupt the principles of that *very* religion it is meant to encourage, by bribing, with a monopoly of worldly honours and emoluments, those who will externally profess and conform to it; that though indeed these are criminal who do not withstand such temptation, yet neither are those innocent who lay the bait in their way; *that the opinions of men are not the object of civil government, nor under its jurisdiction;* that to suffer the civil magistrate to intrude his powers into the field of opinion and to restrain the profession or propagation of principles on supposition of their ill tendency is a dangerous fallacy, which at once destroys all religious liberty, because he being of course judge of that tendency will make his opinions the rule of judgment, and approve or condemn the sentiments of others only as they shall square with or differ from his own; that it is time enough for the rightful purposes of civil government for its officers to interfere when principles break out into overt acts against peace and good order; and finally, that truth is great and will prevail if left to herself; that she is the proper and sufficient antagonist to error, and has nothing to fear from the conflict unless by human interposition disarmed of her natural weapons, free argument and debate; errors ceasing to be dangerous when it is permitted freely to contradict them.

We the General Assembly of Virginia do enact [Be it enacted by the General Assembly] that no man shall be compelled to frequent or support any religious worship, place, or ministry whatsoever, nor shall be enforced, restrained, molested, or burthened in his body or goods, nor shall otherwise suffer, on account of his religious opinions or belief; but that all men shall be free to profess, and by argument to maintain, their opinions in matters of religion, and that the same shall in no wise diminish, enlarge, or affect their civil capacities.

And though we well know that this Assembly, elected by the people for the ordinary purpose of legislation only, have no power to restrain the acts of succeeding Assemblies, constituted with powers equal to our own, and that therefore to declare this act [to be] irrevocable would be of no effect in law; yet we are free to declare, and do declare, that the rights hereby asserted are of the natural rights of mankind, and that if any act shall be hereafter passed to repeal the present or to narrow its operation, such act will be an infringement of natural right.

Note: Spelling as in original. Italics stricken by General Assembly; bracketed material added.
Source: Julian T. Boyd et al., *Papers of Thomas Jefferson,* 2:545–47.

MEMORIAL & REMONSTRANCE AGAINST RELIGIOUS ASSESSMENTS

To the Honorable the General Assembly of the Commonwealth of Virginia
A Memorial and Remonstrance Against Religious Assessments
We the subscribers, citizens of the said Commonwealth, having taken into serious consideration, a Bill printed by order of the last Session of General Assembly, entitled "A Bill establishing a provision for Teachers of the Christian Religion," and conceiving that the same if finally armed with the sanctions of a law, will be a dangerous abuse of power, are bound as faithful members of a free State to remonstrate against it, and to declare the reasons by which we are determined. We remonstrate against the said Bill,

1. Because we hold it for a fundamental and undeniable truth, "that religion or the duty which we owe to our Creator and the manner of discharging it, can be directed only by reason and conviction, not by force or violence." The Religion then of every man must be left to the conviction and conscience of every man; and it is the right of every man to exercise it as these may dictate. This right is in its nature an unalienable right. It is unalienable, because the opinions of men, depending only on the evidence contemplated by their own minds cannot follow the dictates of other men: It is unalienable also, because what is here a right towards men, is a duty towards the Creator. It is the duty of every man to render to

the Creator such homage and such only as he believes to be acceptable to him. This duty is precedent, both in order of time and in degree of obligation, to the claims of Civil Society. Before any man can be considered as a member of Civil Society, he must be considered as a subject of the Governour of the Universe: And if a member of Civil Society, do it with a saving of his allegiance to the Universal Sovereign. We maintain therefore that in matters of Religion, no man's right is abridged by the institution of Civil Society and that Religion is wholly exempt from its cognizance. True it is, that no other rule exists, by which any question which may divide a Society, can be ultimately determined, but the will of the majority; but it is also true that the majority may trespass on the rights of the minority.

2. Because Religion be exempt from the authority of the Society at large, still less can it be subject to that of the Legislative Body. The latter are but the creatures and vicegerents of the former. Their jurisdiction is both derivative and limited: it is limited with regard to the co-ordinate departments, more necessarily is it limited with regard to the constituents. The preservation of a free Government requires not merely, that the metes and bounds which separate each department of power be invariably maintained; but more especially that neither of them be suffered to overleap the great Barrier which defends the rights of the people. The Rulers who are guilty of such an encroachment, exceed the commission from which they derive their authority, and are Tyrants. The People who submit to it are governed by laws made neither by themselves nor by an authority derived from them, and are slaves.

3. Because it is proper to take alarm at the first experiment on our liberties. We hold this prudent jealousy to be the first duty of Citizens, and one of the noblest characteristics of the late Revolution. The free men of America did not wait till usurped power had strengthened itself by exercise, and entangled the question in precedents. They saw all the consequences in the principle, and they avoided the consequences by denying the principle. We revere this lesson too much soon to forget it. Who does not see that the same authority which can establish Christianity, in exclusion of all other Religions, may establish with the same ease any particular sect of Christians, in exclusion of all other Sects? that the same authority which can force a citizen to contribute three pence only of his property for the support of any one establishment, may force him to conform to any other establishment in all cases whatsoever?

4. Because the Bill violates the equality which ought to be the basis of every law, and which is more indispensible, in proportion as the validity or expediency of any law is more liable to be impeached. If "all men are by nature equally free and independent," all men are to be considered as entering into Society on equal conditions; as relinquishing no more, and therefore retaining no less, one than another, of their natural rights. Above all are they to be considered as retaining an "equal title to the free exercise of Religion according to the dictates of Conscience." Whilst we assert for ourselves a freedom to embrace, to profess and to observe the Religion which we believe to be of divine origin, we cannot deny an equal freedom to those whose minds have not yet yielded to the evidence which has convinced us. If this freedom be abused, it is an offence against God, not against man: To God, therefore, not to man, must an account of it be rendered. As the Bill violates equality by subjecting some to peculiar burdens, so it violates the same principle, by granting to others peculiar exemptions. Are the Quakers and Menonists the only sects who think a compulsive support of their Religions unnecessary and unwarrantable? can their piety alone be

entrusted with the care of public worship? Ought their Religions to be endowed above all others with extraordinary privileges by which proselytes may be enticed from all others? We think too favorably of the justice and good sense of these denominations to believe that they either covet pre-eminences over their fellow citizens or that they will be seduced by them from the common opposition to the measure.

5. Because the Bill implies either that the Civil Magistrate is a competent Judge of Religious Truth; or that he may employ Religion as an engine of Civil policy. The first is an arrogant pretension falsified by the contradictory opinions of Rulers in all ages, and throughout the world: the second an unhallowed perversion of the means of salvation.

6. Because the establishment proposed by the Bill is not requisite for the support of the Christian Religion. To say that it is, is a contradiction to the Christian Religion itself, for every page of it disavows a dependence on the powers of this world: it is a contradiction to fact; for it is known that this Religion both existed and flourished, not only without the support of human laws, but in spite of every opposition from them, and not only during the period of miraculous aid, but long after it had been left to its own evidence and the ordinary care of Providence. Nay, it is a contradiction in terms; for a Religion not invented by human policy, must have pre-existed and been supported, before it was established by human policy. It is moreover to weaken in those who profess this Religion a pious confidence in its innate excellence and the patronage of its Author; and to foster in those who still reject it, a suspicion that its friends are too conscious of its fallacies to trust it to its own merits.

7. Because experience witnesseth that eccelsiastical establishments, instead of maintaining the purity and efficacy of Religion, have had a contrary operation. During almost fifteen centuries has the legal establishment of Christianity been on trial. What have been its fruits? More or less in all places, pride and indolence in the Clergy, ignorance and servility in the laity, in both, superstition, bigotry and persecution. Enquire of the Teachers of Christianity for the ages in which it appeared in its greatest lustre; those of every sect, point to the ages prior to its incorporation with Civil policy. Propose a restoration of this primitive State in which its Teachers depended on the voluntary rewards of their flocks, many of them predict its downfall. On which Side ought their testimony to have greatest weight, when for or when against their interest?

8. Because the establishment in question is not necessary for the support of Civil Government. If it be urged as necessary for the support of Civil Government only as it is a means of supporting Religion, and it be not necessary for the latter purpose, it cannot be necessary for the former. If Religion be not within the cognizance of Civil Government how can its legal establishment be necessary to Civil Government? What influence in fact have ecclesiastical establishments had on Civil Society? In some instances they have been seen to erect a spiritual tyranny on the ruins of the Civil authority; in many instances they have been seen upholding the thrones of political tyranny: in no instance have they been seen the guardians of the liberties of the people. Rulers who wished to subvert the public liberty, may have found an established Clergy convenient auxiliaries. A just Government instituted to secure & perpetuate it needs them not. Such a Government will be best supported by protecting every Citizen in the enjoyment of his Religion with the same equal hand which protects his person and his property; by neither invading the equal rights of any Sect, nor suffering any Sect to invade those of another.

9. Because the proposed establishment is a departure from the generous policy, which, offering an Asylum to the persecuted and oppressed of every Nation and Religion, promised a lustre to our country, and an accession to the number of its citizens. What a melancholy mark is the Bill of sudden degeneracy? Instead of holding forth an Asylum to the persecuted, it is itself a signal of persecution. It degrades from the equal rank of Citizens all those whose opinions in Religion do not bend to those of the Legislative authority. Distant as it may be in its present form from the Inquisition, it differs from it only in degree. The one is the first step, the other the last in the career of intolerance. The magnanimous sufferer under this cruel scourge in foreign Regions, must view the Bill as a Beacon on our Coast, warning him to seek some other haven, where liberty and philanthrophy in their due extent, may offer a more certain repose from his Troubles.

10. Because it will have a like tendency to banish our Citizens. The allurements presented by other situations are every day thinning their number. To superadd a fresh motive to emigration by revoking the liberty which they now enjoy, would be the same species of folly which has dishonoured and depopulated flourishing kingdoms

11. Because it will destroy that moderation and harmony which the forbearance of our laws to intermeddle with Religion has produced among its several sects. Torrents of blood have been spilt in the old world, by vain attempts of the secular arm, to extinguish Religious discord, by proscribing all difference in Religious opinion. Time has at length revealed the true remedy. Every relaxation of narrow and rigorous policy, wherever it has been tried, has been found to assuage the disease. The American Theatre has exhibited proofs that equal and compleat liberty, if it does not wholly eradicate it, sufficiently destroys its malignant influence on the health and prosperity of the State. If with the salutary effects of this system under our own eyes, we begin to contract the bounds of Religious freedom, we know no name that will too severely reproach our folly. At least let warning be taken at the first fruits of the threatened innovation. The very appearance of the Bill has transformed "that Christian forbearance, love and charity," which of late mutually prevailed, into animosities and jealousies, which may not soon be appeased. What mischiefs may not be dreaded, should this enemy to the public quiet be armed with the force of a law?

12. Because the policy of the Bill is adverse to the diffusion of the light of Christianity. The first wish of those who enjoy this precious gift ought to be that it may be imparted to the whole race of mankind. Compare the number of those who have as yet received it with the number still remaining under the dominion of false Religions; and how small is the former! Does the policy of the Bill tend to lessen the disproportion? No; it at once discourages those who are strangers to the light of revelation from coming into the Region of it; and countenances by example the nations who continue in darkness, in shutting out those who might convey it to them. Instead of Levelling as far as possible, every obstacle to the victorious progress of Truth, the Bill with an ignoble and unchristian timidity would circumscribe it with a wall of defence against the encroachments of error.

13. Because attempts to enforce by legal sanctions, acts obnoxious to so great a proportion of Citizens, tend to enervate the laws in general, and to slacken the bands of Society. If it be difficult to execute any law which is not generally deemed necessary or salutary, what must be the case, where it is deemed invalid and dangerous? And what may be the effect of so striking an example of impotency in the Government, on its general authority?

14. Because a measure of such singular magnitude and delicacy ought not to be imposed,

without the clearest evidence that it is called for by a majority of citizens, and no satisfactory method is yet proposed by which the voice of the majority in this case may be determined, or its influence secured." The people of the respective counties are indeed requested to signify their opinion respecting the adoption of the Bill to the next Session of Assembly." But the representations must be made equal, before the voice either of the Representatives or of the Counties will be that of the people. Our hope is that neither of the former will, after due consideration, espouse the dangerous principle of the Bill. Should the event disappoint us, it will still leave us in full confidence, that a fair appeal to the latter will reverse the sentence against our liberties.

15. Because finally, "the equal right of every citizen to the free exercise of his Religion according to the dictates of conscience" is held by the same tenure with all our other rights. If we recur to its origin, it is equally the gift of nature; if we weigh its importance, it cannot be less dear to us; if we consult the "Declaration of those rights which pertain to the good people of Virginia, as the basis and foundation of Government," it is enumerated with equal solemnity, or rather studied emphasis. Either then, we must say, that the Will of the Legislature is the only measure of their authority; and that in the plenitude of this authority, they may sweep away all our fundamental rights; or, that they are bound to leave this particular right untouched and sacred: Either we must say, that they may controul the freedom of the press, may abolish the Trial by Jury, may swallow up the Executive and Judiciary Powers of the State; nay that they may despoil us of our very right of suffrage, and erect themselves into an independent and hereditary Assembly or, we must say, that they have no authority to enact into the law the Bill under consideration. We the Subscribers say, that the General Assembly of this Commonwealth have no such authority: And that no effort may be omitted on our part against so dangerous an usurpation, we oppose to it, this remonstrance; earnestly praying, as we are in duty bound, that the Supreme Lawgiver of the Universe, by illuminating those to whom it is addressed, may on the one hand, turn their Councils from every act which would affront his holy prerogative, or violate the trust committed to them: and on the other, guide them into every measure which may be worthy of his blessing, may redound to their own praise, and may establish more firmly the liberties, the prosperity and the happiness of the Commonwealth.

Note: Spelling as in original.
Source: William T. Hutchinson et al., eds., *Papers of James Madison,* 8:298–303.

FIRST AMENDMENT TO THE U.S. CONSTITUTION

Congress shall make no law respecting an establishment of religion, or prohibiting the free exercise thereof; or abridging the freedom of speech, or of the press; or the right of the people peaceably to assemble, and to petition the Government for a redress of grievances.

MEMORIAL FROM THE GENERAL CONVENTION OF
VIRGINIA PRESBYTERIANS

At Bethel, Augusta County
August 13, 1785

To the Honourable the General Assembly of the Commonwealth of Virginia,

The Ministers and Lay Representatives of the Presbyterian Church in Virginia, assembled in Convention, beg leave to address you.

As citizens of the State, not so by accident but choice, and having willingly conformed to the system of civil policy adopted for our government, and defended it with the foremost at the risk of every thing dear to us, we feel ourselves deeply interested in all the measures of the Legislature.

When the late happy Revolution secured to us an exemption from British control, we hoped that the gloom of injustice and usurpation would have been forever dispelled by the cheering rays of liberty and independence. This inspired our hearts with resolution in the most distressful scenes of adversity and nerved our arm in the day of battle. But our hopes have since been overcast with apprehension when we found how slowly and unwillingly, ancient distinctions among the citizens on account of religious opinions were removed by the Legislature. For although the glaring partiality of obliging all denominations to support the one which had been the favourite of government, was pretty early withdrawn, yet an evident predilection in favour of that church, still subsisted in the acts of the Assembly. Peculiar distinctions and the honour of an important name, were still continued; and these are considered as equally partial and injurious with the ancient emoluments. Our apprehensions on account of the continuance of these, which could have no other effect than to produce jealous animosities, and unnecessary contentions among different parties, were increased when we found that they were tenaciously adhered to by government notwithstanding the remonstrances of several Christian societies. To increase the evil a manifest disposition has been shown by the State, to consider itself as possessed of supremacy in *spirituals,* as well as *temporals;* and our fears have been realized in certain proceedings of the General Assembly at their last sessions. The engrossed bill for establishing a provision for the teachers of the Christian religion and the act incorporating the Protestant Episcopal Church, so far as it secures to that church, the churches, glebes, &c. procured at the expense of the whole community, are not only evidence of this, but of an impolitic partiality which we are sorry to have observed so long.

We therefore in the name of the Presbyterian Church in Virginia, beg leave to exercise our privilege as freemen in remonstrating against the former absolutely, and against the latter under the restrictions above expressed.

We oppose the Bill,

Because it is a departure from the proper line of legislation;

Because it is unnecessary, and inadequate to its professed end—impolitic in many respects—and a direct violation of the Declaration of Rights.

The end of civil government is security to the temporal liberty and property of mankind, and to protect them in the free exercise of religion. Legislators are invested with powers from their constituents, for this purpose only; and their duty extends no farther. Religion is altogether personal, and the right of exercising it unalienable; and it is not, cannot, and ought not to be, resigned to the will of the society at large; and much less to the Legislature, which derives its authority wholly from the consent of the people, and is limited by the original intention of civil associations.

We never resigned to the control of government, our right of determining for ourselves, in this important article; and acting agreeably to the convictions of reason and conscience, in discharging our duty to our Creator. And therefore, it would be an unwarrantable stretch of prerogative, in the Legislature, to make laws concerning it, except for protection. And it would be a fatal symptom of abject slavery in us, were we to submit to the usurpation.

The Bill is also unnecessary, and inadequate expedient for the end proposed. We are fully persuaded of the happy influence of Christianity upon the morals of men; but we have never known it, in the history of its progress, so effectual for this purpose, as when left to its native excellence and evidence to recommend it, under the all directing providence of God, and free from the intrusive hand of the civil magistrate. Its Divine Author did not think it necessary to render it dependent on earthly governments. And experience has shown, that this dependence, where it has been effected, has been an injury rather than an aid. It has introduced corruption among the teachers and professors of it, wherever it has been tried, for hundreds of years, and had been destructive of genuine morality, in proportion to the zeal of the powers of this world, in arming it with the sanction of legal terrors, or inviting to its profession by honours and rewards.

It is urged, indeed, by the abettors of this bill, that it would be the means of cherishing religion and morality among the citizens. But it appears from fact, that these can be promoted only by the internal conviction of the mind, and its involuntary choice, which such establishments cannot effect.

We farther remonstrate against the bill as an impolitic measure:

It disgusts so large a proportion of citizens, that it would weaken the influence of government in other respects, and diffuse a spirit of opposition to the rightful exercise of constitutional authority, if enacted into law:

It partially supposes the Quakers and Mennonites to be more faithful in conducting the religious interests of their societies, than the other sects—which we apprehend to be contrary to fact:

It unjustly subjects men who may be good citizens, but who have not embraced our common faith, to the hardship of supporting a system, they have not as yet believed the truth of; and deprives them of their property, for what they do not suppose to be of importance to them:

It establishes a precedent for farther encroachments, by making the Legislature judges of religious truth. If the Assembly have a right to determine the preference between Christianity, and the other systems of religion that prevail in the world, they may also, at a convenient time, give a preference to some favoured sect among Christians:

It discourages the population of our country by alarming those who may have been oppressed by religious establishments in other countries, with fears of the same in this: and by exciting our own citizens to emigrate to other lands of greater freedom:

It revives the principle which our ancestors contested to blood, of attempting to reduce all religions to one standard by the force of civil authority:

And it naturally opens a door for contention among citizens of different creeds, and different opinions respecting the extent of the powers of government.

The bill is also a direct violation of the Declaration of Rights, which ought to be the standard of all laws. The sixteenth article is clearly infringed upon by it, and any explication which may have been given of it by the friends of this measure in the Legislature, so as to justify a departure from its literal construction, might also be used to deprive us of other fundamental principles of our government.

For these reasons, and others that might be produced, we conceive it our duty to remonstrate and protest against the said bill; and earnestly urge that it may not be enacted into a law. . . .

We regret that full equality in all things, and ample protection and security to religious liberty were not incontestibly fixed in the constitution of the government. But we earnestly request that the defect may be remedied, as far as it is possible for the Legislature to do it, by the adopting the bill in the revised laws for establishing religious freedom. (Chap. 82 of the Report.)

That Heaven may illuminate your minds with all that wisdom which is necessary for the important purposes of your deliberations, is our earnest wish. And we beg leave to assure you, that however warmly we may engage in preserving our religion free from the shackles of human authority, and opposing claims of spiritual domination in civil powers, we are zealously disposed to support the government of our country, and to maintain a due submission to the lawful exercise of its authority.

Signed by order of the Convention.

John Todd, Chairman

Attest, Daniel McCalla, Clerk.
Bethel, Augusta County,
13th August, 1785.

Note: Spelling and emphasis as in original. Deletions concerning incorporation.
Source: The Bethel Petition does not appear in the petitions database, although several versions of it adopted by individual churches appear. The text is taken from William Henry Foote, *Sketches of Virginia: Historical and Biographical,* 342–44.

RESOLUTION OF THE BAPTIST GENERAL COMMITTEE

The Basis of the "Spirit of the Gospel" Petitions
August 13, 1785

Resolved, That it be recommended to those counties which have not yet prepared petitions to be presented to the General Assembly against the engrossed bill for a general assessment for the support of the teachers of the Christian religion, to proceed thereon as soon as possible; that it is believed to be repugnant to the spirit of the gospel for the Legislature thus to proceed in matters of religion; that no human laws ought to be established for this purpose, but that every person ought to be left entirely free in respect to matters of religion; that the Holy Author of our religion needs no such compulsive measures for the promotion of His cause; that the Gospel wants not the feeble arm of man for its support; that it has made, and will again through divine power make, its way against all opposition; and that should the Legislature assume the right of taxing the people for the support of the Gospel, it will be destructive to religious liberty.

Note: Emphasis as in original.
Source: Robert B. Semple, *A History of the Baptists in Virginia*, 96. Many modified versions appear in the petitions database.

JEFFERSON'S LETTER TO THE DANBURY BAPTISTS

January 1, 1802

To messers. Nehemiah Dodge, Ephraim Robbins, & Stephen S. Nelson, a committee of the Danbury Baptist association in the state of Connecticut.

Gentlemen

The affectionate sentiments of esteem and approbation which you are so good as to express towards me, on behalf of the Danbury Baptist association, give me the highest satisfaction. my duties dictate a faithful and zealous pursuit of the interests of my constituents, & in proportion as they are persuaded of my fidelity to those duties, the discharge of them becomes more and more pleasing.

Believing with you that religion is a matter which lies solely between Man & his God, that he owes account to none other for his faith or his worship, that the legitimate powers of government reach actions only, & not opinions, I contemplate with sovereign reverence that act of the whole American people which declared that their legislature should "make no law respecting an establishment of religion, or prohibiting the free exercise thereof," thus building a wall of separation between Church & State. Adhering to this expression of the supreme will of the nation in behalf of the rights of conscience, I shall see with sincere satisfaction the progress of those sentiments which tend to restore to man all his natural rights, convinced he has no natural right in opposition to his social duties.

I reciprocate your kind prayers for the protection & blessing of the common father and creator of man, and tender you for yourselves & your religious association, assurances of my high respect & esteem.

Th Jefferson
Jan. 1. 1802.

JEFFERSON TO ATTORNEY GENERAL LEVI LINCOLN

Regarding the Letter to the Danbury Baptists
January 1, 1802

Averse to receive addresses, yet unable to prevent them, I have generally endeavored to turn them to some account, by making them the occasion, by way of answer, of sowing useful truths and principles among the people, which might germinate and become rooted among their political tenets. The Baptist address, now enclosed, admits of a condemnation of the alliance between Church and State, under the authority of the Constitution. It furnishes an occasion, too, which I have long wished to find, of saying why I do not proclaim fastings and thanksgivings, as my predecessors did. The address, to be sure does not point at this, and its introduction is awkward. But I foresee no opportunity of doing it more pertinently. I know it will give great offence to the New England clergy; but the advocate of religious freedom is to expect neither peace nor forgiveness from them. Will you be so good as to examine the answer, and suggest any alterations which might prevent an ill effect or promote a good one, among the people? You understand the temper of those in the North, and can weaken it, therefore, to their stomachs; it is at present seasoned to the Southern taste only. I would ask the favor of you to return it, with the address, in the course of the day or evening. Health and affection.

POSTMASTER GENERAL GIDEON GRANGER TO THOMAS JEFFERSON

Regarding the Letter to the Danbury Baptists
December 31, 1801

G Granger presents his compliments to The Presidt. and assures him he has carefully & attentively perused the inclosed Address & Answer—The answer will undoubtedly give great Offence to the established Clergy of New England while it will delight the Dissenters as they are called. It is but a declaration of Truths which are in fact felt by a great Majority of New England, & publicly acknowledged by near half of the People of Connecticut; It may however occasion a temporary Spasm among the Established Religionists yet his mind approves of it, because it will "germinate among the People" and in time fix "their political Tenets"—He cannot therefore wish a Sentence changed, or a Sentiment expressed equivocally—A more fortunate time can never be expected.—

Source: Julian P. Boyd et al., *Papers of Thomas Jefferson,* 36:256–57.

Notes

Abbreviations

Bergh   Albert Ellery Bergh, ed., *The Writings of Thomas Jefferson*.

DHFFC   Linda Grant de Pauw et al., eds., *The Documentary History of the First Federal Congress*.

DHRC   Merrill Jensen et al., eds., *The Documentary History of the Ratification of the Constitution*.

EVRP   *Early Virginia Religious Petitions*.

Ford   Paul Leicester Ford, ed., *The Writings of Thomas Jefferson*.

Hening   William Waller Hening, ed., *The Statutes at Large, Being a Collection of All the Laws of Virginia from the First Session of the Legislature in the Year 1619*, Vols. 1–13.

JHB   *Journal of the House of Burgesses of Virginia*.

JHD   *Journal of the House of Delegates of Virginia*.

PJM   William T. Hutchinson et al., eds., *Papers of James Madison*.

PTJ   Julian P. Boyd et al., eds., *The Papers of Thomas Jefferson*.

PTJR   Jeffrey Looney et al., eds., *The Papers of Thomas Jefferson: Retirement Series*.

WJM   Gaillard Hunt, ed., *The Writings of James Madison*.

Introduction

1. Jefferson to Dr. Benjamin Rush, September 23, 1800, in *PTJ*, 32:168; Jefferson to Danbury Baptists, January 1, 1802, in *PTJ*, 36:258.

2. *Reynolds v. United States*, 98 U.S. 145 (1879); *McGowan v. Maryland*, 366 U.S. 420, 437 (1961). For example, Pfeffer, "Madison's 'Detached Memoranda,'" 285; Marty, "Virginia Statute," 1; Peterson and Vaughan, *Virginia Statute*, x; Stokes, *Church and State*, 1:366; and Butler, *Awash*, 265.

3. Miller, *First Liberty*, 69; "State of the First Amendment"; Haynes, "Surprising Support."

4. "Praying Against the National Prayer Breakfast," *American Spectator*, February 1, 2012.

5. *Wallace v. Jaffree*, 472 U.S. 38, 99 (1985) (Rehnquist dissenting). For example, Hamburger, *Separation*; and Dreisbach, *Forgotten*.

6. For example, *Elk Grove v. Newdow*, 542 U.S. 1, 45–46 (2004) (Thomas concurring).

7. McConnell, "Establishment," 2207; Dreisbach, *Thomas Jefferson*, 51 (emphasis original).

8. *Abington School District v. Schempp*, 374 U.S. 203, 305 (1963) (Goldberg concurring).

9. See, for example, Green, *Second*; Myerson, *Endowed*; and Sehat, *Myth*.

10. Gaustad, *Sworn*, 69.

1. Thomas Jefferson's Religion and Religious Liberty

1. Jefferson to Danbury Baptists, January 1, 1802, in *PTJ*, 36:258; Jefferson to John Adams, January 11, 1817, in Ford, 10:73; Jefferson to M[argaret Bayard] Harrison Smith, August 6, 1816, in Bergh, 15:60.

2. For example, Schaaf, *Franklin, Jefferson*, 142 ("To anyone who questioned whether or not Thomas Jefferson was a Christian, his own words should lay the matter to rest"). Jefferson to Charles Thomson, January 9, 1816, in Bergh, 14:385 (emphasis original); Jefferson to William Short, October 31, 1819, in Ford, 10:144; Jefferson to William Short, August 4, 1820, in Bergh, 15:259–61; Jefferson to John Adams, April 11, 1823, in Bergh, 15:428–30.

3. Brutus, *Serious Facts*, 11, 2; *Boston Independent Chronicle*, May 11–14, 1801. For example, *Mississippian and State Gazette* (Jackson), October 6, 1858 (public professor of Christianity).

4. Green, *Second*, 23; Jefferson, *Autobiography*, 8. Compare Baird, *Religion in the United States*, 263 (days of fasting/prayer during Revolution evidence that the United States is a "Christian nation").

5. See, for example, http://mediamatters.org/blog/201006250027; http://wthrockmorton.com/2011/04/20/david-barton-on-thomas-jefferson-in-the-year-of-our-lord-christ/; and www.huffingtonpost.com/chris-rodda/no-mr-beck-jefferson-did_b_622122.html, responding to such claims by David Barton and Glenn Beck.

6. A number of books analyze Jefferson's religious beliefs. The most accessible, a short monograph, is Eugene Sheridan's excellent *Jefferson and Religion*. Edwin Gaustad's *Sworn on the Altar of God* is also a good treatment of the subject. Several shorter works deserve a strong recommendation: Onuf, "Thomas Jefferson's Christian Nation"; Conkin, "Religious Pilgrimage of Thomas Jefferson"; and Neem, "Beyond the Wall."

7. Meade, *Old Churches*, 1:191; Brenner, *Jefferson & Madison*, 16 (vestryman of St. Anne's parish in Albemarle in 1774); Randall, *Life of Thomas Jefferson*, 1:17, 3:555; http://classroom.monticello.org/kids/gallery/image/376/Jefferson-Family-Book-of-Common-Prayer/; Gould, "Religious Opinions," 197.

8. See, generally, Malone, *Jefferson the Virginian*, 22–48. Maury, "To Christians of Every Denomination."

9. S. Randolph, *Domestic Life*, 34 (sister "gratified" young Tom by singing hymns). Granddaughter Ellen Coolidge, Letterbook, www.monticello.org/site/jefferson/quotations-music#_note-2; *PTJ*, 1:537; John Adams to Abigail Adams, August 14, 1776, in C. Taylor, *Adams Papers*; Rodda, *Liars for Jesus*, 1:458; Myerson, *Endowed*, 5. Barton, *Original*, 101, for example, omits any discussion of Jefferson's proposal for the obverse image on the national seal.

10. Jefferson to John Page, July 15, 1763, in *PTJ*, 1:10.

11. McGarvie, *One Nation*, 5; www.monticello.org/site/jefferson/william-small.

Compare Fea, *Was America*, 203 ("schooled by Anglican ministers at the College of William and Mary"). Jefferson to Frances Eppes, January 19, 1821, in Bergh, 15:306; Wilson, *Jefferson's Literary Commonplace Book*, 25, 28.

12. Jefferson to J. P. P. [Peter] Derieux, July 25, 1788, in *PTJ*, 13:418; Gould, "Religious Opinions," 201.

13. Blosser, "Pursuing Happiness," 213, 214, quoting Tillotson; Buckley, "Religious Rhetoric," 55, 56, quoting Tillotson; Jefferson to Peyton Randolph, July 23, 1770, in *PTJ*, 1:51. George Washington might be better described as a latitudinarian (see Fea, *Was America*, 182; cf. Buckley, "Religious Rhetoric," 55).

14. Jefferson to Robert Skipwith, enclosure, August 3, 1771, in *PTJ*, 1:79–80; Jefferson, *Notes*, 285; Jefferson to Peter Carr, August 10, 1787, in *PTJ*, 12:15. See also Jefferson to John Adams, August 15, 1820; in Bergh, 15:273–74 (empiricist). Jefferson to J. P. P. [Peter] Derieux, July 25, 1788, in *PTJ*, 13:418.

15. Jefferson to William Short, October 31, 1819, in Ford, 10:144; Jefferson to William Short, April 13, 1820; in Bergh, 15:245; Jefferson to John Adams, April 11, 1823, in Bergh, 15:425; Jefferson to Salma Hales, July 26, 1818, Library of Congress, American Memory, http://hdl.loc.gov/loc.mss/mtj.mjtbib023250 image 1029.

16. Jefferson uses the phrase on several occasions (see, for example, Jefferson to Martin van Buren, June 29, 1824, in Ford, 10:307). In each case, it is difficult to read too much into the expression, whereas his rejection of Jesus's resurrection, divinity, etc., were clear and emphatic.

17. Jefferson to John Adams, January 11, 1817, in Ford, 10:73; Jefferson to M[argaret Bayard] Smith, August 6, 1816, in Bergh, 15:60; Jefferson to Edward Dowse, April 19, 1803, in Bergh, 10:378. Steven Green notes that "Philip Hamburger [in] disput[ing] the sincerity of the Republican defense of church-state separation during the 1800 election . . . understates the philosophical commitment of the Republicans while he overstates the purity of motive of the orthodox clergy." Green, *Second*, 105, citing Hamburger, *Separation*, 111–20; see also Peterson, *Jefferson Image*, 93.

18. Jefferson to Benjamin Waterhouse, July 19, 1822, in Bergh, 15:391; Jefferson to Charles Clay, January 29, 1815, in *PTJR*, 8:212; Jefferson to George Thacher, January 26, 1824, in Ford, 10:289; Jefferson to Ezra Styles, June 25, 1819, in Bergh, 15:203.

19. Jefferson to Isaac Story, December 5, 1801, in *PTJ*, 36:30; Jefferson to John Adams, March 14, 1820, in Bergh, 15:240–41.

20. Jefferson to Miles King, September 26, 1814, in *PTJR*, 7:705; Jefferson to Ezra Styles, June 25, 1819, in Bergh, 15:203–4 (a good example of Bergh's excessive capitalization); Jefferson to James Fishback, draft, September 27, 1809, in *PTJR*, 1:564; Jefferson to Thomas Parker, May 15, 1819, Library of Congress, American Memory, http://hdl.loc .gov/loc.mss/mtj.mtjbib023495 image 555.

21. Jefferson, *Notes*, 287.

22. Jefferson to Mathew Carey, November 11, 1816, in Ford, 10:67–68; Notes, *Writings*, 286; Memorial & Remonstrance Against Religious Assessments (hereafter M&R), ¶ 11, appendix; Gaustad, *Sworn*, 35; *Portland (ME) Eastern Argus*, February 8, 1805; *Providence Phoenix*, February 9, 1805, reprinting *Pittsfield Sun*.

23. Conkin, "Religious Pilgrimage," 33–34, 35; Jefferson to M[argaret Bayard] Smith, August 6, 1816, in Bergh, 15:60.

24. Jefferson to Francis Hopkinson, March 13, 1789, in *PTJ*, 14:650; Statute for Establishing Religious Freedom, appendix.

25. See Jefferson to James Madison, December 16, 1786, in *PTJ*, 10:602; Jefferson to George Wythe, August 13, 1786, in *PTJ*, 10:243; Jefferson to Judge William Johnson, June 12, 1823, in Bergh, 15:441; Jefferson to Charles Clay, January 29, 1815, in *PTJR*, 8:212; "Syllabus of an Estimate of the Merit of the Doctrines of Jesus, Compared with Those of Others," April 1803, in Peterson, *Writings*, 1125–26; Jefferson to John Adams, June 15, 1813, in *PTJR*, 6:193; Jefferson to Levi Lincoln, August 26, 1801, in *PTJ*, 35:147.

26. Dwight, *Duty of Americans*, 20; *Connecticut Courant* (Hartford), September 15, 1800. Forrest Church suggests that the author of the final piece, signed only "Burleigh," was Theodore Dwight, Timothy's brother (Church, *So Help Me God*, 188). There is an unfortunate "modern" quality to Dwight's political attacks: "Let us hear no more, at such times, of amiability and gentleness—or candor, liberality, and moderation—of conciliating, mild and generous feeling. Such qualities are now not virtues, but vices" (quoted ibid., 189).

27. Mason, "Voice of Warning to Christians" (1800); Linn, *Serious Considerations*, 22; Gould, "Religious Opinions," 191; Baird, *Religion in the United States*, 230. See also O'Brien, "Religious Issue in the Presidential Campaign"; and Schulz, "Of Bigotry in Politics and Religion."

28. Jefferson to Joseph Priestly, March 21, 1801, in *PTJ*, 33:393. While Jefferson was attacked for his lack of orthodoxy, it is noteworthy that John Adams believed that his own apparent orthodoxy, in particular announcing a national day of prayer and fasting, cost him the 1800 election. Later he reflected that "nothing is more dreaded than the national government meddling with religion" (John Adams to Benjamin Rush, June 12, 1812, quoted in Church, *So Help Me God*, 219).

29. Jefferson to Charles Clay, January 29, 1815, in *PTJR*, 8:212.

30. Onuf, "Thomas Jefferson's Christian Nation," 22, quoting Jefferson to George Wythe, August 13, 1786, and Jefferson to John Adams October 28, 1813 (emphasis Onuf).

31. Jefferson to Marquis de Chastellux, Enclosure, September 2, 1785, in *PTJ*, 8:470; Jefferson to Jeremiah Moor, August 14, 1800, in *PTJ*, 32:102–3; Observations on Jefferson's Draught of a Constitution for Virginia, ca. October 15, 1788, in *PJM*, 11:288; Jefferson to P. H. Wendover, unsent, March 13, 1815, in *PTJR*, 8:342. Compare Butler, "Coercion, Miracle, Reason," 29–30 (Jefferson called for separation of "church and state," not "religion").

32. Jefferson to John Adams, August 15, 1820, in Bergh, 15:274; Jefferson to John Adams, April 11, 1823, in Bergh, 15:426–27, 429; Jefferson to William Short, August 4, 1820, in Bergh, 15:259–61.

33. Jefferson to John Adams, April 11, 1823, in Bergh, 15:429. Kristin Swenson, a religious studies and Bible scholar, confirms that Jefferson's translation, while far from definitive, is not entirely unfair (communication with the author). Jefferson to Miles King, September 26, 1814, in *PTJR*, 7:705; Neem, "Republican Reformation," 95, quoting *Notes on the State of Virginia*.

34. "Syllabus," in Peterson, *Writings*, 1125–26; Jefferson to William Short, August 4, 1820, in Bergh, 15:260; Jefferson to John Adams, October 12, 1813, in *PTJR*, 6:550; Sanford, *Religious Life*, 170; Jefferson to Miles King, September 26, 1814, in *PTJR*, 7:705;

Jefferson to John Adams, November 13, 1818, in Ford, 10:114; Jefferson to Isaac Story, December 5, 1801, in *PTJ*, 36:30. Compare Sheridan, *Jefferson and Religion*, 66 (believes with doubts), and Brodie, *Thomas Jefferson*, 170, 377 (abandoned belief). Neem, "Republican Reformation," 96–97 ("could never convince himself," but "express[ed] hope").

35. Summary View, in *PTJ*, 1:135; Novak, "How Did Virginians," 28. For example, Jefferson, *Notes*, Query XVII, 285; and M&R, ⁋ 1, appendix. Neem, "Republican Reformation," 95; Jefferson, *Notes*, Query XVIII, 289.

Dreisbach fairly notes the irony that Jefferson's "statutory recognition of the deity and Jefferson's assertion that religious liberty is derived from the 'plan of the holy author of our religion' would surely offend strict separationists today" (Dreisbach, "Thomas Jefferson and Bills," 188).

36. Jefferson to John Adams, April 11, 1823, in Bergh, 15:427; Jefferson to David Barrow, May 1, 1815, in *PTJR*, 8:455.

37. Jefferson to Joseph Priestley, April 9, 1803, in Bergh, 10:374; "Syllabus," in Peterson, *Writings*, 1124.

38. Jefferson, Second Inaugural Address, in Ford, 8:347–48; Jefferson to New York Society of Tammany, February 29, 1808, Library of Congress, American Memory, http://hdl.loc.gov/loc.mss/mtj.mtjbib018312 image 1249; Jefferson to Joseph Priestley, April 24, 1803, Library of Congress, American Memory, http://hdl.loc.gov/loc.mss/mtj.mtjbib012342 image 207; Jefferson to William Stephens Smith, July 9, 1786, in *PTJ*, 10:117; Jefferson, First Annual Message to Congress, December 8, 1801, in *PTJ*, 36:58.

39. For a discussion of Franklin's religious views, see Gaustad, *Faith*, 59–71; Waldman, *Founding Faith*, 20–24; Mapp, *Faiths of Our Fathers*, 22–40. Malone, *Jefferson the President*, 199 n. 24, citing Manasseh Cutler, January 3, 1803.

40. For example, Jefferson to Thomas Parker, May 15, 1819, Library of Congress, American Memory, http://hdl.loc.gov/loc.mss/mtj.mtjbib023495 image 555. Jefferson to Martha Jefferson, December 11, 1783, in *PTJ*, 6:380; Neem, "Beyond the Wall," 148.

41. Jefferson to John Adams, August 22, 1813, in Ford, 9:418; Gaustad, *Faith*, 98; Conkin, "Religious Pilgrimage," 41.

42. Very little has been written about Paine's influence on Jefferson's religious views; given that Paine's religious works had made him a political liability in America, Jefferson certainly did not write about this. Still, it is an issue worthy of some consideration. A century ago, Leslie Hall noted that some of Paine's work on religion "might have been written by Jefferson" (Hall, "Religious Opinions," 176).

43. Jefferson to Joseph Priestley, April 9, 1803, in Bergh, 10:375; Sheridan, *Jefferson and Religion*, 49, 41; Gaustad, *Sworn*, 104; "Syllabus," in Peterson, *Writings*, 1124, 1125; Jefferson to Edward Dowse, April 19, 1803, in Bergh, 10:377; Jefferson to Benjamin Waterhouse, June 26, 1822, in Ford, 10:220; Conkin, "Religious Pilgrimage," 37–38.

44. Jefferson to John Adams, October 12, 1813, in *PTJR*, 6:549; Jefferson to William Short, April 13, 1820, in Bergh, 15:244.

45. Jefferson to Van der Kamp, April 25, 1816, in Bergh, 15:2–3 (another example of Bergh's excessive capitalization and "correction" of Jefferson's work); Jefferson to Samuel Wells and Gabriel Lilly, April 1, 1818, in Peterson, *Writings*, 1414.

46. *Niles National Register* 23, no. 1 (September 4, 1847); Gaustad, *Sworn*, 123, 131.

47. Jefferson to Benjamin Rush, April 21, 1803, in Bergh, 10:380 (emphasis original);

Jefferson to Francis Adrian Van der Kemp, July 30, 1816, in Adams, *Jefferson's Extracts*, 375; Jefferson to William Short, April 13, 1820, in Bergh, 15:244; "Syllabus," in Peterson, *Writings*, 1124–25.

48. Jefferson to Michael Megear, May 29, 1823, in Bergh, 15:434. It is sometimes noted that Jefferson's *Philosophy of Jesus* states on the title page that it was "for the use of the Indians unembarrassed with matters of fact or faith beyond the level of their comprehensions." There is, though, no evidence that Jefferson actually intended it for missionary work; it seems that he was ironically referring to other "Indians," federalists who had questioned his religion and threatened to undermine the republic (Sheridan, *Jefferson and Religion*, 44–49). By comparison, Madison argued that restrictions on religious liberty would encourage foreign nations, not yet exposed to Christian truths, to restrict the access of Christian missionaries (M&R, ¶ 12, appendix).

49. Jefferson, *Notes*, Query XIV, 273; Jefferson to William Baldwin, unsent, January 19, 1810, in *PTJR*, 2:157; Jefferson to Samuel Greenhow, January 31, 1814, in *PTJR*, 7:178. Jefferson's concern for the delicate minds of children parallels the care exhibited by the modern Supreme Court to prevent government endorsement of religion from being imposed on children in the context of mandatory school attendance. Compare *Lee v. Weisman*, 505 U.S. 577, 596–97 (1992): "The atmosphere at the opening of a session of a state legislature where adults are free to enter and leave with little comment and for any number of reasons cannot compare with the constraining potential of one school event most important for the student to attend" (same *Board of Education v. Mergens*, 496 U.S. 226, 287 [1990]; and *Edwards v. Aguillard*, 482 U.S. 578, 583–84 [1987]).

50. Jefferson to Moses Robinson, March 23, 1801, in *PTJ*, 33:424; Jefferson, March 4, 1801, First Inaugural Address, in *PTJ*, 33:150.

51. Jefferson to William Carver, December 4, 1823, in Ford, 10:285; Jefferson to Benjamin Waterhouse, January 8, 1825, in Ford, 10:336; Jefferson to James Smith, December 8, 1822, in Bergh, 15:409; Jefferson to Benjamin Waterhouse, June 26, 1822, in Ford, 10:220 (emphasis original).

52. Gaustad, *Faith*, 120, quoting Barbara M. Cross, ed., *The Autobiography of Lyman Beecher* (Cambridge: Belknap Press of Harvard University Press, 1961), 1:251–53 (emphasis original); Beecher, *Lectures on Political Atheism*, 320; Hatch, *Democratization*, 64; Church, *So Help Me God*, 272.

53. Jefferson to Thomas Cooper, November 2, 1822, in Ford, 10:242; Virginia Statute, appendix.

54. Kessler, "Locke's Influence," 245.

55. Jefferson to Jared Sparks, November 4, 1820, in Bergh, 15:288; Jefferson, *Notes*, Query XVII, 285. Compare Isaac Backus, Draft for a bill of Rights for the Massachusetts Constitution (1779): "As . . . nothing can be true religion but a voluntary obedience unto his [God's] revealed will, . . . every person has an unalienable right to act in religious affairs according to the full persuasion of his own mind, where others are not injured thereby" (quoted in Hamilton and Steamer, "Religious Origins," 1775).

56. M&R ¶ 1, appendix; Rakove, "Beyond Locke," 47; Virginia Statute, appendix; Jefferson to John Adams, October 28, 1813, in *PTJR*, 6:565.

57. Jefferson to DeWitt Clinton, May 24, 1807, in Ford, 9:63; Kramnick and Moore, *Godless*, 44–45. See also M&R, ¶ 8, appendix.

58. *Maryland Gazette*, issue 2798, August 28, 1800 (reprinting the Statute); *Portland (ME) Eastern Argus*, November 16, 1804.

59. Quoted in Church, *So Help Me God*, 197; Bishop, *Oration Delivered in Wallingford*.

60. Jefferson to Horatio Gates Spafford, March 17, 1814, in *PTJR*, 7:248; Jefferson to Alexander von Humboldt, December 6, 1813, in *PTJR*, 7:29; M&R, ¶ 7, appendix.

61. For example, Buckley, "Religious Rhetoric," 74. Neem, "Beyond the Wall," 142. See also Samuelson, "Jefferson and Religion," 151. Jefferson to Jacob De La Motta, September 1, 1820, Library of Congress, American Memory, http://hdl.loc.gov/loc.mss/mtj .mtjbib023880 image 224.

62. Jefferson to Benjamin Rush, September 23, 1800, in *PTJ*, 32:168; Gaustad, *Faith*, 50; *PTJ*, 1:531 (scraps accompanying Jefferson's work on Committee of Religion); Jefferson to Baltimore Baptist Association, October 17, 1808, Library of Congress, American Memory, http://hdl.loc.gov/loc.mss/mtj.mtjbib019183 image 671; Wortman, "Solemn Address," 1488. Justice Welch, relying heavily on Madison, made this point in the Cincinnati Bible case: "United with government, religion never rises above the merest superstition; united with religion, government never rises above the merest despotism" (*Board of Education of the City of Cincinnati*, 23 Ohio St. 211, 248–49 [1872]).

63. Jefferson, *Autobiography*, 40 (spelling as in original); *PTJ*, 1:551 n. 2; Jefferson, *Notes*, Query XVII, 285; Jefferson to Chesterfield Virginia Baptist Associations, November 21, 1808, Library of Congress, American Memory, http://hdl.loc.gov/loc.mss/ mtj.mtjbib019322 image 1012; Madison to Edward Everett, March 19, 1823, in *WJM*, 9:126–27.

64. Hutson, "Thomas Jefferson's Letter," 775–90; Hutson, "Wall of Separation," 139, 163. Compare Hutson, "Wall of Separation" to "Letter of Concern from the Scholars Listed Below." Jefferson to Levi Lincoln, January 1, 1802, in *PTJ*, 36:256; Gideon Granger to Jefferson, December 31, 1801, in *PTJ*, 36:256; Levy, *Jefferson and Civil Liberties*, 8, quoting James M. O'Neill, *Religion and Education under the Constitution* (New York: Harper, 1949), 81–82, 83; and Edwin S. Corwin, "The Supreme Court as National School Board," *Law and Contemporary Problems* 14 (Winter 1949): 14; Jefferson to Benjamin Rush, April 21, 1803, in Bergh, 10:381.

65. Madison to William Bradford, April 1, 1774, in *PJM*, 1:112–13; *Everson v. Board of Education*, 330 U.S. 1, 34 (1947) (Rutledge, Frankfurter, Jackson, Burton dissenting); Gaustad, "Thomas Jefferson, Religious Freedom," 683. See also Brant, "Madison: On the Separation," 3 ("To James Madison, author of the American Bill of Rights, freedom of religion was the fundamental item upon which all other forms of civil liberty depend").

2. Virginia's Establishment and the Revolutionary Battle for Religious Liberty

1. Jefferson, *Notes*, Query XVII, 287.

2. Articles, Instructions and Orders, November 20, 1606, in Hening, 1:68–69; Second Charter to the Treasurer and Company, May 23, 1609, in Hening, 1:97–98; Bond, *Spreading the Gospel*, 10.

3. Brydon, *Mother Church*, 1:119–21; Hall, *Vestry Book*, xxiii; Hening, 1 (1643):277; Bond, *Spreading the Gospel*, 12–13; Hening, 1 (1659):532–33.

4. Jefferson, *Notes*, Query VII, 283.

5. Brydon, *Mother Church*, 1:375; Nelson, *Blessed Company*, 126; Clergy of New York and New Jersey to Earl of Hillsborough, October 12, 1771, in Davies, *Documents*, vol. 3, *Transcripts, 1771*, 209.

6. Gundersen, "Search for Good Men," 453–55; Meade, *Old Churches*, 1:163; Bishop of London to Rev. Philip Doddridge, May 11, 1751, quoted in Isaac, "Religion and Authority," 6; Madison to Robert Walsh, Jr., March 2, 1819, in *PJM*, Retirement Series, 1:491.

7. Nelson, *Blessed Company*, 126, 4–5; D. Holmes, "Episcopal Church," 264; Gundersen, "Search for Good Men," 453, 458; Gundersen, *Anglican Ministry*, 230; Nelson, *Blessed Company*, 407 n. 53. See also Bonomi, *Under the Cope of Heaven*, 61.

8. Baird, *Religion in the United States*, 228; Meade, *Old Churches*, 15–16; Gewehr, *Great Awakening*, 36–38; Hening, 3 (1696):151–53; Willison, *Patrick Henry*, 73–82; Beeman, *Patrick Henry*, 15–21; Isaac, "Religion and Authority."

9. Isaac, *Transformation*, 144; Foote, *Sketches*, 212 (Virginians largely indifferent according to Presbyterian Samuel Davies); Longmore, "All Matters and Things," 787 ("fear that a bishop would displace" gentry); Middleton, "Colonial Virginia Parson," 426 (bishop opposed "largely for political reasons"); Brant, "Madison: On the Separation," 4.

10. Seiler, "Anglican Parish," 132; Meade, *Old Churches*, 1:151–53; Hening, 3 (1705):288, and 6 (1753):326; J. Greene, "Foundations of Political Power," 490; Sydnor, *American Revolutionaries*, 89–90; Ragosta, *Wellspring*, 38; Scott, *History of Orange County*, 50.

11. Nelson, *Blessed Company*, 14, 7, 15; Hening: 1 (1643):240 (presentments); 2 (1676):359 (exemption levies); 3 (1696):149–50 (marriage); 6 (1748):31–33 (poor administration, binding out); 6 (1748):112 (manumitted slaves); 6 (1748):81–85 (marriage); 7 (1757):93 (militia); 8 (1769):374–77 (bastard children). Seiler, "Anglican Church," 148 (workhouses); Gundersen, *Anglican Ministry*, 183, citing Leonard Wood Labaree, ed., *Royal Instructions to British Colonial Governors, 1670–1776* (New York: D. Appleton-Century, 1935), 2:492.

12. Waddell, *Annals*, 59; Hening: 7 (1759):302–3, 8 (1769):432–33; Van Horne, *Correspondence of William Nelson*, 158–59 and n. 2; Brydon, *Mother Church*, 2:122–28 (western vestries occasionally dominated by non-Anglicans); Isaac, "Religion and Authority."

13. E. Randolph, *History of Virginia*, 158; Brydon, *Mother Church*, 2:44 (attendance law not enforced); Roeber, *Faithful Magistrates*, 142; Nelson, *Blessed Company*, 245–48; Gewehr, *Great Awakening*, 128; Howison, *History of Virginia*, 2:175 (Presbyterian Morris paid twenty fines); Isaac, "Rage of Malice," 140–41 (Baptists presented in Orange County); Ragosta, *Wellspring*, appendix; Fristoe, *Concise History*, 64; Gundersen, *Anglican Ministry*, 183; Campbell, *Colonial Caroline*, 226.

14. Thompson, *Presbyterians in the South*, 54–56; Davis, "Struggle for Religious Freedom," 27; McIlwaine, *Struggle of Protestant Dissenters*, 54; Foote, *Sketches*, 212–14.

15. Foote, *Sketches*, 135–38, 164–66 (British governor supported Rodgers but could not convince Council); Fristoe, *Concise History*, 67–68, 69–70. See also Amelia County: Baptists, Petition, *JHB*, February 24, 1772, 185–86 (one meeting house permitted per county); Thompson, *Presbyterians in the South*, 54–55.

16. Gewehr, *Great Awakening*, 74–75; Foote, *Sketches*, 213; *Virginia Gazette* (Purdie and Dixon), February 20, 1772; Foote, *Sketches*, 138.

17. Young, *Westward into Kentucky*, 128; Campbell, *History of the Colony*, 566. See also Ireland, *Life of the Reverend*, 155; and, generally, Spangler, *Virginians Reborn*, 119–20.

18. Gewehr, *Great Awakening*, 40–42; Najar, "Sectarians and Strategies," 122.

19. Gewehr, *Great Awakening*, 47; Foote, *Sketches*, 122, 124–25; Gewehr, *Great Awakening*, 50, 68–69.

20. Cobb, *Rise of Religious Liberty*, 111–12; Thom, *Struggle for Religious Freedom*, 34–35 (510–11); Najar, "Sectarians and Strategies," 115, 126–27; generally, Spangler, *Virginians Reborn*.

21. Bonomi, *Under the Cope of Heaven*, 89; Benedict, *General History*, 2:553; Campbell, *History of the Colony*, 562, quoting Jonathan Boucher.

22. Jefferson, *Notes*, Query XVII, 283; *PTJ*, 1:539 (55,000 dissenters); Tucker, *Life of Thomas Jefferson*, 1:97n, 19n; Prufer, "Franchise in Virginia," 260–65.

23. *Virginia Gazette* (Rind), July 21, 1768, 2–3.

24. Semple, *History of the Baptists*, 481–82, 20; Edwards, *Materials*, 3:75–76, 25–26, 82; "Persecution of Baptists," *Religious Herald*, 6, no. 14 (April 6, 1871); Little, *Imprisoned Preachers*, 227, 517–18. Waller had been an unconverted reprobate known primarily for hard drinking and florid cussing until he happened to sit on a jury in the Spotsylvania trial of Baptist preachers; he was so impressed by their demeanor in the face of persecution that he experienced a dramatic conversion, becoming one of the most powerful preachers in Virginia (Semple, *History of the Baptists*, 24n*). The persecution is documented at length in Ragosta, *Wellspring*, 28–36, 171–80.

25. Semple, *History of the Baptists*, 460, 400, 20; Ireland, *Life of the Reverend*, 156.

26. Fristoe, *Concise History*, 71–72; Edwards, *Materials*, 3:29–30, 54, 70, 90, 82; Thom, *Struggle for Religious Freedom*, 17 (493); Gewehr, *Great Awakening*, 119–20; Little, *Imprisoned Preachers*, 391, 176–77, 465, 192, 520; Semple, *History of the Baptists*, 20, 29; Campbell, *Colonial Caroline*, 222; Caroline County Order Book (1768), 142, 183.

27. Ireland, *Life of the Reverend*, 114–15; Spangler, "Presbyterians, Baptists," 162.

28. Ragosta, *Wellspring*, 32–36; Terman, "American Revolution," 327–28; Sprague, *Annals of the American Pulpit*, vol. 6, *Baptists*, 81 (quoting Samuel Harris); Orange County Order Book, No. 8 (1769–77), October 28, 1773, 287.

29. J. Taylor, *Lives*, 126; Rutland, *Bill of Rights*, 89; Ireland, *Life of the Reverend*, 136; Doares, "Alternative of Williams-Burg," 21.

30. Isaac, *Transformation*, 177; Ireland, *Life of the Reverend*, 155.

31. Adair, "James Madison's Autobiography," 198; Madison to William Bradford, January 24, 1774, in *PJM*, 1:105–6; Ragosta, *Wellspring*, 22, 25; *PTJ*, 1:535–39.

32. Baptist Petition (May 26, 1770), *EVRP*; Longmore, "All Matters and Things," 777; *JHB*, May 26, 1770, 179; *JHB*, June 1, 1770, 198; *JHB*, June 18, 1770, 242.

33. Lunenburg Baptists (February 12, 1772), Mecklenburg Baptists (February 22, 1772), Amelia Baptists (February 24, 1772), Sussex Baptists (February 24, 1772), Caroline Baptists (March 14, 1772), *JHB*, 30, 160–61, 182–83, 185–86, 245; Loudon County (May 1774), *JHB*, 92; *Virginia Gazette* (Rind), March 26, 1772; Petition of Lunenburg Baptists, *JHB*, February 12, 1772, 160–61; *JHB*, May 12, 1774, 92; Thomas, *Virginian Baptist*, 33; Bedford County (May 17, 1774), *EVRP*; *JHB*, May 26, 1770, 20.

34. *Virginia Gazette* (Rind), March 26, 1772; Isaac, *Transformation*, 219–22; Brydon, *Mother Church*, 2:376–80; Longmore, "All Matters and Things," 793.

35. Madison to William Bradford, April 1, 1774, in *PJM*, 1:112; Jefferson, *Autobiography*, 34.

36. *Meherrin Baptist Meeting Book*, 28–29 (entry after September 1774); Miscellaneous Petition (June 5, 1775), *EVRP*.

37. The Library of Congress database has only a summary of this petition from the *Journal of the Virginia Convention* (Miscellaneous Petition [August 16, 1775]). A full copy is available in Scribner and Tarter, *Revolutionary Virginia*, 3:441–42. *Virginia Gazette* (Pinkney), August 31, 1776, 3:3. See also Resolution of the Hartwood Baptist Church (September 16, 1775) ("lawful" for Christians "to take up arms in the present dispute with Great Britain and her colonies"), in Minute Book, 7. Henry, *Patrick Henry*, 1:317; James, *Documentary History*, 53.

38. Jefferson to Thomas Nelson, May 16, 1776, in *PTJ*, 1:292; Bearss, *Dictionary of Virginia*, 3:103.

39. Edmund Pendleton to William Woodford, March 16, 1776, in Mays, *Letters and Papers*, 1:158–59; *Virginia Gazette* (Purdie), March 15, 1776, Supplement, 1–2; *Virginia Gazette* (Purdie), March 22, 1776; *Virginia Gazette* (Dixon and Hunter), March 23, 1776, 3. Loyalism among southern dissenters is discussed in Ragosta, *Wellspring*, 101–7.

40. *Virginia Gazette* (Purdie), April 26, 1776. Other scholars have noted that mobilization required the cooperation of the "lower" class, resulting in significant class conflict in Virginia (see, for example, McDonnell, *Politics of War*; and Holton, *Forced Founders*). Those conflicts, though, generally concerned mobilization and were resolved by concessions over the means or terms of enlistment. The negotiation between religious dissenters and the Establishment cut across mobilization and politics, particularly religious freedom. In both cases, those that challenged Establishment authority became more engaged politically (see, for example, Rozbicki, *Culture and Liberty*). Douglas Bradburn makes a similar point about the politicization that accompanied transformation of "subjects" into "citizens" (*Citizenship Revolution*).

41. *PTJ*, 1:329–45.

42. *PJM*, 1:170–75; *PTJ*, 1:363.

43. Adair, "James Madison's Autobiography," 199; *PJM*, 1:171–79; *Virginia Gazette* (Dixon & Hunter), July 20, 1776; Henry, *Patrick Henry*, 1:450; Curry, *First Freedoms*, 135.

44. For example, George Washington to John Hancock, September 2, 1776; George Washington to John Hancock, December 5, 1776, in Crackel, *Papers of George Washington*. See, generally, Lengel, *Glorious Struggle*.

45. Prince William County (June 20, 1776), *EVRP* (emphasis added). The petition in the Library of Congress database is damaged; language supplemented from Ryland, *Baptists of Virginia*, 98.

46. Miscellaneous (October 16, 1776); Miscellaneous (October 24, 1776), *EVRP*. Virginia's population at the time was about 400,000–600,000, of which approximately 40–45 percent was enslaved. Assuming that adult, white, males fit for military service accounted for one in five of the remainder, and recognizing that not all signatories were white males, the petition likely garnered over 10 percent of that population.

47. *Virginia Gazette* (Purdie), October 18, 1776 (emphasis original); Miscellaneous Petition (October 24, 1776); Albemarle, Amherst, Buckingham Counties (October 22, 1776) (two petitions of the same date), *EVRP*; *Virginia Gazette* (Purdie), November 8, 1776.

48. *JHD*, October 11, 1776, 9; Mapp, *Virginia Experiment*, 448.

49. Albemarle County Instructions, *PTJ*, 6:288 (September-October 1776).

50. *JHD*, November 6, 1776, 58; *PTJ*, 1:530; *JHD*, November, 19, 1776, 85.

51. *JHD*: November 19, 1776, 85, and November 29, 1776, 101; Whitsitt, *Life and Times*, 53; *JHD*: November 20, 1776, 102–3, December 2, 1776, 106, October 25, 1776, 36, and December 2, 1776, 105; Whitsitt, *Life and Times*, 54; *JHD*, December 4, 1776, 110.

52. Whitsitt, *Life and Times*, 54, 57; *PTJ*, 1:533–34 n. 1; Hening, 9 (1776):164–66; Jefferson, *Autobiography*, 34. Jefferson's original draft of the bill also called for repeal of a Virginia law against apostasy (which did not originate in Parliament). For unknown reasons, this language was not included in the final version (*PTJ*, 1:530–34). The bill was also silent as to the licensing of ministers and other local regulations. While these restrictions were not enforced during the war, any ambiguity was removed by adoption of Jefferson's Statute in 1786.

53. Jefferson Notes on Religion, Library of Congress, American Memory, http://memory .loc.gov/master/mss/mtj/mtj1/001/1400/1449.jpg. The Library of Congress places these notes with Jefferson's notes on the Statute from 1779; the *Papers of Thomas Jefferson* places them as part of the 1776 legislative debate (see *PTJ*, 1:536–37). *PTJ*, 1:531 n. 1.

54. Jefferson Notes on Religion, Library of Congress, American Memory, http:// memory.loc.gov/master/mss/mtj/mtj1/001/1400/1450.jpg. See *PTJ*, 1:537–38. For evidence of Locke's influence, see Jefferson notes on Locke and Shaftesbury, in *PTJ*, 1:544–45. See, for example, Howell, *Early Baptists*, 122 (Baptist Convention proposed Statute in 1777; Jefferson and Madison drafted at Reuben Ford's request in 1778); and Patton, *Triumph*, 51–52 (nothing in bill not from 1776 Presbyterian petition). Smylie, "From Revolution to Civil War," 52; Howell, *Early Baptists*, 113, 124; Thom, *Struggle for Religious Freedom*, 77 (553); James, *Documentary History*, 62ff.; Johnson, *Virginia Presbyterianism*, 76ff; *PJM*, 8:297.

55. Jefferson Notes on Religion, Library of Congress, American Memory, http:// memory.loc.gov/master/mss/mtj/mtj1/001/1400/1449.jpg. See *PTJ*, 1:537. Jefferson, *Notes*, Query XVII, 286. Voltaire wrote that "if one religion only were allowed in England, the government very possibly would become arbitrary; if there were but two, the people would cut one another's throats; but, as there is such a multitude, they all live happy, and in peace" (Voltaire, "Letter on the Presbyterians," 218–19). Adam Smith made the point in 1776: "The interested and active zeal of religious teachers can be dangerous and troublesome only where there is, either but one sect tolerated in the society, or where the whole of a large society is divided into two or three great sects" (*Inquiry into the Nature*, 2:382). (The author thanks Iain McLean for this observation.) It is unlikely that Jefferson had a copy of Smith in November of 1776, although Madison may have seen it by the time the *Federalist* was prepared.

56. *PTJ*, 1:662.

57. Jefferson, *Autobiography*, 35; Hening, 9 (1776):165.

58. Mecklenburg County (May 29, 1777), *EVRP*; Cumberland County (May 21, 1777, and November 6, 1777), ibid.; Lunenburg County (December 11, 1777), ibid. (petition missing, summary like Mecklenburg petition); Westmoreland County (October 9, 1778), ibid.; *Virginia Gazette* (Dixon and Hunter), March 28, 1777; Mecklenburg County (May 29, 1777), *EVRP*.

59. Compare Hening: 7 (1757):93; 9 (1775):28, 89; 9 (1776):139–40; 9 (1777):267; 9 (1777): 312, 387; 9 (1777): 337–48. Miscellaneous Petition (October 29, 1778), *EVRP*; Hening, 10 (1779):28; compare Hening, 7 (1769):311; 9 (1775):32; 10 (1780):288–90, 361–63.

60. *JHD*, June 12, 1779, 50; Essex County (October 22, 1779), *EVRP* (marked, apparently by Committee on Religion, as "rejected"). Lancaster County (October 20, 1779), ibid. See also Culpeper County (October 21, 1779), ibid.; Lunenburg County (November 3, 1779), ibid.; Amherst County (November 10, 1779), ibid. Compare *Virginia Gazette* (Dixon & Nicolson), August 14, 1779, September 11, 1779, September 18, 1779, *Virginia Gazette* (Clarkson and Davis), November 6, 1779, and *Virginia Gazette* (Clarkson and Davis), October 30, 1779. *JHD*, October 25, 1779, 28. Miscellaneous Petition (October 24, 1776), *EVRP* (Presbyterian); Goochland County (December 25, 1776), *EVRP* (Baptist); Miscellaneous Petition (June 3, 1777), *EVRP* (Presbyterian); John Todd to Jefferson, August 16, 1779, in *PTJ*, 3:68.

61. Scribner and Tarter, *Revolutionary Virginia*, 7:153; *Virginia Gazette* (Purdie), February 21, 1777; Honyman, *Diary*, (March 4, 1777), 115–16; McIlwaine, *Journals of the Council*, 2:74, January 28, 1778; Moore, "Jeremiah Walker," 719, 725; Benedict, *General History*, 2:390–92 (Walker "all-powerful in Associations and other places among the Baptists"); Henry, *Patrick Henry*, 2:134; Newman, *History of the Baptist Churches*, 368.

62. See, generally, Ragosta, *Wellspring*, 87–107.

63. E. Randolph, *History of Virginia*, 263–64, 194; Mays, *Letters and Papers*, 2:488–89. Compare Morgan, *Patrick Henry*, 275 (accepting Randolph's characterization).

64. Miscellaneous Petition (May 26, 1784), *EVRP*; Powhatan County (November 6, 1783), ibid.; Mecklenburg County (May 29, 1777), ibid. Rozbicki makes the point more generally, suggesting that the growth of liberty during this period was often the result of an entrenched hierarchy being forced by necessity to give the privileges which they enjoyed to a broader group (*Culture and Liberty*).

65. Jefferson, *Notes*, Query XVII, 285, 287, 283.

66. Caroline County (November 8, 1780), *EVRP*. The seven counties in which overseers managed poor relief were Rockbridge, Botetourt, Montgomery, Washington, Greenbrier, Augusta, and Frederick (Hening, 10 [1780]: 288–90). In 1782, Shenandoah, Henry, Monongalia, Ohio, and Berkeley were added (Hening, 11 (1782):62).

3. The Virginia Statute for Establishing Religious Freedom

1. Miscellaneous Petition (June 3, 1782); Amelia (May 1783); Powhatan (November 16, 1783); Prince Edward (November 22, 1781); Essex (May 30, 1783); Amelia (May 31, 1783), *EVRP*.

2. David Griffith to John Buchanan, Fall 1783, quoted in Meade, *Old Churches*, 2:264–65; *Virginia Gazette or American Advertiser*, September 13, 1783.

3. Richard Henry Lee to Madison, November 26, 1784, in *PJM*, 8:149.

4. Warwick (May 15, 1784); Lunenburg (November 8, 1783); Amherst (November 27, 1783) (spelling as in original); Powhatan (June 4, 1784), *EVRP*. The Library of Congress database describes the Powhatan petition as a request for a new Baptist church; the text shows that it supports a general assessment, and the House of Delegates saw it as such

(*JHD*, June 4, 1784, 48–49). Nor does this petition appear to come from Baptists; Joseph Eggleston, later a member of Congress from adjacent Amelia County and reportedly an Episcopalian, is a signatory.

5. Lunenburg (November 8, 1783); Lunenburg (November 15, 1783); Amherst (November 27, 1783); Warwick (May 15, 1784); Powhatan (June 4, 1784); Miscellaneous Petition (June 4, 1784); Isle of Wight (November 4, 1784); Amelia (November 8, 1784), *EVRP*. For example, *Virginia Gazette or American Advertiser* (September 13, 1783, November 15 and 22, 1783) (responding to a November 8 letter opposed to a general assessment because "the Church and the State, are two societies, and in their nature and designs, as different as Heaven and earth").

6. *JHD*: May 27, 1784, 30, June 8, 1784, 57–58, June 28, 1784, 111; Madison to Jefferson, July 3, 1784, in *PJM*, 8:93–94. On December 8, 1784, Jefferson wrote to Madison in code that "what we have to do . . . is *devoutly to pray* for *his* [Henry's] *death*" (*PTJ*, 7:558; italics originally in cipher). This unkind reference is often misattributed to the general-assessment debate, but Jefferson was referring to efforts to reframe the Virginia constitution opposed by Henry.

7. *JHD*, November 11, 1784, 17; Richard Henry Lee to Madison, November 26, 1784, in *PJM*, 8:149, 8:390 (Harrison); Brant, *James Madison: The Nationalist*, 343 (John Marshall, Philip Barbour, Joseph Jones, William Norvell, Henry Tazewell); Hunt, "James Madison," 1:168 (Spencer Roane); Edmund Pendleton to Richard Henry Lee, February 28, 1785, in Mays, *Letters and Papers*, 2:474 (Edmund Pendleton); John Page to Jefferson, August 23, 1785, in *PTJ*, 8:428–29; Washington to George Mason, October 3, 1785, in Rutland, *Papers of George Mason*, 2:832 (spelling and emphasis as in original); Madison to Jefferson, January 9, 1785, in *PTJ*, 7: 594.

8. For example, Kidd, *Patrick Henry*, 168; Dreisbach, "George Mason's," 226; McLoughlin, "Role of Religion," 213; Muñoz, "Religion and the Common Good," 3; and Drakeman, *Church, State*, 114. Washington to George Mason, October 3, 1785, in Rutland, *Papers of George Mason*, 2:832; Eckenrode, *Separation*, 85, quoting Beverley Randolph.

The divisiveness of religious disputes has also often been an issue in modern constitutional debates. Justice Jackson, for example, argued that the First Amendment "was intended not only to keep the states' hands out of religion, but to keep religion's hands off the state, and, above all, to keep bitter religious controversy out of public life" (*Everson*, 330 U.S. 1, 26–27 [1947] [Jackson dissenting]). This factor has tended to disappear from recent decisions.

9. *JHD*, November 17, 1784, 25.

10. Miscellaneous Petitions (November 12, 1784), *EVRP*. The 1779 proposal would have required churches to endorse five doctrines to receive tax revenues, including a future state of rewards and punishments, Christianity as the "true Religion," and the Old and New Testaments as divinely inspired (*JHD*, October 25, 1779, 28; Buckley, *Church and State*, 56–57).

11. Miscellaneous Petitions (November 11, 1784), *EVRP*; James, *Documentary History*, 131; Madison to Jefferson, January 9, 1785, in *PTJ*, 7:594.

12. Rice, "Memorials," 38.

13. Brant, "Madison: On the Separation," 7–8, citing John Blair Smith to Madison, June 21, 1784, in *PJM*, 8:80–82. That letter focuses on incorporation and does not discuss

the assessment. Madison to James Monroe, April 12, 1785, in *PJM*, 8:261; Madison to Richard Henry Lee, November 14, 1784, in *PJM*, 9:431 (a "Schism will take place" between Episcopalians and Presbyterians). For earlier Presbyterian petitions opposing a general assessment, see Miscellaneous Petition (October 24, 1776); Miscellaneous Petition (June 3, 1777); and Miscellaneous Petition (May 26, 1784), *EVRP*.

14. John Blair Smith to Madison, June 21, 1784, in *PJM*, 8:80–82.

15. Miscellaneous Petitions (June 4, 1784), *EVRP*; Madison to Jefferson, July 3, 1784, in *PTJ*, 7:360–61; Jefferson to Madison, December 8, 1784, in *PTJ*, 7:558 (italics originally in cipher).

16. *JHD*: November 17, 1784, 25, December 11, 1784, 62. Compare *JHD*: December 11, 1784, 62, December 13, 1784, 65, December 17, 1784, 71, December 18, 1784, 72, December 20, 1784), 73, December 22, 1784, 75, and November 17, 1784, 25, December 21, 1784, 74.

17. Hening, 11 (1784):532–35; *JHD*, December 24, 1784, 79; Mazzei, *Researches*, 161; Edmund Pendleton to Richard Henry Lee, February 28, 1785, in Mays, *Letters and Papers*, 2:474; Madison to Jefferson, January 9, 1785, in *PTJ*, 7:594; Madison to James Madison Sr., January 6, 1785, in *PJM*, 8:217.

18. Madison to Jefferson, January 9, 1785, in *PTJ*, 7:594.

19. *JHD*, December 16, 1784, 68; Hening, 11 (1784):503–4; Bennett, *Memorials*, 210.

20. Rockingham, *JHD*, November 18, 1784, 26; see also *Virginia Gazette and Weekly Advertiser*, November 13, 1784 (100 Botetourt County citizens oppose). See Lunenburg, Mecklenburg, and Amelia and Halifax, *JHD*, November 20, 1784, 29; Dinwiddie, Amelia, and Surry, *JHD*, December 3, 1784, 51; *Virginia Gazette and Weekly Advertiser*, November 20, 1784 (Prince Edward residents support); Madison to Jefferson, January 9, 1785, in *PJM*, 8:229.

21. *PJM*, 8:198; *JHD*, December 24, 1784, 78–79; Madison to George Mason (namesake of Madison's colleague of 1784), July 14, 1826, Library of Congress, American Memory, http://memory.loc.gov/cgi-bin/ampage image 611.

22. Compare *JHD*, November 11, 1784, 17, and December 24, 1784, 78–79.

23. Burkitt, *Concise History*, 79; James, *Documentary History*, 137–38; Resolution of the Baptist General Committee, August 13, 1785, appendix.

24. *Virginia Gazette* (Dixon and Hunter), March 28, 1777; L. Greene, *Writings of the Late Elder John Leland*, 181.

25. Surry (October 26, 1785); Caroline (October 27, 1785), *EVRP*; *PJM*, 8:297. For example, Southampton (November 29, 1785) (David Barrow), *EVRP*.

26. Hanover Presbytery Minutes, May 19, 1785; Foote, *Sketches*, 341–44, 342–43. (The original of this petition does not appear in the Library of Congress database; Foote, *Sketches*, 342–44, provides a copy.) Memorial from the General Convention of Virginia Presbyterians, August 13, 1785 (Bethel), appendix. For example, Miscellaneous Petitions (November 12, 1785) (multiple sources referring to Bethel meeting), Frederick and Berkeley (November 12, 1785), Prince Edward (November 12, 1785), Berkeley (November 18, 1785); Miscellaneous Petitions (November 2, 1785), *EVRP*; Madison to Jefferson, August 20, 1785, in *PTJ*, 8:413–16, 415 (italics originally in cipher).

27. *PJM*, 8:297–98. The 1790 census showed Virginia with a population of 747,550, of which 292,627 were slaves. Assuming adult white males comprised one-fourth of the remainder (a conservative estimate), the figure is less than 115,000. While some women

and blacks undoubtedly signed these petitions, they would not account for a large share of signatories. George Nicholas to Madison, April 22, 1785, *PJM*, 8:264; editorial note, 8:295; M&R, *PJM*, 8:298–304 (internal quote from the Virginia Declaration of Rights), appendix.

28. For example, Kidd, *Patrick Henry*, 170–71. Accomack (October 28, 1785). Chester-field (November 14, 1785) (spelling as in original), *EVRP*. For example, Memorial from the General Convention of Virginia Presbyterians, August 13, 1785 (Bethel), appendix; Nansemond (October 27, 1785); Northumberland (November 28, 1785) (versions of Baptist Spirit of the Gospel petition), *EVRP*.

Hamburger simply confuses the role of the evangelical dissenters in arguing that they "did not demand a separation of church and state" but sought an end to discrimination and "a freedom from legislation that took cognizance of religion, . . . a request that law take no notice of religion" (*Separation*, 89, 94).

29. James, *Documentary History*, 139; Rives, *History of the Life*, 1:632; Madison, "Detached Memorandum," 492; Foote, *Sketches*, 346, 431; Madison to Jefferson, January 22, 1786, in *PJM*, 8:473.

30. *PTJ*, 2:548; *JHD*, December 16, 1785, December 17, 1785, 93–94; *Journal of the Senate*, December 23, 1785, 61. Statute text in Documentary Appendix. The Statute received Senate approval on January 16 (now celebrated as "Religious Freedom Day"), but the Speaker's signature was not attached until January 19 (*JHD*, January 19, 1786, 146).

31. Madison to Jefferson, January 22, 1786, in *PJM*, 8:474; Dreisbach, "Thomas Jefferson and Bills," 170 n. 60 ("most significant amendment"); Gaustad, *Sworn*, 65 ("probably pained Jefferson most"). In his Letter to the Danbury Baptists, Jefferson reiterated that "the legitimate powers of government reach actions only, & not opinions." Jefferson's views in this regard did not go unchallenged; see, for example, Hamburger, *Separation*, 71 n. 7, citing *Considerations on an Act of the Legislature of Virginia, Entitled, An Act for the Establishment of Religious Freedom* (Philadelphia, 1786), 12, but he prevailed in the Virginia Statute.

32. Buckley, *Church and State*, 158 n. 45; Madison, "Detached Memorandum," 494; Novak, "How Did Virginians," 26; Jefferson, *Autobiography*, 40; Madison, "Detached Memorandum," 492.

33. *PTJ*, 2:550–52; Mazzei, *Researches*, 158; *PTJ*, 2:552–53. For example, *Morning Chronicle and London Advertiser*, August 30, 1786 (text from Richard Price). Madison to Jefferson, January 22, 1786, in *PTJ*, 9:196.

34. Miller, *First Liberty*, 153; Gaustad, *Faith*, 34.

35. The post-Revolution process of evangelicals disassociating themselves from separation of church and state (Ragosta, *Wellspring*, 163–64) accelerated after the Supreme Court's school integration and school prayer decisions in the 1950s and 1960s (for example, Jeffries and Ryan, "Political History"; and S. Gordon, *Spirit of the Law*, 92–93).

36. Samuelson, "Jefferson and Religion," 151; Kramer, "Free Church."

37. *Rosenberger v. University of Virginia*, 515 U.S. 819, 854 (1995) (Thomas concurring); *Wallace v. Jaffee*, 472 U.S. 38, 91–114 (1985) (Rehnquist dissenting); Malbin, *Religion and Politics*; R. Smith, "Getting Off on the Wrong Foot"; Cord, *Separation*, 19–21; Laycock, "'Nonpreferential' Aid," 877.

38. For example, Laycock, "'Nonpreferential' Aid," 896–99.

39. Washington to George Mason, October 3, 1785, in Rutland, *Papers of George Mason*, 2:832; *Rosenberger*, 515 U.S. at 869 n. 1 (Souter, Stevens, Ginsburg, Breyer dissenting); *Rosenberger*, 515 U.S. at 853 n.1 (Thomas concurring).

40. Cord, *Separation*, 20–21; Dreisbach, "Thomas Jefferson and Bills," 167; *Rosenberger*, 515 U.S. at 855 (Thomas concurring); Hamburger, *Separation*, 104 n. 34, quoting Madison to Richard Henry Lee, November 14, 1784.

41. Curry, *First Freedoms*, 145; Edmund Pendleton to Richard Henry Lee, February 28, 1785, in Mays, *Letters and Papers*, 2:474; Richard Henry Lee to Madison, November 26, 1784, in *PJM*, 9:149–50; Miscellaneous Petition, November 12, 1784; *JHD*, November 12, 1784, 19 ("all who profess the public worship of the Deity"); Madison to Jefferson, January 9, 1785, in *PTJ*, 7:595.

Similarly, objections to a proposal for an assessment in Georgia "were not based on its exclusion of non-Christians" (Myerson, *Endowed*, 261, citing Samuel Boykin, *History of the Baptist Denomination of Georgia* [Atlanta: Harrison, 1881], 1:262). A Connecticut general assessment scheme was opposed both because of de facto discrimination and because "it is unjust to apply the monies of those who pretend to no religion and were paid by them for other purposes to the support of religion they do not believe in when it is known to be contrary to their desire" (McLoughlin, *New England Dissent*, 2:1040, quoting resolution of First and Second Baptist Churches of Groton).

42. Madison to Richard Henry Lee, November 14, 1784, in *PJM*, 9:430–31; *PTJ*, 1:531 n. 1.

43. Hanover Presbytery Minutes, May 19, 1785; Botetourt (November 29, 1785); Orange (November 17, 1785), *EVRP*.

44. Madison to Jefferson, January 9, 1785, in *PTJ*, 7:592. See also Archibald Stuart to Jefferson, October 17, 1785, in *PTJ*, 8:645 (extravagance and dissipation, excellent tax revenues, good tobacco prices). Grigsby, *History of the Virginia Federal Convention*, 2:122–30. See also Dreisbach, "Thomas Jefferson and Bills," 168–69 (opposition to tax was a "significant consideration often overlooked by modern commentators").

45. Washington to George Mason, October 3, 1785, in Rutland, *Papers of George Mason*, 2:831–32. When multiple copies of a petition from the same county were received on a single day, they were counted as one petition unless their content was clearly different. For example, Goochland (November 2, 1785), *EVRP* (M&R); and Goochland County (November 2, 1785), ibid. ("Spirit of the Gospel"). The eleven "miscellaneous petitions" received on November 12, 1785, endorsing the Presbyterian Bethel resolution, without an indication of county of origin, were treated as one petition. Some petitions appear in the *JHD* without being survived by a hard copy.

46. Foote, *Sketches*, 431; Madison to James Monroe, May 29, 1785, in *PJM*, 8:286. See also Madison to James Monroe, April 28, 1785, in *PJM*, 8:272 (James Pendleton, colonel in the Revolution, former sheriff of Culpeper, lost for support of assessment); Mays, *Letters and Papers*, 2:478; Buckley, *Church and State*, 117 n. 11 (John Marshall, Philip Barbour, John Coleman, James Pendleton, and George Slaughter).

47. Dreisbach, "Thomas Jefferson and Bills," 203. See also Cord, *Separation of Church*, 222; and Cord, "Founding Intentions," 49.

48. Dreisbach, "Thomas Jefferson and Bills," 192–93. My thanks to Daniel Clinkman for pointing out Pendleton's interest in the Levitical Laws.

49. Myerson, *Endowed*, 115–21; Green, *Second*, 41–42. See also, for example, *PTJ*, 2:558 (marriage law liberalizing).

50. Hening, 12 (1785):27–30; *JHD*: December 30, 1785, 117, January 16, 1786, 141, January 6, 1787, 142; Hening, 12 (1786):266; *Perry v. Commonwealth*, 44 VA 632, 642 (1846); Stokes and Pfeffer, *Church and State*, 52.

51. Jefferson to Madison, December 16, 1786, in *PTJ*, 10:604; Madison, "Detached Memorandum," 492.

4. The First Amendment to the U.S. Constitution

1. Generally Maier, *Ratification*.

2. Jefferson to Madison, December 20, 1787, in *PTJ*, 12:440.

3. For example, Labunski, *James Madison*; Veit, Bowling, and Bickford, *Creating the Bill of Rights*; Cogan, *Complete*; and Schwartz, *Bill of Rights*.

4. 330 U.S. 1, 11, 13 (1947); *Everson*, 330 U.S. at 33 (Rutledge, Frankfurter, Jackson, Burton dissenting) (ftnt. omitted); *McGowan v. Maryland*, 366 U.S. 420, 437 (1961).

5. *Wallace v. Jaffree*, 472 U.S. 38, 92, 106 (1985) (Rehnquist dissenting).

6. Myerson, *Endowed*, 138–39 (oath).

7. Madison to Jefferson, October 17, 1788, in *PTJ*, 14:19. See also Madison's response to a call for a bill of rights in the Virginia Ratification Convention (June 12, 1788, *DHRC*, 10:1223).

8. Madison to Jefferson, October 24, 1787, in *PTJ*, 12:280; *PTJ*, 12:284; Jefferson to Madison, December 20, 1787, in *PTJ*, 12:440. Madison heard about the lack of a bill of rights from other sources as well, for example, George Lee Turberville to Madison, December 11, 1787, in *PJM*, 10:316 ("principal objection that the opponents bring forward . . . is the total want of a Bill of Rights").

9. Madison to Jefferson, December 20, 1787, in *PJM*, 10:332.

10. Madison to Jefferson, April 22, 1788, in *PTJ*, 13:98; Jefferson to Alexander Donald, February 7, 1788, in *PTJ*, 12:571; Speech of Patrick Henry, June 9, 1788, in *DHRC*, 9:1051–52; Madison to Jefferson, July 24, 1788, in *PTJ*, 13:412–13.

11. Jefferson to Madison, July 31, 1788, in *PTJ*, 13:440, 442.

12. Madison to Jefferson, October 17, 1788, in *PTJ*, 14:18; Madison to Jefferson, December 8, 1788, in *PJM*, 11:383. See also Madison to Jefferson, March 29, 1789, in *PJM*, 12:38 ("detaching the deluded opponents from their designing leaders"); and Antieau, Downey, and Roberts, *Freedom*, 126 (Daniel Carroll thought religious liberty amendment most important to conciliate people).

13. U.S. Constitution, art. I, § 8. Madison's arguments for a bill of rights, June 8, 1789, in *PJM*, 12:196–209, 205; and August 15, 1789, *PJM*, 12:339.

14. General Defense of the Constitution, June 12, 1788, in *PJM*, 11:130; Madison to Jefferson, October 17, 1788, in *PTJ*, 14:18. Cord cites Madison's view that there is "not a shadow of a right in the general government to intermeddle with religion," as applying only to establishment of a single sect (Cord, *Separation*, 8). That reading is inconsistent with both the language and Madison's views expressed in the Memorial & Remonstrance and elsewhere.

15. Madison to Jefferson, October 17, 1788, in *PTJ*, 14:18; *DHRC*, 10:1553; Cogan, *Complete*, 11–13.

16. Jefferson to Madison, March 15, 1789, in *PTJ*, 14:660, 659.

17. Jefferson sent an extract of his December 20, 1787, letter to Madison to a Marylander, Uriah Forrest, then resident in London, with an admonition that the letter could be used but without attribution. Daniel Carroll, a delegate to the Philadelphia Convention active in Maryland's ratification, informed Madison that a letter from Jefferson had been "shown at Annapolis," that expressed concern with a lack of a bill of rights, particularly religious freedom (Carroll to Madison, May 28, 1788, in *PJM*, 11:64–65). See also *DHRC*, 10:1708 n 5. *Proceedings and Debates*, 254; Price, "There Ought to Be," 438.

18. Jefferson to William Stephens Smith, November 13, 1787, in *PTJ*, 12:356–56; Jefferson to William Stephens Smith, February 2, 1788, in *PTJ*, 12:558; Jefferson to Edward Carrington, May 27, 1788, in *PTJ*, 13:208; Jefferson to Francis Hopkinson, March 13, 1789, in *PTJ*, 14:650. See also Jefferson to C. W. F. Dumas, February 12, 1788, in *PTJ*, 12:583.

19. Price, "There Ought to Be," 438. See Conley, "Rhode Island," 152 ("primarily rights-related"). Murrin, "Massachusetts," 95. See also Collier, "Liberty, Justice," 116 ("in Virginia, New York, and Massachusetts, Federalists seeking election to Congress had to promise to bring amendments forward"). Cogan, *Complete Bill of Rights*, 11–12 (Maryland [minority statement], Massachusetts [minority statement], New Hampshire, New York, North Carolina, Pennsylvania [minority statement], Rhode Island, and Virginia called for religious freedom amendment).

20. "Centinel," *Philadelphia Freeman's Journal*, October 24, 1787, in *DHRC*, 13:466; "An Old Whig, No. 5," Fall 1787; Herbert J. Storing, *The Complete Anti-federalist* (Chicago: University of Chicago Press, 1981): 3.3.25–29, in Kurland and Lerner, *Founders' Constitution*, 5:86–87; "A [Maryland] Farmer, No. 7," April 11, 1788, in Storing, *Complete Antifederalist*, 5:1:105–7, in Kurland and Lerner, *Founders' Constitution*, 5:87.

21. Madison's arguments for a bill of rights, June 8, 1789, in *PJM*, 12:196–209, 198, 205, 207; Speech of Madison, August 15, 1789, in *PJM*, 12:339. See also Madison to Richard Peters, August 19, 1789, in *PJM*, 12:347.

22. Madison to Richard Peters, August 19, 1789, in *PJM*, 12:347 (emphasis original).

23. James Madison Sr. to Madison, January 30, 1788, in *PJM*, 10:446. Others also warned Madison of Leland's opposition (*DHRC*, 4:253–54 [Joseph Spenser to Madison, enclosing Leland's objections to the Constitution]). The most thorough treatment of Madison's electoral alliance with Leland is provided in Scarberry, "John Leland and James Madison." Compare Ryland, *Baptists of Virginia*, 134; and Sprague, *Annals of the American Pulpit*, 6:180.

24. Madison to George Eve, January 2, 1789, in *PJM*, 11:404–5; Labunski, *James Madison*, 175; Madison to George Washington, November 20, 1789, in *PJM*, 12:453.

25. *PJM*, 12:196–209. *Philadelphia Independent Gazetteer*, February 10, 1789, reprinting *Virginia Independent Chronicle*, January 13, 1789; *New Jersey Journal*, February 18, 1789; *New Hampshire Spy*, March 6, 1789.

26. *Reynolds v. United States*, 98 U.S. 145, 163, 164 (1879). Justice Field dissented on a technical point in *Reynolds*, but joined the decision's relevant portions. *Everson v. Board of Education*, 330 U.S. 1 (1947). See, for example, Butler, *Awash*, 265 ("The Virginia debate and the Act for Establishing Religious Freedom directly affected the conceptualization

and passage of the First Amendment to the Constitution"); Peterson and Vaughan, *Virginia Statute*, x; Marty, "Virginia Statute Two Hundred Years Later," 1 ("The Virginia event, by common consent, was the most decisive element in an epochal shift in the Western world's approach to relations between civil and religious spheres of life"); Pfeffer, "Madison's 'Detached Memoranda,'" 285 ("Nor can there be any doubt that together, the 'Memorial and Remonstrance' and the Virginia Statute furnished a historic basis for the adoption" of the First amendment); and Stokes, *Church and State*, 1:366 (the Statute "influenced the American theories of Church-State separation and religious freedom more than any other historical factor").

27. Magrath, "Chief Justice Waite," provides an informative discussion of the Waite/ Bancroft cooperation. See also Drakeman, "*Reynolds v. United States.*"

28. Connecticut Fundamental Orders (1639) (Christian); Delaware Constitution, art. 22 (1776) (oath for office includes trinity, Old and New Testaments); Georgia Constitution, art. VI (1777) (Protestant office holders); Maryland Declaration of Rights, art. 33 (1776) (Christians protected); Massachusetts Constitution, art. 3 (1780) (Protestant religion); New Hampshire Constitution, art. 6 (1784) (Christians protected); New Jersey Constitution, art. 19 (1776) (Protestants protected); New York Constitution, art. 42 (1777) (anti-Catholic); North Carolina Constitution, art. 32 (1776) (Protestant office holders); Pennsylvania Constitution, § 10 (1776) (belief in God, old and new testaments to hold office); South Carolina Constitution, arts. 3, 12 (1778) (Protestant office holders), in Thorpe, *Federal and State Constitutions*. While its charter seemed to prohibit such actions, Rhode Island legislatively restricted the franchise to Protestants (Conley, "Rhode Island," 144).

29. For example, *Wallace v. Jaffree*, 472 U.S. 38, 92 *et seq.* (1985) (Rehnquist dissenting); *Cutter v. Wilkinson*, 544 U.S. 709, 726–27 (2005) (Thomas concurring); *Elk Grove Unified School Dist. v. Newdow*, 542 U.S. 1, 50 (2004) (Thomas concurring). Dreisbach, "Church-State Debate," 155; Hamburger, *Separation*, 2.

30. D. Gordon, "Constitutional *Res Gestae*," 21; *Van Orden v. Perry*, 545 U.S. 677, 731 (2005) (Stevens dissenting); West, "Case Against," 620; Miller, *First Liberty*, 299; Curry, *First Freedoms*, 193. See also Drakeman, *Church, State*, 328 (had to be "noncontroversial").

31. Martis and Elmes, *Historical Atlas*, 6–7; John Adams to Patrick Henry, June 3, 1776, in Taylor, *Adams Papers*; Baird, *Religion*, 242; Dreisbach, "Virginia's Contribution," 186; *New England Chronicle* (published as *Boston Independent Chronicle*), April 6, 1780, 1; *Columbian Herald or the Patriotic Courier of North-America*, May 29, June 5, June 8, and June 12, 1786. See also *Considerations on an Act of the Legislature of Virginia; Massachusetts Centinel*, April 26, 1786, referring to articles in *Halifax Journal* and *Nova Scotia Gazette*.

32. See *Wallace v. Jaffree*, 472 U.S. at 97 (Rehnquist dissenting) ("Madison was undoubtedly the most important architect"). *Arizona Christian School Tuition Organization v. Winn*, __U.S. __, Slip Op. 09–987 (April 4, 2011), 13 ("Madison . . . went on to become, as *Flast* put it, 'the leading architect of the religion clauses of the First Amendment'"), quoting *Flast v. Cohen*, 393 U.S. 83, 103 (1968).

33. Myerson, *Endowed*, 153–54, 173. See also Green, *Second*, 63–64.

34. Jefferson to Madison, March 15, 1789, in *PTJ*, 14:660. Smith argues that "enactors of the religion clause simply were not concerned with . . . the question of Congress's power over religion in federally controlled areas," citing federalists' argument that

Congress had no express power over religion (S. Smith, *Foreordained*, 28). This ignores the views of antifederalists and federalists like Madison who were increasingly concerned about the "necessary and proper" clause.

35. Curry, *First Freedoms*, 202.

36. Adams and Emmerich, *Nation Dedicated*, 47.

37. Cogan, *Complete*, 12 (Pennsylvania minority proposal); Drakeman, *Church, State*, 229, 328; Brant, "Madison: On the Separation," 15.

38. *DHFFC*, 4:10–11; Brant, "Madison: On the Separation," 19. Notably, a 1776 proposal from John Dickinson that the states of the confederacy be prohibited from compelling attendance at or support for religion was rejected for impinging states' rights (Green, *Second*, 55).

39. *DHFFC*, 4:28–29, 11:1261–62.

40. Ibid., 11:1261–61. See also Curry, *First Freedoms*, 203. Lash, "Second Adoption," 1101.

41. *DHFFC*, 11:1284, 4:36, 39.

42. Drakeman, *Church, State*, 209; *DHFFC*, 1:151; Virginia General Assessment bill (1784); Delaware 1776, art. 29: "no establishment of any one religious sect in this State in preference to another," in Thorpe, *Federal and State*, 1:567–68; Georgia 1798: "No one religious society shall ever be established in this State, in preference to another" (ibid., 2:800–801); New Jersey 1776, art. XIX: "no establishment of any one religious sect in this Province, in preference to another" (ibid., 5:2597–98); Baird, *Religion*, 104; Cord, *Separation*, 6–7. Some sources further twist this nonpreferentialist view into an argument that the First Amendment was intended only to prohibit discrimination among Christian sects. For example, Colwell, *Position of Christianity*, 23 (excluding Catholics and Mormons from his definition of Christians, 20); editorial, "No Room for the Ten Commandments," *Washington Times*, February 8, 2011 (Jefferson only sought to prevent government "showing favor to particular Christian denominations"). www.washingtontimes.com/news/2011/feb/8/no-room-for-the-ten-commandments/print/. Not only are such claims devoid of textual support, but Jefferson was clear that religious freedom was "to comprehend, within the mantle of it's protection, the Jew and the Gentile, the Christian and Mahometan, the Hindoo, and infidel of every denomination" (*Autobiography*, 40). The Memorial & Remonstrance also expressly attacked the effort to "establish Christianity, in exclusion of all other Religions" (appendix).

43. *DHFFC*, 1:151, 4:46, 1:158.

44. Ibid., 4:46, 1:158, 138.

45. Levy, *Establishment*, 83; Landholder, December 17, 1787, quoted in Kurland and Lerner, *Founders' Constitution*, 4:14.

46. Madison Speech, August 17, 1789, in *PJM*, 12:344.

47. *DHFFC*, 4:47–48; Levy, *Establishment*, 83; Cogan, *Complete*, 7–8; *DHFFC*, 1:189, 192.

48. *DHFFC*, 1:151. See also Drakeman, *Church, State*, 206 (Madison's effort to reinsert "national" "seems clearly to be an effort to address any concern that church-state practices in the various states would be affected by the amendment"). August 15, 1789 speech, *DHFFC*, 11:1262. (It is also worth noting that this excerpt from the debates differs significantly from other reports, and some have suggested that it may be an erroneous quotation, not an unknown phenomenon in the late eighteenth century.) *DHFFC*, 11:1284–92; Madison, "Detached Memorandum," 494.

49. Hamburger, *Separation*, 106–7; *Wallace v. Jaffree*, 472 U.S. at 98–99 (Rehnquist dissenting); Brant, "Madison: On Separation," 17. See also *Everson*, 330 U.S. at 60 n. 55, 37 (Rutledge, Frankfurter, Jackson, Burton dissenting) ("Madison's entire thesis, as reflected throughout the Remonstrance and in his other writings, . . . was altogether incompatible with acceptance of general and 'nondiscriminatory' support." "[T]he Remonstrance is at once the most concise and the most accurate statement of the views of the *First Amendment's* author concerning what is 'an establishment of religion'").

50. Dreisbach, "Thomas Jefferson and Bills," 195; Brant, "Madison: On the Separation," 17–18, citing *Annals of Congress* (House), January 25, February 2, 1790; Church, *Separation*, 60; Brant, "Madison: On the Separation," 3.

51. For example, *Wallace v. Jaffree*, 472 U.S. at 98 (Rehnquist dissenting). *PJM*, 12:205, 339.

52. Compare Bradley, *Church-State*, 13, 19. Cogan, *Complete*, 61 (in suggesting the "Congress shall make no law" language, Samuel Livermore understood that multiple establishments in Massachusetts and Connecticut could be "construed into a religious establishment.") Levy, *Original Intent*, 189–94; Drakeman, *Church, State*, 228 n. 119.

53. Jefferson Second Inaugural Address, March 4, 1805, in Ford, 8:344; Curry, *First Freedoms*, 209; Drakeman, *Church, State*, 231; Miller, *First Liberty*, 120. Compare Jeffries and Ryan, "Political History," 296 n. 81. S. Smith, *Foreordained*, 33–34; Antieau, Downey, and Roberts, *Freedom*, 153–54.

54. Witte, *Religion*, 21; Jeffries and Ryan, "Political History," 292.

55. *Walz*, 397 U.S. 664, 682 (1970) (Brennan concurring) (citations omitted). A similar distinction can be applied to Donald Drakeman's criticism of Justice Douglas for rejecting the history of state tax exemptions for religious institutions in *Walz* (1970) and then relying on the history of Jefferson's and Madison's impact on the First Amendment (Drakeman, *Church, State*, 78). The two are fundamentally different. In analyzing the original meaning of the First Amendment, state provisions tell us little about that question, while Jefferson's and Madison's views are central.

56. *Wallace v. Jaffree*, 452 U.S. at 92 (Rehnquist dissenting); Buckley, "Great Religious Octopus," 335.

57. Knox, *Vindication*, 8.

5. From the First Amendment to *Reynolds*

1. Danbury Baptist Association to Jefferson (after October 7, 1801), in *PTJ*, 35:408; Madison, "Detached Memorandum," 492.

2. *Reynolds v. United States*, 98 U.S. 145 (1879); Hamburger, *Separation*, 11.

3. Dreisbach, *Thomas Jefferson*, 54.

4. Ahlstrom, *Religious History*, 380; *Washington, DC, National Intelligencer*, September 14, 1811.

5. See, generally, Thorpe, *Federal and State*: CN, 1:519–20, 536; DE, 1:566, 567–68, 568; GA, 2:779, 789, 801, 810, see also 843; ME, 3:1647, 1661; MD, 3:1689–90, 1705, 1715, 1745; MA, 3:1890, 1908, 1912–14, 1922; NH, 4:2472, 2477, 2491–92; NJ, 5:2597, 2599; NY, 5:2638; NC, 5:2793, 2799, 2793, 2802; PA, 5:3085, 3100; SC 6:3247, 3255, 3264, 3263 (oath);

VT, 6:3740, 3752, 3757, 3767. McLoughlin, *New England Dissent*, 2:894 (NH); A. Holmes, *Collection* (Rhode Island); *State ex rel. M'Cready v. Hunt*, 20 SCL (2 Hill) 1, 66 (S.C. Ct. App. 1834), quoted in Underwood, "Without Discrimination," 58; Green, *Second*, 31, citing Curry, *First Freedoms*, 134–92; see McLoughlin, *New England Dissent*, 2:843–44. Green, *Second*, 33; Sehat, *Myth*, 54–55 (Sehat's illuminating discussion of how these principles were applied, and misapplied, is discussed below); Mulder, *Controversial Spirit*, 104.

6. Philip Schaff, "Religious Vitality and Church-State Separation," in *America: A Sketch of Its Political, Social, and Religious Character* (1854; repr., Cambridge: Belknap Press of Harvard University Press, 1961), 72–81, quoted in Allitt, *Major Problems*, 4; Underwood, "Without Discrimination," 61. See also Ramsay, *History of South-Carolina*, 2:139, South Carolina formed a new constitution "in conformity to that of the United States [and] . . . adapted to the new order of things."

7. *Proceedings and Debates*, 219, 238–39 (emphasis original); *Fayetteville Observer*, September 1, 1835.

8. Rhode Island, art. 1.3 (1842), Thorpe, *Federal and State*, 6:3222, 7:4015 (WV 1861–63, art. II, § 9).

9. *Debates of the Convention*, 492, 529.

10. *Republican Notes*; Stokes and Pfeffer, *Church and State*, 52; Strout, "Jeffersonian Religious Liberty," 209–10; Butterfield, "Elder John Leland," 210–11; Stokes and Pfeffer, *Church and State*, 178–79; Green, *Second*, 37 (Vermont); see McLoughlin, *New England*, 2:809–11. *New-Hampshire Patriot and State Gazette*, September 22, 1842; Stokes and Pfeffer, *Church and State*, 245–48; Thorpe, *Federal and State*, KY, 3:1274, AL, 1:97.

11. *Abington School District v. Schempp*, 374 U.S. 203, 214 (1963) (ftnt. omitted); *Wallace*, 472 U.S. at 99, 99 n. 4 (Rehnquist dissenting).

12. For newspapers that reprinted and/or commented favorably on Jefferson's Statute in the years before 1879, see, for example, *State Gazette of South Carolina*, August 10, 1786; *Massachusetts Centinel*, November 18, 1786 (well received abroad); *Cumberland Gazette* (Portland, ME), December 1, 1786 (well received abroad); *New York Journal*, January 9, 1788 (reporting its printing in *American Museum* of November 1787); *Herald of Liberty*, April 1, 1799, 2:60 (from *Aurora*) (quoting Statute in opposition to Sedition Act); *Maryland Gazette*, August 28, 1800 (politics "converted the elegant reasoning of Jefferson against *religious establishments*, into a blasphemous argument against religion itself," reprints, from *Federal Gazette*); *City Gazette and Daily Advertiser* (Carolina), August 18, 1800 (consistent with Christian principles); *Carolina Gazette*, October 2, 1800 (favorable comment in election piece); *Salem Gazette* (*Salem Register*), March 3, 1803; *New-Hampshire Gazette*, September 27, 1803; *Bennington (VT) World*, July 11, 1804; *Worcester (MA) National Aegis*, December 19, 1804; *Aurora General Advertiser*, March 5, 1806 (favorable comment); *Portland (ME) Eastern Argus*, November 10, 1808 (reprinting address of Baltimore Baptist Association to Jefferson, same *Washington, DC, National Intelligencer and Washington Advertiser*, November 19, 1808); *Pittsfield (MA) Sun*, November 7, 1810 ("celebrated 'Act for Establishing Religious Freedom' drawn up by the luminous and immortal pen of Thomas Jefferson" in article about Memorial & Remonstrance); *Bridgeport (CN) Republican Farmer*, November 21, 1810 (same as *Sun*, November 7); *Rhode-Island Republican*, November 21, 1810 (Baptist role in defeat of assessment and passage of Statute) (from *Richmond Enquirer*); *Portsmouth (NH) People's Advocate*,

November 30, 1816 (reprints under title "Seek Not to Lay a Restraint on the Mind . . ."); *Boston Daily Advertiser*, September 25, 1822 (eulogy to Judge Roane, who referred to statute as "that sublime act") (from *Richmond Enquirer*); *Haverhill Gazette* (as *Salem Gazette*), October 1, 1822 (same); *Philadelphia Reformer*, November 1, 1825 ("nothing more important in a state than the free enjoyment of religious opinions, without the interruption of legislative authorities") (from *Gospel Luminary*); *Aurora & Franklin Gazette* (Philadelphia), March 4, 1826; *United States' Telegraph* (Washington, DC), June 27, 1826; *Richmond Enquirer*, July 4, 1826 (preamble); *Vermont Patriot & State Gazette*, July 4, 1826 ("justly procured for him the applause of the world") (from the *Enquirer*); *Columbia Telescope, and South Carolina State Journal*, July 4, 1826) (same); *Charleston (SC) City Gazette*, July 13, 1826 (quoting Jefferson on key accomplishments) (from *Richmond Enquirer*, July 7, 1826); *Richmond Enquirer*, July 14, 1826 (reporting on eulogy) (numerous same omitted); *Augusta Chronicle*, July 22, 1826 (same *Vermont Patriot*, July 4); *Boston Gospel Advocate and Impartial Investigator*, November 11, 1826 (same as *Reformer*, November 1); *Columbia Telescope and South Carolina State Journal*, November 21, 1826; *Richmond Enquirer*, February 12, 1829 (reporting on publication of *Writings of Thomas Jefferson*: statute "always held by Mr. Jefferson to be one of his best efforts in the cause of liberty . . . and it is certainly the strongest *legal* barrier that could be erected against a connection between Church and State"); *Portland (ME) Eastern Argus*, February 27, 1829 (same); *Ohio State Journal* 18, no. 42 (April 30, 1829) (reporting on publication of *Writings*); *Raleigh Register, and North-Carolina Gazette*, April 29, 1830; *Pensacola Gazette and Florida Advertiser*, May 15, 1830; *The American Almanac and Repository of Useful Knowledge*, 1836 (reprints operative paragraph); *Vermont Gazette*, January 3, 1843; *Louisville Christian Observer*, May, 1, 1852 (reprinting portions); *Mississippian and State Gazette*, February 14, 1855 (response to anti-Catholic, anti-immigrant, quotes operative paragraph); *Texas State Gazette* (Austin), July 7, 1855 (reprints); *Liberator*, December 28, 1855; *Christian Review*, April 1 (1858), 199 ("unanswerable arguments"); *New York Herald*, August 15, 1859 (Jefferson and Madison two great law-givers of the Revolution); *Middletown (NY) Banner of Liberty*, August 17, 1859; *Boston Investigator*, December 4, 1861 (requests to reprint), December 11, 1861 (reprints); *Columbus (OH) Crisis*, December 26, 1861; *Daily Arkansas Gazette*, June 7, 1871. Scores of additional passing references appear in reported July Fourth and Jefferson birthday toasts, obituaries, and references to the inscription on Jefferson's tomb.

For newspapers that reprinted or commented favorably on Madison's Memorial & Remonstrance, see, for example, *Boston Independent Chronicle*, May 11–14, 1801; *Washington, DC, National Intelligencer and Washington Advertiser*, October 24, 1810 (reprints, led to Statute from the "luminous and immortal pen of Thomas Jefferson") (from *Richmond Enquirer*); *Pittsfield (MA) Sun*, November 7, 1810 (same as *Washington, DC, National Intelligencer*, October 24); *Bridgeport (CN) Republican Farmer*, November 21, 1810 (same); *Rhode-Island Republican*, November 21, 1810 (same); *Essex Register*, December 8, 1810 (same); *Hartford (CN) American Mercury*, June 17, 1817; *Niles Weekly Register* (Baltimore), July 5, 1817; *Brattleboro (VT) American Yeoman*, July 11, 1817; *Norfolk (VA) American Beacon and Commercial Diary*, July 12, 1817; *Bridgeport (CN) Republican Farmer*, November 21, 1820; *Baltimore Patriot*, November 7, 1826 (quoted in antislavery piece); *Columbia Telescope and South Carolina State Journal*, November 21, 1826 (reprints, "under the influence of the public sentiment thus manifested, the celebrated bill 'establishing religious freedom' enacted into a permanent barrier against future attempts on the rights of conscience") (from *Richmond Enquirer*); *Vermont Chronicle*, January 30, 1829 (quotes and notes pamphlet available); *Vermont Gazette*, January 27, 1829 (reprints), February 24, 1829 (comments, noting reprinted in *Vermont Telegraph*); *Buffalo (NY) Gospel Advocate and Impartial Investigator*, February 21, 1829 (from *Hartford Times*); *New York Correspondent*, April 4, 1829 (reprints); *New York Free Enquirer*, April 22, 1829 (Senator Johnson's report on Sunday mail relied on M&R, reprints); *Boston Christian Watchman*, January 20, 1832 (reprints); *Boston Recorder*, January 25, 1832; *Boston Christian Review*, March 1, 1837 (eulogy of Madison by John Quincy Adams, citing to Benedict's *A General History of the Baptist Denomination in America*, 2 vols., 1813 for text of M&R); *Boston Investigator*, April 7, 1847, April 14, 1847 (reprints); *Southern Literary Magazine* 14, no. 6 (June 1848) ("A memorial, celebrated for its dignity of tone, and strength of argument"); *Christian Review*, April 1, 1858, 199 ("unanswerable arguments"); *Washington, DC, Daily National Intelligencer*, July 16, 1866 (M&R reprinted in Rives, "diffused extensively throughout the State, and caused the ultimate defeat of the" general assessment).

For newspapers that reprinted or commented favorably on Jefferson's Letter to the Danbury Baptists, see, for example, *New York American Citizen and General Advertiser*, January 18, 1802; *Boston Independent Chronicle*, January 25, 1802; *Salem Register*, January 25, 1802 ("Religion is a matter which lies solely between man and his God"); *New Jersey Journal*, January 26, 1802; *Boston Constitutional Telegraph*, January 27, 1802; *Hartford (CT) American Mercury*, January 28, 1802; *Boston Independent Chronicle*, January 28, 1802 (summary); *Salem Gazette*, January 28, 1802; *Salem Register*, January 28, 1802; *Rhode Island Republican*, January 30, 1802; *Charleston City Gazette*, January 30, 1802; *Walpole (NH) Farmer's Weekly Museum*, February 2, 1802 (quoting but without "wall of separation"); *New London (CN) Bee*, February 3, 1802; *Carolina Gazette*, February 4, 1802; *Stoningtonport (CT) Patriot, or Scourge of Aristocracy*, February 5, 1802; *The Temple of Reason*, February 6, 1802; *New Hampshire Gazette*, February 9, 1802; *Sun*, February 15, 1802; *Newark Centinel of Freedom*, February 23, 1802; *Rhode-Island Republican*, February 27, 1802; *Daily South Carolinian* (Columbia), May 4, 1855; *Delaware State Reporter*, May 8, 1855; *Boston Investigator*, May 30, 1855, January 9, 1869 (from *Richmond Whig*), June 9, 1869 (reprints with Jefferson letter to Levi Lincoln).

13. *Aurora*, August 18, 1800, in Rosenfeld, *American Aurora*, 839; *Richmond Enquirer*, August 29, 1826; *Boston Investigator*, May 30, 1855; *Massachusetts Centinel*, April 26, 1786 (referring to an earlier article in the *Halifax Journal*); *Southern Literary Magazine* 14, no. 6 (June 1848).

14. *Boston Independent Chronicle*, May 11–14, 1801; *Oration Delivered in Tammany Hall*, 23 (emphasis original).

15. Toulmin, *Thoughts on Emigration*, 36–38, 94; Stuart, *Three Years*, 2:50. Edward Oliphant also reprinted key portions of the Statute in reporting to Britons on the American experiment (*History of North America*, 317).

16. Myerson, *Endowed*, 210, 251, quoting William Duane's "Federalism vs. Republicanism" (October 14, 1800); *Charleston Carolina Gazette*, August 21, 1800; Hamburger, *Separation*, 111–20.

17. *Times and District of Columbia Daily Advertiser*, October 28, 1800; *Wellsboro (PA) Tioga Eagle*, October 11, 1843; *Louisiana Advertiser* (New Orleans), October 21, 1826

(eulogy reprinted from the *Boston Courier*); *Illinois Gazette* (Shawnee-town), March 21, 1829; "Progress of Democracy, v. Old Fogy Retrogrades," *New York Democrat's Review*, April 1852; *New York Workingman's Advocate*, March 12, 1831; *New-Hampshire Statesman and State Journal*, July 16, 1843; Baptist General Meeting of Correspondence of Virginia, Robert Semple, Moderator, to Jefferson, October 24, 1808, Library of Congress, American Memory, http://hdl.loc.gov/loc.mss/mtj.mtjbib019212 image 732; *Boston Democrat*, April 8, 1809; *Portland (ME) Eastern Argus*, November 10, 1808.

18. *Carolina Gazette*, June 12, 1800 (reprinting Boston paper from May 8, 1800). See also *Raleigh Register, and North-Carolina Weekly Advertiser*, July 8, 1800; *Constitutional Telegraph*, August 23, 1800; *Portsmouth (NH) Herald of Gospel Liberty*, February 2, 1809; *South Carolina Gazette and Timothy's Daily Adviser*, 58:6333, July 26, 1800 (attack); *Political Magazine and Miscellaneous Repository, Containing Ancient and Modern . . .*, August 1, 1800 (attack); *Ohio Repository*, December 7, 1826; *Portland (ME) Eastern Argus*, September 30, 1833 (tomb inscription); *Raleigh Register, and North-Carolina Gazette*, April 29, 1830 (reprinted *Pensacola Gazette and Florida Advertiser*, May 15, 1830); *Pittsfield (MA) Sun*, May 18, 1843; *Wisconsin Democrat*, July 13, 1843 (tomb inscription).

19. *Richmond Enquirer*, July 25, 1826 (memorial services at Fredericksburg, reprinted from the *Herald*); *Richmond Enquirer*, August 8, 1826 (services at Suffolk); *New Hampshire Gazette*, 1:48, August 23, 1826 (funeral oration by Governor Tyler quoting preamble); *Selection of Eulogies*, 87; *United States' Telegraph* (Washington, DC), June 27, 1826 (emphasis original). *Columbia Telescope and South Carolina State Journal*, July 4, 1826; *Vermont Patriot & State Gazette*, July 4, 1826; *Augusta (GA) Chronicle*, July 22, 1826.

20. *Boston Recorder*, January 25, 1832; *Boston Christian Watchman*, November 25, 1820; *Hartford (CT) Times and Weekly Advertiser (Hartford Times)*, June 8, 1829; *New York Herald*, August 15, 1859, reprinted: *Middletown (NY) Banner of Liberty*, August 17, 1859. *Philadelphia North American and United States Gazette*, August 4, 1874; *Washington, DC, Daily National Intelligencer*, September 6, 1854 (quote); *Herald of Liberty*, April 1, 1799, from *Aurora*; *Texas State Gazette* (Austin), July 7, 1855.

21. Jefferson to Rabbi Mordecai Manuel Noah, May 28, 1818, Library of Congress, American Memory, http://hdl.loc.gov/loc.mss/mtj.mtjbib023207 image 924; Jefferson to Jared Sparks, November 4, 1820, in Bergh, 15:288; Sehat, *Myth*, 62–63; *Columbus (OH) Crisis*, December 26, 1861; *Boston Investigator*, December 4, 1861; *New York Independent*, March 24, 1870.

22. *Columbian Herald or the Patriotic Courier of North-America*, May 29, June 5, June 8, June 12, 1786; *Connecticut Courant*, April 20, 1803. For example, *Evening Post (New-York Evening Post)*, September 23, 1802 ("The writings of Mr. Jefferson, upon civil and religious freedom, are pretty well known, his conduct in time of danger and peril has been hinted at, but is not so generally known"); Baird, *Religion in the United States*, 241, 252.

23. Bancroft, *History of the United States*, 10:224–25. Interestingly, Bancroft's brother-in-law corresponded with Jefferson concerning the Unitarian sermons of Aaron Bancroft, George's father. Jefferson praised Aaron's "efforts to restore us to primitive Christianity, in all the simplicity that it came from the lips of Jesus," and expressed the hope "that the same free exercise of private judgment which gave us our political reformation will extend it's effects to that of religion." (Jefferson to John Davis, January 18, 1824, in Ford, 9:287–88).

24. Hildreth, *History of the United States*, 3:384; Howison, *History of Virginia*, 2:298–302, 333, 297; Burk, Jones, and Girardin, *History of Virginia*, 348.

25. See Drakeman, *Church, State*, 45–57. Waite also relied upon Howison, *History of Virginia*; and Semple, *History of the Baptists*. Drakeman, "Reynolds v. United States," 710–11, 716; *Board of Education of the City of Cincinnati v. Minor*, 23 Ohio St. 211, 253 (1872).

26. *Vermont Patriot & State Gazette*, June 22, 1835 (reprinted from *Hartford Patriot and Baltimore Republican*).

27. *Los Angeles Times*, November 15, 1887. See also *San Francisco Daily Evening Bulletin*, January 10, 1879 (Statute "the true distinction between what properly belongs to the Church and what to the state."); *St. Louis Globe-Democrat*, January 19, 1879 (quoting Statute and Danbury); *American Catholic Historical Researches* 18, no. 2 (April 1901), (reprinting Danbury); Swaney, "Religious Freedom," 636–37; Max J. Kobler, "Phases in the History of Religious Liberty in America, with Special Reference to the Jews," *Publications of the American Jewish Historical Society* 11 (1903):66, quoted in Strout, "Jeffersonian Religious," 224; Joseph Fort Newton, "Thomas Jefferson and the Religion of America," *Forum* (December 1927), 891–93, 894, quoted in Strout, "Jefferson's Statute," 7.

28. Hamburger, *Separation*, 270–71; S. Gordon, *Mormon*, 78, 77. Compare Drakeman, *Church, State*, 71 ("As Philip Hamburger has demonstrated, the strict separationist view that was adopted by Chief Justice Waite in Reynolds had settled into the American zeitgeist by the latter portion of the nineteenth century"); and ibid., 70 n. 202 (Hamburger underestimates influence of eighteenth-century Presbyterians/Baptists).

29. Dreisbach, *Religion and Politics*, xi, 2, 23 n. 4, 124, 177–89, 2, 21. Adams's sermon is also discussed in Green, *Second*, 98–103.

30. Madison to Jasper Adams, 1832, in *WJM*, 9:486–87.

31. *Wallace*, 472 U.S. at 104 (Rehnquist dissenting), citing *Commentaries on the Constitution of the United States*, 5th ed. (1891): 2:630–32. See Howard, "Supreme Court," 333 (emphasis Story). *Lynch v. Donnelly*, 465 U.S. 668, 678 (1984).

32. Story, *Commentaries*, 2:1873; Dreisbach, *Religion and Politics*, 47.

33. Tucker, *View of the Constitution*, 375, quoting Richard Price, 376, 373; Kramer, "Free Church." See discussion in Myerson, *Endowed*, 256–58.

34. *Wallace*, 472 U.S. at 105 (Rehnquist dissenting), quoting Cooley, *Treatise*, 470; Cooley, *Treatise*, 467, 469; Story, *Commentaries*, 2:1847; *Wallace*, 472 U.S. at 106. See also Green, *Second*, 360 ("Cooley's *Treatise* . . . quickly became the most influential constitutional law book of the final third of the century"). Story's views are discussed further in Sekulow, *Witnessing*, 26 (Story was "expositing the Constitution from a conservative, New England perspective"). Green, *Second*, 190–203.

35. Green, *Second*. See also Lash, "Second Adoption."

36. Compare Sehat, *Myth*; *County of Allegheny v. ACLU*, 492 U.S. 573, 604–5 (1989). Sehat's analysis also has important implications for the theory that the Constitution should be interpreted based upon its "original intent," discussed briefly in chapter 7.

37. Jon Meacham notes a parallel pattern after World War II: "As the nation grew more broadly religious, fueled in part by the Cold War against 'godless Communism,' the Supreme Court, led by Justice Hugo Black, the former Klansman from Alabama, excavated Jefferson's letter to the Danbury Baptists and with it his wall between church and state—or at least what the court thought his wall was" (Meacham, *American Gospel*, 172).

38. Martin, *Genuine Information*, 80 (emphasis original). H. Abbot, NC Ratifying Convention (July 30, 1778), Kurland and Lerner, *Founders' Constitution*, 5:Am. 1, Doc. 52. Amos Singletary of Massachusetts, an outspoken critic of the Constitution, said that he "hoped to see Christians (in power), yet by the Constitution, a Papist or an Infidel was as eligible as they" (Kurland and Lerner, *Founders' Constitution*, 2: art. 1, § 2, clause 3, document 11). Story, *Commentaries*, 2:1847; Kramnick and Moore, *Godless Constitution*.

39. For example, Dreisbach, *Religion*, 15, citing Jasper Adams. Myerson, *Endowed*, 141–44, 146.

40. *Church and State*, 40; Sheldon, "Religion and Politics," 92; Dreisbach, *Forgotten Founders*. For example, Green, *Second*, 81–118. *Rodman v. Robinson*, 47 S.E. 19, 20–21 (N.C. 1904).

41. Schaff, *Church and State*, 40.

42. Onuf, "Thomas Jefferson's Christian Nation," 31.

43. Articles of Confederation, http://avalon.law.yale.edu/18th_century/artconf.asp; Green, *Second*, 31. See also Kramnick and Moore, *Godless Constitution*, 26–45.

44. Washington's Farewell Address (1796), http://avalon.law.yale.edu/18th_century/washing.asp; Northwest Ordinance, http://avalon.law.yale.edu/18th_century/nworder.asp; Jefferson to Moses Robinson, March 23, 1801, in *PTJ*, 33:424.

45. Madison to Jasper Adams, 1832, in *WJM*, 9:486; *Board of Education of the City of Cincinnati v. Minor*, 23 Ohio St. 211, 243–44 (1872). Hamilton draft of Washington's Farewell Address, July 1796, Online Library of Liberty http://oll.libertyfund.org/?option=com_staticxt&staticfile=show.php%3Ftitle=1385&chapter=92647&layout=html&Itemid=27. See also Waldman, *Founding Faith*, 162. Muñoz, "Religion and the Common Good," 2, 6.

There may have developed some split on this matter between Virginian Baptists (including John Leland, who returned to New England in 1791) and New England Baptists, with the latter more willing to accept generic government support of religion in the name of civic virtue.

46. McGarvie, *One Nation*, 73, quoting Ely from Robert S. Handy, *A Christian America* (New York: Oxford University Press, 1971), 50; *Boston Constitutional Telegraph*, November 26, 1800 (attributed to Charles Pinckney). See also Myerson, *Endowed*, 205.

47. Jefferson to Marquis de Chastellux, Enclosure, September 2, 1785, in *PTJ*, 8:470; Cooley, *Treatise*, 468 (clergy at one time ineligible for office in Delaware, Kentucky, Louisiana, North Carolina, South Carolina, Tennessee, Texas, and Virginia); Jefferson to Jeremiah Moor, August 14, 1800, in *PTJ*, 32:102–3.

Today, ministers may participate in politics with the caveat that neither churches nor charities can claim tax-exempt status if funds are used for overtly political purposes, including a minister's campaigning on church business. See *Tax Guide for Churches and Religious Organizations*, Internal Revenue Service (2010).

48. Jefferson to P. H. Wendover, March 13, 1815 (unsent), in *PTJR*, 8:340–42; Jefferson to M[argaret Bayard] Harrison Smith, August 6, 1816, in Bergh, 15:60.

49. M&R, ❡ 6, appendix; *Treaty of Peace and Friendship between the United States of America and the Bey and Subjects of Tripoli of Barbary* (1796), art. 11. From "Religious Liberty" (1856), in Black, *Essays and Speeches* (1886), 51, 53, quoted in *McCollum*, 333 U.S. at 244 n.8 (Frankfurter, Jackson, Rutledge, Burton dissenting) (emphasis original). *Wash-*

ington, DC, National Intelligencer, September 14, 1811 ("Pagans, Turks, Jews and christians should be equally protected"). *Board of Education of the City of Cincinnati v. Minor,* 23 Ohio St. 211, 248 (1872) (emphasis original).

50. Jefferson, *Autobiography,* 1821. Ragosta, *Wellspring of Liberty,* 139–46. *New York Herald,* August 15, 1859; *Middletown (NY) Banner of Liberty,* August 17, 1859; Washington to the Hebrew Congregation in Newport, Rhode Island, August 18, 1790, in Crackel, *Papers of George Washington,* Presidential Series, 6:285.

51. The breadth of the "Christian nation" movement in the nineteenth century, and its inconsistency with the Founding era, is discussed at length in Green, *Second;* and Fea, *Was America.*

52. Thorpe, *Federal and State,* ME 3:1646; IL 2:985; IN 2:1073, IA 2:1136, KS 2:1222. See also AR (1868) 1:306; GA (1865): 2:809–10; LA (1879) 3:1450; MD (1851) 3:1713; MI (1857) 4:1991; MS (1868) 4:2069; MO (1865) 4:2191; NE (1866–67) 4:2349; NV (1864) 4:2402; NY (1821) 5:2639; NC (1868) 5:2800; OH (1851) 5:2913; SC (1868) 6:3281; VA (1870) 7:3873.

53. Thorpe, *Federal and State,* PA, 5:3081, 5:3092, 5:3121; VT, (1777) 6:3740; (1786) 6:3749; (1793) 6:3762; *Report of the Debates in the Convention of California,* 416–17; Meacham, *American Gospel,* 78. Compare Miller, *First Liberty,* 109. *Report of the Debates and Proceedings of the Convention for the Revision of the Constitution of the State of Indiana, 1850,* 852–56; *Debates and Proceedings of the Constitutional Convention of the State of Illinois,* 1:233, 235, 277, 2:1560.

54. Thorpe, *Federal and State,* 3:1646; 3:1647; 6:3222; *Debates and Proceedings of the Constitutional Convention of the State of Illinois,* 1:233. See also *Debates and Proceeding of the Minnesota Constitutional Convention,* 208–10 (Delegates Flaundrau, Sherburne, Curtiz: preamble is not "part of the Constitutional law; it is merely placed there to make it read better").

This view of the null effect of preambles was particularly stressed by conservative supporters of states' rights because of their disdain for the implications of the federal Constitution's reliance on "We the People" (Gutzman, *Virginia's American Revolution,* 169, citing *PJM,* 17:307–50).

55. *People v. Ruggles,* 8 Johns. R. 290 (N.Y. 1811), in Kurland and Lerner, *Founders' Constitution,* amendment 1, doc. 62; *Report of the Proceedings and Debates,* 575, 463; S. Gordon, "Long Nineteenth Century," 428; Green, *Second,* 169, quoting *State v. Chandler,* 2 Harr 553, 562–63 (Del. 1837); *Church of the Holy Trinity v. United States,* 143 U.S. 457, 471 (1892); Brewer, "The Pew to the Pulpit," 9; *Brewer Family Papers,* 3:138, quoted in Green, *Second,* 375–76. In the modern era, Justice Douglas made a similar clarification: Having said in *Zorach v. Clauson,* 343 U.S. 306, 313 (1952), that "we are a religious people whose institutions presuppose a Supreme Being," he explained ten years later in *Engel v. Vitale* that "if a religious leaven is to be worked into the affairs of our people, it is to be done by individuals and groups, not by the Government" (*Engel v. Vitale,* 370 U.S. 421, 443 [1962]) [Douglas concurring]).

56. Blakely, *American State Papers,* 250. See Stokes and Pfeffer, *Church and State,* 566–67; Humphrey, *Nationalism and Religion,* 479 (at least nine efforts to add "God" or "Christian" to Constitution). Hamburger, *Separation,* 296–302.

57. Scully, *Religion and the Making,* 120; *Catholic World* 433, 434–35 (1876), quoted in

McCollum, 333 U.S. at 218 (Frankfurter, Jackson, Rutledge, Burton concurring). *The Works of James Abram Garfield* (ed. Hinsdale, 1883), 2:783, quoted in *Everson*, 330 U.S. at 61 n. 56 (Rutledge, Frankfurter, Jackson, Burton dissenting); *Abington v. Schemp*, 374 U.S. at 273 (Brennan concurring), quoting Teddy Roosevelt; Jeffries and Ryan, "Political History," 285 n. 18. See, for example, Thorpe, *Federal and State*: GA (1877): art. I, § 1, para XIV, 2:843; IN (1851): art. I, § 6, 2:1074; LA (1864): art. 146, 3:1446; MI (1825): art. I, § 5, 4:1931; MN (1857): art I, § 16, 4:1993; OH (1851), art. 6:2, 5:2925; OR (1857): art. I, § 5, 5:2998; Hamburger, *Separation*, 193, 251. See also Feldman, *Divided*, 74 (Blaine Amendment was Republican electoral ploy to pit Democrat Catholics against Democrat Protestants). Beecher quoted in S. Gordon, *Mormon*, 197. *Texas State Gazette* (Austin), 6:46:353, July 7, 1855.

58. For example, Neem, *Creating a Nation*. Green, *Second*, 173–74.

59. *Reynolds v. United States*, 98 U.S. at 163, 164, 165 (1879); Plöchl, "Thomas Jefferson," 183.

6. Federal Control

1. *Everson*, 330 U.S. at 39 (Rutledge, Frankfurter, Jackson, Burton dissenting). See also *id.* at 33 ("No provision of the Constitution is more closely tied to or given content by its generating history . . . the long and intensive struggle for religious freedom in America, more especially in Virginia") (ftnt. omitted). *McGowan v. Maryland*, 366 U.S. 420, 437 (1961). For example, Butler, *Awash*, 265; Marty, "Virginia Statute," 1; Pfeffer, "Madison's 'Detached,'" 285; and Stokes, *Church and State*, 1:366. For the broad cultural significance of the Jeffersonian vision, see, for example, Miller, *First Liberty*, 69–70.

2. By its terms, it applies only to "Congress," but its broad application to the federal government has never been seriously questioned. See, for example, *McCreary County v. ACLU*, 545 U.S. 844, 877 (2005); and *Abington v. Schempp*, 374 U.S. 203, 222 (1963). Otherwise, the executive and judicial branches would be free to restrict speech, the press, the right of assembly, and free exercise of religion. Jefferson explained in a draft of his Letter to the Danbury Baptists that since federal authority arises from laws passed by Congress, and Congress is by the First Amendment "inhibited from acts respecting religion and the Executive authorized only to execute their acts," the President is equally bound (*PTJ*, 36:255). Madison thought the greater likelihood of abuse lay with Congress, but also understood the protections to apply to the Executive (Maier, *Ratification*, 451). The textual limitation might owe something to the fact that when the amendments were introduced Madison intended this provision to be incorporated into the text of article I, rather than appended as part of a separate "Bill of Rights."

3. See, for example, Curtis, *No State Shall*. See also *O'Neil v. Vermont*, 144 U.S. 323, 361, 370 (1892) (Field, Harlan dissenting).

4. *Slaughter-House Cases*, 83 U.S. 36 (1873); *Gitlow v. New York*, 268 U.S. 652, 666 (1925). Arguably the Court's willingness to incorporate fundamental liberties into the Fourteenth Amendment dates to *Chicago, Burlington & Quincy Railroad Co. v. City of Chicago*, 166 U.S. 226 (1897). *Palko v. Connecticut*, 302 U.S. 319, 325 (1937). For incorporation debate generally, see, for example, Curtis, *No State Shall*; Fairman, *Fourteenth Amendment*; Amar, *Bill of Rights*; Rosenthal, "New Originalism."

5. *Cantwell v. Connecticut*, 310 U.S. 296 (1940); *Everson v. Board of Education*, 330 U.S. 1 (1947).

6. *Elk Grove Unified School Dist. v. Newdow*, 542 U.S. 1, 45–46 (2004) (Thomas concurring); *Cutter v. Wilkinson*, 544 U.S. 709, 727–28 (2005) (Thomas concurring). See also Jeffries and Ryan, "Political History," 295; Amar, *Bill of Rights*, 33–34; Witte, *Religion*, 139; S. Smith, *Foreordained*, 53; and Snee, "Religious Disestablishment," 371–407.

7. *Elk Grove*, 542 U.S. at 50; Lash, "Second Adoption," 1091–92. *Zelman*, 536 U.S. at 679 n. 4, quoting Amar, "Bill of Rights as a Constitution," 1159. See also S. Smith, *Foreordained*, 5.

8. *Zelman v. Simmons-Harris*, 536 U.S. 639, 679 (2002) (Thomas concurring); Amar, *Bill of Rights*, 246. See also Amar, "Bill of Rights as a Constitution"; S. Smith, *Foreordained*, 30.

9. *Elk Grove*, 542 U.S. at 51 (emphasis original), citing Potter Stewart in dissent in *Abington School District v. Schempp*, 374 U.S. 203, 310 (1963); Amar, "Bill of Rights as a Constitution," 1158.

10. *Barron v. Baltimore*, 32 U.S. 243, 250 (1833) ("no expression indicating an intention to apply them to the state governments").

11. Amar, *Bill of Rights*, 246.

12. For example, Kauper, *Religion*, 46 ("the language is not clearly stated as merely a limitation on the power of Congress to interfere with state religious establishments. It is a direct and substantive limitation on the power of Congress").

13. Compare *Elk Grove*, 542 U.S. at 50 (Thomas concurring); and S. Smith, *Foreordained*, 17–18. Compare Hamburger, *Separation*, 19, 54–55. Speeches of Madison, August 15, 1789, *PJM*, 12:339; June 8, 1789, in *PJM*, 12:205; Lash, "Second Adoption," 1092–93 (Madison argued no federal power); Cogan, *Complete*, 12.

14. *Philadelphia Freeman's Journal*, October 24, 1787, in *DHRC*, 13:466. The language used by "Centinel II" is from the Pennsylvania declaration of rights, a provision praised by Jefferson (Jefferson, *Notes*, 286–87).

15. Amar, "Bill of Rights as a Constitution," 1157; Lash, "Second Adoption," 1088–89, 1091–92. See also Jeffries and Ryan, "Political History," 292.

16. *Zelman*, 536 U.S. at 678; Virginia Statute, appendix; Letter to the Danbury Baptists, appendix.

17. Mr. Tennent's Speech on the Dissenting Petition, January 11, 1777, in Jones, "Writings of the Reverend," 197 (emphasis original); *Abington*, 374 U.S. at 256 (Brennan concurring), quoting *McGowan*, 366 U.S. at 464 (1961) (Frankfurter).

18. Amar, "Bill of Rights as a Constitution," 1158 n. 132, citing discussion of Senator Howard; Jeffries and Ryan, "Political History," 296 n. 80; Lash, "Second Adoption," 1143, citing *Cong. Globe*, 42nd Cong., 1st sess. (March 31, 1871); 1144–45, citing *Cong. Globe*, 43rd, 1st sess. (1874); 1143, quoting *Cong. Globe*, 38th Cong., 1st sess., 1202 (1864).

19. Jeffries and Ryan, "Political History," 296. 4 Cong. Rec. 5585 (August 14, 1876); Lash, "Second Adoption," 1147, 1150, quoting Senator Eaton, 4 Cong. Rec. 5592 (1876).

20. *County of Allegheny v. Greater Pittsburgh ACLU*, 472 U.S. 573, 659 (1989) (Kennedy, White, Rehnquist, Scalia dissenting). As a practical matter, Jefferson was not as opposed to the exercise of federal authority as is sometimes suggested (see, for example, Balogh, *Government Out of Sight*).

21. *DHFFC*, 4:10–11; Madison Speech, August 17, 1789, in *PJM*, 12:234; Madison, "Detached Memorandum," 492; Jefferson to Samuel Miller, January 23, 1808, in Ford, 9:174.

22. Jefferson to Madison, March 15, 1789, in *PTJ*, 14:659; Madison to Jefferson, October 17, 1788, in *PJM*, 11:298 (emphasis original); Madison to Richard Peters, August 19, 1789, in *PJM*, 12:347.

23. *McDonald v. City of Chicago*, 561 U.S. 3025 (2010).

24. *McDonald*, 561 U.S. at __, Slip Op. 08–1521 at 7, 5 (Thomas concurring). Cf. Washington to Touro Synagogue in Rhode Island, August 18, 1790, in Crackel, *Papers of George Washington, Presidential Series*, 6:285: Jews "possess alike liberty of conscience and immunities of citizenship."

25. *Everson*, 330 U.S. at 15–16; *Everson*, 330 U.S. at 31–32 (Rutledge, Frankfurter, Jackson, Burton dissenting); *McCollum*, 333 U.S. at 212; *Engel v. Vitale*, 370 U.S. at 431; *Abington*, 374 U.S. at 217.

26. Jeffries and Ryan, "Political History," 282, 328–29, 344; ibid., 335 ("segregation provided the original impetus for Christian academies, opposition to the secularization of public education gave them sustenance").

27. S. Gordon, *Spirit of the Law*, 84–92; Sehat, *Myth*, 228–29.

28. *Wallace v. Jaffree*, 472 U.S. at 92 *et seq.* (Rehnquist dissenting); *Cutter v. Wilkinson*, 544 U.S. at 726–27 (Thomas concurring); Zagari, "Founding," 10. See also Formisano and Pickering, "Christian Nation," 220–21, citing Hamburger, *Separation*, 481.

29. Dreisbach, Hall, and Morrison, *Forgotten*, xiv–xv. See also Hall, "Jeffersonian Walls," 605. For example, *Wallace*, 472 U.S. at 98 (Rehnquist dissenting) (compromise).

30. *Abington*, 374 U.S. at 214; *Wallace*, 472 U.S. at 99, 99 n. 4 (Rehnquist dissenting); Green, *Second*, 36.

31. Cord, *Separation*, 20–21; *Rosenberger*, 515 U.S. at 854–56 (Thomas concurring); M&R, appendix; *Everson*, 330 U.S. at 60 n. 55 (Rutledge, Frankfurter, Jackson, Burton dissenting); *PTJ*, 1:531 n. 1.

32. *Wallace*, 472 U.S. at 99; *Board of Education v. Louis Grumet*, 512 U.S. 687, 732 (1994) (Scalia, Rehnquist, Thomas dissenting); *DHFFC*, 1:151; compare *Wallace*, 472 U.S. at 97. *Wallace*, 472 U.S. at 106. For example, Brant, "Madison: On Separation," 17. *Landholder*, no. 7, December 17, 1787, quoted in Kurland, *Founders' Constitution*, 4:14. See, generally, Laycock, "Nonpreferential."

Rehnquist's dictionary citation is curious in any case. He noted Webster's definition of "establishment" as "the act of establishing, founding, ratifying or ordaining" and used Webster's example of "[t]he episcopal form of religion, so called, in England" (Webster's seventh definition). *Wallace*, 472 U.S. at 106. See Webster, *American Dictionary*, 1:676. It is not clear that a prohibition on Congress "ratifying or ordaining" religion would require only nonpreferentialism. Moreover, the definition from Webster's *American Dictionary* includes: "2. Settlement; fixed state. . . . 3. Confirmation; ratification of what has been settled or made. . . . 4. Settled regulation; . . . 5. Fixed or stated allowance for subsistence; income; salary."

33. Adams, *Nation Dedicated*, 70. See *Everson*, 330 U.S. at 15–16 ("No person can be punished for entertaining or professing religious beliefs or disbeliefs").

34. Madison, "Detached Memorandum," 494–95; Murray, *Religious Liberty*, 131;

Torasco v. Watkins, 367 U.S. 488, 495 (1961); Paul Freund and Robert Ulich, *Religion and the Public Schools* (1965), 14, quoted in Jeffries and Ryan, "Political History," 321–22.

35. For example, Colwell, *Position of Christianity*, 23; Cord, "Founding Intentions," 50–51. Christian preferentialism is also inconsistent with the understanding that absence of test oaths meant that Jews, Muslims, and atheists could hold office. See, for example, Cogan, *Complete*, 62–68. For example, "Prominent Pastor Calls Romney's Church a Cult," *New York Times*, October 7, 2011. See U.S. Census Bureau, *Statistical Abstract* (2011), table 75, 61 (more than 36 million Americans nonmonotheists in 2008; almost 43 million non-Christians).

36. For example, *Wallace*, 472 U.S. at 101–3 (Rehnquist dissenting).

37. Kauper, *Religion*, 86.

38. Madison, "Detached Memorandum," 494. For example, Jon Meacham at Pew Center on Religion and Public Life, December 2006, http://pewforum.org/Church-State -Law/The-Christmas-Wars-Religion-in-the-American-Public-Square.aspx.

39. Curry, *First Freedoms*, 148; Lash, "Power and the Subject of Religion," 1117; Greenawalt, "Common Sense," 497; *Rosenberger*, 515 U.S. at 872 n. 2 (Souter, Stevens, Ginsburg, Breyer dissenting), quoting *Lee v. Weisman*, 505 U.S. 577, 626 (1992) (Souter concurring); Curry, *First Freedoms*, 221.

40. Dreisbach, *Religion and Politics*, 21; Madison to Jasper Adams, 1832, in *WJM*, 9:487. Mead, "Neither Church," 350; Myerson, *Endowed*, 234–35.

41. *Wallace*, 472 U.S. at 92 (Rehnquist dissenting); Hutson, "Thomas Jefferson's Letter," 775–90. Jefferson to Levi Lincoln, January 1, 1802, in *PTJ*, 36:256; *Reynolds*, 98 U.S. at 164.

42. Jefferson, *Autobiography*, 8.

43. Jefferson took some care in this area as both of his predecessors issued religious proclamations, and, even in 1805, Washington's practice was imbued with near-divine authority.

44. Second Inaugural, in Ford, 8:344; Jefferson to Rev. Samuel Miller, January 23, 1808, in Ford, 9:174–75 (emphasis and spelling as in original); Madison, "Detached Memorandum," 494. Compare O'Neill, "Nonpreferential," 277 ("inaccurate" to say "Jefferson considered a presidential Thanksgiving proclamation as a law respecting an establishment of religion").

45. Documentary Appendix. For example, Leland, *Virginia Chronicle*, 22n+; L. Greene, *Writings of the Late Elder John Leland*, 181; Miscellaneous Petition (November 12, 1784); Madison Proclamation of Thanksgiving, July 23, 1813, in *PJM*, Presidential, 6:459.

46. Madison Proclamation of Thanksgiving, July 23, 1813, in *PJM*, Presidential, 6:458–59; Madison to Edward Livingston, July 10, 1822, in *WJM*, 9:101 (emphasis original); Madison, "Detached Memorandum," 494 (emphasis original).

47. Jefferson's First Inaugural Address, March 4, 1801, *PTJ*, 33:150. *Boston Independent Chronicle*, March 16, 1801, omission by *Columbian Centinel*; Church, *So Help Me*, 248; Jefferson's Second Inaugural Address, http://avalon.law.yale.edu/19th_century/jefinau2 .asp. Madison contributed to this aspect of Jefferson's Second Inaugural. See Madison memoranda of February 8, 1805, in *PJM*, Secretary of State, 9:21; and February 21, 1805, in *PJM*, Secretary of State, 9:59.

48. Dreisbach, *Thomas Jefferson,* 57.

49. Madison, "Detached Memorandum," 494; *Bridgeport (CN) Republican Farmer,* 1:50:2, October 24, 1804; 2:44:1, October 2, 1805 (second emphasis added). Compare *Van Orden v. Perry,* 545 U.S. 677, 723 (2005) (Stevens, Ginsburg dissenting): "[W]hen public officials deliver public speeches, we recognize that their words are not exclusively a transmission from the government because those oratories have embedded within them the inherently personal views of the speaker as an individual member of the polity" (ftnt. omitted). Myerson's otherwise excellent analysis fails to make this distinction, suggesting that Jefferson's inaugural addresses were "references by government" (*Endowed,* 233).

50. Madison, "Detached Memorandum," 495; *Engel,* 370 U.S. at 432.

51. Madison, "Detached Memorandum," 495.

52. Jefferson, *Autobiography,* 8; compare Dreisbach, "Thomas Jefferson and Bills," 194 (Bill 85 shows Jefferson and Madison "misrepresented").

53. Minutes of the Board of Visitors of the University of Virginia, October 7, 1822, in Bergh, 19:413–14. Justice Thomas is fond of citing an earlier Jefferson education proposal that implied a slightly broader role for religion. *Rosenberger v. Rectors and Visitors,* 515 U.S. 819, 859 n. 4 (1995) (Thomas concurring). While the significance of the earlier scheme can be argued, Jefferson's plans for UVA obviously evidence his considered judgment.

54. Jefferson to Thomas Cooper, November 2, 1822, in Ford 10:243; Levy, *Establishment,* 73; Jefferson, Minutes of the Board of Visitors, October 7, 1822, in Bergh, 19:414–16.

55. Minutes of the Board of Visitors of the University of Virginia, October 7, 1822, in Bergh, 19:416; Jefferson to Thomas Cooper, October 7, 1814, in *PTJR,* 8:12. See Brant, "Madison: On Separation," 20.

56. "Report of the Commission Appointed to Fix the Site of the University of Virginia" (August 4, 1818), quoted in Lee, *Crusade Against Ignorance,* 116; Jefferson to Arthur Spicer Brockenbrough, April 21, 1825, Library of Congress, American Memory, http://hdl.loc.gov/loc.mss/mtj.mtjbib025371 image 156 (emphasis original); Madison to Edward Everett, March 19, 1823, in *WJM,* 9:125 (emphasis added); Madison to Frederick Beasley, December 22, 1824, in *WJM,* 9:211.

57. Hunt, *First Forty Years,* 13–14; Hutson, *Religion and the Founding,* 89. Smith also said that the services were "very little like a religious assembly"; "being seen" appeared to be the primary purpose. Rodda, *Liars,* 445–46, makes much of this, but this seems irrelevant. After all, government officials should not be in the position of judging which services are sufficiently pious to preclude their presence on government property.

58. Cutler and Cutler, *Life, Journals,* 2:66. Cutler quoted in Church, *So Help Me,* 258–59.

59. Jefferson to Thomas Cooper, November 2, 1822, in Ford, 10:242–43. *County of Allegheny v. ACLU,* 492 U.S. 573, 593–94, quoting *Lynch,* 465 U.S. at 687 (O'Connor concurring); Statute, appendix.

60. *Rosenberger,* 515 U.S. 819 (1995); *Widmar v. Vincent,* 454 U.S. 263 (1981). These access cases must be distinguished from "government speech" cases. Thus, while UVA cannot discriminate if it chooses to allocate student fees to a host of student groups, that does not mean that it cannot "discriminate" in choosing which professorships to fund, as with Jefferson's decision not to fund a divinity professor. The latter involves direct government action or speech ("endorsement" one might say) and is not a question of impartial-

ity to private religious and nonreligious activity (see *Pleasant Grove City v. Summum*, 555 U.S. 460 [2009]). A more serious issue arises when a facially neutral program results in a disproportionate allocation of government funds to religious institutions. This difficult question has not been adequately addressed.

61. *McCollum*, 333 U.S. at 248 (Reed dissenting). Bartrum, "Historiography," 111. By characterizing the release-time program in *McCollum* as merely a matter of facility use, Reed missed the more serious problem of endorsement of religion when government mandated attendance at public school and released students only if they attended religious services. *Zorach*, 343 U.S. at 324–25 (Jackson dissenting).

62. 463 U.S. 783, 789 (1983). Following Justice Brennan's dissent, 463 U.S. at 795, *Marsh* has been largely treated as a narrow, historic exception. For example, see Note, "Office of the House," 1421–53; Lund, "Legislative Prayer"; Klukowski, "In Whose Name." Even in the early republic, chaplains were not uncontroversial; Kentucky, for example, initially rejected legislative chaplains because of apparent inconsistency with separation (Robertson, *Should Churches be Taxed?*, 61, citing Niels H. Sonne, *Liberal Kentucky, 1780–1828* [Berkeley: University of California Press, 1939], 7).

63. Drakeman, *Church, State*, 17.

64. Madison to Edward Livingston, July 10, 1822, in *WJM*, 9:100; Madison, "Detached Memorandum," 493; Brant, "Madison: On the Separation," 22. See, for example, Barton, *Original*, 209; and Cord, *Founding Intentions*, 50. Justices have also made too much of Madison's participation as one member of this committee (for example, *Marsh v. Chambers*, 463 U.S. at 788 n. 8).

65. *Marsh*, 463 U.S. at 793, 794–95; *Simpson v. Chesterfield County Board of Supervisors*, 404 F.3d 276 (4th Cir. 2005); *Pelphrey v. Cobb County, Ga.*, 547 F.3d 1263 (11th Cir. 2008); *Hinrichs v. Bosma*, 400 F. Supp. 2nd 1103, 1129 (S.D. Ind. 2005), dismissed for lack of standing, 506 F.3d 584 (7th Cir. 2007); *Wynne v. Town of Great Falls*, 376 F.3d 292 (4th Cir. 2004); *Joyner v. Forsyth*, No. 10–1232 (4th Cir. 2011), cert. denied, 565 U.S. __, No. 11–546 (2012); *Snyder v. Murray City Corp.*, 159 F.3d 1227, 1228 n. 3 (10th Cir. 1998).

66. Statute, appendix; Petition from Baptist Convention (December 25, 1776), *Virginia Gazette* (Dixon and Hunter), March 28, 1777.

67. Madison, "Detached Memorandum," 493–94. Oregon, for example, has privately funded chaplains (Note, "Officer of the House," 1429–30). When an objection to paid chaplains was made in the 1877 Georgia constitutional convention, it was agreed that delegates could open deliberations with prayer if they so chose (*Journal of the Constitutional Convention* [Atlanta: 1877], 24).

68. Madison, "Detached Memorandum," 494.

69. Ibid., 493. House chaplains have included "Baptist (7), Christian (1), Congregationalist (2), Disciples of Christ (1), Episcopalian (4), Lutheran (1), Methodist (16), Presbyterian (15), Roman Catholic (1), Unitarian (2), and Universalist (1)." (http://chaplain.house.gov/chaplaincy/history.html).

70. Madison, "Detached Memorandum," 494.

71. Dreisbach, *Real Threat*, 75; Cord, "Founding Intentions," 51.

72. Cord, *Separation*, 39.

73. *Everson*, 330 U.S. at 43 n. 35 (Rutledge, Frankfurter, Jackson, Burton dissenting), citing *Reuben Quick Bear v. Leupp*, 210 U.S. 50 (1908).

74. Madison Memorandum to Jefferson, October 1, 1803, in *PJM*, Secretary of State, 5:480. Richardson, *Compilation of the Messages* (October 17, 1803), 1:359.

75. Richardson, *Compilation of the Messages* (February 28, 1811), 1:490; *Annals of Congress* 22 (March 2, 1811): 1104–5; Madison to Jesse Jones and Others, June 3, 1811, in *PJM*, Presidential, 3:324.

76. Madison to Jesse Jones and Others, June 3, 1811, in *PJM*, Presidential, 3:324.

77. Richardson, *Compilation of the Messages* (February 21, 1811), 1:490; *Annals of Congress* 22 (February 23, 1811): 997–98; Eisgruber and Sager, *Religious Freedom*, 235.

78. Currie, *Constitution in Congress*, 318, 320; *Annals of Congress* 22 (February 21, 1811): 985. Compare bill Jefferson signed: 2 Stat. 356. Compare Drakeman, *Church, State*, 284–85 (Senator Johnson, supporting incorporation of DC Baptists, acted inconsistently with Madison).

79. *Davis v. Beason*, 133 U.S. 333, 342–43 (1890) (polygamy); *Sherbert v. Verner*, 374 U.S. 398 (1963); *Church of the Holy Trinity v. United States*, 143 U.S. 457, 471 (1892); *Watchtower Society v. Village of Stratton*, 536 U.S. 150 (2002); *Employment Decision v. Smith*, 494 U.S. 872 (1990); *City of Boerne v. P. F. Flores*, 521 U.S. 507 (1997); *Abington*, 374 U.S. at 254 (Brennan concurring), quoting *Cantwell*, 310 U.S. at 303–4.

The Court's recent decision to exempt ministerial hiring and firing from the reach of the Equal Employment Opportunities Act touches on these cases only in passing. Apparently the Court believed that the choice of a minister so deeply "affects the faith and mission of the church itself," that it could not be compared to religiously-motivated actions that had been held subject to facially neutral laws (*Hosanna-Tabor Evangelical Lutheran Church and School v. EEOC*, __ U.S. __, Slip Op. 10–553 [2012], 15).

80. Jefferson to Madison, July 31, 1788, in *PTJ*, 13:442–43; Jefferson, Notes on Religion, 1776, in *PTJ*, 1:547–48.

81. *Sherbert*, 374 U.S. at 406. Much of the "dissonance between theory and practice" identified by Sehat, *Myth*, 237, might fall into a similar category and require searching inquiry into whether a real discrimination based on religion was being made in a facially neutral statute.

82. *Abington*, 374 U.S. at 234–35 (Brennan concurring) (ftnts. omitted).

83. Drakeman, *Church, State*, 17.

7. Jefferson's Enduring Legacy

1. Jefferson to Madison, September 6, 1789, in *PJM*, 12:385; Madison to Jefferson, February 4, 1790, in *PJM*, 13:19; Jefferson to Samuel Kercheval, July 12, 1816, in Ford, 10:42–43; Report of the Commissioners Appointed to Fix the Site of the University of Virginia, December 8, 1818, quoted in Lee, *Crusade Against Ignorance*, 119–20; Rakove, *Original Meanings*, xv.

2. Statute, appendix; Jefferson to the Society of the Methodist Episcopal Church at New London, CN, February 4, 1809, Library of Congress, American Memory, http://hdl .loc.gov/loc.mss/mtj.mtjbib019696 image 559.

3. Jefferson, Notes on Epitaph, in *Writings*, 706.

4. Madison, "Detached Memorandum," 492.

5. Rakove, *Original Meanings*, 367.

6. *Everson*, 330 U.S. at 33 (Rutledge, Frankfurter, Jackson, Burton dissenting) (ftnt. omitted); *Wallace v. Jaffree*, 472 U.S. at 113; *Lee v. Weisman*, 505 U.S. 577, 632 (1992) (Scalia dissenting), quoting *New York Trust Co. v. Eisner*, 256 U.S. 345, 349 (1921).

7. Coxe, *American Citizen*, October 21, 1787.

8. Boyle and Sheen, *Freedom of Religion*, 155; *McCreary County v. ACLU*, 545 U.S. at 882 (O'Connor concurring).

9. See, for example, Muñoz, "Religion and the Common Good," 1; Jeffries and Ryan, "Political History," 286 (*Everson* "treated the history of the United States as if it were the history of Virginia"); Novak, "Christmas Wars," Pew Center on Religion and Public Life, December 2006, www.pewforum.org/Church-State-Law/The-Christmas-Wars-Religion -in-the-American-Public-Square.aspx (need to consider one hundred Founders, not just the most irreligious). See, for example, Whittington, "New Originalism." The "new originalism" is also subject to the textualist objection: "Nothing but the text itself was adopted by the people." Joseph Story, *Commentaries on the Constitution of the United States*, 1st ed. (1833): 1:389; Madison to Spencer Roane, May 6, 1821, in *WJM*, 9:61.

10. Koppelman, *Phony*, 737–38; *Abington*, 374 U.S. at 234–35 (Brennan concurring) (ftnts. omitted); Koppelman, *Phony*, 745; Jefferson to William Johnson, June 12, 1823, in Bergh, 15:449.

11. Rakove, *Original Meanings*, 340.

12. *Federalist* No. 37

13. Mark DeWolfe Howe, *The Garden and the Wilderness: Religion and Government in American Constitutional History* (Chicago: University of Chicago Press, 1965), 4, quoted in Levy, *Original*, 313.

14. Wood, "No Thanks."

15. Ibid.

16. Sehat, *Myth*, 6. See also Meacham, *American Gospel*, 232 ("The intensity with which the religious right attempts to conscript the Founders into their cause indicates the importance the movement ascribes to historical benediction by association with the origins of the Republic").

17. *Everson*, 330 U.S. at 8.

18. Mazzei, *Researches*, 166.

19. Lincoln to Henry L. Pierce, April 6, 1859, in *Collected Works of Abraham Lincoln*, ed. Roy P. Basler, 3:376.

20. Miller, *First Liberty*, 69–70, 271–72.

21. Adams, *Nation Dedicated*, 51.

22. *Southern Literary Magazine* 6, no. 9 (September 1840); Peterson, *Jefferson Image*, 9.

23. Jefferson to Madison, December 16, 1786, in *PTJ*, 10:604.

24. Pfeffer, *Liberties of an American*, 32; Thom, *Struggle for Religious Freedom*, 78 (554); United Nations, International Covenant on Civil and Political Rights, http://treaties.un .org/doc/Publication/UNTS/Volume%20999/volume-999-I-14668-English.pdf.

25. Jefferson to Chesterfield Virginia Baptist Associations, November 21, 1808, Library of Congress, American Memory, http://hdl.loc.gov/loc.mss/mtj.mtjbib019322 image 1012.

Bibliography

Adair, Douglass. "James Madison's Autobiography." *William and Mary Quarterly*, 3rd ser., 2, no. 2 (April 1945): 191–209.

Adams, Arlin M., and Charles J. Emmerich. *A Nation Dedicated to Religious Liberty: The Constitutional Heritage of the Religious Clauses*. Philadelphia: University of Pennsylvania Press, 1990.

Adams, Dickinson, and Ruth W. Lester, eds. *Jefferson's Extracts from the Gospels*. Papers of Thomas Jefferson. 2nd ser. Princeton: Princeton University Press, 1983.

Ahlstrom, Sydney E. *A Religious History of the American People*. 2nd ed. New Haven: Yale University Press, 2004.

Allitt, Patrick, ed. *Major Problems in American Religious History*. Boston: Houghton Mifflin, 2000.

Amar, Akhil Reed. "The Bill of Rights as a Constitution." *Yale Law Journal* 100 (1991): 1131–210.

———. *The Bill of Rights: Creation and Reconstruction*. New Haven: Yale University Press, 1998.

Annals of the Congress of the United States. 11th Cong., 3rd sess. Washington: Gales and Seaton, 1853.

Antieau, Chester James, Arthur T. Downey, and Edward C. Roberts. *Freedom from Federal Establishment: Formation and Early History of the First Amendment Religion Clauses*. Milwaukee: Bruce, 1964.

Baird, Robert. *Religion in the United States of America*. Edited by Edwin S. Gaustad. 1844. Reprint, New York: Arno Press, 1969.

Balogh, Brian. *A Government Out of Sight: The Mystery of National Authority in Nineteenth-Century America*. New York: Cambridge University Press, 2009.

Bancroft, George. *History of the United States from the Discovery of the American Continent*. Vol. 10. Boston: Little, Brown, 1875.

Barton, David. *Original Intent: The Courts, the Constitution, & Religion*. Aledo, TX: Wallbuilder Press, 2000.

Bartrum, Ian. "Of Historiography and Constitutional Principle: Jefferson's Reply to the Danbury Baptists." *Journal Church and State* 51, no. 1 (2009): 102–25.

Basler, Roy P., ed. *Collected Works of Abraham Lincoln*. New Brunswick, NJ: Rutgers University Press, 1953.

Bearss, Sara B., ed. *Dictionary of Virginia Biography*. Richmond: Library of Virginia, 2006.

Beecher, Lyman. *Lectures on Political Atheism and Related Subjects, Beecher's Works*. Vol. 1. Boston: John P. Jewett, 1852.

Beeman, Richard R. *Patrick Henry: A Biography*. New York: McGraw-Hill, 1974.

Benedict, David. *A General History of the Baptist Denomination in America.* 2 vols. 1813. Reprint, Freeport, NY: Books for Libraries Press, 1971.

Bennett, William W. *Memorials of Methodism in Virginia.* Richmond, 1871.

Bergh, Albert Ellery, ed. *The Writings of Thomas Jefferson.* 20 vols. Washington, DC: Thomas Jefferson Memorial Association, 1907.

Bishop, Abraham. *Oration Delivered in Wallingford, on the 11th of March 1801.* Bennington: Anthony Haswell, 1801.

Blakely, William Addison, ed. *American State Papers and Related Documents on Freedom in Religion.* Washington, DC: Review and Herald, 1949.

Blosser, Jacob M. "Pursuing Happiness in Colonial Virginia: Sacred Words, Cheap Print, and Popular Religion in the Eighteenth Century." *Virginia Magazine of History and Biography* 118, no. 3 (Fall 2010): 210–45.

Bond, Edward L. *Spreading the Gospel in Colonial Virginia: Preaching Religion and Community.* Lanham, MD: Lexington Books, 2005.

Bonomi, Patricia. *Under the Cope of Heaven: Religion, Society, and Politics in Colonial America.* New York: Oxford University Press, 1986.

Boyd, Julian P., et al., eds. *The Papers of Thomas Jefferson.* Princeton: Princeton University Press, multiple volumes, 1950–.

Boyle, Kevin, and Juliet Sheen, eds. *Freedom of Religion and Belief: A World Report.* London: Routledge, 1997.

Bradburn, Douglas. *The Citizenship Revolution: Politics & the Creation of the American Union 1774–1804.* Charlottesville: University of Virginia Press, 2009.

Bradley, Gerald V. *Church-State Relationships in America.* New York: Greenwood Press, 1987.

Brant, Irving. *James Madison: The Nationalist.* Indianapolis: Bobbs-Merrill, 1948.

———. "Madison: On the Separation of Church and State." *William and Mary Quarterly,* 3rd ser., 8, no. 1 (January 1951): 3–24.

Brenner, Lenni, ed. *Jefferson & Madison on Separation of Church and State: Writings on Religion and Secularism.* Fort Lee, NJ: Barricade Books, 2004.

Brodie, Fawn M. *Thomas Jefferson: An Intimate History.* New York: Norton, 1974.

Brutus, Marcus. *Serious Facts, Opposed to "Serious Considerations": Or The Voice of Warning to Religious Republicans.* Pamphlet. October 1800.

Brydon, George MacLaren. *Virginia's Mother Church and the Political Conditions Under Which It Grew.* 2 vols. Richmond: Whittet and Shepperson, 1947.

Buckley, Thomas E. *Church and State in Revolutionary Virginia, 1776–1787.* Charlottesville: University Press of Virginia, 1977.

———. "'A Great Religious Octopus': Church and State at Virginia's Constitutional Convention, 1901–1902." *Church History* 72, no. 2 (June 2003): 333–60.

———. "The Religious Rhetoric of Thomas Jefferson." In *The Founders on God and Government,* edited by Daniel L. Dreisbach, Mark D. Hall, and Jeffrey H. Morrison, 53–82. Lanham, MD: Rowman & Littlefield, 2004.

Burk, John, Skelton Jones, and Louis Hue Girardin. *The History of Virginia.* 4 vols. Petersburg, VA: M. W. Dunnavant, 1816.

Burkitt, Lemuel. *A Concise History of the Kehukee Baptist Association, From Its Original Rise down to 1803.* Halifax, NC: A. Hodge, 1803.

Butler, Jon. *Awash in a Sea of Faith: Christianizing the American People*. Cambridge: Harvard University Press, 1990.

———. "Coercion, Miracle, Reason: Rethinking the American Religious Experience in the Revolutionary Age." In *Religion in a Revolutionary Age*, edited by Ronald Hoffman and Peter J. Albert, 1–30. Charlottesville: University Press of Virginia, 1994.

Butterfield, L. H. "Elder John Leland, Jeffersonian Itinerant." *American Antiquarian Society Proceedings* 62, no. 2 (October 1952): 155–242.

Campbell, Charles. *History of the Colony and Ancient Dominion of Virginia*. Philadelphia: Lippincott, 1860.

Campbell, T. E. *Colonial Caroline: A History of Caroline County, Virginia*. Richmond: Dietz Press, 1954.

Church, Forrest. *So Help Me God: The Founding Fathers and the First Great Battle over Church and State*. Orlando: Harcourt, 2007.

Cobb, Sanford H. *The Rise of Religious Liberty in America: A History*. 1902. Reprint, New York: Burt Franklin, 1970.

Cogan, Neil H., ed. *The Complete Bill of Rights: The Drafts, Debates, Sources, and Origins*. New York: Oxford University Press, 1977.

Collier, Christopher. "Liberty, Justice, and No Bill of Rights: Protecting Natural Rights in a Common-Law Commonwealth." In *The Bill of Rights and the States: The Colonial and Revolutionary Origins of American Liberty*, edited by Patrick T. Conley and John P. Kaminski, 100–122. Madison, WI: Madison House, 1992.

Colwell, Stephen. *The Position of Christianity in the United States, in Its Relations with Our Political Institutions, and especially with Reference to Religious Instruction in the Public Schools*. New York, 1853.

Conkin, Paul K. "The Religious Pilgrimage of Thomas Jefferson." In *Jeffersonian Legacies*, edited by Peter S. Onuf, 19–49. Charlottesville: University of Virginia Press, 1993.

Conley, Patrick T. "Rhode Island: Laboratory for the 'Lively Experiment.'" In *The Bill of Rights and the States: The Colonial and Revolutionary Origins of American Liberty*, edited by Patrick T. Conley and John P. Kaminski, 123–61. Madison, WI: Madison House, 1992.

Considerations on an Act of the Legislature of Virginia, Entitled an Act for the Establishment of Religious Freedom. Philadelphia: Robert Aitken, 1786.

Cooley, Thomas M. *A Treatise on the Constitutional Limitations Which Rest upon the Legislative Power of the States of the American Union*. Boston: Little, Brown, 1868.

Cord, Robert L. "Founding Intentions and the Establishment Clause: Harmonizing Accommodation and Separation." *Harvard Journal of Law and Public Policy* 10, no. 1 (1987): 47–52.

———. *Separation of Church and State: Historic Fact and Current Fiction*. New York: Lambeth Press, 1982.

Coxe, Tench. *An American Citizen, IV: On the Federal Government*. Pamphlet. Philadelphia, October 21, 1787.

Crackel, Theodore J., ed. *The Papers of George Washington Digital Edition*. Charlottesville: University of Virginia Press, Rotunda, 2008.

Currie, David P. *The Constitution in Congress: The Jeffersonians, 1801–1829*. Chicago: University of Chicago Press, 2001.

Curry, Thomas J. *The First Freedoms: Church and State in America to the Passage of the First Amendment.* New York: Oxford University Press, 1986.

Curtis, Michael Kent. *No State Shall Abridge—The Fourteenth Amendment and the Bill of Rights.* Durham, NC: Duke University Press, 1986.

Cutler, William Parker, and Julia Perkins Cutler, eds. *Life, Journals and Correspondence of Rev. Manasseh Cutler, LL.D.* Cincinnati: Robert Clarke, 1888.

Davies, K. G., ed. *Documents of the American Revolution, 1770–1783.* Colonial Office Series. Shannon, Ireland: Irish University Press, 1973.

Davis, Robert P. "The Struggle for Religious Freedom (1611–1776)." In *Virginia Presbyterians in American Life: Hanover Presbytery (1755–1980),* edited by Davis, James H. Smylie, Dean K. Thompson, Ernest Trice Thompson, and William Newton Todd, 3–44. Richmond: Hanover Presbytery, 1982.

Debates of the Convention for the Revision and Amendment of the Constitution of the State of Louisiana, Assembled at Liberty Hall, New Orleans, April 6, 1864. New Orleans: W. P. Fish, 1864.

Debates and Proceedings of the Constitutional Convention of the State of Illinois, convened at the City of Springfield, Tuesday, December 13, 1869. Springfield: E. I. Merritt & Brother, 1870.

The Debates and Proceeding of the Minnesota Constitutional Convention. St. Paul: Earle S. Goodrich, 1857.

de Pauw, Linda Grant, et al., eds. *The Documentary History of the First Federal Congress.* Multiple volumes. Baltimore: Johns Hopkins University Press, 1972–.

Doares, Robert. "The Alternative of Williams-Burg." *Colonial Williamsburg* 28, no. 2 (Spring 2006): 20–25.

Drakeman, Donald L. *Church, State, and Original Intent.* New York: Cambridge University Press, 2010.

———. "*Reynolds v. United States:* The Historical Construction of Constitutional Reality." *Constitutional Commentary* 21 (Winter 2004): 697–726.

Dreisbach, Donald L. "Church-State Debate in the Virginia Legislature: From the Declaration of Rights to the Statute for Establishing Religious Freedom." In *Religion and Political Culture in Jefferson's Virginia,* edited by Garrett Ward Sheldon and Daniel L. Dreisbach, 135–65. Lanham, MD: Rowman and Littlefield, 2000.

———. "George Mason's Pursuit of Religious Liberty in Revolutionary Virginia." *Virginia Magazine of History and Biography* 108, no. 1 (2000): 5–44.

———. *Real Threat and Mere Shadow: Religious Liberty and the First Amendment.* Vol. 5 of *The Rutherford Institute Report.* Westchester, IL: Crossway Books, 1987.

———, ed. *Religion and Politics in the Early Republic: Jasper Adams and the Church State Debate.* Lexington: University Press of Kentucky, 1996.

———. "Thomas Jefferson, a Mammoth Cheese, and the 'Wall of Separation between Church and State.'" In *Religion and the New Republic: Faith in the Founding of America,* edited by James H. Hutson, 65–114. Lanham: Rowman and Littlefield, 2000.

———. "Thomas Jefferson and Bills Number 82–86 of the Revision of the Laws of Virginia, 1776–1786: New Light on the Jeffersonian Model of Church-State Relations." *North Carolina Law Review* 69 (1990–91): 159–211.

———. *Thomas Jefferson and the Wall of Separation between Church and State.* New York: New York University Press, 2002.

———. "Virginia's Contribution to the Enduring Themes of Religious Liberty in America." In *From Jamestown to Jefferson: The Evolution of Religious Freedom in Virginia*, edited by Paul Rasor and Richard E. Bond, 166–91. Charlottesville: University of Virginia Press, 2011.

Dreisbach, Daniel L., Mark David Hall, and Jeffrey H. Morrison, eds. *The Forgotten Founders on Religion and Public Life*. Notre Dame: University of Notre Dame Press, 2009.

Dwight, Timothy. *The Duty of Americans at the Present Crisis . . . Preached on the Fourth of July 1798*. New Haven: Thomas and Samuel Green, 1798.

Early Virginia Religious Petitions. Library of Congress. www.memory.loc.gov/ammem/collections/petitions/Eckenrode.

H. J. *Separation of Church and State in Virginia: A Study in the Development of the Revolution*. 1910. Reprint, New York: Da Capo Press, 1971.

Edwards, Morgan. *Materials towards a History of the Baptists in the Provinces of Maryland, Virginia, North Carolina, South Carolina, Georgia*. Vol. 3. 1772. Microfilm. Special Collections, University of Virginia, Charlottesville.

Eisgruber, Christopher L., and Lawrence G. Sager. *Religious Freedom and the Constitution*. Cambridge: Harvard University Press, 2007.

Fairman, Charles, Stanley Morrison, and Leonard William Levy. *Fourteenth Amendment and the Bill of Rights: Incorporation Theory*. New York: Da Capo Press, 1970.

Fea, John. *Was America Founded as a Christian Nation?: A Historical Introduction*. Louisville, KY: Westminster John Knox Press, 2011.

Feldman, Noah. *Divided by God: America's Church State Problem – and What We Should Do about It*. New York: Farrar, Strauss and Giroux, 2005.

Foote, William Henry. *Sketches of Virginia Historical and Biographical*. 1850. Reprint, Richmond: John Knox Press, 1966.

Ford, Paul Leicester, ed. *The Writings of Thomas Jefferson*. 10 vols. New York: G. P. Putnam's Sons, 1899.

Formisano, Ronald P., and Stephen Pickering. "The Christian Nation Debate and Witness Competency." *Journal of the Early Republic* 29 (Summer 2009): 219–48.

Fristoe, William. *A Concise History of the Ketocton Baptist Association*. 1808. Reprint, Harrisonburg, Va.: Sprinkle Publications, 2002.

Gaustad, Edwin S. *Faith of the Founders: Religion and the New Nation 1776–1826*. Waco, TX: Baylor University Press, 2004.

———. *Sworn on the Altar of God: A Religious Biography of Thomas Jefferson*. Grand Rapids, MI: William B. Eerdmans, 1986.

———. "Thomas Jefferson, Religious Freedom, and the Supreme Court." *Church History* 67, no. 4 (December 1998): 682–94.

Gewehr, Wesley M. *The Great Awakening in Virginia, 1740–1790*. Durham: Duke University Press, 1930.

Gordon, Daniel. "A Constitutional *Res Gestae*: Ending the Dueling Histories of *Everson* and *McCollum* and the Nazi State." *Widener Law Journal* 16, no. 1 (2006): 1–42.

Gordon, Sarah Barringer. "The Long Nineteenth Century (1789–1920)." In *The Cambridge History of Law in America*, vol. 2, edited by Michael Grossberg and Christopher Tomlins, 417–48. Cambridge: Cambridge University Press, 2008.

———. *The Mormon Question: Polygamy and Constitutional Conflict in Nineteenth-Century America*. Chapel Hill: University of North Carolina Press, 2002.

———. *The Spirit of the Law: Religious Voices and the Constitution in Modern America.* Cambridge: Belknap Press of Harvard University Press, 2010.

Gould, William D. "The Religious Opinions of Thomas Jefferson." *Mississippi Valley Historical Review* 20, no. 2 (September 1933): 191–208.

Green, Steven K. *The Second Disestablishment: Church and State in Nineteenth-Century America.* New York: Oxford University Press, 2010.

Greenawalt, Kent. "Common Sense about Original and Subsequent Understanding of the Religion Clauses." *University of Pennsylvania Journal of Constitutional Law* 8 (May 2006): 479–512.

Greene, Jack P. "Foundations of Political Power in the Virginia House of Burgesses, 1720–1776." *William and Mary Quarterly* 3rd ser., 16, no. 4 (October 1959): 485–506.

Greene, L. F., ed. *The Writings of the Late Elder John Leland, Including Some Events in His Life, Written by Himself, with Some Additional Sketches.* New York: G. W. Wood, 1845.

Grigsby, Hugh Blair. *History of the Virginia Federal Convention of 1788.* Virginia Historical Society, Collections, New Series, X. Richmond, 1891.

Gundersen, Joan R. *The Anglican Ministry in Virginia 1723–1766: A Study of a Social Class.* New York: Garland, 1989.

———. "The Search for Good Men: Recruiting Ministers in Colonial Virginia." *Historical Magazine of the Protestant Episcopal Church* 48 (1979): 453–64.

Gutzman, Kevin R. C. *Virginia's American Revolution: from Dominion to Republic, 1776–1840.* Lanham, MD: Lexington Books, 2007.

Hall, J. Leslie. "The Religious Opinions of Thomas Jefferson." *The Sewanee Review* 21:2 (April 1913): 164–76.

Hall, Mark David. "Jeffersonian Walls and Madisonian Lines: The Supreme Court's Use of History in Religion Clause Cases." *Oregon Law Review* 85 (2006): 563–614.

Hamburger, Philip. *Separation of Church and State.* Cambridge: Harvard University Press, 2002.

Hamilton, Marci A., and Rachel Steamer. "The Religious Origins of Disestablishment Principles." *Notre Dame Law Review* 81 (2006): 1775–91.

Hanover Presbytery Minutes: 1755–1823, May 19, 1785. Microfilm reel P278a. Union Theological Seminary, Richmond.

Hatch, Nathan O. *The Democratization of American Christianity.* New Haven: Yale University Press, 1989.

Haynes, Charles C. "Surprising Support for Separating Church from State." First Amendment Center, www.firstamendmentcenter.org/surprising-support-for-separating-church-from-state.

Hening, William Waller, ed. *The Statutes at Large, Being a Collection of all the Laws of Virginia from the First Session of the Legislature in the Year 1619, Vols. 1–13.* Heritage Books, CD-ROM #0878. 2003.

Henry, William Wirt. *Patrick Henry: Life, Correspondence and Speeches.* 3 vols. New York: Scribner's Sons, 1891.

Hildreth, Richard. *The History of the United States of America.* Vol. 3. New York: Harper and Brothers, 1856.

Holmes, Abiel. *Collection of the Massachusetts Historical Society.* Ser. 3, no. 5 (1836): 243–44.

Holmes, David L. "The Episcopal Church and the American Revolution." *Historical Magazine of the Protestant Episcopal Church* 67 (1978): 261–91.

Holton, Woody. *Forced Founders: Indians, Debtors, Slaves, & the Making of the American Revolution in Virginia.* Chapel Hill: University of North Carolina Press, 1999.

Honyman, Robert. *Diary, 1776–1782.* Accession 28855, Personal Papers Collection, Library of Virginia, Richmond.

Howard, A. E. Dick. "The Supreme Court and the Serpentine Wall." In *The Virginia Statute for Religious Freedom: Its Evolution and Consequences in American History,* edited by Merrill D. Peterson and Robert C. Vaughan, 313–49. Cambridge: Cambridge University Press, 1988.

Howell, Robert Boyle C. *The Early Baptists of Virginia.* 1864. CD-ROM, Baptist Standard Bearer. 2005.

Howison, Robert R. *History of Virginia, from Its Discovery and Settlement by Europeans to the Present Time.* Vol. 2. Richmond: Drinker and Morris, 1848.

Humphrey, Edward Frank. *Nationalism and Religion in America, 1774–1789.* New York: Russell and Russell, 1965.

Hunt, Gaillard, ed. *The First Forty Years of Washington Society: Portrayed by the Family Letters of Mrs. Samuel Harrison Smith (Margaret Bayard) from the Collection of her Grandson, J. Henley Smith.* New York: Scribner's Sons, 1906.

———. "James Madison and Religious Liberty." *Annual Report of the American Historical Association for the Year 1901* (Washington, DC, 1902): 1:165–71.

———, ed. *The Writings of James Madison.* New York: G. P. Putnam's Sons, 1900.

Hutchinson, William T., et al., eds. *Papers of James Madison.* Multiple volumes. Chicago: University of Chicago Press; Charlottesville, University of Virginia Press, 1962–.

Hutson, James. *Religion and the Founding of the American Republic.* Washington: Library of Congress, 1998.

———. "Thomas Jefferson's Letter to the Danbury Baptists: A Controversy Rejoined." *William and Mary Quarterly,* 3rd ser., 56, no. 4 (October 1999): 775–90.

———. "'A Wall of Separation': FBI Helps Restore Jefferson's Obliterated Draft." *Library of Congress Information Bulletin* 57, no. 6 (June 1998): 136–63.

Ireland, James. *The Life of the Reverend James Ireland.* 1819. Reprint, Harrisonburg, VA: Sprinkle Publications, 2002.

Isaac, Rhys. "'The Rage of Malice of the Old Serpent Devil': The Dissenters and the Making and Remaking of the Virginia Statute for Religious Freedom." In *The Virginia Statute for Religious Freedom: Its Evolution and Consequences in American History,* edited by Merrill D. Peterson and Robert C. Vaughan, 139–69. Cambridge: Cambridge University Press, 1988.

———. "Religion and Authority: Problems of the Anglican Establishment in Virginia in the Era of the Great Awakening and the Parsons' Cause." *William and Mary Quarterly,* 3rd ser., 30, no. 1 (January 1973): 3–36.

———. *The Transformation of Virginia, 1740–1790.* New York: Norton, 1982.

James, Charles F. *Documentary History of the Struggle for Religious Liberty in Virginia.* Lynchburg, VA: J. P. Bell, 1900.

Jefferson, Thomas. *Autobiography.* In *Thomas Jefferson, Writings,* edited by Merrill D. Peterson, 3–101. New York: Library of America, 1984.

———. *Notes on the State of Virginia*. In *Thomas Jefferson, Writings*, edited by Merrill D. Peterson, 123–325. New York: Library of America, 1984.

Jeffries, John C., Jr., and James E. Ryan. "A Political History of the Establishment Clause." *Michigan Law Review* 100 (November 2001): 279–370.

Jensen, Merrill, et al., eds. *The Documentary History of the Ratification of the Constitution*. Multiple volumes. Madison: Wisconsin Historical Society Press, 1976–.

Johnson, Thomas Cary. *Virginia Presbyterianism and Religious Liberty in Colonial and Revolutionary Times*. Richmond: Presbyterian Committee of Publication, 1907.

Jones, Newton B., ed. "Writings of the Reverend William Tennent, 1740–1777." *South Carolina Historical Magazine* 61 (July-October 1960): 189–209.

Journal of the Constitutional Convention of Georgia. Atlanta: 1877.

Journal of the House of Burgesses of Virginia. Heritage Books, CD-ROM #1547. 2000.

Journal of the House of Delegates of Virginia. Early American Imprints, Series 1.

Journal of the Senate of the Commonwealth of Virginia; begun and held in the City of Richmond, On Monday, the 17th day of October, in the year of our Lord Christ, 1785. Richmond: Thomas W. White, 1827.

Kauper, Paul G. *Religion and the Constitution*. Baton Rouge: Louisiana State University Press, 1964.

Kessler, Sanford. "Locke's Influence on Jefferson's 'Bill for Establishing Religious Freedom.'" *Journal of Church and State* 25 (1983): 231–52.

Kidd, Thomas S. *Patrick Henry: First among Patriots*. New York: Basic Books, 2011.

Klukowski, Kenneth A. "In Whose Name We Pray: Fixing the Establishment Clause Train Wreck Involving Legislative Prayer." *Georgetown Journal of Law and Public Policy* 6 (2008): 219–82.

Knox, Reverend Samuel. *A Vindication of the Religion of Mr. Jefferson and a Statement of his Services in the Cause of Religious Liberty*. Baltimore: W. Pechin, 1800.

Koppelman, Andrew. "Phony Originalism and the Establishment Clause." *Northwestern University Law Review* 103, no. 2 (2009): 727–50.

Kramer, Reverend John W. "The Free Church in the Free American State: Part II." *American Church Review* (July 1877): 321.

Krammick, Isaac, and R. Laurence Moore. *The Godless Constitution: A Moral Defense of the Secular State*. New York: Norton, 2005.

Kurland, Philip B., and Ralph Lerner, eds. *The Founders' Constitution*. 5 vols. Chicago: University of Chicago Press, 1987.

Labunski, Richard. *James Madison and the Struggle for the Bill of Rights*. New York: Oxford University Press, 2006.

Lash, Kurt T. "Power and the Subject of Religion." *Ohio State Law Journal* 59 (1998): 1069–154.

———. "The Second Adoption of the Establishment Clause: The Rise of the Nonestablishment Principle." *Arizona State Law Journal* 27 (1995): 1085–154.

Laycock, Douglas. "'Nonpreferential' Aid to Religion: A False Claim about Original Intent." *William and Mary Law Review* 27 (1985–86): 875–923.

Lee, Gordon C. *Crusade against Ignorance: Thomas Jefferson on Education*. New York: Teachers' College, 1967.

Leland, John. *The Virginia Chronicle: With Judicious and Critical Remarks under XXIV Heads*. Norfolk: Prentis and Baxter, 1790.

Lengel, Edward G., ed. *This Glorious Struggle: George Washington's Revolutionary War Letters.* Charlottesville: University of Virginia Press, 2010.

"A Letter of Concern from the Scholars Listed Below." Press release, Americans United for Separation of Church and State. July 29, 1998.

Levy, Leonard W. *The Establishment Clause: Religion and the First Amendment.* 2nd ed. Chapel Hill: University of North Carolina Press, 1994.

———. *Jefferson and Civil Liberties: The Darker Side.* Cambridge: Belknap Press of Harvard University Press, 1963.

———. *Original Intent and the Framers' Constitution.* New York: Macmillan, 1988.

Linn, William. *Serious Considerations on the Election of a President: Addressed to the Citizens of the United States.* Trenton: Sherman, Mersmon and Thomas, 1800.

Little, Lewis Peyton. *Imprisoned Preachers and Religious Liberty in Virginia.* 1938. Reprint, Gallatin, TN: Church History Research and Archives, 1987.

Longmore, Paul K. "'All Matters and Things Relating to Religion and Morality': The Virginia Burgesses' Committee for Religion, 1769 to 1775." *Journal of Church and State* 38 (1996): 775–97.

Looney, Jeffrey, et al., eds. *The Papers of Thomas Jefferson: Retirement Series.* Multiple volumes. Princeton: Princeton University Press, multiple volumes, 2004–.

Lund, Christopher. "Legislative Prayer and the Secret Costs of Religious Endorsements." *Minnesota Law Review* 94 (2010): 972–1050.

Madison, James. "Detached Memorandum." In "Aspects of Monopoly One Hundred Years Ago," *Harper's Monthly Magazine,* March 1914, 489–95.

Magrath, C. Peter. "Chief Justice Waite and the 'Twin Relic': *Reynolds v. United States.*" *Vanderbilt Law Review* 18 (1965): 507–43.

Maier, Pauline. *Ratification: The People Debate the Constitution, 1787–1788.* New York: Simon and Schuster, 2010.

Malbin, Michael J. *Religion and Politics: The Intentions of the Authors of the First Amendment.* Washington: American Enterprise Institute, 1978.

Malone, Dumas. *Jefferson the President: First Term, 1801–1805.* Boston: Little, Brown, 1970.

———. *Jefferson the Virginian.* Boston: Little, Brown, 1970.

Mapp, Alfred J. *The Faiths of Our Fathers: What America's Founders Really Believed.* Lanham, MD: Rowman and Littlefield, 2003.

———. *The Virginia Experiment: The Old Dominion's Role in the Making of America (1607–1781).* Richmond: Dietz Press, 1957.

Martin, Luther. *The Genuine Information Delivered to the Legislature of the State of Maryland, Relative to the Proceedings of the General Convention.* Philadelphia: Eleazer Oswald, 1788.

Martis, Kenneth C., and Gregory A. Elmes. *The Historical Atlas of State Power in Congress, 1790–1990.* Washington, DC: Congressional Quarterly, 1993.

Marty, Martin E. "Virginia Statute Two Hundred Years Later." In *The Virginia Statute for Religious Freedom: Its Evolution and Consequences in American History,* edited by Merrill D. Peterson and Robert C. Vaughan, 1–21. Cambridge: Cambridge University Press, 1988.

Mason, John Mitchell. "The Voice of Warning to Christians" (1800). In *Political Sermons of the American Founding Era, 1730–1805,* edited by Ellis Sandoz. 2nd ed., 2:1447–76. Indianapolis: Liberty Fund, 1998.

Maury, James. *To Christians of Every Denomination among Us, Especially Those of the Established Church, an Address*. Annapolis: Anne Catharine Green, 1771. Early American Imprints, series 1, no. 42253 (filmed).

Mays, David John, ed. *The Letters and Papers of Edmund Pendleton, 1734–1803*. Charlottesville: University Press of Virginia, 1967.

Mazzei, Philip. *Researches on the United States*. Translated by Constance D. Sherman. Charlottesville: University Press of Virginia, 1976.

McConnell, Michael W. "Establishment and Disestablishment at the Founding, Part I: Establishment of Religion." *William and Mary Law Review* 44 (2002–3): 2105–8.

McDonnell, Michael A. *The Politics of War: Race, Class, & Conflict in Revolutionary Virginia*. Chapel Hill: University of North Carolina Press, 2007.

McGarvie, Mark Douglas. *One Nation under Law: America's Early National Struggle to Separate Church and State*. DeKalb: Northern Illinois University Press, 2004.

McIlwaine, Henry R., ed. *Journals of the Council of the State of Virginia*. Vol. 2 (October 6, 1777–November 30, 1781). Richmond: Virginia State Library, 1932.

———. *The Struggle of Protestant Dissenters for Religious Toleration in Virginia*. Johns Hopkins University Studies, Historical and Political Science, 12th ser., no. 4. Baltimore: Johns Hopkins University Press, 1894.

McLoughlin, William G. *New England Dissent 1660–1833*. 2 vols. Cambridge: Harvard University Press, 1971.

———. "The Role of Religion in the Revolution." In *Essays on the American Revolution*, edited by Stephen G. Kurtz and James H. Hutson, 197–255. Chapel Hill: University of North Carolina Press, 1973.

Meacham, Jon. *American Gospel: God, the Founding Fathers, and the Making of a Nation*. New York: Random House, 2006.

Mead, Sidney E. "Neither Church nor State: Reflections on James Madison's 'Line of Separation.'" *Journal of Church and State* 10 (1968): 349–63.

Meade, Bishop William. *Old Churches, Ministers and Families of Virginia*. 2 vols. 1857. Reprint, Baltimore: Genealogical Publishing, 1978.

Meherrin Baptist Meeting Book (1771–1884). Virginia Baptist Historical Society, University of Richmond, Richmond.

Middleton, Arthur Pierce. "The Colonial Virginia Parson." *William and Mary Quarterly*, 3rd ser., 26, no. 3 (July 1969): 425–40.

Miller, William Lee. *The First Liberty: Religion and the American Republic*. New York: Knopf, 1987.

Minute Book of Hartwood Baptist Church, 1775–1861. Virginia Baptist Historical Society, University of Richmond, Richmond.

Moore, John S. "Jeremiah Walker in Virginia." *Virginia Baptist Register* 15 (1976): 719–44.

Morgan, George. *The True Patrick Henry*. Philadelphia: Lippincott, 1907.

Mulder, Philip N. *A Controversial Spirit: Evangelical Awakenings in the South*. Oxford: Oxford University Press, 2002.

Muñoz, Vincent Philip. "Religion and the Common Good: George Washington on Church and State." In *The Founders on God and Government*, edited by Daniel L. Dreisbach, Mark D. Hall, and Jeffry H. Morrison, 2–22. Lanham: Rowman and Littlefield, 2004.

Murray, Bruce T. *Religious Liberty in America: The First Amendment in Historical and Contemporary Perspective.* Amherst: University of Massachusetts Press, 2008.

Murrin, John M. "Massachusetts: From Liberties to Rights, The Struggle in Colonial Massachusetts." In *The Bill of Rights and the States: The Colonial and Revolutionary Origins of American Liberty,* edited by Patrick T. Conley and John P. Kaminski, 63–69. Madison, WI: Madison House, 1992.

Myerson, Michael. *Endowed by Their Creator.* New Haven: Yale University Press, 2012.

Najar, Monica. "Sectarians and Strategies of Dissent in Colonial Virginia." In *From Jamestown to Jefferson: The Evolution of Religious Freedom in Virginia,* edited by Paul Rasor and Richard E. Bond, 108–37. Charlottesville: University of Virginia Press, 2011.

Neem, Johann N. "Beyond the Wall: Reinterpreting Jefferson's Danbury Address." *Journal of the Early Republic* 27 (Spring 2007): 139–54.

———. *Creating a Nation of Joiners: Democracy and Civil Society in Early National Massachusetts.* Cambridge: Harvard University Press, 2008.

———. "A Republican Reformation: Thomas Jefferson's Civil Religion and the Separation of Church and State." In *A Companion to Thomas Jefferson,* ed. by Francis D. Cogliano, 91–109. Chichester, UK: Wiley-Blackwell, 2011.

Nelson, John K. *A Blessed Company: Parishes, Parsons and Parishioners in Anglican Virginia, 1690–1776.* Chapel Hill: University of North Carolina Press, 2001.

Newman, A. H. *A History of the Baptist Churches in the United States.* New York: Christian Literature, 1894.

Note. "'An Office of the House Which Chooses Him, and Nothing More': How Should *Marsh v. Chambers* Apply to Rotating Chaplains?" *University of Chicago Law Review* 73 (2006): 1421–53.

Novak, Michael. "How Did Virginians Ground Religious Rights?" *Human Rights Review* 4, no. 3 (April–June 2003): 17–33.

O'Brien, Charles F. "The Religious Issues in the Presidential Campaign of 1800." *Essex Institute Historical Collections* 107 (January 1971): 82–93.

Oliphant, Edward. *The History of North America and Its United States.* Edinburgh: J. Johnstone, 1800.

O'Neill, James M. "Nonpreferential Aid to Religion Is Not an Establishment of Religion." *Buffalo Law Review* 2 (1952): 242–78.

Onuf, Peter. "Thomas Jefferson's Christian Nation." In *Religion, State, and Society: Jefferson's Wall of Separation in Comparative Perspective,* edited by Robert Fatton Jr. and R. K. Ramazani. New York: Palgrave MacMillan, 2009.

An Oration Delivered in Tammany Hall, in Commemoration of the Birthday of Thomas Paine. Published under the direction of the Committee of Management. New York: Evans and Brooks, 1832.

Patton, Jacob Harris. *The Triumph of the Presbytery of Hanover; or, Separation of Church and State in Virginia.* New York: Anson D. F. Randolph, 1887.

Peterson, Merrill D. *The Jefferson Image in the American Mind.* Charlottesville: University of Virginia Press, 1998.

———, ed. *Thomas Jefferson: Writings.* New York: Library of America, 1984.

Peterson, Merrill D., and Robert C. Vaughan, eds. *The Virginia Statute for Religious*

Freedom: Its Evolution and Consequences in American History. Cambridge: Cambridge University Press, 1988.

Pfeffer, Leo. *Liberties of an American: The Supreme Court Speaks.* Boston: Beacon Press, 1957.

———, "Madison's 'Detached Memoranda': Then and Now." In *The Virginia Statute for Religious Freedom: Its Evolution and Consequences in American History,* edited by Merrill D. Peterson and Robert C. Vaughan, 283–312. Cambridge: Cambridge University Press, 1988.

Plöchl, Willibald M. "Thomas Jefferson, Author of the Statute of Virginia for Religious Freedom." *Jurist* 3 (1943): 182–230.

Price, William S., Jr. "'There Ought to Be a Bill of Rights:' North Carolina Enters a New Nation." In *The Bill of Rights and the States: The Colonial and Revolutionary Origins of American Liberty,* edited by Patrick T. Conley and John P. Kaminski, 424–42. Madison, WI: Madison House, 1992.

Proceedings and Debates of the Convention of North Carolina. Edenton: Hodge and Wills, 1789.

Prufer, Julius F. "The Franchise in Virginia from Jefferson through the Convention of 1829." *William and Mary Quarterly* 2nd ser., 7, no. 4 (October 1927): 255–70.

Ragosta, John A. *Wellspring of Liberty: How Virginia's Religious Dissenters Helped Win the American Revolution & Secured Religious Liberty.* New York: Oxford University Press, 2010.

Rakove, Jack N. "Beyond Locke, Beyond Belief: The Nexus of Free Exercise and Separation of Church and State." In *Religion, State, and Society: Jefferson's Wall of Separation in Comparative Perspective,* edited by Robert Fatton Jr. and R. K. Ramazani, 37–52. New York: Palgrave Macmillan, 2009.

———. *Original Meanings: Politics and Ideas in the Making of the Constitution.* New York: Knopf, 1996.

Ramsay, David. *The History of South-Carolina.* Charleston: David Longworth, 1809.

Randall, Henry S. *The Life of Thomas Jefferson.* 3 vols. Philadelphia: Lippincott, 1865.

Randolph, Edmund. *History of Virginia.* Edited by Arthur H. Shaffer. Charlottesville: University Press of Virginia, 1970.

Randolph, Sarah N. *The Domestic Life of Thomas Jefferson, Compiled from Family Letters and Reminiscences.* 1871. Reprint, Charlottesville: University Press of Virginia, 1978.

Report of the Debates in the Convention of California on the Formation of the State Constitution, in September and October, 1849. Washington: John T. Towers, 1850.

Report of the Debates and Proceedings of the Convention for the Revision of the Constitution of the State of Indiana, 1850. Indianapolis: A. H. Brown, 1850.

Report of the Proceedings and Debates of the Convention of 1821, Assembled for the Purpose of Amending the Constitution of the State of New York. Albany: E. E. Hosford, 1821.

Republican Notes on Religion; And, an Act Establishing Religious Freedom, Passed in the Assembly of Virginia, in the Year 1786. Danbury, CN: Thomas Rowe, 1803.

Rice, John Holt. "Memorials to the General Assembly of Virginia." *Literary and Evangelical Magazine* 9, no. 1 (January 1826): 30–47.

Richardson, James D. *A Compilation of the Messages and Papers of the Presidents.* 10 vols. U.S. Congress, 1900.

Rives, William C. *History of the Life and Times of James Madison.* Vol. 1. Boston: Little, Brown, 1859.

Robertson, D. B. *Should Churches Be Taxed?* Philadelphia: Westminster Press, 1968.

Rodda, Chris. *Liars for Jesus: The Religious Right's Alternate Version of American History.* Vol. 1. Self-published, 2006.

Roeber, A. G. *Faithful Magistrates and Republican Lawyers: Creators of Virginia Legal Culture, 1680–1810.* Chapel Hill: University of North Carolina Press, 1981.

Rosenfeld, Richard N. *American Aurora.* New York: St. Martin's Press, 1997.

Rosenthal, Lawrence. "The New Originalism Meets the Fourteenth Amendment: Original Public Meaning and the Problem of Incorporation." *Journal of Contemporary Legal Issues* 18 (Spring 2009): 361–408.

Rozbicki, Michal Jan. *Culture and Liberty in the Age of the American Revolution.* Charlottesville: University of Virginia Press, 2011.

Rutland, Robert Allen. *The Birth of the Bill of Rights, 1776–1791.* New York: Collier Books, 1962.

———, ed. *The Papers of George Mason: 1725–1792.* Vol. 2. Chapel Hill: University of North Carolina Press, 1970.

Ryland, Garnett. *The Baptists of Virginia, 1699–1926.* Richmond: Virginia Baptist Board of Missions and Education, 1955.

Samuelson, Richard. "Jefferson and Religion: Private Belief, Public Policy." In *The Cambridge Companion to Thomas Jefferson,* edited by Frank Shuffelton, 143–54. Cambridge: Cambridge University Press, 2009.

Sanford, Charles B. *The Religious Life of Thomas Jefferson.* Charlottesville: University Press of Virginia, 1984.

Scarberry, Mark S. "John Leland and James Madison: Religious Influence on the Ratification of the Constitution and on the Proposal of the Bill of Rights." *Penn State Law Review* 113, no. 3 (2009): 733–800.

Schaaf, Gregory. *Franklin, Jefferson, & Madison: On Religion and the State.* Sante Fe: CIAC Press, 2004.

Schaff, Philip. *Church and State in the United States.* New York, 1888.

Schwartz, Bernard, ed. *The Bill of Rights: A Documentary History.* New York: Chelsea House, 1971.

Schulz, Constance B. "'Of Bigotry in Politics and Religion': Jefferson's Religion, the Federalist Press, and the Syllabus." *Virginia Magazine of History and Biography* 91 (January 1993): 73–91.

Scott, W. W. *A History of Orange County in Virginia.* Richmond: Everett Waddey, 1907.

Scribner, Robert L., and Brent Tarter, eds. *Revolutionary Virginia: The Road to Independence.* 8 vols. Charlottesville: University Press of Virginia, 1977.

Scully, Randolph Ferguson. *Religion and the Making of Nat Turner's Virginia: Baptist Community and Conflict, 1740–1840.* Charlottesville: University of Virginia Press, 2008.

Sehat, David. *The Myth of American Religious Freedom.* New York: Oxford University Press, 2011.

Seiler, William H. "The Anglican Church: A Basic Institution of Local Government in Colonial Virginia." In *Town and County: Essays on the Structure of Local Government in the American Colonies,* edited by Bruce C. Daniels, 134–59. Middletown, CN: Wesleyan University Press, 1978.

———. "The Anglican Parish in Virginia." In *Seventeenth-Century America: Essays in Colonial History,* edited by James Morton Smith, 119–42. Chapel Hill: University of North Carolina Press, 1959.

Sekulow, Jay Alan. *Witnessing Their Faith: Religious Influence on Supreme Court Justices and their Opinions.* Lantham, MD: Rowman and Littlefield, 2006.

Semple, Robert B. *A History of the Baptists in Virginia.* Revised and extended by G. W. Beale. 1894. Reprint, Cottonport, LA: Polyanthos, 1972.

Sheridan, Eugene R. *Jefferson and Religion.* Charlottesville: Thomas Jefferson Memorial Foundation, 1998.

Smith, Adam. *An Inquiry into the Nature and Causes of the Wealth of Nations.* 2nd ed. London: W. Strahan and T. Cadell, 1778.

Smith, Rodney. "Getting off on the Wrong Foot and Back on Again: A Reexamination of the History of the Framing of the Religion Clauses of the First Amendment and a Critique of the *Reynolds* and *Everson* Decisions." *Wake Forest Law Review* 20 (1984): 569–643.

Smith, Steven D. *Foreordained Failure: The Quest for a Constitutional Principle of Religious Freedom.* New York: Oxford University Press, 1995.

Smylie, James H. "From Revolution to Civil War (1776–1861)." In *Virginia Presbyterians in American Life: Hanover Presbytery (1755–1980),* 45–102. Richmond: Hanover Presbytery, 1982.

Snee, Joseph M. "Religious Disestablishment and the Fourteenth Amendment." *Washington University Law Quarterly* 4 (December 1954): 371–407.

Spangler, Jewell L. "Presbyterians, Baptists, and the Making of a Slave Society in Virginia, 1740–1820." Ph.D. diss., University of California, San Diego, 1996.

———. *Virginians Reborn: Anglican Monopoly, Evangelical Dissent, and the Rise of the Baptists in the Late Eighteenth Century.* Charlottesville: University of Virginia Press, 2008.

Sprague, William B. *Annals of the American Pulpit.* Vol. 6, *Baptists.* New York: Robert Carter and Brothers, 1865.

"State of the First Amendment." First Amendment Center, Freedom Forum. www.firstamendmentcenter.org/madison/wp-content/uploads/2011/07/sofa-2011-report.pdf.

Stokes, Anson Phelps. *Church and State in the United States.* Vol. 1. New York: Harper and Brothers, 1950.

Stokes, Anson Phelps, and Leo Pfeffer. *Church and State in the United States.* Rev. ed. New York: Harper and Row, 1964.

Story, Joseph. *Commentaries on the Constitution of the United States.* 2 vols. 3rd ed. Boston: Little, Brown, 1858.

Strout, Cushing. "Jeffersonian Religious Liberty and American Pluralism." In *The Virginia Statute for Religious Freedom: Its Evolution and Consequences in American History,* edited by Merrill D. Peterson and Robert C. Vaughan, 201–35. Cambridge: Cambridge University Press, 1988.

———. "Jefferson's Statute and the Glorious First." *Proteus* 4, no. 2 (1987): 5–12.

Stuart, James. *Three Years in North America*. Vol. 2. Edinburgh: Robert Cadell, 1833.

Swaney, W. B. "Religious Freedom." *Virginia Law Review* 12, no. 8 (June 1926): 632–44.

Sydnor, Charles S. *American Revolutionaries in the Making: Political Practices in Washington's Virginia*. New York: Free Press, 1965.

Taylor, C. James, ed. *The Adams Papers Digital Edition*. Charlottesville: University of Virginia Press, Rotunda, 2008. http://rotunda.upress.virginia.edu/founders/ADMS.html

Taylor, James B. *Lives of Virginia Baptist Ministers*. 2nd ed., rev. Richmond: Yale and Wyatt, 1838.

Terman, William Jennings, Jr. "The American Revolution and the Baptist and Presbyterian Clergy of Virginia: A Study of Dissenter Opinion and Action." Ph.D. diss., Michigan State University, 1974.

Thom, William Taylor. *The Struggle for Religious Freedom in Virginia: The Baptists*. Johns Hopkins University Studies, Historical and Political Science, series 18, nos. 10–11–12. Edited by Herbert B. Adams. 1900. Reprint, New York: Johnson Reprint Corp., 1973.

Thomas, David. *The Virginian Baptist*. Early American Imprint Series 1, no. 13651. Baltimore: Enoch Story, 1774.

Thompson, Ernest Trice. *Presbyterians in the South*. Vol. 1, *1607–1861*. Richmond: John Knox Press, 1963.

Thorpe, Francis Newton. *The Federal and State Constitutions, Colonial Charters, and Other Organic Laws of the State, Territories, and Colonies now or heretofore forming the United States of America*. 7 vols. Washington: U.S. Government Printing Office, 1909.

Toulmin, Henry. *Thoughts on Emigration: To which are added, Miscellaneous Observations relating to the United States of America: and a Short Account of the State of Kentucky*. Pamphlet. London, October 1792.

Tucker, George. *The Life of Thomas Jefferson, Third President of the United States, with Parts of His Correspondence Never Before Published and Notices of his Opinions in Questions on Civil Government, National Policy and Constitutional Law*. Philadelphia: Covey, Lea and Blanchard, 1837.

Tucker, St. George. *View of the Constitution of the United States with Selected Writings*. Indianapolis: Liberty Fund, 1999.

Underwood, James Lowell. "'Without Discrimination or Preference': Equality for Catholics and Jews under the South Carolina Constitution of 1790." In *The Dawn of Religious Freedom in South Carolina*, edited by James Lowell Underwood and W. Lewis Burke, 58–94. Columbia: University of South Carolina Press, 2006.

Van Horne, John C., ed. *Correspondence of William Nelson as Acting Governor of Virginia, 1770–1771*. Charlottesville: University Press of Virginia, 1975.

Veit, Helen E., Kenneth R. Bowling, and Charlene Bangs Bickford. *Creating the Bill of Rights: The Documentary Record from the First Federal Congress*. Baltimore: Johns Hopkins University Press, 1991.

Voltaire, "Letter on the Presbyterians." In *The Works of Voltaire: A Contemporary Version*, edited by John Morley, 21 vols., 19:216–19. E. R. DuMont, 1901.

Waddell, Joseph A. *Annals of Augusta County, Virginia, From 1726 to 1871*. 1902. Reprint, Bridgewater, VA: C. J. Carter, 1958.

Waldman, Steven. *Founding Faith: Providence, Politics, and the Birth of Religious Freedom in America*. New York: Random House, 2008.

West, Ellis. "The Case Against a Right to Religion-Based Exemptions." *Notre Dame Journal of Law, Ethics, and Public Policy* 4 (1990): 591–638

West, Thomas G. "Religious Liberty: The View from the Founding." In *On Faith and Free Government,* edited by Daniel C. Palm, 3–27. Lanham, MD: Rowman and Littlefield, 1997.

Whitsitt, William H. *The Life and Times of Judge Caleb Wallace.* Louisville: John P. Morton, 1888.

Willison, George F. *Patrick Henry and His World: A Biography.* Garden City, NY: Doubleday, 1969

Wilson, Douglas L., ed. *Jefferson's Literary Commonplace Book.* Princeton: Princeton University Press, 1989.

Witte, John, Jr. *Religion and the American Constitutional Experiment.* 2nd ed. Boulder: Westview Press, 2005.

Whittington, Keith E. "The New Originalism." *Georgetown Journal of Law & Public Policy* 2 (2004): 599–613.

Wood, Gordon S. "No Thanks for the Memories." *New York Review of Books,* January 13, 2011.

Wortman, Tunis. "A Solemn Address to Christians and Patriots." In *Political Sermons of the American Founding Era, 1730–1805,* edited by Ellis Sandoz, 2nd ed., 2:1477–527. Indianapolis: Liberty Fund, 1998.

Young, Chester Raymond, ed. *Westward into Kentucky: The Narrative of Daniel Trabue.* Lexington: University Press of Kentucky, 2004.

Zagari, Rosemarie. "Founding Intentions." *New Republic,* September 9, 1985, 10–11.

Index

Virginia Law Review, 148
Volney, Comte de, 17
Voltaire, 677, 245n55

Waddell, James, 52
Wafford, Thomas, 52
Waite, Morrison, 113, 114, 130, 137, 147, 167,
 260n28
Wallace, Caleb, 63
Wallace v. Jaffree, 3, 153, 212
Waller, John, "Swearing Jack," 52
Walker, Jeremiah, 67, 70
Walz v. Tax Commission, 129
Warren, Earl, 2, 102
Washington, George, 47, 61, 103, 112,

158–60, 192; and general assessment,
 79–80, 94, 97
Watkins, Thomas, 49
Weber, William, 52
West, Ellis, 114
Will, George, 182
William and Mary, College of, 10, 11, 43,
 45, 46
Williams, Roger, 140
Witherspoon, Jonathan, 45
Witte, John, 128
Wood, Gordon, 217
Wortman, Tunis, 36

Zelman v. Simmons-Harris, 176

Recent Books in the JEFFERSONIAN AMERICA Series

Douglas Bradburn
*The Citizenship Revolution:
Politics and the Creation of the
American Union, 1774–1804*

Clarence E. Walker
*Mongrel Nation: The America Begotten
by Thomas Jefferson and Sally Hemings*

Timothy Mason Roberts
*Distant Revolutions: 1848 and the
Challenge to American Exceptionalism*

Peter J. Kastor and François Weil, editors
*Empires of the Imagination: Transatlantic
Histories of the Louisiana Purchase*

Eran Shalev
*Rome Reborn on Western Shores:
Historical Imagination and the
Creation of the American Republic*

Leonard J. Sadosky
*Revolutionary Negotiations:
Indians, Empires, and Diplomats
in the Founding of America*

Philipp Ziesche
*Cosmopolitan Patriots: Americans
in Paris in the Age of Revolution*

Leonard J. Sadosky, Peter Nicolaisen,
Peter S. Onuf, and Andrew J.
O'Shaughnessy, editors
*Old World, New World: America
and Europe in the Age of Jefferson*

Sam W. Haynes
*Unfinished Revolution: The American
Republic in a British World, 1815–1850*

Michal Jan Rozbicki
*Culture and Liberty in the Age of
the American Revolution*

Ellen Holmes Pearson
*Remaking Custom: Law and Identity
in the Early American Republic*

Seth Cotlar
*Tom Paine's America: The Rise and
Fall of Transatlantic Radicalism*

John Craig Hammond and
Matthew Mason, editors
*Contesting Slavery: The Politics of Bondage
and Freedom in the New American Nation*

Ruma Chopra
*Unnatural Rebellion: Loyalists in
New York City during the Revolution*

Maurizio Valsania
*The Limits of Optimism: Thomas
Jefferson's Dualistic Enlightenment*

Peter S. Onuf and Nicholas P. Cole,
editors
*Thomas Jefferson, the Classical
World, and Early America*

Hannah Spahn
Thomas Jefferson, Time, and History

Lucia Stanton
"Those Who Labor for My
Happiness": Slavery at
Thomas Jefferson's Monticello

Robert M. S. McDonald, editor
Light and Liberty: Thomas Jefferson
and the Power of Knowledge

Catherine Allgor, editor
The Queen of America: Mary
Cutts's Life of Dolley Madison

Peter Thompson and
Peter S. Onuf, editors
State and Citizen: British America
and the Early United States

Maurizio Valsania
Nature's Man: Thomas Jefferson's
Philosophical Anthropology

John Ragosta
Religious Freedom: Jefferson's
Legacy, America's Creed